FROM THE DEEP OCEAN ABOVE

MANKIND'S UNHEEDED MESSAGE
TO ITSELF

RESEARCHED,
COMPILED, BRAIN-STORMED,
AND WRITTEN PRO SE

BY

BARD A. MADSEN

Copyright 2015

ISBN #

Library of Congress #

Cover : God's Tough-Love Carolina Bays
Back-Cover : Dorje, found in Jan. 2012

Please keep this book in your scram bag, so
when the Space fall occurs again, the
Initiates to the upcoming cycle, will have a
chance not to fall back into the rut Mankind
has been stuck in for far too long.

It is highly recommended to listen to good ol' Classic
Rock-n-Roll, such as Dio, while reading this material!

http://sites.google.com/site/fromthedeepoceanabove/

or search with quotes "From The Deep Ocean Above"

fromthedeepoceanabove@gmail.com

FROM THE DEEP OCEAN ABOVE

MANKINDS UNHEEDED MESSAGE TO ITSELF

I come to make contact again. Apologetically, I cross the dark, inky Ocean to make my Iron point achieve its mark. It has been an arduously long and pseudo-morphing journey, but I fear my words will become awash and diluted further. Therefore, take note – once again – for it is prudent to your existence. My origin is as immaterial, as is your present disconnection to material ! At the height of your glory, the majority are misled, when it is so simple. Hark ! I call thee to at least become aware of the manner of your destruction, and not die with strife in your hearts – the stakes are consciousness or dark oblivion. You have the superior weapon! Pick it up and think with the utmost haste, or, be grievously wounded once again.

You already know me, and yet you look away from the sky above, allowing others to mask my true nature. As many as possible, must be made aware and retain this knowledge, in order to sustain themselves without any help. In order to rebuild and pass on the key to other initiates before the next Space Fall passes.

Denial, will never achieve corrected excellence. Even the old narrative sent by your ancestors, has been displaced, disallowed, and has not been deciphered and disclosed. It has been supplanted by another kind of mythological viewpoint that futilely apes an answer. In reality, what was written to you is now regarded as nothing but fantasy, when the inverse is true.

Those were messages in bottles, left floating atop the waters, waiting for the reader to open them and understand the message within. A sender and a receiver must have the same key to learn, to live and to continue searching. Then, and only then, will you attain true understanding.

The first thing I recall was the Sun in my Eyes and watching the Green Countryside move by while on a Train. Before first grade I watched the Thor cartoons in a caretaker's garage. I realized then, that the story line had to have more behind it, yet all I was told was that it pertained to my own heritage. At Seven years of age, I watched, with the utmost fascination, the first Men to land on the Moon ; live on television. I was alone that night and mesmerized at the bravery and such technology. A year later, I had a step father ; the only one who ever talked to me as a kid on an adult level. He was a geologist and his dad presided over a major research center. Their family heritage also Nordic, going so far back, that he had a trunk half-full of swords that must have dated back a thousand years. Their family name was engraved on most of them. One stands out in my mind. The blade itself looked like a wave ; a Serpent Shape Undulating back and forth possibly Seven times.

That Halloween, under the Stars, I asked him the reason behind the Tradition of Trick-or-Treating. He told me about Harvard astronomer, Dr. Whipple and the Taurid Stream. How, in ancient times this extensive Meteor Shower (Shooting Stars), dominated the Skies, frightening all Mankind at this very time of year. The psychological Impact of the sight, had been so great, it still had its own ramifications carried over to this day. "If you look closely," he said, while pointing toward the horizon, "you can see the high pointed Pyramidal shape of its remnant - the Zodiacal Light."

Many adversities in Life later (around 1984), in a used book store, I found "World's in Collision" for fifty cents. Was it Fiction or Verity? I couldn't figure it out, because it spoke of Venus being the cause. I didn't accept the theory that our sister planet could be captured recently and have a similar orbit - yet there was something in it that Rang of Truth. Not long after that I found "The Cosmic Serpent" in a grocery store, but couldn't afford it. I searched the libraries, locating only one copy down town. I read just over half of it, then it was due to go back. I called to find out if I could re-check it out, but the answer was no. I dropped it off in a mailbox.

Most of my Life I lived in large metroplexes, and never could get libraries to do inter-library loans for me. In the one's I visited, it always seemed the best books were missing entirely (likely stolen). Later I moved to the country. I was taken aback at the small library that seemed to have more DVD's than books. I asked the librarian if they offered inter-library loans, and to my surprise, an extremely joyous voice replied. "Sure do! What would you like to order up"? I told him I'd really have to think about it, since I was so used to hearing, "No"!

1

Having half forgotten about the opportunity of the inter-library loans and staring at the search engine blank entry it hit me to look for something interesting after so many years of closed doors. It didn't take long from starting at Petroglyphs and Barringer Crater to a seemingly obscure site about a group of scientist purporting that Space Falls have happened a number of times in human history, with their pictures and all the blurry images of books they had written. It was perfect. Soon the librarian had a list – books arrived - and I began reading them from cover to cover. I took copious notes, while adding to my list from the bibliographies within them, and books the author's mentioned in the text that sounded good.

At about the end of the Seventh book, I set it down and began thinking on the entirety of what it said. Then it occurred to me, this was the book from way back when ; that I only had the opportunity to read half of – "*The Cosmic Serpent*"! After a lengthy memory of making a whole day of just getting that book the first time I started to contemplate if it could really be true, could Traditions have possibly Recorded Real Factual and Eyewitness Accounts of these Space Falls ? And what an Abyss of time and effort would one have to expend to delve into the unfathomable immensely of the rehashed 'Myth word' to Verily get the Truth one way or another ?

In this book I have endeavored to take the Confusion Out of the subject of Mythology. It took the rest of the day to come to a conclusion of, if I wanted to go that far to find out. After that, I switched back and forth between the topics of Dry Science and Mythology, even at times reading each depending on which room the book was located or just for a change. Almost the next book "The Cycle of Cosmic Catastrophes" talked about the Carolina Bays and I knew instantly, This Is It ! I know this pattern, it Came From Above as if a liquid to liquid transfer. And on top of that I just happen to be located close to where it must have hit, in whatever fashion and flew off to create them. Then came the realization from satellite imagery that I live within what surely looks like a Complex Crater that to my knowledge hasn't been discovered and the waves of it are evident by driving around, this research for pure entertainment was becoming too strange.

The search for Traditions started out badly and sort of expected even though the *Iliad* most assuredly had been written, and excellently well if I may add, about Celestial Phenomena, it only had a faint echo of the celestial message left. Next I chose the Norse Traditions, which are a completely different style and yet found nothing conclusive. I realized I would have to find the oldest, and likely the most expensive material possible, to round up a consensus. Not long after that I started running out of science books I found Cuneiform and Hieroglyphic Text and the libraries wouldn't lend those.

At this point I'm hooked beyond doubt and resorted to buying books and to my surprise no one seems to want to read that stuff. There were quite a few, one hundred year old plus books, that I bought that are obviously printed in sheets, folded, and then bound in which I had to cut the fold to open the pages to read them. Come to find out the best information has already been researched by extremely well learned Men and Women back between 1860 and 1922 and excavations were cut off by the Wars I & II. Cuneiform and Hieroglyphs are the perfect medium because it can't possibly be corrupted throughout the Millennia and was Textualized from the Traditional Verbal Legends that were ages old at 6,000 years BP (Before Present).

By the half way point, of reading through the one hundred plus books listed in the Bibliography at the end of this book it was a certainty that I would have to compile a book about this subject ; even if it is just for me ; or to publish a book, that I would positively like to read myself. I have no doubt that it will have as many facets of views, as the number of readers. I hope that All will Understand I Honestly had no idea how Deep this was going to go. By the time I realized it myself, it was too late to turn back and forget it. Instead of being offended, rest assured that the ancient religions that may still exist ; though in altered states or expanded forms ; they are inexorably related to each other and Irrefutably all whistling the same tune. They are all chanting the same refrain of the Celestial Events of the Past, it Echoes Globally to this day and to my tangible knowledge appears to be mostly Ignored.

What you have here, is a compellation of extracts of the most vivid and widely acknowledged written records of Man's history at my disposal, from as far back as 13,000 years BP. I am sure that the message will still be conveyed, even if a reader cursorily skips some of the technical names appearing within the quoted texts. I left them intact for the curious, the learned, and of course because of the problematic flow that would occur if extracted. It is curious that the Verity is also sounded out within the etymology of many names of people, places, and things, that changed little throughout the innumerable generations of the re-telling of the story.

I am positive that this so-called 'fringe science' will flow in our mainstream consciences very soon, as did the 'KT Boundary' being accepted as instrumental in the demise of the dinosaurs. The premise is that a Space Fall (Comet strike) happened at the Great Lakes of North America, some 13,000 years BP. It broke up the Laurentide Ice Sheet causing a Great Conflagration, Flooding, Tsunamis, reverberating global Earthquake, and Bombardment of Ice then, veiled the atmosphere. This added another millennium to the Ice Age (that was ebbing), thus killing off the Clovis people and approximately thirty-five species of large animals, like the Mammoth, and Saber Tooth Cat, in North America alone. Many Prestigious University studies have confirmed the initial evidence of Black Mats, nano-Diamonds, Metallic and Carbon spherules, that are all indicators of Extraterrestrial Catastrophic Cosmic remains. It isn't my place to try to convince the reader with other's copyrighted Scientific Proofs of such things, thus I highly recommend reading from some of the relative titles found in my Bibliography and of Scientific Papers for more Convincing Detains.

The following is the only known fictional part of this book. I personally liked the style and subject matter. I believe it sets the tone well for what will follow ; and it reflects the predominant Traditions of western society in which I was raised, but it is but a springboard to other pools of information around the World. Elizabeth Rundle Charles wrote it in 1864.

Initial extract of the Introduction, by Professor Henry B. Smith:

It is the High Office of History to Restore the Past to a New Life. All Great Events have a Twofold Life ; once, as they actually occurred, and again, as they are revived upon the historic page for the Benefit of After Times. The historian must first of all give an accurate record of Facts in their just order ; but more than this is needed, if the Past is to speak Persuasively to the Present. It must be so Reanimated as to bring to view living Men and Scenes, that the imagination may be enlisted and the pulse quickened. To the Sharp Outline of Fact, fiction may add its embellishments, and thus allure many who would Otherwise Pass Carelessly by the Great Lessons of Human History.

The Early Dawn

Period – The Second Century

One Midsummer Eve, more than seventeen centuries ago, the red gleams of a huge bonfire contended with the pale moonbeams in clothing with fantastic light and shade the gigantic piles of granite which crest, as with a natural fortress, that point of the Cornish coast now called Trerhyn Castle. The wild flickerings of the flames leaded high enough at times even to touch

4

with their fiery glow the edges of the mysterious Logan Rock which crowns the summit. That it was no mere bonfire of marry-makers might be easily seen in the earnest faces and grave movements of the men gathered round it. They were not mingled in a confused throng, nor scattered in irregular groups, but moved solemnly round the fire from east to west, following the course of the sun, now hidden from their gaze beneath that shore less Ocean whose waves Thundered ceaselessly against the base of the cliff on which they were assembled. Their steps were the slow and measured movements of a sacred mystic dance ; and as they circled round the blaze they sang a wild monotonous chant, to which the minor intervals gave, not the plaintive tenderness of a major melody broken by a minor fall, but rather the abrupt and savage restlessness of a combined wail and war-cry. From time to time the song rose with the flames into a defiant shout, and then sank again into the low crooning of a dirge ; the steps of the singers changing with the music from a rapid march to the slow tramp of a funeral procession. The sacred music of that old British race resolved itself into no calm, restful, major close. Theirs was the worship of a conquered race, and of a proscribed religion. Driven by the Romans from their temples in the interior of the island – temples, whose unhewn and gigantic grandeur not even the persistency of Roman enmity could ruin – this little band of the old lords of the land had met in that remote recess, not yet trodden by the conqueror's feet, to celebrate the rites of their own proscribed Druid priesthood.

There, under the shadow of that grand natural fortress, to us so like one of their own Druid temples, they had kindled on May Day the sacred "Fire of God ;" and there on Midsummer Eve they now gathered round the "Fire of Peace." At length the rites, endeared to them as the last relics of their national existence, were finished ; the wild chant was silent, succeeded by the ceaseless roar of the breakers : and the torches were kindled at the sacred fire, to relight once more, from a sacred fire, to relight once more, from a sacred source, the household fires that night extinguished. One by one the little British company dispersed, and could be traced along the cliffs, or inland across the unbroken moorland, by the glare of their torches.

The Druid was left alone. A solemn, solitary figure, he stood on the deserted space by the decaying fire, his fine form still erect, although the long beard, characteristic of his priestly office, was snow – white with age. The fitful glow of the expiring embers threw a mysterious light on the folds of his white robe, and gleamed on the rays of the broad golden circlet which bound his brow. Turning from the fire he looked across the sea, scarcely more solitary or wild than the rugged shore on which he lingered.

It was always a dreary moment to him when the solemn rites were over, and the worshippers were gone. A few minutes since he had stood before the

5

awe – stricken throng as one altogether apart and exalted, a medium of intercourse with the unknown supreme powers, a representative of the majesty so dimly understood, so vividly dreaded ; and their faith had thrown back a reflected reality on his. But now he stood alone, a mortal man to whom the unseen was indeed as invisible which his presence inspired in others, but which he had found it so hard to maintain in himself. His people looking with dim and longing eyes into the infinite, at least saw him ; whilst he saw only a blank infinity.

Musing thus, he gazed on that restless, boundless Ocean, the broad sweep of whose waves measured the long path of moonlight with their perspective of diminishing curves. Could it be possible, he thought, that at the end of that radiant pathway human eyes (were they but pure enough) might see the silvery outlines of that " Isle of the Brave," where he taught his people the spirits of their dead were resting ? Could it be that the waves which broke with that wild and wistful music at his feet might sound in human ears (were they but worthy to hear) the echoes of those deathless shores in the far west, where perhaps they had received their first impulse ?

Thus he stood musing, until his reverie was broken by the sound of footsteps close at hand. Turning hastily round, he saw between him and the fire a dark form wrapped in a Roman mantle. " Who art thou," he asked abruptly, " Thou hast tracked us thus to our last refuge ? Thou hast lighted on what may prove to thee a treasure better than any of the mines thy people grudge us. Doubtless, thou seest, " he added bitterly, " that I am one of that proscribed Druid priesthood whom, unarmed and defenseless, your Roman armies so much dread. Denounce me to the rulers, if thou wilt. I will follow thee without a struggle. Of what avail to me is life ? "

" I am no Roman, " said the stranger sadly. " On my people also the wrath of those irresistible legions has fallen. I also am one of the priesthood of a proscribed religion, and of a conquered race. Far in the East my people had once a city beautiful beyond all the earth, and a temple where white – robed priests, mitered with gold, ministered and sacrificed to Him whose name must not be uttered. Our temple is burned with fire, our city is laid waste, and trodden under foot of strangers ; our people are scattered east and west, and I among them. I had lost my way to–night on this wild coast, as I was journeying to the port near this, whither of old our fathers came to traffic, when, seeing the unusual gleam of this fire, I came to learn what it meant. Thou seest no ally of the Romans in me."

The Druid was appeased, and laying aside his priestly vestments, he appeared in the ordinary Celtic plaid worn by his tribe. The two men ; and, piling up the scattered logs on the dying embers, they agreed to remain together there until the dawn should throw sufficient light on their path to

6

enable them to travel safely along those rugged cliffs against which the waves, now hidden in the shades of the night, seemed to roar and chafe, like raging and disappointed beasts of prey. " Your priestly vestments remind me strangely, " said the Hebrew, when they were reseated by the fire, " of the sacred robes my father's wore of old. Whence did your religion come ?" " The sources of sacred things are hidden in the night, " Replied the Druid. " Some say our religion was taught direst from heaven ; some, that it was brought, before the memory of man, from a land the far East. Whence after the great flood the father and mother of our race came forth." " In those distant ages," said the Jew, " doubtless your forefathers and ours were one. Since you had a priesthood, had you then also a temple and sacred rites ?" " We had many temples," was the reply ; " gigantic circles of stone, as unhewn and as enormous as these amidst which we stand. Huge reminders of the solemn cliffs and mountains set up in unrivalled majesty on the solitary sweeps of our great inland plains ; roofed by the heavens, and floored by a bare unsmoothed earth. I laugh when I see the pigmy temples in which these Romans bow down before their little men and women gods." " You had, then no graven images ?" " Of old we had none ; and never any in our temples. We have but one image of the Highest ; if indeed," he added, in a low and awed voice, " he is only an image ! Our worship is directed to the sun. In his eternal course from east to west our sacred dances move. At his rising we rejoice. When in flowery May his beams once more begin to make the earth fruitful, we kindle in his honour the ' Fire of God," and begin our year anew. When he has risen in midsummer to his highest seat in the heavens, and reigns in his fullest might, we kindle the sacred ' Fire of Peace,' as to – night, in honour of his peaceful and consummated dominion." " Since, then, you had temples, had you also sacrifices ?" " We had," was the solemn reply ; " but not such as those of the Romans ; not only the white steer from the herd, or the spotless lamb from the flock. We offered to our gods costlier sacrifices than these, and dearer life." " What life, then ?" said the Jew, in horror. " The only life worthy to be accepted for the life of man," was the reply ; " the only life worthy to be offered to the Immortal." " Your altars were stained with human blood ! " said the Jew, with a shudder ; " your people had indeed, then, a different law from mine. But to whom," he continued, after a pause, " did you offer these terrible offerings ?" " The various tribes of our race had various names for him," said the Druid, in a low voice. " Some called him Hu, and some Dhia or Dhe, and some Be'al, the life of all life, the source of all being."

The Jew started as the name, denounced by his prophets, and abhorred by his race, fell on his ear, yet strangely blended with a word like the incommunicable name he might not utter, the mysterious Jah. " It is very

7

strange ! " he said, at length. " Your words sound to me like an echo of the utterance of the prophets of my people, resounding through the ages as the waves through one of these Ocean caverns, and broken into strange discords and wild confusion. " " Had you then no sacred writings ?" " We have none," said the Druid. " Our aged priests teach the sacred words in solemn chants to the priestly neophytes, and initiate them in the sacred rites. So we were taught ; so shall we teach those that follow, if the world or our race is to endure." " But," said the Jew, " did you ever shrink from the sufferings of the victims as you sacrificed them, or think whether there might not be some pity in the Eternal which might revolt from such rites." " Am I not a man ?" was the reply. " Doubtless my heart often ached at the sufferers were, for the most part, criminals, or captives taken in war ; and what was I, to be wiser than the aged who taught me ? "

The remembrance of the sacred name, revealed to the law-giver of his nation, rushed in on the heart of the Jew – of " Jehovah Elohim," the eternal and the mighty, " merciful and gracious, long – suffering, abounding in goodness and truth, yet by no means clearing the guilty ;" and with it came the recollection of that ritual so stern in its demands for the acknowledgment of sin, and of the forfeited right of the sinner to life, yet so jealous in its guard for that human life it declared forfeit. " Are you sure that your God hears you when you thus invoke and sacrifice to him ?" he said, after a pause. "We assure the people of these things," was the evasive reply ; " and also of rewards and punishments in the world beyond. The people need the barriers of such belief to keep them from crime." " But you do not teach what you do not believe ?" " Belief is not so easy for the instructed," was the reply. " Who that has looked into the depth of life can rest and believe like the ignorant ?" " Our faith," said the Jew, mournfully, " was a faith for all ; our most sacred truths were for the peasant as well as the priest. Among us the seers revealed what they had seen, and the prophets believed what they taught."

The Druid listened long with grave interest as the Hebrew spoke of that God who was revealed to his people as at once so awful and so near ; before whom, the prophet said, " The Holy Hosts above veil their faces," and yet of whom the shepherd – king could say," He is my Shepherd." At length he said, -- " But since you had such revelations, and such a faith, and were a nation so honored by the Highest, how can it be that you are a banished man like me ? What does this mean ?" " I know not, or at least, I can only partly conjecture," was the sad reply. " Our people had sinned, and our God is one who will not clear the guilty. Once before, our fathers were driven from their homes into that yet further East whence first they came, and our holy and beautiful house was burned with fire. But then, in their exile they had prophets and promises, and a limit fixed to their disgrace, at the end of which they were indeed restored. Scattered hither and thither we lose the record of our lineage. Our glory is all in the past. In all the future I can see no vision of hope. It seems to me, sometimes, almost as if our nation had made a shipwreck in the night on some unknown shore, nor any light in view, save in that distant past to which the blazing ruins of our temple warn us we may not return."

"Yet," resumed the Druid, " had it been otherwise with your nation, scarcely would your prosperity have brought hope to the world, to other races, or to mine. You say it was to your nation only God spoke ; to your nation alone the promises were made, which in some incomprehensible way you have lost. The world, then, has lost little in your fall." " I know not," replied the Jew. " Our prophets spoke of the veil being rent from all people, and of all nations coming to the brightness of the rising of a king who was to reign over ours." " Did this King then never come ?" " How can he have come ?" said the Jew, with a strange impatience. " How should I then be here, an exile without a country ? And was not our King to come as a Conqueror and a Redeemer for our nation,--as a Sun, flashing his unquestionable glory on all nations ? There is, indeed," he added, a fanatical sect who sprang from our race, who assert that our King has come, and that it is for rejecting him we are rejected. But who can believe this ?"

" It would be terrible, truly, for your people to believe it," said the Druid. " Those amongst you who think thus must be a mourning and wretched company." " Nay," was the answer, " they are not. Their delusion leads them to profess themselves the most blessed of men. They think that he whom they call King and Lord, who not much more than a hundred years ago was crucified by the Romans in our city, has arisen from the dead, and lives in heaven. And they say they are glad to die to depart to him." " Their hope extends then beyond death," said the Druid, abstractly. " There are then some who think they know of one who has visited the ' Isle of the Brave,' and has come back to tell what he saw ! "

As they spoke, the dawn began to break over the green slopes of the shore on a promontory of which they sat. One by one the higher points of that magnificent series of rock – bastions which guard our country from the Atlantic, like a fortress of God, caught the early sunbeams. Soon the Ocean also was bathed in another Ocean of Light, broken only by the shadow of the cliffs, or by the countless purple cups of shade, which gave an individual existence to every one of those wonderful translucent green waves.

The two priests of the two religions moved slowly across the pass between the rocks which separate the natural castled bulwark, where they had passed the night, from the green slopes of the coast within. " See," exclaimed the

Druid, " how the fire, which during the hours of darkness was all our light, now lies a faint red stain on the daylight ; whilst the waves, which all the night roared around us like angry demons, quietly heave in the sunshine. The earth has her dawns renewed continually. Will no new sun ever rise for man ? Must the golden dawn for us be always in the past ?"

Too deep a shadow rested for the Jew on the glorious predictions of his prophets for him to give any answer ; and silently they went along the cliffs. When they had walked inland thus for some time, they saw before them a labourer, in an earth – stained and common dress, going to his work in one of the mines which of old had tempted the Phoenicians to those very shores. This miner was evidently young, and had the lithe grace of the South about his form and movements. As he walked he sang, and the tones of his rich Southern tenor rose clear and full through the clear morning air. The cadence was different from any music the Druid had ever heard. There was a repose about the melody, quite foreign to the wild wails or war songs of his people. And as they drew near, the language was to him as strange. They stepped on softly behind the singer, and listened. " Strange words to hear in such a place," murmured the Jew at length. " They are Greek – the language of a people who dwelt still, in East, near the home of my forefathers."

They drew near and greeted the stranger. There was a gentle and easy courtesy in his manner as he returned their salutations, which, in a son of the North, would have betokened high breeding, but in him might be merely the natural bearing of his acute and versatile race. He willingly complied when the Jew asked him to repeat his song, which he translated thus to the Druid :-

Glory to God in the highest, And on earth peace, Good-will among men, We praise Thee, We bless Thee, We worship Thee for thy great glory, O Lord, heavenly King, O God the Father ruling all, O Lord the only-begotten Son, Saviour, Messiah, With the Holy Spirit. O Lord God, Lamb of God, Son of the Father, Who takest away the sins of the world, Receive our prayer. Thou who sittest at the right hand of the Father, Have mercy on us, For Thou only art holy—Thou only art the Lord, Saviour, and Messiah--- To the glory of God the Father. Amen.

~ End of Extract ~

As you read on, there are key words to keep in mind when reading the following types of material. I have Capitalized the ones I feel are Celestial in Nature and some to Emphasize those things that might otherwise be missed, particularly if read too fast. This may be very unconventional, but the benefits far outweigh cosmetic considerations. The material is not broken up into chapters, but book titles and the text will appear as it was translated with a minimal number of my own interjections, i.e., [my comments bracketed thus].

I have spent, literally years of continuous sleepless nights and days, trying to come up with a way to ease into this subject to no avail ! Much of the material has been loosely grouped together, even though the reader will find that the author's of some of the quoted material, will themselves, jump around place-to-place, speaking of the similarities in symbolism recurring over disjointed parts of the World. It seems to go with the territory, when the territory is the entire Planet!

Without giving away the conclusions presented, the main underlying theme in the literature I have compiled is quite simple. Mankind is Deathly Worried about the Sun disappearing and not coming back and it is Not about the Diurnal or the Seasonal Cycles, the stories evolved to fit Orderly Nature after the True Meaning had been lost over time.

It has been said that the Comet showed up 40,000 years BP on account of its spread out debris field with its Northern and Southern distinct Streams. The only thing that I have thought could push the date back is the Lascaux Cave Art (in France), which is approximately 17,000 BP. The reason being, it contains one depiction showing an Auroch with Seven marks to indicate the Pleiades and another that renders a Bull killing Man and a Bird of the Pleiades. My contention is, that the largest of the "recent" Floods and Mass Destructions, had to coincide with the formation of the Carolina Bays and the extinction of the Mega Fauna at around 13,000 BP. Unless, that was the moment of perturbation between the streams.

Many other stories of Man's distant past describe this, and other events, with the same kind of story line ; but with different characters and themes, which include the 'Great Beast' originating from the Pleiades. From the ancient traditions of the 'Old World' this small cluster of Stars is situated on the back of Taurus the Bull and are known as the Maidens, Eggs, Birds, Children, Brood, Angels, Hosts, and more. As said, some of these recurring and key words are Capitalized to remind the reader not to miss them, as they are part of a larger story ; one even retained in the etymology of the names which reaffirm the Validity of the tale throughout time.

There may be other Streams from Comets, although the vast majority of texts point to the Taurids. Some only seem to hint at the Leonids that can be

11

intermixed with both by Constellation and the 'Precessional Time Stamp', as are many of the mythological associations that promote the cause of preserving the message. This could be similar to how song lyrics, having words with multiple connotations, become favorites among very different groups of people having radically different World views. I use that only as an example, but warn that overemphasizing that possibility can lead to denial illusory correlation, meaning, one thinks they can read into it whatever they want, without limit, i.e., relinquishing the original temporal context altogether.

Precession is a complex phenomenon in which the Earth's axis wobbles as does a top when it slows down from spinning perfectly steady and this changes when the equinoxes and solstices occur as to the backdrop of the stars and changes the pole star over time. This wobbles' frequency is very slow and takes 25,772 years to make one revolution, which equals to 2,148 years per constellation. The ancient sages were intensely interested in where the Sun was as to the Constellations at the Spring Equinox, which is when the Northern and Southern hemispheres of the Earth get equal amount of Sun light and summer is approaching the Northern hemisphere. How they actually accomplished this as far as I know has not come down to us from the horary past, they most likely took note of the Constellation opposite at Midnight and that would tell them where the Sun was at noon the day of the Spring Equinox. For example, if Scorpio is the Constellation at midnight upon the Spring Equinox then the opposite would be Taurus, meaning the Sun's House or Mansion it resided in would be Taurus and that would mean that within The Great Year it would be approximately 2,500 BC or 4,500 years BP.

When the Hebrews were starting out it was the age of the Ram, and Jesus at Pieces, and we are now in the age of Aquarius. It is all very fascinating that it gives us a time stamp of events of extreme antiquity and even the end Paleolithic time as if a message from a time machine written in the sky via the words handed down to us from as far back as the Space Fall of 13,000 years ago. The ancient sages obviously had a profound reason to watch the skies so intently and invent mathematics to find out that the Sun moves one degree every 72 years and in all probability for calculating other important things in the sky. Today this has evolved into astrology in which one finds in the newspaper every day. That being your sign is where the sun was in the month you were born on an annular basis, but the precession of the Spring Equinox shows where the Sun was over extreme human perception of time. These are called ages and also ages mean the number of Space falls that separated each age of Man and not the just the different signs of the Constellations.

12

Some of the most prominent Allegories for The Comet or if one prefers of
the Progenitor of 2P / Encke ; Inner Solar System Space Debris : the
Northern and Southern Taurid Stream called by the ancients the Dragon,
Serpent, Feathered Serpent, Winged Bull, Goat-Fish, Fish, Leopard,
Rabbit, and Boar, and others. Mankind in the Horary Past didn't have
terminology for 'Fantastic Phenomena' that threatened his very Existence,
so he used metaphorical language related to things he saw around him.
Rabbits are fast, or, like the anecdote my dad use to tell me, "When I say
Rabbit you Jump !" If *one* animal or inanimate object didn't fit the scheme,
people pieced them together into 'Compound Creatures' [See above picture
of a Chimera] that we have all been told Are Not Real (and therefore
meaningless ?) ! In addition, Figurative Idioms are used for which the
familiar meanings have been lost, yet if thought out, reveal Truths revealed
in some part of the expression. Nevertheless, this can also be used as an
avenue for denying the eyewitness testimony on record as Poppycock that
from the Dutch : 'pappekak' for 'soft dung'.

This Book will Prove Otherwise from the sheer number of independent,
yet similar narratives impossible to have that been prospectively orchestrated
to undermine any future religious belief system, thus inadvertently
promoting iconoclastic ideals and retroactively anticipating modern
historical events that Prove the Wild Imaginary Fictional Stories are True !

13

One more thing before we get to the good stuff. Most of the scholarly work cited here comes from the late 19th & early 20th Centuries no longer constrained by copyright law. Frankly, I haven't searched the last century with nearly as much vigor, but it seems that the best stuff comes from the oldest books. That fact has the huge benefit of coming from people who lived in times before space travel, with the majority also never having seen an airplane, which restricted them from certain misconceptions about the information even inadvertently.

The message is ultimately an Explicit Warning and with Surprising Detail of Where, When, How, on Whom (people with Feelings), and Even Where the remainder Went ! After one reads enough of these allegorical texts, it becomes readable in many evidential places, for example, the once common practice of placing an image of a Cock atop a Weathervane ! I can't even pick up a current *International Topography Magazine* without seeing right through a story or picture within it. This quest has change the way I view the World beyond a doubt. A crucial thing to remember as you read, is most of what is said is about what is *Above* (the Ocean of the Cosmos) even though reflected by images of things on Earth. A Sea Monster then, should not be expected to rise from Earth's waters, but appear in the atmospheric Waters (the Sky ; Outer Space).

Scholars of the 19th Century were just waiting for a Huge Snake to be dug up any moment in the waves of Egypt sand, just as some diligently watch the ripples of the Loch Ness hoping for a similar sight. Without a Doubt, the ancients use the terms: Ocean, Sea, Lake, Pond, Stream, or Water as representations of the Sky and Outer Space Above ! The texts repeatedly say as much, Listen… Open Your Eyes, it is a gift of Knowledge and is for Mankind's very Survival even though the messengers are long gone.

If I recall correctly *The Library of the Sibylline Oracles* burned down at approximately 500 BC. Someone realized the magnitude of loss, and decreed that extant fragments be collected and restored to preserve the information as well as possible. Below are extracts from that intensive project. I believe that the bodings from the prognosticating Priestesses ; said to be under the influence of the volcanic vapors at Delphi, and the Temple of Apollo, the Sun God. The one who slew the Python, for instance, to be Ancient Knowledge but put to use in theatrical forms, fortune telling, and epics of Apocalyptic Proportions – the End of the World. In other words, "spin-doctored" proclamations of past tragedies meant to be credulous to those in the future.

The Sibylline Oracles (Books III. – V.),
by H. N. Bate, 1918

Woe to thee, Libya, woe, Sea and Land. Daughters of the West, to how
bitter a day shall ye come, and ye shall come under the pursuing of grievous
conflict, hard and terrible : A dread judgment shall there be once more, and
ye shall all be driven to Destruction, for that ye laid waste the holy house of
the immortal, and gnawed it grievously with Teeth of Iron. Therefore shalt
thou see thy land full of dead bodies slain by war, by Every On Set of God,
by Famine and Pestilence, and by foes of savage heart and all thy land shall
be Desolate, and thy cities forsaken. But in the West a Star shall Shine,
which Men will call the Long-Haired Star, a sign of the Sword, of Famine
and Death to Men, of the slaughter of great captains and Men of renown.

Sicyon with brazen Trumpeting shall Boast her Loudest over thee,
Corinth ; but the Flute shall give back the same note in answer.

For to all nations that dwell on the Earth shall the Most High send a Dread
Stroke of Calamity.

God shall make the Whole Heaven as brass above, and send Drought upon
the Whole Earth, and it shall be as Iron.

Fiery Swords shall Fall from Heaven on the Earth : Great Flashing Torches,
Flaming through the Midst of them ; and the Earth, Mother of all things,
shall be Shaken in those days by the Hand of the Immortal, and the fishes of
the sea and all the beasts of the Earth and the myriad of tribes of birds, and
every soul of Man and every Sea Shall Shudder before the Face of the
Immortal, and there shall be Great Fear.

God shall give judgment upon All, by war, by Sword, by Fire and
drenching rain ; and Brimstone shall Fall from Heaven, with Stones of Hail
Great and Grievous : and Death shall overtake the four-footed Beasts.

The babe shall lie down with the Dragon and the Asp.

I will tell thee an unerring sign, whereby to know when to find of all things
shall come on Earth. When by night in the Starry Heavens Swords are seen
Westward And Eastward, then shall a Dust Fall from Heaven over All the
Earth and the Light of the Sun shall Fail from Heaven in his mid course, and
suddenly the Moon-rays shall shine out and come upon the Earth ; there shall

16

be a sign of dripping of Blood from the Rocks ; and in a cloud ye shall see a Warring of footmen and horse ; like a hunting of beasts in the likeness of a Mist ; this is the End of All Things . . . .

From Asia a king shall come, lifting up a Mighty Sword, in countless ships, walking on the wet ways of the Sea, and cutting through a high-peaked Mountain in his voyaging, him trembling Asia shall receive back, as he flees for refuge from the war.

Samos, banks of Sand shall Cover it All, and Delos shall no more answer its name, but Wholly Deleted.

A Bolt from Above shall Destroy.

I long, thrice wretched, to see the works of the Thracians, even the wall from Sea to Sea, dragged down to the dust by a Blast of Air, Falling like a River into the Sea where the cormorant drive for fish.

One day shall the Voice of God be Heard from Heaven as a Peal of Thunder. The rays of the Sun shall Fail, the Moon shall not give her bright Light, in the time of the end, when God shall rule. There shall be Thick Darkness over all the Earth : . . . .

And then a Wintry Blast shall blow over the Earth, and the plain shall be filled once more with evil war. For Fire shall rain down from the floor of Heaven upon Men, and Fire, Water, Thunderbolts, gloom, and war and a Mist of slaughter to destroy all kings together and all Men of might.

A Fell Dragon breathing out grievous war, ...

Woe to thee, Lylia, for the ills devised against thee by the Sea, which shall invade thy land of his own accord, and with a Dread Shaking of the Earth, . .

But when after the fourth year a great Star shines, which shall of itself destroy the Whole Earth . . . . And from Heaven a Great Star shall Fall on the Dread Ocean and burn up the Deep Sea, ...

Be afraid, ye Indians and high-hearted Ethiopians : For when the Fiery Wheel of the Ecliptic . . . . and Capricorn . . . . and Taurus among the Twins encircles the Mid-Heaven, when the Virgin ascending and the Sun fastening the Girdle Round his Forehead dominates the Whole

17

Firmament ; there shall be a Great Conflagration from the Sky, Falling on the Earth ; and in the Warring Stars there shall be a New Portent, so that the Whole land of Ethiopia shall perish in Fire and groaning.

A rain of Burning Fire shall Fall from the clouds : men shall no more reap fair Fruit from the Earth ; all shall be unsown, unploughed, till Men take knowledge of him who governs all things, ...

And then in his answer the immortal God who dwells on high shall Hurl from the Sky a Fiery Bolt on the head of the unholy : and Summer shall change to Winter in that day. And then great woe shall befall mortal Men : for he that Thunders from on high shall destroy all the shameless, with Thundering and Lightnings and Burning Thunderbolts upon his enemies, and shall make an end of them for their Ungodliness, so that the corpses shall lie on the Earth more countless than the sand.

There shall be Fire over the Whole Earth and a Great Sign of a Sword with a Trumpet, at the rising of the Sun : and All the Earth Shall Hear Loud Wailing and a Mighty Noise.

The Seven Sisters Pleiades - with Missing Darker Electra

New Materials for the History of Man,
by Robert Grant Haliburton, 1863
(Derived from a Comparison of the Calendars & Festivals of Nations)

If the Festivals of the Greeks, Romans, Persians, Egyptians, and Goths, could be arranged with exactness in the same form with these Indian tables, there would be found, I am persuaded, a striking resemblance among them ; and an attentive comparison of them all might throw great light on the religion, and, perhaps, on the history, of the primitive World.

– Sir William Jones on the Lunar Year of the Hindoos.

Thor's 540 halls, multiplied by 48, make 25,920. 72 descendents of Noah, 72 priests of Apis. [Numbers that correspond with the Precession.]

The Pleiades were regarded as the Stars of Death.

In India, November is called 'The Month of the Pleiades'.

In European Calendars, the last day of October, and the first and second days of November, are designated as the festival of 'All Halloween', 'All Saints', and 'All Souls'. Though they have hitherto never attracted any special attention, and have not been supposed to have been connected with each other, they originally constituted but one commemoration of three days' duration, Known Among Almost All Nations as 'The Festival of the Dead', or the 'Feast of Ancestors'. It is now, or was formerly, observed at or near the beginning of November by the Peruvians, the Hindoos, the Pacific Islanders, the people of the Tonga Islands, The Australians, the ancient Persians, the ancient Egyptians, and the Northern nations of Europe, and continued for three days among the Japanese, the Hindoos, the Australians, the ancient Romans, and the ancient Egyptians.

The Universality of Primitive Superstitions and Customs of the Habit of Saying "God bless you" to a person who Sneezes, is referred to by Homer, and found in Europe, Asia, Africa, Polynesia, and America and even traced to the Arctic regions, that Death and Disease are Not the Result of Natural, but of Supernatural, Causes ; and that when a person Sneezes, he is Liable to be a Victim of the Spirits, or as the Celtic race express it, "to be carried off by the Fairies." [This could be the Dry Mist of the Conflagration at the time of the Deluge and Pestilence from the Comet.]

In the ancient calendar in India, the year commenced in the month of November, which bears the name 'Cartiguey', i.e., the 'Pleiades'. In the ancient Egyptian Calendar the same resemblance can be traced between the name of the Pleiades, which among the Hebrews and Chaldeans is 'Athor-aye', with that of the Egyptian month of November, which is 'Athor', meaning 'The Night'. The Arab name for the 'Pleiades', 'Atauria', also suggests a resemblance. In November, took place the Primeval Festival of the Dead, clad in a veil of Egyptian Mythology. The Isia, the solemn mourning for the God Osiris, 'the Lord of Tombs', lasted for three days, and began at Sunset, like the 'Lemuria' of the Romans, and the Festival of the Dead among the Persians and other nations. The singular custom of counting the day from the Sunset of the preceding day, or the Nocturnal System, was so universal, that many consider it proof of the unity of origin of our race. The Bible tells us "the evening and the morning were the first day" (Genesis 1 : 5). The Babylonians also started their days at Sunset. But the first day of our Festival of the Dead, is a still stronger illustration, as it is called Halloweve. [This probably means we were hit on the incoming dark side the first time at -13K Years BP and outgoing in the day time as with the 2300 BC Icarus / Phaethon Myth Event.]

The Indigenous Australians also consecrate Three Days to the Memory of the Dead, as a Vernal New Year's Celebration, regulated by the time-honoured Pleiades at the end of October, in which they paint a white stripe over their arms, legs, and ribs, they appear, as they dance by the Fires at night, like so many Skeletons Rejoicing. [They are propitiating that the Death Star would pass.]

The rising of the Pleiades in November on the Tonga Islands is connected with their Festival of the Dead and a first Fruits celebration (also called "the blossoming of the reeds.") in which vast numbers attend a sumptuous banquet and ceremony viewed as a national acknowledgement to the Gods. When the prayers were finished, and the banquet ended, a usage prevailed resembling much the Popish custom of mass for souls in purgatory. Each one returned to his home of family *marae*, there to offer special prayers for the spirits of Departed Relatives. [This was originally from the Flood.]

In Peru, we find the primitive calendar of two seasons marked by a New Year's Festival of the Dead, occurring in November, and celebrated at precisely the same time as in Europe and Polynesia. The month in which occurs is called 'Ayamarca', from 'Aya', 'a Corpse', and 'Marca', 'Carrying in Arms', because they celebrated the solemn Festival of the

20

Dead, with tears, lugubrious songs, and plaintive music ; and it was customary to visit the Tombs of Relations, and to leave in them food and drink. [There must be some reason this month is recalled as the one, "Of Carrying Corpses in their Arms!"] It is worthy of remark that the feast was celebrated among the ancient Peruvians at the same period, and on the same day, that Christians solemnize "The Commemoration of the Dead" (2nd November).

In Persia, we find a singular light thrown on the ancient calendar, November was consecrated to the Angel who presided over Agriculture and Death, or called 'Mordad', 'The Month of the Angel of Death'. It is called by some writers the Nouruz of the Magi, because the Maji still adhered to the Primitive New Year's Festival. It commenced in the evening with a Halloween, which was regarded as peculiarly sacred. Bonfires are lighted at this Festival as they are in Britain, and in most portions of the Globe, at this season of the year.

We now turn to Mexico, and there we find that 'The Great Festival' of the Mexican cycle was held on the 17th of November, and was regulated by the Pleiades. It began at Sunset ; and at Midnight as that Constellation approached the Zenith, a human victim was offered up to Avert the Dread Calamity which they believed impended over the human race. They had a Tradition that at the time the World had been previously Destroyed ; and they dreaded lest a similar Catastrophe would, at the end of a cycle, Annihilate the human race.

Now it is most remarkable to find that the Egyptians, with their Isia, or New Year's Festival of Agriculture, and of the Dead, that took place on the 17th day of November, associated Traditions as to the Deluge, and it is still more surprising to find that the 17th day of November is the Very Day on which, the Bible tells us, the Deluge took place. The Deluge commenced on the 17th of the second month of the Jewish year (i.e., November) ; the Ark rested on Mount Ararat on the 17th day of the 7th month; and the Dove returned with the olive branch on the 17th day of the 11th month.

The ceremony of the Secular Fire among the Aztecs, the oldest, the most solemn, the most sacred of all in their calendar, seems to imply the same thing of them; for that was celebrated at Midnight; that is, though the ceremony itself began at Sunset, the consummation or conclusion, by the Lighting Anew of the Secular Fire, took place at Midnight.

21

The spirits of the Dead, which among almost all savage races, are supposed to reappear in the form of Snakes (hence the Greek Python Ob, the Serpent, i.e., the Dead), are at large as "Flying Dragons on the Ayre." In Cornwall it is the opinion of the Vulgar, that "It is usual for Snakes to meet in companies." on Midsummer Eve ; when by joining their heads together, by their hissing they form bubbles which harden into the magic "Snake Stone," the sacred amulet of northern nations. [Still common (late 20th Century) of the Finnish to pour molten lead into water on Midsummer Eve.]

Many of the northern nations of Europe have retained traces of the ancient year, not only in the Festivals of All Halloween, All Saints, and All Souls, but also in the very name of November, which was called among the Anglo-Saxons, the Dutch, the Danes, and the Swedes, the month of Blood or of Sacrifice.

The Festival of Kali the Goddess of Death, and the spouse of Siva, "the Destroyer," takes place in Hindostan in November (the month of the Pleiades).

No clue has been supplied to the belief of the ancient Persians, that winter comes up from hell at the beginning of November, "The Month of Death" (Morda), which is also known among the Arabs as Rajeb ("the Month of Fear").

Proserpine wedded Pluto in November.

All the Myths, therefore, connected with the Festival of the Dead, show that that commemoration and its rites were inherited by All Nations from a Common Source. Even in minute details we have Unanswerable Proof of this. The Japanese, at the end of their Festival of the Dead, "speed the parting guests" by the same means that were in vogue among the ancient Romans at the end of their Lemuria, by Casting Stones into the Air, to frighten home any stray ghosts inclined to linger after the close of the Feast of Ancestors. Even the duration of the Festival is so similar throughout the World, that this resemblance alone would Prove the Common Origin of the Feast of Ancestors. It is Impossible that Accident can have Caused the inhabitants of Australia, the Sandwich Islands, Japan, Hindostan, Ceylon, ancient Persia, Egypt, Greece, and Rome, as well as of Northern Europe, to hold this Festival for Three Days. Captain Cook, struck by the remarkable resemblance between the Festivals of the Pacific Islanders, arrived at a conclusion, which may be extended to the whole human race, when he suggested "the reasonableness of tracing such singularly resembling customs to a Common Source."

Virgil quote : "A Bull with Gilded Horns opens the Year is White."

"On Ida's Summit, with his mighty mother, young Bacchus leads the Frantic Train, and through the Echoing Woods the Rattling Timbrels "Sound." Then the Curetes Clash'd their Sounding Arms, and raised, with joyful voice, the song to Bacchus, ever young ; while the Shrill Pipe Resounded to the praise of Cybele, and the gay Satyrs tripp'd in jocund dance, such dance as Bacchus loves." - Mr. Fader's translation Mystery of the Cabiri.

"Come, hero Dionusus, to thy Temple on the Sea Shore ; come, Heifer-footed deity, to thy sacrifice, and bring the graces in thy Train ! Hear us, O Bull, worthy of our veneration ; hear us, O Illustrious Bull !"

The reverence paid to the Seven Stars was almost Universal – and probably referred Not to the Sun and Moon, and the five planets, as has been hitherto supposed, but to the Seven Pleiades. It was conspicuous in the ancient Mysteries, and its traceable in the circular dance of the priests representing the course of the Stars. But the most striking evidence of its influence throughout the Globe, is that a reference to the Seven Stars, or to the Number Seven, Pervades the Symbolism of Almost All Races, in Europe, Asia, Africa, Australia, and America, even still lingering among our Freemasons, with whom the Seven Stars are a Conspicuous and probably not very intelligible emblem. But as this reverence for the Number Seven, or for Seven Stars, is found in Every Quarter of the Globe, and the Pleiades are Almost Everywhere the Subjects of Veneration, or at least of observation, we can Scarcely Doubt that the Wide-Spread Symbol of the Seven Stars can Only Refer to the Pleiades.

Among the Greeks and Romans the five intercalation days at the end of the 360 day year were called Stained or Polluted by Death, which is precisely the same name by which they were known among the Yucatan Indians. They were also known among the former as Unlucky Days. This name was clearly connected with the Dead, as it was applied to the Sceleratae Portae of Rome, through which funerals passed. Don Juan Pio Perez of Yucatan, speaking of the Yucatan calendar, says "Five Supplementary Days were Added at the End of each Year, which made part of no month, and which for that reason they called 'days without names.'" "They called them also

23

Wayab, or Uayab Jaab. The word Uayab may be derived from Uay, which means to be Destroyed, Wounded, Corroded by the Caustic Juice of plants, or with Lye and other Strong Liquids." If this was the real meaning of the name, these days that were "Stained" by Death. Also, in India, the Festival evidently fell on the days called Dagda or Burned. [Like the Venomous Blood of Tiamat's Host and Acidic American Legends.]

On this account, the Yucatan Indians Feared those days, believing them to be Unfortunate, and to carry Danger of Sudden Death, Plague, and other Misfortunes. For this reason these Five days were assigned for the celebration of the God Mam ("Grandfather"). On the first day they carried him about and Feasted him with great magnificence ; on the second day they diminished the solemnity ; on the third day they brought him down from the altar, and placed him in the middle of the temple ; on the fourth day they placed him at the threshold of door ; and on the fifth day, the ceremony of taking leave (or the dismissal) took place, that the New Year might commence the following day. [Grandpa is actually a mummy.]

These Unlucky Days were regarded in the Old as well as the New World, as Stained by the Shadow of Death. They were not numbered with the months, nor included in the days of the year. It is not a little remarkable that to a Curse, similar to that of the Patriarch Job, the Egyptians attributed the Very Origin of these Five Unlucky Days. Plutarch tells us that the Sun, enraged with Chronos (Saturn, Time, or the year) and Rhea (the Starry Heavens), for begotten the five planets, for whom there was no space in the year or in the Heavens, uttered a Curse that they should neither be born in a month, nor in the year. Therefore Hermes, as a return to Rhea for past favour, played at dice with the Moon, and won back the 72nd part of each day of the year of 360 days, i.e., 5 days, which thenceforward constituted those five epagomenae, or "days without name," which neither formed a part of the months, nor of the year. To show how striking is the identity between the imprecation which forms the basis of this Myth, and that of Job against the day of his birth, we have only to imagine the Sun using the very words of the Patriarch to curse those ill-omened birthdays of the planets. [The days of the week which is the substitute for the forgotten meaning.]

"After this opened Job his mouth, and cursed his day. And Job spoke and said : Let the day perish wherein I was born, and the night wherein it was said : 'A man-child is brought forth.' Let that day be Darkness ; let not God inquire after it from above, neither let the Light Shine upon it. Let Darkness

and the Shadow of Death claim it for their own ; let a Cloud Dwell Upon
it ; let all that maketh Black the day Terrify it. As for that night, let Thick
Darkness seize upon it ; let it not rejoice among the days of the year ; let not
come into the number of the months. Lo, let that night be Desolate ; let no
joyful voice come therein. Let them curse it that curse the day, who are
ready to Rouse Up Leviathan [Dragon]. Let the Stars of the twilight thereof
be Dark ; let it look for Light, but have none ; neither let it behold the
eyelids of the morning;"   Job 3 : 1-9 [1917]

The Egyptian month of Athyr must have been connected with the
Constellation of Taurus, it is the month in which the Pleiades are most
distinct and Hesychius says that in the Egyptian "Athyr meant both a month
and a Bull," and Plutarch says that the Phoenicians called a Bull Thor
(Taurus).

Everything connected with the year and its festivals was Concealed by the
Priests with the Most Watchful Jealousy, and was Veiled from the Eyes of
Men in Allegories and Myths. Even when the Mystic Secret was partially
disclosed to the Initiated, it was Guarded by the Terrors of Superstition and
by the Sanctity of Oaths, which it was Death to Violate. The stories of the
wandering Io, of Proserpine, Osiris, Menu, and the Phoenix, show this
tendency to convert simple Truths connected with Astronomy or Natural
Phenomena, into Gods or Fables. The memory of these Secrets, so
carefully guarded, must have Gradually Faded Away ; but the Myths, in
which they were Concealed, must have Outlived their own history and
Meaning, and must have long lingered after the Key that could Unlock their
Mystic Treasures had been Lost and Forgotten.

The ancient Mysteries represented the Death and Revival of the Stars, the
Bull put to Death and is Resurrected, as the Myth of Osiris whose soul
resides in a Bull being Lost and Found with the setting and rising of the
Pleiades. And of Proserpine the daughter of Ceres and a Bull sinking down
into Hell and Rising Again ; as well as the Two Festivals of the German
Goddess of Life and Death, all had their origin in the appearance and
disappearance of the Stars in Taurus. That the initiated at the ancient
Mysteries really learned something as to the Astronomical Basis of their
Religion, we have every reason to infer ; but it is plain that Herodotus and
many other ancient authors were either Ignorant, or Prudently Silent as to
the Secret Sources of Classical Mythology. Chaeremon and others,
however, according to Eusebius, not only Believed, but also Declared that
the Egyptians held that the Stars were the Only Deities, and that All

Festivals had been instituted originally in their honor ; that "the heroes whose names appear in the almanacs, are nothing else than charms for the cures of evils, and observations of the rising and settings of Stars." They also believed "that the Legends about Osiris and Isis and All other their Mythological Fables have reference either to the Stars, their appearances and occultations, and the periods of their risings, or to the increase and decrease of the Moon, or to the cycles of the Sun, or the diurnal and nocturnal hemispheres." [Or The Comet]

It is therefore plain that my conclusions, based on the times of observance of Festivals and on their Connection with the Year of the Pleiades, are borne out by the opinions of the ancients themselves. But their view of the Astronomical Character of Egyptian Mythology, supplies a Clue to what has hitherto Evaded All Enquiry. If the very deities of the Egyptians were merely representatives of the Stars, and of the year, then their symbols must also have had a Hidden Meaning connected with the year or its seasons. The Crux Ansata, or the T or Tau, surmounted by a ring, and the Sacred Beetle, the Scarabaeus, were the most Mysterious and the most Conspicuous Emblems of the Egyptians. I have found that they were in reality the same. In seeking for the Meaning of the Scarabaeus, it has escaped notice that it was the Hieroglyphic for the Letter T, and that its Egyptian name was Thore. On examining a Scarabaeus in my possession, I found out the reason for its name, and of its Significance. On the back of the beetle a T or Tau is most clearly marked. [Symbolizing Life or Death] [Pass or Strike]

Hills and Mountains in England known as Tor and Arthur's seat.

The Mexican Sacrifice which was made with an Axe of Obsidian.

In alluding to the Light which I believe these investigations into the times of observance of the Festivals of nations, are likely to throw on the subject of the Deluge, I do so with a Good Deal of Hesitation, first, because this event being connected with sacred history should be inquired into with all due reverence, and secondly, because it is a matter which a large number of earnest and good men Believe Should Beyond Pale of Scientific Enquiry. Yet it Must be Allowed that the history of the Deluge has often Proved the Stumbling Block of Science, and the apology of the skeptic. I feel but little sympathy with that want of faith, which forgetting that Christianity owes, not only its existence, but also its Protection to the Deity, often seeks to Defend Revelation by Attempting to Preclude All Honest and Fair Investigation, and by Exhibiting a Bitterness and a Want of Charity, which seems too often peculiar to theological controversies, and which would Not be Tolerated in the Ordinary Affairs of Every Day Life. To rebuke the fears of his followers, the great Head of the Church walked in safety over the waves ; and we may be sure that the truth of Christianity will never founder, whatever may be the Foreboding of the timid or the Unbelieving.

. . . . to throw a new light on the history of the human race . . . .

The peculiarity which Greswell, as other writers, has noticed in the Traditions of the Aztecs, the Connection of the Midnight Culmination of the Pleiades with the Deluge and with the end of a cycle, I found even more remarkable than has been supposed, and that the Hebrews, the Egyptians and the Mexicans must have attached the memory of that event to the same day and probably to the Same Phenomenon. I found Greswell saying, "We commend this fact to the attention of Astronomers." The Fact is certain that the Culmination of this particular Constellation (the Pleiades) was one of the Phenomena presented by the Heathens, to which the Aztecs in particular, "for some reason or other, looked with peculiar interest and attached peculiar importance." Knowing as I did that the Midnight Culmination of the Pleiades was Connected with a Primitive Year beginning in November, and hence had nothing whatever to do with the miracle alluded to by Greswell, and that with that month the Hebrews and Egyptians Connected the Beginning of the Deluge, I felt that I had accidently met with a most Marvelous Fact, that once established a Connection between our account of the Deluge and the Traditions of the Heathen nations and of Primeval Antiquity. It was plain that if the latter were, to some extent, Astronomical rather than historical, our account of it must to a certain degree partake of the same character. At any rate no candid enquirer could meet with a Fact like that, and Shut His Eyes to its Importance and Significance, or Forbear to Allude to It, for Fear of the Odium that the Discussion of this Subject is apt to Entail upon anyone who does not accept literally all the incidents and details of the history of the Deluge. These facts have forced themselves upon my attention. They are so palpable that one could even commence these investigations without having his attention drawn to the Connection of the Traditions of all nations as to the Deluge, with Primitive Festivals and with the idea of time ; and no person could pursue the enquiry without coming to the conclusion that our history of that event is Almost Identical with the Traditions of Primeval Antiquity on the subject. I feel convinced that whatever prejudices may be created by the facts I mention, Further Enquiry Will Fully Substantiate My Conclusions ; and that the Day Will Come when it will Universally be Conceded that our narrative of the Deluge

27

was neither description of that event, that was in accordance with the ideas of Primitive Antiquity on the subject.

In the Japanese Lanthorn Festival they believe that for three days in every year the spirits of Deceased relatives return to their former homes and the grave yards are lighted with lanthorns and regaled with Feasts, and welcomed with Festivals and are sent home to the world of spirits in a boat made of straw, which is lighted with tapers to cheer the souls on their Dark journey.

The Cauldron of Medea was well known to the early inhabitants of Britain as the Cauldron of the Year and of the Flood, which was "regarded as an emblem of the Deluge itself," which was "kept boiling for a year and a day" (Davies Druids)

The letter A = Ataur and = to Egyptian crux ansata

[The ancient Phoenician / Greek Alphabet started with the letter A, upside-down is the Constellation Taurus, which does look like the inverted Capital letter A and representing the Bull with nose and horns also that the last letter was T or Tau with the U as the symbol shape of Omega, this is also the same as the Hebrew from Aleph to Tav which correspond to numbers such as the Sumerians related Gods to numerals. So, the saying, "I am the Alpha and Omega," (Revelation 21 : 6) would start and end with the same reference as to the Taurids. Creation according to most Traditions starts as the rebirth of the World after the Catastrophe, so technically, it is the ending and beginning: or the causation and afterward clearing or uplifting of the Sky resulting in the Resurrection of Verdure and Animal Life.]

[Note : Within the next image the Sky Mountain is shown, not yet demonstrated in the literature, and the Constellation of Leo in which they represent the Comet and the Time that the Space Fall happened (Actually when the earth began to recover.) via Precession of the Equinoxes to approximately 12,000 years BP.]

28

Astronomical Myths, based on Flammarion's History of the Heavens," by John Frederick Blake, 1877

No longer some little neighbouring lights shine down upon us from a solid vault ; but we find ourselves launched into the <u>Sea</u> of Infinity ; with power to gaze into its almost Immeasurable <u>Depths</u>. [19th Century telescope]

Cassiopeia seated and holding a Lotus flower in her hand. [The Lotus flower represents the birth of the New Sun after atmospheric loading.]

Hercules [Constellation] kneeling down to pick up Stones to Throw.

Orion the guardian. [Against the Bull]

Both the Persians and the Chinese noted four bright Stars, which they said watched over the rest, Taschter over the East, Sateris over the West, Venaud over the South, and Hastorang over the North. Now we must understand these points to refer to the Sun, the East being the Spring Equinox, the West the Autumnal Equinox, and the North and South the Summer and Winter Solstices. Which would have corresponded to Aldebaran, the Antares, Regulus, and Fomalhaut, four Stars of the first magnitude.

Draconis a the Tail of the Dragon was the pole star in 2850 BC.

Among the Jews there seems to be some remarkable connection between their patriarchs and the signs, through the history of that connection may not well be made out. The Twelve signs are mentioned as being worshiped, along with the Sun and Moon, in the book of Kings. But what is more remarkable is the dream of Joseph, in which the Sun and the Moon and the other eleven Stars worshipped him, coupled with the various designations or descriptions given to each son in the blessing of Jacob. In Reuben we have the Man who is said to be "unstable as water," in which we may recognize Aquarius. In Simeon and Levi "the Brethren," we trace the Twins. Judah is the "Lion." Zebulun, "that dwells at the Haven of the Sea," represents Fishes. Issachar is the Bull, or "strong ass couching down between two burdens." Dan, "the Serpent by the way, the Adder in the path," represents the Scorpion. Gad is the Ram, the leader to a flock or troop of sheep. Asher the Balance, as the weigher of bread. Naphtali, "the Hind let loose," is the Capricorn, Joseph the Archer, whose bow abode in strength. Brujanin the Crab, changing from morning to evening, and Dinah, the only daughter, represents the Virgin. [Personally, I do not belive this is entirely correct.]

There is doubtless something far-fetched in some of these comparisons, but when we consider the care with which the number Twelve was retained, and that the four signs – namely, Judah a Lion, Reuben a Man, Ephraim a Bull, and Dan a Scorpion – and notice the numerous traces of astronomical culture in the Jewish ceremonies, the Seven lights of the candlestick, the Twelve Stones of the High Priest, the feasts at the two Equinoxes, the ceremonies connected with the Ram and a Bull, we cannot doubt that there is Something More than Chance in the Matter, but rather conclude that we have an

30

example of the process by which, in the hands of the Egyptians themselves, Astronomical representations became at last actually defined.

It has been thought possible indeed to assign definitely each God of the Egyptians to one of the Twelve Zodiacal signs. The Ram was consecrated to Jupiter Ammon, who was represented with a Ram's head and horns. The Bull became the God Apis, who was worshipped under that similitude. The Twins correspond to Horus and Harpocrates, two sons of Osiris. The Crab was consecrated to Anubis or Mercury. The Lion belonged to the Summer Sun, Osiris ; the Virgin to Isis. The Balance and the Scorpion were included together under the name of Scorpion, which animal belongs to Typhon, as did all dangerous animals. The Archer was the image of Hercules, for whom the Egyptians had great veneration. The Capricorn was consecrated to Pan or Mendes. The Waterer – or Man carrying a water-pot – is found on many Egyptian monuments.

Among the Most Remarkable of the Constellations is a group of Seven Stars arranged in a kind of triangular cluster, and known as the Pleiades. It is not, strictly speaking, one of the Constellations, as it forms only part of one. We have seen that one of the ancient Signs of the Zodiac is the Bull, or Taurus ; the group of Stars we are now speaking of forms part of this, lying towards the Eastern part in the shoulders of the Bull. The Pleiades scarcely escape anybody's observation now, and we shall not be, therefore, surprised that they have Always Attracted Great Attention. So Great Indeed has been the Attention Paid to Them that Festivals and Seasons, Calendars and Years, have by many nations been regulated by their rising or culmination, and they have thus more mixed up with the early history of Astronomy, and have left more marks on the records of past nations, Than Any Other Celestial Object, except the Sun and Moon. [And the Comet that appeared to come out of the Pleiades.]

It is possible that Taurus, the German Their, somehow got connected with the letter "tau" in Greek, which seems itself connected with the sacred scarabaeus of Tau-beetle of Egypt ; but the nature of the connection is by no means obvious. Mr. Haliburton even suggests that the "tors" and "Arthur's seat," which are names given to British hill-tops, may be Connected with the "high places," of the Worship of the Pleiades, but of this we have no proof. Among the customs possibly derived from the ancients, through the Phoenicians, though now adopted as conveying a different meaning in a Christian sense, is that of the "hot cross bun," or "Bull cake." It is found on Egyptian monuments, signifying the four quarters of the year, and

31

sometimes stamped with the Head and Horns of the Bull. It is found among ourselves too, essentially Connected with the Dead, and something similar to it appears in the "soul cake" connected originally with All Souls' Day.

Among the Scotch it was Traditionally thought that on New Year's Eve the Candlemas Bull can be seen, rising at twilight and sailing over the Heavens – a very near approach to a matter-of-fact statement.

The Greeks called it the Galaxy, the Chinese and Arabians call it the River of Heaven. It is the Path of Souls among the North American Indians. [Yet others, milk way, wolf tracks, bird migration, and male/female shape at a Norwegian website. The Galaxy can be confused with the Zodiacal Stream that would have crossed approximately perpendicular to the Milky Way.]

They decreed that the Earth constituted the Universe, that the Heavens were made for it, that God, the angels, and the saints inhabited an eternal abode of joy situated above the Azure sphere of the fixed Stars, and they embodied this gratifying illusion in all their illuminated manuscripts, their calendars, and their church windows. The doctors of the Church all acknowledged a plurality of Heavens, but they differed as to the number. Those who wished to have everything as complete as possible combined the system of Ptolemy with that of the Fathers of the Church, and placed in the centre of the Earth the Infernal Regions which they surrounded by a circle. Another circle marked the Earth itself, and after that the surrounding Ocean, marked as Water, then the circle of Air, and lastly that of Fire. Enveloping these, and following one after the other, were the Seven circles of the Seven planets ;

the eighth represented the sphere of the fixed Stars on the Firmament, then came the ninth heaven, then a tenth, the coelum cristallinum, and lastly an eleventh and outermost, which was the empyreal Heaven, where dwelt the Cherubim [Winged Bull] and Seraphim [Serpent - Dragon], and above all the spheres was a throne on which sat the Father, as Jupiter Olympus.

We are led on to examine some of these Legends, that we may appreciate how far a Knowledge of Astronomy will Effect the Eradication of Errors and Fantasies which, Under the Aspect of Truth, have So Long Enslaved The People. No doubt the authors of the Legendary Stories Knew Well Enough their Allegorical Nature ; but those who received them supposed that they gave True Indications of the Nature of the Earth and World, and therefore accepted them as Facts. Thus a Great Amount of Darkness has Obscured Scientific Knowledge.

Among the ancient nations people used to come to the assistance of the Moon, by making a Confused Noise with all kinds of instruments, when it was eclipsed. It is even done now in Persia and some parts of China [19th Century], where they fancy that the Moon is Fighting with a Great Dragon, and they think the noise will make him loose his hold and take flight. Among the East Indians they have the same belief that when the Sun and the Moon are eclipsed, a Dragon is seizing them, and Astronomers who go there to observe eclipses are troubled by the fears of their native attendants, and by their endeavors to get into the Water as the best place under the circumstances. [Probably expecting Fire from Heaven to proceed next, including, the innate fear of the reoccurrence of a previous disaster blocking out the Sun!]

The ancients divided Comets into different classes, the chief points of distinction being derived from the shape, length, and brilliancy of the Tails. Pliny distinguished Twelve kinds, which he thus characterized :- "Some frighten us by their blood-coloured Mane ; their Bristling Hair rises towards the Heaven. The Bearded ones let their Long Hair Fall Down like a Majestic Beard [White Bearded Americans]. The Javelin-Shaped ones seem to be projected forwards like a Dart, as they rapidly attain their shape after their first appearance ; if the Tail is shorter, and terminates in a point, it is called a Sword ; this is the palest of all the Comets ; it has the appearance of a Bright Sword without any diverging rays. The plate or disc derives its name from its shape, its colour is that of amber, it gives out some diverging rays from its sides, but not in large quantity. The cask has really the form of a cask, which one might suppose to be Staved in Smoke enveloped in Light.

33

The retort imitates the figure of a Horn, and the lamp that of a Burning Flame. The Horse-Comet represents the Mane of a Horse which is Violently Agitated, as by a circular, or rather cylindrical, motion. Such a Comet appears also of singular Whiteness, with Hair of a Silver hue ; it is so Bright that one can Scarcely Look At It. [Possibly mistaken for the Sun in Legends of rising in the West as a very near Comet or a Bolide.] There are Bristling Comets, they are like the Skins of Beasts with their Hair on, and are surrounded by a Nebulosity. Lastly, the Hair of the Comet sometimes takes the form of a Lace." Pingre, a celebrated historian of Comets, tell us that one of the first Comets noticed in history is that which appeared over Rome forty years before Christ, and in which the Roman people imagined they saw the soul of Caesar endowed with divine honours. Next comes that which threw its Light on Jerusalem when it was being besieged and remained for a whole year above the city, according to the account of Josephus. It was of this kind that Pliny said it "is of so great a Whiteness that one can scarcely look at it, and one may see in it the Image of God in human form."

It is well known that the year 1000 AD was for a long time predicted to be the End of the World. In this year the Astronomers and Chroniclers registered the Fall of an Enormous Burning Meteor and the Appearance of a Comet. Pingre says : "On the 19th of the calends of January" – that is the 14th of December – "the Heavens being dark, a kind of Burning Sword Fell to Earth, leaving behind it a Long Train of Light. Its Brilliancy was such that it Frightened not only those who were in the fields, but even those who were shut up in their houses. This Great Opening in the Heavens was Gradually Closed, and then was seen the Figure of a Dragon, whose Feet were Blue, and whose Head kept Continually Increasing. A Comet having appeared at the same time as this Chasm, or Meteor, they were Confounded."

In the early months of 1472 appeared a Large Comet, which historians agree in saying was Very Horrible and Alarming. Belleforest said it was a Hideous and Frightening Comet, which Threw its Rays from East to West, giving Great cause for Fear to great people, who were not Ignorant that Comets are the Menacing Rods of God, which Admonish those who are in Authority, that they may be Converted.

The most Frightful of Comets of this period, according to Simon Goulart, was that of 1527. "It put some into so Great a Freight that they Died ; others Fell Sick. It was seen by several thousand people, and appeared very long, and of the Colour of Blood. At the summit was seen the Representation of a Curved Arm, holding a Large Sword in its Hand, as it would Strike ; at the top of the point of the Sword were Three Stars, but that which touched the point was more Brilliant than the others. On the Two sides of the Rays of the Comet were seen Large Hatchets, Poignards, Bloody Swords, among which were seen a great number of Men Decapitated, having their Heads and Beards Horribly Bristling."

It has always been known that very soon after these Miserable Portents Afflictions, effusion of human blood, massacres, Deaths of great monarchs, kings, princes, and rulers, seditions, treacheries, raids, Overthrowing of empires, kingdoms, or villages ; hunger and scarcity of provisions, Burning and overthrowing of towns ; Pestilences, Widespread Mortality, both of Beasts and Men ; in fact all sorts of Evils and Misfortunes take place. Nor can it be doubted that all these Signs and Prodigies give Warning that the End of the World is Come, and with it the Terrible Last Judgment of God. A remarkable Comet, however, which appeared in 1680, was not without its Fears for the Vulgar. We are told that it was recognized as the same which appeared the year of Caesar's death, then in 531, and afterwards in 1106, having a period of about 575 years. The Terror it produced in the towns was Great ; timid spirits saw in it the Sign of a New Deluge, as they said Water was always announced by Fire. Of this same Comet Bernouilli wrote, "That if the body of the Comet is not a Visible Sign of the Anger of God, the Tail may be." It was this too that suggested to Whiston the idea that he put forward, not as a superstitious, but as a physical speculation, that a Comet approaching the Earth Was The Cause of the Deluge.

The story in Herodotus, who tells us, that the Sun, in the space of 11,340 years [Amazing Correspondence.], four times inverted his course, and rose in the West. But what I mainly depend on, is that discourse in Plato, who relating some very ancient Traditions (as he expressly says they are, and delivered by our first parents to their posterity) about the primitive state of things, and what a mighty and remarkable change was effected by a certain mighty and remarkable alternation in the Heavenly motions.

The first of the year at November 17 th corresponding to the rising of the Pleiades can be traced back to 1300 BC among the Egyptians and Hindoo.

Among the earliest Egyptians the year was of 360 days, which were reckoned in the months, and five days were added each year, between the

35

commencement of one and the end of the other, and called unlucky days. It was the belief of the Egyptians that these five days were the birthdays of their principal Gods ; Osiris being born on the first, Anieris (or Apollo) on the second, Typhon [Dragon] on the third, Isis on the fourth, Nephys (or Aphrodite) on the fifth. These appear to have some relation with similar unlucky days among the Greeks and Romans, and other nations. [Must have been 5 days instead of 3 for the Festival of the Dead or one today as Halloween, a degradation of memory thus the disconnection of Trick-or- Treaters.]

Every Twelve years the Babylonians expected to have the same weather repeated. When we connect this with their observations on the varying brightness of the Sun, especially at the commencement of the year on the first of Nisan, which they record at one time as "bright yellow" and at another as "spotted," and remember that modern [19th century] researchers have shown that weather is certainly in some way dependent on the solar spots. [Modern 11 year Solar cycle ; plus one would have to have some kind of filter to see this, either atmospheric at Sunrise or Sunset, colored glass, lenses, or Camera Obscura Image. If one had positional sheets Karnak would have multiple possibilities of image sizes throughout the Temple. In the Pyramid Texts they seem to describe the Suns images as if they could view the limb and spots ! Notes of Pyramid Text lost due to computer crash.]

Pliny, Macrobius, and Suidas, do all agree, that the Egyptians of old computed a lunar month for a year. Explaining long Biblical ages of Men. Strabo says, that the chain of Mountains which ran eastward from Cappadocia and Comagena, are first called Taurus and that the Gordyean Mountains are contiguous to the Taurus Mountains and that Mount Ararat belongs to Armenia.

The very name of Typhon also, according to some learned Men, signifies a Deluge or Inundation ; whence the Egyptian priests (as Plutarch says) called the Sea Typhon. Typhon (whom the Latin poets more frequently call Typhoeus) is represented as a Monstrous Giant who Fought Against Heaven, and was at last Overcome by Jupiter, and, as On says, lies now submersed in Water. From all which it appears very probable, that he was one of those Giants who, as the scriptures says, were in the Earth before the Flood ; one of those mighty Men which were of old, Men of renown, whose wickedness was so exceedingly great, as might easily give occasion to the ancient Tradition of their fighting against God. And lastly, Typhon's being said to be overcome and Submersed in Water seems evidently to proceed from his perishing in the Deluge.

Now the only assignable cause, is that of the impulse of a Comet with little or no atmosphere, or of a central solid hitting obliquely upon the Earth along some parts of its present Equator. So that it is plain that the Comet did descend into our region either at, or very near the time when the flood of Noah began.

A New Theory of the Earth, by William Whiston, 1696

"I have evidently shown, that in case a Comet passed by, before the Earth, in its annual course, on the 17th day of the second month from the Autumnal equinox, or November 28, in the 2349 th year before the Christian era. It is true, when upon a mere supposition of such a passing by of a Comet, I had in my own mind observed the phenomena relating to the deluge to answer to admiration, I was not a little surprised, and pleased at such a discovery. It gave me no small satisfaction to see, that, upon a possible and easy hypothesis, I could give so clear an account of those things which had hitherto proved so hard, no to say inexplicable and could show the exact coincidence of the particulars with the sacred history, and the phenomena of nature. I thought to be able to proceed so far, was not only more than had been yet done, more than was generally expected ever would be done ; but abundantly sufficient to the best of purposes, to clear the Holy Scriptures from the imputations of ill-disposed Men, and to demonstrate the account of the deluge to be in every part neither impossible nor unphilosophical. But proceeding in some farther thoughts and calculations on the said hypothesis, to my exceeding great content and admiration, I found all things to correspond so strangely, and the time of the year by several concurring ways to be so exactly fixed, agreeably to the sacred history thereby ; that, as I saw abundant reason myself to rest satisfied of the reality, as well as probability of what I before barely supposed ; so I thought the producing the particulars I had discovered, might afford evidence to the minds of others and go a great way to the entire establishing the certainty of that, of whose great probability the correspondence of the several phenomena of the Deluge had before afforded sufficient satisfaction."

The Elder Edda of Saemund Sigfusson

Translated from the original Old Norse text into
English, by Benjamin Thorpe, the Younger Edda of
Snorre Sturleson and I. A. Blackwell, 1907

Of Ragnarok ; or the Twilight of the Gods ; and the Conflagration of the Universe

In the first place will come the winter, called Fimbul-winter, during which snow will fall from the four corners of the World ; the frost will be very severe, the wind piercing, the weather tempestuous, and the Sun impart no Gladness. Three such Winters shall pass away without being tempered by a Single Summer. Three other Similar Winters follow, during which war and discord will spread over the Whole Globe. Brethren for the sake of mere gain shall kill each other, and no one shall spare either his parents or his children. Then shall happen such things as may truly be accounted great prodigies. The Wolf shall Devour the Sun, and a severe loss will that be for Mankind. The other Wolf will take the Moon, and this too will cause great mischief. Then the Stars shall be Hurled from the Heavens, and the Earth so Violently Shaken that Trees will be Torn up by the Roots, the tottering Mountains Tumble headlong from their foundations, and all bonds and fetters be shivered in pieces. Fenrir then breaks loose, and the Sea Rushes

39

Over the Earth, on account of the Midgard Serpent turning with a Giant Force, and Gaining the Land. [Tsunami]

The Wolf Fenrir advancing, opens his enormous mouth ; the lower jaw reaches to Earth, and the upper one to Heaven, and would in fact reach still father were there space to admit of it. Fire flashes from his eyes and nostrils. The Miggard Serpent, placing himself by the side of the Wolf, Vomits forth Floods of Poison which overwhelm the Air and the Waters. Amidst this devastation Heaven is Cleft in Twain, and the Sons of Muspell ride through the Breach. Surtur rides first, and both before and behind him Flames of Burning Fire. His Sword Outshines the Sun itself.

Broken was the outer wall of the AEsir's burgh. The Vanir, foreseeing conflict, tramp o'er the plains. Odin cast his Spear, and mid the people hurled it : that was the first Warfare in the World. [Kaali Meteorite]

She knows that Heimdall's Horn is hidden under the Heaven-Bright holy Tree. A River she sees flow, with foamy fall, from Valfather's pledge. Understand ye yet, or what?

She saw a Hall standing, far from the Sun, in Nastrond ; its doors are Northward turned, venom-drops fall in through its apertures : entwined is that Hall with Serpent's backs.

Easily to be known is, by those who to Odin come, the Mansion by its aspect. A Wolf hangs before the Western door, over it an Eagle hovers.

Fixed on the hook the shield of Men, the Serpent's slayer, the Ox's Head. Gaped at the bait the Foe of Gods, the Encircler beneath of every land. [The Great Serpent that encircles the Solar System with Tail in Mouth.]

They had far journeyed before Odin's son cast one look backward : he from the caverns saw, with Hymir from the East, a Troop [Host] of Many-Headed Monsters coming.

From his shoulders he lifted the Kettle [Druid Ark of Darkness] down ; Miollnir hurled forth towards the savage crew, and slew all the Mountain-Giants, who with Hymir had him pursued.

40

In his strength exulting he to the God's council came, and had the Kettle, which Hymir had possessed, out of which every God shall with OEgir drink at every harvest-tide.

Thor.
Thou now remindest me how I with Hrungnir (Serpent) fought, that stout-hearted Jotun, whose head was all of Stone ; yet I made him Fall, and Sink before me. What meanwhile didst thou, Harbard (Abyss) ?

Harbard.
Sprightly Women we had, had they but been meek ; shrewd ones we had, had they been kind. Of sand a rope they twisted, and from the Deep valley dug the Earth : to them all I alone was superior in cunning. I rested with the Sisters Seven, and their love and pleasures shared. What meanwhile didst thou, Thor?

Thor.
I slew Thiassi, that stout-hearted Jotun (Giant) : up I cast the eyes of Allvaldi's son into the Heaven serene : they are signs the greatest of my deeds. What meanwhile didst thou, Harbard?

Harbard.
Great seductive arts I used against the riders of the night, (Giantesses, Witches, ect.) When from their husbands I enticed them. A mighty Jotun I believe Hlebard to be : a Magic Wand he gave me, but from his wits I charmed him.

Thor.
In the East I was, and slew the Jotun brides, crafty in evil, as they to the Mountain went. Great would have been the Jotun race, had they all lived ; and not a Man left Midgard. Also a River I defended, when the Sons of Svarang me assailed, and with Stones pelted me, though in their success they little joyed : they were the first to sue for peace.

Frey.
Why shall I tell thee, thou young man, my mind's great trouble ? For the Alf's Illuminator Shines every day, yet not for my pleasure. In Gymir's courts I saw walking a maid for whom I long. Her arms gave forth Light wherein Shone All Air and Water.

Gerd.

What is that Sound of Sounds, which I now Sounding Hear within our dwelling? The Earth is Shaken, and with it all the house of Gymir Trembles.

Skirnir.

The Ring too I will give thee, which was Burnt with the young son of Odin. Eight of equal weight will from it drop, every ninth night.

Skirnir.

Seest thou this Sword, young maiden ! Thin, Glittering-Bright, which I have here in hand ? Beneath its edge shall the old Jotun Fall : thy sire is death-doomed. With a Taming-Wand I smite thee, and I will tame thee, maiden ! To my will. Thou shalt go tither, where the son's of Men shall never more behold thee. On an Eagle's Mount thou shalt early sit, looking and turning towards Hel. Food shall to thee more loathsome be than is to any one the Glistening Serpent among Men.

Vindkald.

Tell me, Fiolsvith ! ect., what those Dogs are called, that chase away the Giantesses, and safety to the fields restore ?

Oceans Tower with Storms to Heaven itself, Flow O'er the Land ; the Air is Rent : thence come the snows and rapid winds ; then it is decreed that the rain should cease.

Then shall another come, yet mightier, although I dare not his name declare. Few may see further forth than when Odin meets the Wolf.

Fire I see burning, and the Earth Blazing ; many will have their lives to save. Bear thou the cup to Ottar's hand, the mead with venom mingled, in an evil hour !

A Ring is on the Hilt, courage in the midst, in the point terror for his use who owns it : along the edge a Blood-Stained Serpent lies, and on the guard the Serpent Casts its Tail.

The prince would neither the blood-fine pay, nor for the slain indemnity would give. They might expect, he said, a terrific storm of grey Arrows, and Odin's ire.

Then Gleamed a Ray from Logafioll, and from that Ray Lightnings issued ; then appeared, in the Field of Air, a helmed band of Valkyriur : Their corsets were with blood besprinkled, and from their Spears Shone Beams of Light.

So happy I shall not sit at Sefafioll, neither at morn nor night, as to feel joy in Life, if o'er the people plays not the prince's Beam of Light ; if his war-steed runs not under the chieftain hither, to the Gold bit accustomed ; if in the king I cannot rejoice.

So himself Helgi among warriors bore, as the towering Ash is among thorns, or as the Fawn, moistened with dew, that more proudly stalks than all the other beasts, and its Horns Glisten against the Sky.

'Tis No Delusion which thou thinkest to see, nor of Mankind the End, although thou seest us, although our Horses we with spurs urge on, nor to warriors is a home-journey granted.

Time 'tis for me to ride on the Reddening ways : let the Pale Horse tread the Aerial Path. I towards the West must go over Vindhialm's Bridge, ere Salgofnir awakens heroes.

There stands a Hall on the High Hindarfiall, without 'tis all with Fire Surrounded ; Sagacious Men have it constructed of the Resplendent Radiance of the Flood.

The Fire began to Rage, and the Earth to Tremble, High Rose the Flame to Heaven itself : there ventured few chiefs of people through that Fire to ride, or to leap over.

When they came he threw the Serpent into that Deep Ocean by which the Earth is Engirdled. But that Monster has grown to such an Enormous Size that, Holding his Tail in his Mouth, he Encircles the Whole Earth.

Frigga has a Horse that can run through the Air and Water, called Hofvarpnir. Once, as she drove out, certain Vanir saw her Car in the Air, when one of them exclaimed, "What flieth there ? What goeth there ? In the Air Aloft what Glideth ?" "She answered," 'I fly not though I go, And Glide Through the Air On Hofvarpnir, whose sire's Hamskerpir, and dam Gardrofa.' [Bolide]

43

Loki suspected of Plunging the Heaven into Darkness by permitting the Giant to carry away the Sun and Moon.

For what thou tookest for a Cat was in reality the Great Midgard Serpent that Encompassed the Whole Earth, and he was then barely long enough to enclose it between his Head and Tail, so high had thy hand raised him up towards Heaven.

"Hermod then pursued his journey until he came to the barred gates of Hel. Here he alighted, girthed his saddle tighter, and remounting, clapped both spurs to his horse, who cleared the gate by a tremendous leap without touching it. Hermod then rode on to the palace, where he found his brother Baldur occupying the most distinguished seat in the Hall, and passed the night in his company. The next morning he besought Hele (Death) to let Baldur [The Sun] ride home with him, assuring her that nothing but Lamentations were to be heard among the Gods. Hela answered that it should now be tried whether Baldur was so beloved as he was said to be. "If therefore," she added, 'All things in the World, both living and lifeless, Weep for him, then shall he return to the AEsir [Heaven], but if any one thing speak against him or refuse to Weep, he shall be kept in Hel.'

Astrology & Religion Among the Greeks and Romans, by Franz Cumont, 1912

During the period of the French Revolution Charles-Francois Dupuis, in three bulky volumes "On the Origin of all Forms of Worship" (1794), Developed the Idea that the Primary Source of Religion was the Spectacle of Celestial Phenomena and the Ascertainment of their Correspondence with Earthly Events, and he undertook to show that the Myths of all peoples and all times were nothing but a set of Astronomical Combinations. According to him, the Egyptians, to whom he assigned the foremost place among "the Inventors of Religions," had conceived, some Twelve or Fifteen Thousand Years Before Our Era [13,000 years BP Comet Strike.], the division of the Ecliptic into Twelve Constellations corresponding to the Twelve months.

Giving up the Firmament of Primitive Cosmogonies, Seleucus of Seleucia opened the infinite spaces of a limitless Universe to the Courses of the Stars. Recurring to a bold hypothesis of Aristarchus of Samos, and advancing new

44

arguments in its support, he showed that the Sun is the center of the World, and that the Earth has a double motion, revolving round the Sun and spinning on its own axis.

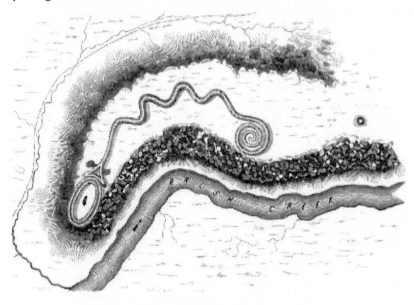

Serpent Mound Ohio
[Eating the Sun, Bolide, the Earth Ark / Egg]

Legends, Traditions, & Laws of the Iroquois or Six Nations and History of the Tuscarora Indians, by Elias Johnson – a Native Chief, 1881

"According to the Cosmogony of the Tuscarora the Bad Minded attempted to conceal the land Animals in the Ground, so as to deprive Men of the means of Subsistence. Afterwards, the Iroquois, in the age of Monsters they called one Oyahguaharh, supposed to be some Great Mammoth, who was Furious against Men, and Destroyed the Lives of many Indian Hunters, but he was at length Killed, after a Severe Contest.

A Great Horned Serpent also next appeared on Lake Ontario who, by means of his Poisonous Breath, Caused Disease, and Caused the Death of Many. At length the old Women congregated, with one accord, and prayed to the Great Spirit that he would send their grand-father, The Thunder, who would get to their relief in this, their sore time of trouble, and at the same

45

time burning tobacco as burned offerings. So finally the Monster was compelled to retire in the Deeps of the Lake by Thunder Bolts. Before this Calamity was forgotten Another happened. A Blazing Star Fell into their village, situated on the banks of the St. Lawrence, and Destroyed the people. Such a phenomenon caused a Great Panic and Consternation and Dread, which they regarded as Ominous of their Entire Destruction. Not long after this prediction of the Blazing Star it was verified. These tribes, who were held together by feeble ties, fell into dispute and wars among themselves, which were pursued through a long period, until they had utterly destroyed each other, and so reduced their numbers that the lands were again over-run with wild beasts.

At this period there were six families that took refuge in a large Cave in a Mountain, where they dwelled for a long time. The Men would come out occasionally to hunt for food. This Mammoth Cave was situated at or near the falls of the Oswego River. Taryenya-wa-gon (Holder of the Heavens) extricated these six families from this subterraneous bowels and confines of the Mountain. They always looked to this divine messenger, who had Power to Assume Various Shapes, as emergency dictated, as the friend and patron of their nation. As soon as they were released he gave them instructions respecting the mode of hunting, matrimony, worship, and bid them to disperse as the Six Nations and they entered into an agreement to preserve the chain of alliance which should not be extinguished under any circumstance. He took his position, sometimes, on the Top of High Cliffs, Springing, if need be, Over frightful chasms ; and Flew, as it were, Over Great Lakes in a wonderful Canoe of Immaculate Whiteness and of magic power. [Bolide]

A wise leader Hiawatha and people became Alarmed by the sudden news of the approach of a Furious and Powerful Enemy from North of the Great Lakes. As the Enemy Advanced, they made an Indiscriminate Slaughter of Men, Women, and Children. The people fled from their villages a short time before them, and there was no heart in the people to make a stand against such Powerful and Ruthless Invaders. In the Emergency, they fled to Hiawatha for his advice. He counseled them to call a general council of all the tribes from East to West. "For," said he, "our strength is not in the war club and arrows alone, but in wise counsels." He appointed a place on the banks of Onondaga Lake for the meeting. It was clear eminence from which there was a wide prospect. Runners were dispatched in every direction, and the chiefs, warriors, and headmen forthwith assembled in great numbers, bringing with them, in the general Alarm, their Women and children.

46

Fleets of Canoes were seen on the bosom of the Lake, and every interior warpath was kept open by the foot-prints of the different tribes, hurrying to obey the summons of Hiawatha. When the White Canoe of the venerable chief appeared, a Shout of welcome Rang among those in the hills. The day was calm and serene. No wind ruffled the lake, and scarcely a cloud floated in the Sky above. But while the Wise Man was measuring his steps toward the place designated for the council, and while ascending from the Water's Edge, a Low Sound was Heard, as if it were caused by the Approach of a Violent, Rushing Wind. Instantly All Eyes were Turned Upwards, where a small and compact mass of Cloudy Darkness Appeared. It gathered in Size and Velocity as it approached, and appeared to be directed inevitably to Fall in the midst of the assembly. Everyone fled in consternation but Hiawatha and his daughter. He stood erect, with ornaments waving in his frontlet, and besought his daughter calmly to await the issue, "for it is Impossible," said he, "to Escape the Power of the Great Spirit. If he has determined our Destruction we cannot, by running, fly from him."

She modestly assented and they stood together, while Horror was depicted in the faces of the others. But the force of the Descending Body was that of a Sudden Storm. They had hardly taken the resolution to halt when an Immense Bird, with long, extended wings, Came Down with swoop. This Gigantic Agent of the Sky came with such force that the assembly felt the Shock. The girl in a Nature, and embodied in the combination of the Terrestrial and Celestial Nature, Was Beautiful and Fascinating in her looks and form, was Borne Away by the Celestial Bird to be seen No More upon the Earth." [Verdure and Animals were Vanquished.]

Myths & Marvels of Astronomy,
by Richard A. Proctor, 1903

Cicero in a argument against the pretensions of astrologers asks : 'What Contagion can reach us from the planets, whose distance is almost Infinite ?'

No one who considers the wonderful accuracy with which, nearly two thousand years before the Christian era, the Chaldeans had determined the famous cycle of the Saros (the eclipse cycle), can doubt that they must have observed the Heavenly bodies for centuries before they could have achieved such a success ; and the Study of the Motions of the Celestial Bodies compels 'Men to trouble themselves' about the famous Ratio of the

Circumference to the Diameter of a Circle. [Pie] What the actual extent of their Astronomical Knowledge may have been it would be difficult to say. But it is certain, from the Exact Knowledge which later Chaldeans possessed respecting Long Astronomical Cycles, that Astronomical Observations must have been carried on continuously by that people for many hundreds of years. It is highly probable that the Astronomical Knowledge of the Chaldeans in the days of Terah and Abraham was Much More Accurate than that possessed by the Greeks even after the time of Hipparchus. It has been remarked that, though Hipparchus had the enormous advantage of being able to compare his own observations with those recorded by the Chaldeans, he estimated the length of the year less correctly than the Chaldeans. It has been thought by some that the Chaldeans were acquainted with the True System of the Universe, but I do not know that there are sufficient grounds for this supposition. Diodorus Siculus and Apollonius Myndius mention, however, that they were able to Predict the Return of Comets, and this implies that their Observations had been continued for many centuries with Great Care and Exactness. [The Exact Sciences in Antiquity by O. Neugebauer 1952 is a great source of Babylonian and Egyptian Mathematics which shows even Pythagoras borrowed his ideas, they were probably trying to calculate the orbit of 2P/Encke precisely. And one quote : "Without Violent Catastrophes there would hardly be any Archeology".]

Myths of the North American Indians,
by Lewis Spence, 1914

The Horn of the Great Prince of Serpents was suppose to dwell in the Great
Lakes.

"Many years ago the Great Spirit called all his people together, and,
standing on the precipice of the Red Pipe-Stone Rock, he broke a piece from
the wall, and, kneading it in his hands, made a huge pipe, which he
Smoked Over them, and to the North, South, East, and West. He told
them that this Stone was Red, that it was their Flesh, that of it they might
make their pipes of peace ; but it belonged equally to all ; and the war-club
and the scalping-knife must not be raised on this ground. And he Smoked
his pipe and talked to them till the last whiff, and then his Head Disappeared
in a Cloud ; and immediately the whole surface of the Rock for several miles
was Melted and Glazed. Two great ovens were opened beneath, and two
Women (guardian spirits of the place) entered them in a Blaze of Fire ; and

they are heard there yet, and answer to the invocation of the priests, or medicine-men, who consult them on their visits to this sacred place.

The principal deity of the Navaho Indians of New Mexico, Ahsonnutli, was regarded as the Creator of the Heavens and Earth. He was suppose to have placed Twelve Men at each of the cardinal points to Uphold the Heavens. He was believed to possess the Qualities of Both Sexes [Like the Egyptian Blue Headed Ptah.], and is entitled the Turquoise Man-Woman.

The Sacred Tree, or the Tree in Religion & Myth, by Mrs. J. H. Philpot, 1897

In parts of Estonia the peasants even within the 19th century regarded trees as sacred, carefully protected them, hung them with wreaths, and once a year poured fresh Bullock's blood about their roots, in order that the Cattle might thrive. [Forgotten meaning of appeasing the Bull not to kill the Trees / Life.]

The Oak played a salient part in the old Druidical worship, and Pliny even derives the name Druid from the Greek word for Oak, as some still connect it with Darach, the Celtic word for that Tree. The important rites with which the Mistletoe was severed from the parent tree and dedicated at the altar furnish evidence of the veneration paid to the Spirit of the Tree, who, according to the teaching of the Druids, retreated into the Parasite-Bough when the Oak leaves withered. [Mistletoe tiny orbs probably represent the Pleiades because they were instrumental in killing Baldr, the Norwegian Sun God, and similar to the eggs of the fowl's brood which is more prominent.]

The Laurel played an essential part in the Oracular Ceremonial of Delphi.

The great creative God Brahma, who, by the Light of his Countenance, Dispelled the Primeval Gloom, and by his divine immanence evoked the Earth from the Primeval Ocean, is represented in Hindu Theology as having emanated from a Golden Lotus which had been quickened into Life when the spirit of Om moved over the Face of the Waters.

The custom of making offerings to the Tree is in no doubt of Great Antiquity. In the Legend of the Golden Fleece, Phryxus, having been carried by the fabled Ram across the Hellespont, sacrificed it to Ares, and hung its priceless fleece on the boughs of a sacred Beech-Tree [This Tree keeps its Golden Leaves through the winter.], whence it was subsequently recovered by Jason. When the good ship Argo was built, Athena introduced into it by way of amulet a beam hewn in the grove of Dodona, which in the subsequent voyage constantly gave the Argonauts warning and advice.

Inscribed in the Chaldean sacred Texts it is mentioned of the use of "green branches" in religious ceremonies. At the feast of tabernacles the Israelites were enjoined to "take the boughs of goodly trees, branches of Palm-Trees, and the boughs of thick trees and willows of the brook, and rejoice before the Lord."

The conception of the Tree as the symbol of Fertility seems to be still more clearly emphasized in the Assyrian cylinders and bas-reliefs, where it is conventionally represented as a Date-Palm between two personages, who approach it from either side bearing in their hands a cone similar to the inflorescence of the male Date-Palm. Mr. Tylor suggests that these

personages, variously represented a king or priests, Genii with wings and heads of Eagles, or Mythical Animals, may represent the fertilizing wings or divinities, whose procreative influence was typified by the artificial fecundation of the Palm, a procedure which is necessary for its successful culture, and which we know from Herodotus to have been familiar to the Babylonians. The design is usually surmounted by the Winged Disc representing the Sun, and whole is not improbably meant to symbolize the mystery of procreation, in which the Male element enshrined in the Sun, and the Female element inhabiting the Tree are appropriately represented.

The idea of the Tree-Oracle was familiar to other branches of the Semitic race, and is expressed in their common Tradition of a Tree of Knowledge. Several allusions to Oracular Trees are met with in the Old Testament. That Jehovah should speak of Moses out of the Burning-Bush, if not to be regarded as a case in point, was at any rate quite in conformity with surrounding Tradition, for there is no doubt that the belief in Trees as places of divine revelation was very prevalent in Canaan. The famous Holy Tree near Shechem, called the Tree of the Soothsayers in Judges 9 : 6-15 & 37, and the Tree or Trees of the revealer in Genesis 12 : 6 and Deuteronomy 11 : 30, must have been the seat of a Canaanite Tree-Oracle. The prophetess Deborah gave her responses under a palm near Bethel, which, according to sacred Tradition, marked the grave of the nurse of Rachel. And David, when he inquired of the Lord as to the right moment for attacking the Philistines, received the signal in "the Sound of a going in the tops of the Mulberry-Trees 2 Samuel 5 : 24.

The Tradition of a Universe-Tree is found also in China and Japan. The Legends of the latter country speak of an enormous Metal Pine which grows in the North at the Center of the World.

The beautiful conception met with in some of the above Traditions, by which the Stars were compared at once to Gems and to the Fruits of a Mighty Tree, is frequently encountered in ancient literature. The Arabians represented the Zodiac as a Tree with Twelve branches, of which the Stars were the Fruit, and a somewhat similar idea appears in the Apocalyptic Tree of Life, which "bare Twelve manner of Fruits, and yielded her Fruit every Month." Revelation 22 : 2. The Babylonian hero Gilgamesh, in his wanderings beyond the Gates of Ocean, came upon a forest, which : To the forest of the Tree of Gods in appearance was equal ; Emeralds it carried as its Fruit ; the branch refuses not to support a canopy ; crystal they carried as shoots, Fruits they carry and to the sight it is glistening.

Tree Worship in the Americas

The Myths of Mexico & Peru, by Lewis Spence, 1914

Tezcatlipoca (Fiery Mirror) [Bolide, as if reflecting the Sun Light.] the great God of the air, like the Hebrew Jahveh, also an Air-God, he carried a Mirror or shield, from which he took his name, and which he was supposed to see reflected the actions and deeds of Mankind. Tezcatlipoca was usually depicted as holding in his right hand a Dart in an atlatl (spear-thrower), and his Mirror-shield with four [Ages] spare Darts in his left. The worship of Tezcatlipoca was regarded as compulsory, and to some extent as a safeguard against the Destruction of the Universe. Tezcatlipoca was much more than a mere personification of wind, and if he was regarded as a Life-giver he had also the power of Destroying Existence. In fact on occasion he appears as an Inexorable Death-Dealer, and as such was styled Nezahualpilli (The Hungry Chief) and Yaotzin (The Enemy). Perhaps one of the names by which he was best known was Telpochtli (The Youthful Warrior), from the fact that his reserve of strength, his vital force, never diminished, and that his youthful and boisterous vigor was apparent in the Tempest. One of his names, Yoalli Ehecatl, signifies "Night Wind." He is also the God of human sacrifice par excellence.

Among the American tribes, especially those of the northern continent, the Serpent is regarded with the deepest veneration as the symbol of Wisdom and magic. From these sources come success in war. The Serpent also typifies the Lightning, the symbol of the Divine Spear, the apotheosis of warlike might. Fragments of Serpents are regarded as powerful war-physic among many tribes. Atatarho, a Mythical wizard-king of the Iroquois, was clothed with living Serpents as with a robe, and his Myth throws Light on one of the names of Huitzilopochtli's mother, Coatlantona (Robe of Serpents). Huitzilopochtli's image was surrounded by Serpents, and rested on Serpent-Shaped supporters. His Scepter was a single Snake, and his great drum was of Serpent skin. The name Huitzilopochtli signifies "Humming-Bird to the left," from the circumstance that the God wore the feathers of the Humming-Bird on his left leg, he also flourished a shield and Spear of a Blue colour. In American Mythology the Serpent is closely associated with the Bird. Thus the name of the God Quetzalcoatl is translatable as "Feathered Serpent," and many similar cases where the conception of Bird and Serpent have been unified could be adduced. Huitzilopochtli was War-God of the Aztecs, and was supposed to have led them to the site of Mexico from their Original Home in the North.

In the days of Quetzalcoatl there was abundance of everything necessary for subsistence. The maze was plentiful, the calabashes were as thick as one's arm, and cotton grew in all colors without having to be dyed. A variety of birds of rich plumage filled the air with their songs, and Gold, Silver, and precious Stones were abundant. In the reign of Quetzalcoatl there was Peace and Plenty for all Men.

It is highly probable that Quetzalcoatl was a deity of the pre-Nahua people of Mexico and was regarded by the Aztec race as a God of somewhat alien character. He was regarded as "The Father of the Toltecs," and, Legend says, was the Seventh and youngest son of the Toltec Abraham, Iztacmixcohuatl. Tezcatlipoca banished Quetzalcoatl and his exile Wrought Peculiar Changes upon the Face of the Country. He secreted his Gold and Silver, Burned his palaces, transformed the cacao-trees into mesquites, and ordered all the birds of rich plumage and song to quit from the neighborhood of Tollan. The magicians begged him to return, but he refused on the ground that the Sun required his presence. Proceeding on his way accompanied by musicians who played the Flute he became fatigue crossing the Sierra Nevada (Mountain of Snow), where All the Pages who accompanied him died of Cold. He regretted this misfortune exceedingly, and wept, lamenting their fate with most bitter tears and mournful songs.

55

Arriving at the Sea-Shore, he embarked upon a Raft of Serpents, Floating Away to the East.

Some American tribes also, notably the Pueblo Indians of Arizona, the Serpent has a Solar significance, and with Tail in Mouth symbolizes the annual round of the Sun. The Snake, besides being symbolized by Lightning in many American Mythologies, is also symbolical of Water, which is well typified in its Sinuous Movements. (And also the Sinuous Shape of rivers.) The Hopi Indians of Mexico at the present day also symbolize the Sun as a Serpent with its Tail in Mouth.

The chief Goddess of maize was Chicomecohuatl (Seven-Serpent), her name being an allusion to the fertilizing power of Water, which element the Mexicans symbolized by the Serpent.

The Myth of Nanahuatl tells how before the Sun was created humanity dwelt in Sable and Horrid Gloom. Only a human sacrifice could hasten the appearance of the Luminary.

Mictlantecutli (Lord of Hades) was God of the Dead and of the Grim and Shadowy realm to which the souls of Men repair after their mortal sojourn. He is represented in the Pinturas as a Grisly Monster with capacious mouth, into which fall the spirits of the Dead. His terrible abode was sometimes alluded to as Tlalxicco (Navel of the Earth), but the Mexicans in general seem to have thought that it was situated in the Far North, which they regarded as a place of Famine, Desolation, and Death. [Great Lakes]

The Sun was regarded by all of the Mexican and Central American peoples, as a supreme deity, or rather the principle source of Subsistence and Life. He was the primary source of being, and the heart, the symbol of Life, was looked upon as his special sacrifice. The hearts of animals they had slain for cooking and even the hearts of the victims to Tezcatlipoca and Huitzilopochtli were first held up to the Sun as if he had a primary right to the sacrifice. It was supposed that the Luminary rejoiced in offerings of blood, and that it constituted the only food which would render him sufficiently vigorous to undertake his daily journey through the Heavens. He is often depicted in the Pinturas as licking up the gore of the sacrificial victims with his long tongue-like rays. The Sun must fare well if he was to continue to give Life, Light, and Heat to Mankind. The Mexicans believed that the Luminary they knew had been preceded by Four Others [Ages], each of which had been Quenched by some Awful Cataclysm of Nature.

Eternity had, in fact, been broken up into Epochs, marked by the Destruction of Successive Suns. In the period preceding that in which they lived, a Mighty Deluge had Deprived the Sun of Life, and some such Catastrophe was apprehended at the end of every "sheaf" of fifty-two years.

The Mexican idea of the creation. "In the year and in the day of the Clouds," writes Garcia in his Origin de los Indias, professing to furnish the reader with a translation of an original Mixtec Picture-Manuscript, "Before ever were years or days, the World lay in Darkness. All things were Order less, and a Water covered the Slime and Ooze that the Earth then was." This picture is common to almost all American creation-stories. The red Man in general believed the habitable Globe to have been Created from the Slime which arose above the Primeval Waters.

One of the most complete creation-stories in Mexican Mythology is that given by the half-blood Indian author Ixtlilxochitl, who, we cannot doubt, received it directly from native sources. He states that the Toltecs credited a certain Tloque Nahuaque (Lord of All Existence) with the creation of the Universe, the Stars, Mountains, and animals. At the same time he made the first Man and Woman, from whom all the inhabitants of Earth are descended. This "First Earth" was Destroyed by the "Water-Sun." At the commencement of the next epoch the Toltecs appeared, and after many wanderings settled in Huehue Tlapallan (Very Old Tlapallan). Then followed the Second Catastrophe, that of the "Wind-Sun." The remainder of the Legend recounts how Mighty Earthquakes Shook the World and Destroyed the Earth-Giants (Quinames) were Analogous to the Greek Titans, and were a source of great uneasiness to the Toltecs.

The Sun-God of the Maya who's Hieroglyph is the Sun-Sign, Kin, only accepted human blood for food and must be fed full with this terrible fare or perish, Dragging the World of Men with him into a Fathomless Abyss of Gloom.

In the "Popol Vuh", written in a dialect of the Maya-Kiche, we are told that the God Hurakan, "the Mighty Wind", Passed over the Universe still wrapped in Gloom. He called out "Earth," and the solid land appeared. Then the chief Gods took counsel among themselves as to what should next be made. They agreed that animals should be Created. This was accomplished, and they next turned their attention to the framing of Man. They made a number of manikins carved out of wood. But these were irreverent and angered the Gods, who resolved to bring about their

57

Downfall. Then Hurakan (The Heart of Heaven) caused the Waters to be Swollen, and a Mighty Flood came upon the Manikins. Also a Thick Resinous Rain Descended upon them. The Bird Xecotcovach tore out their eyes, the Bird Camulatz cut off their heads, the Bird Tecumbalam broke their bones and sinews and ground them into powder. Then all sort of beings, great and small, Abused the Manikins.

[The above noses from the 19th Century are identical to waves in the Codex Nuttall of the same region. Tsunami Gods ? In the 21st Century they are repositioned with the "wave crest" pointing up and called 'upper lips'.]

Symbolism of the East & West,
by Mrs. Murray – Aynsley, 1900

St, Green George Day around Easter no surprise High Jacked from Jack in
the Green May pole celebration. Now Arbor Day in the USA (1900!) All
Saints' Day, the Christian substitute for the Roman festival of Pomona, and,
in these islands [UK], also, of the first day of the Celtic Feast of Saman
(Shaman, Shony), the Lord of Death. It follows All Hallow Even, or
Halloween, the Christian substitute for the Vigil of Saman, and precedes
All Souls' Day, the Christian substitute of the second day of the Druidical
Feast of Saman.

[The Celtic Samhain marked the Death of Summer and the meaning of
October 31 Saman (the Lord of Death), and would call together all the souls
that had Died and permit them to roam among the living and the living
would dress up as Zombies so that they would Blend In and thus not be
haunted during the Festival. Probably the meaning of Trick or Treat / ghost
or live person / spirit or neighbor / impact or pass.]

When an eclipse of the Moon is expected, many of the natives of Hindostan
hasten down to the nearest river or tank and remain in the Water the whole
time of its duration, imagining that some Dire Misfortune would Befall
Them were they to omit to do so. This Indian superstition probably took its
rise in the idea that one should not look at this phenomenon directly, but
indirectly – that is to say, one should not contemplate the luminary itself at
such times, but regard only its Reflection in the Water. [I have the feeling
that was the primary function of the pools in the temple courtyards and to re-
enact the past holy events in Manmade Lakes such as in Karnak, Egypt.]

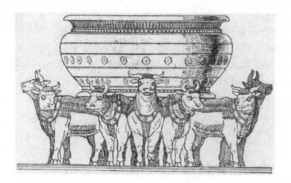

59

In European common life, when passing the wine, or dealing a pack of cards, we constantly hear it said that this should be done "the Way of the Sun," and some persons deem it Most Unlucky if, through inadvertence, the bottle be sent round the other way.

The Swastika [Triskelion] was the emblem of Thor, the chief God of their Mythology – their God of the Air, of Thunder and Lightning as well as of Fire.

In Tumulus of Norway, and in Denmark, and North Germany are found Stone Eggs. It is well known to all who have ever been in India that no Hindu, except a Pariah (or outcast), will eat a Hen's Egg or even keep Fowls. The Saiva sect is said to regard the Hen's Egg as a symbol of creation ; the Bull also was an Emblem used in the Same Connection ; it is one of the Emblems of Siva. The figure of a Bull is invariably placed in the porch or within the precincts of temples dedicated to that God.

At Miaco, in Japan, there is a Pagoda in honour of a Bull ; the animal is represented standing on a broad square altar of massive Gold, a rich collar is round its neck, but the object which principally attracts attention is an Egg, which it holds between its fore feet, and is in the Act of Striking with its Horns. According to the Legend, the Entire World during the time of Chaos was Enclosed in that Egg, which Floated upon the surface of the Waters. The Moon, by its influence and the power of its Light, drew up Earthly matter from the bottom of the Waters, which became hard Rock, on which the Egg rested. The Bull, finding this Egg, Broke It with its Horns, and from the shell burst forth the World ; the breath of the Bull produced Man. Such is the explanation of these objects as given by Japanese Learned Men.

A sect called the Smarta Brahmans may be distinguished from other Brahmans by three horizontal marks of pounded sandal-wood on their foreheads and a round spot in the centre. They worship the Triad of Brahma, Siva, and Vishnu, under the Mystical Syllable A U M, and while admitting them to be co-equal, exalt Siva as their chief deity. They are also called Advaitas (advait, unique, alone), as they believe God and matter to be identical, and that everything is but an atom of the divinity – they themselves being parts of the Supreme Being. The founder of this sect was Sankarach-arya, and their Guru or teacher, is styled the Sringiri-Swami. In this invocation A, the first letter, stands for the Creator ; U, the second, for the Preserver ; and M, the third, for the Destroyer – or Brama, Vishnu, Siva. An Old Passage in the Puranas says : "All the rites ordained in the

60

Vedas, the sacrifices to Fire, and all sacred purifications shall pass away, but the word AUM shall never pass away, for it is the symbol of the Lord of All Things."

A superstition of the same nature is held by the people of the Fiji Islands. They worship a God they call Ndengei under the form of a Large Serpent, and believe that immediately after Death the spirit of the deceased person goes to him for purification or to receive sentence, but that it is not permitted, however, to all spirits to reach the judgment seat of Ndengei. They say that an Enormous Giant Armed with an Axe is constantly upon the watch on the road thither, ready to attack and wound all that attempt to reach him, and that no wounded person can go forward to Ndengei, but is doomed to wander about in the Mountains. To escape unscathed from the Giant's Axe is ascribed solely to good luck.

In the Book of Revelation (Chap. XXII) is mentioned "the Tree of Life, which bore Twelve manner of Fruits and yielded her Fruit every month, and the Leaves of the Tree were for the Healing of the Nations." One of the notions of the primitive Aryan cosmogony was that of a Prodigious Tree which overshadowed the Whole World. The Oak was sacred to Thor, the Scandinavian God of Fire, because of the red colour of its fresh-cut bark.

Snake worship is still to be found [1900] in Indian throughout the length and breadth of the land, from Naga-kovil (Temple of the Snake in the extreme South) to the frontiers of Central Asia ; in fact, almost wherever there is a Hindu population, either its actual presence or its former existence may be seen or traced. Commencing at the extreme North, we find that the earliest form of religion in Kashmir is supposed to have been Naga or Snake worship, since when Buddhism, Hinduism, and again Naga worship are said to have prevailed in that valley.

It seems highly probable that the Parak or head dress worn by the Women of Ladakh (who are Buddhists) should be held to be a remnant of Serpent Worship in the Himalayas. This ornament has precisely the form of a Cobra ; the extremity of the Tail is fastened to the hair on the forehead, and the broad flat hood of the Snake descends behind to the waist of the wearer. It is most usually made of leather, on which are sewn at intervals rough pierced Turquoises [Blue Sky] and brooches of Silver [Moon] or Gold [Sun], according to the wealth and position of the wearer ; but every Woman, however poor, possesses a Parak of some kind.

It is remarkably singular to find in a Teutonic language the Indian word for a Snake. It would seem scarcely necessary to remind our readers that the German word for a Viper is Natter. At the foot of the Simplon, where the people are of German origin, is a little village called Naters, to which is attached the following Legend :- Close to this village, on the Mountain side, is a Deep Cavern, which Tradition states was formerly inhabited by a Horrible Dragon (Dragons and Serpents are synonymous in such tales), who subsisted upon human flesh and any cattle or sheep which he could plunder. He daily devoured a shepherd or one of his flock. The tale goes on to relate that a Blacksmith, who for some crime had been condemned to Death, told the magistrate of the place, on the eve of his execution, that he would Kill the Dragon if he were promised a free pardon should he escape with his Life from the encounter. The combat took place, the Blacksmith using a Sword which he had Forged for the occasion. The Battle lasted an hour or more, when the spectators, seeing that both Man and Dragon were prostrate on the ground, approached them, but with fear and trembling. They found both incapable of further effort – the Dragon was Dead and the Man had fainted away. Doubtless Naters derived its name from this Legend.

The late General Sir Alexander Cunningham, in the Preface to his Bhilsa Topes, identifies this latter form with the Buddhist symbol of Dharma, identifying it with nature defiled.

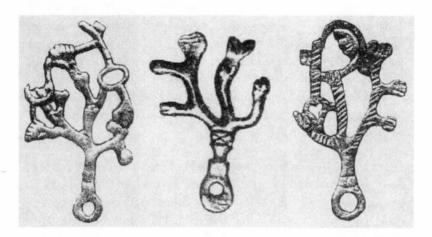

Above are figured several forms of an amulet still in use at Naples. In all of these we find the Tree, the Serpent, an Arm, and hand holding a Horn (The Horn of Plenty ?) within which is a half Moon, the emblem of Janara or the Moon, also a Key, the emblem of Janus or the Sun, who was fabled to have taught Men to build houses and to close them with doors. (Janua) being also the Sun, it was considered suitable that he should have the Keys of the Doors of Heaven, in order that he might open them at Dawn and close them at Sunset. Neapolitan Women of the lower class are in the habit of making use of this word Janara (the Moon, the wife of Janus) as an epithet of reproach ; if angry with one of their own sex they will call her a Janara – a Witch.

Odin was the Storm God, the name Woden or Wuotan denotes the Strong and Furious Goer : Gothic, Wods ; Norwegian, o'dr, Enraged. According to this view, the name may therefore be closely allied to the Lowland Scotch word wud, Mad or Furious. A Jacobite song of 1745 says, "the Women are a' gane wud." There is also a Scotch proverb, "Dinna put a knife into a wud Man's hand." Odin, as the Storm God, may well be supposed to have ridden like one wud : he has been considered to be the Wild Huntsman of the German Legends. If so, the Legend of the Erl King or Wild Huntsman probably came from the same source as Odin's Wild Hunt. He, and his wife Freyja, are fabled to have had two sons, Baldr and Hermond. The tale runs thus : Freyja had made All Created things swear that they would never hurt Baldr [The Sun], "that whitest and most beloved of the Gods ;" however there was one little shoot "that growth East of Valhalla [Heaven], so small and delicate that she forgot to take its oath." It was the Mistletoe, and with a branch of that feeble plant, flung by the Hand of blind Hodr, Balr was Struck Dead. He then descended into the Gloomy Snake-Covered Helheim, whither Hermond (Baldr's brother) made a violent but unsuccessful ride from Star-Spangled Valhalla, mounted on Sleipner, his father's horse [with eight legs.], in order to obtain his brother's body. The Hel Jagd, as it is called in some parts of Germany, has by others been styled the English Hunt. Both refer to the Nether World. And that Great Britain was formerly supposed to be the Land of the Departed Souls.

" A Myth is a Narrative framed for the purpose of Expressing some general Truth."

"A Symbol is a Silent Myth" William Fleming "The Thoughts of all the greatest and Wisest Men have been Expressed through Mythology."

- Ruskin

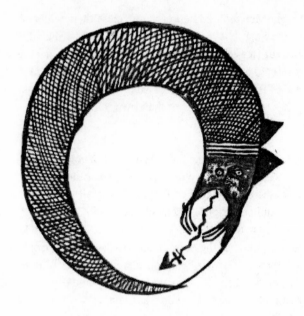

The Myths of the New World a Treatise on the Symbolism & Mythology of the Red Race of America, by Daniel G. Brinton, 1896

Myths, subtle nets of the Devil spread to catch human souls.

Apollo and the Dragon, the victory of the Lord of Bright Summer over the Demon of Chilling Winter. [Late explanation, the Clouds vs. Sun also.]

On the altar of Mixcoatl, God of hunting, the Aztec priest tore the heart from the human victim and smeared with the spouting blood the Snake that coiled its length around the idol.

When the whites first heard the uncouth gutturals of the Indians, it was Piously suggested, that they were from the Devil for the Annoyance of the Missionaries.

The similarity of Myths around the World some have interpreted as psychological parallels as proofs of the unity of the soul of Man obliged or inclined to follow the same paths when setting forth on that quest which has for its goal the Invisible World and the Home of the Gods.

The Heavens, the upper regions, are in Every Religion the supposed abode of the Divine.

The dualistic form, on one hand the good spirit with his legions of angles, on the other the evil one with his swarms of fiends, representing the World as the scene of their unending conflict, Man as the Unlucky Football who gets All the Blows. [Yin & Yang]

The Aztec priests never chanted more regretful dirges than when they sang of Tulan, the cradle of their race, where once it dwelt in Peaceful indolent happiness, whose land abounded with limpid Emeralds, Turquoise, Gold, and Silver. [Verdure, Blue Skies, Sun, and Moon]

A Serpent with Wings, who proceeded with such Velocity that he Pierced Rocks and Walls.

In the Cosmical Pictographs of the Mayas and Nahuas the Tree stands in the centre of the Universe, its branches rise to the fertilizing rain clouds, while its trunk is rooted in the vase of Primeval Waters from which all things took their origin.

Kepler : "The universe is a harmonious whole, the soul of which is God ; numbers, figures, the Stars, All Nature, indeed, are in Unison with the Mysteries of Religion ?"

The "Sacred Pole" of the Omahas typified the Cosmic Tree, the centre of the four winds and the home of the Thunder Bird.

The Fox is always cunning, the Wolf ravenous, the Owl gloomy and wise, and the Ass foolish in many nations nursery rhymes.

The Serpent, its sinuous course is like nothing so much as that of a winding River, which therefore we often call Serpentine.

The Algonkins and the Dakotas words of which express the Supernatural in its broadest sense, are also used as terms for Serpent.

The Serpents annually rejuvenated skin probably led to its adoption as a symbol of time among the Nahuas ; or, perchance, as they reckoned by Suns, and figure of the Sun, a circle, corresponds to nothing animate but a Serpent with its Tail in its Mouth.

65

A close analogy which the Serpent in its motion, its quick spring, and mortal bite, has to zig-zag course, the rapid flash, and the sudden stroke of the electrical discharge. It is associated with the Descent of Fire from Heaven, Lightning and Meteorites. The Algonkins in 1637 when asked of their opinion of the nature of Lightning, " It is an Immense Serpent, which the Manito is vomiting forth ; you can see the twists and folds that he leaves on the trees which he strikes."

The tale of the Horned Serpent figured extensively in the Legends of the Algonkins, the Shawnee, the Creeks, and the Cherokees.

The hero Michabo of an Algonkin Tradition appears in conflict with the Shining prince of Serpents who lives in the Lake and Floods the Earth with its Waters, and destroys the Reptile with a Dart.

The names Quetzalcoatl, Gucumatz, and Kukulkan are all titles of the God of the air in the languages of Central America, All Signifying the "Bird-Serpent." The "masters" in native magic craft explained to the bishop Nunez de le Vega that this Compound Symbolism was to represent "the Snake with Feathers which moves in the Waters," that is the Heavenly Waters, the clouds and the rains. Quetzalcoatl, also having the attribute of a Rattlesnake disappeared, sailing towards the East in a Bark [Boat] of Serpent Skins. These are also attributed to the ruler of the Winds and Lightning, but they don't always sail East, so they must be describing something else. They were also known as the God of Riches and Mythologists have likened it to other tales of the Greeks and ancient Germans and that of the Golden color of the Liquid Fire that is the process of making precious Metal and also to the Bright Lightning. So it was in Peru, where the God of Riches was worshipped under the image of a Rattle Snake Horned and Hairy, with a Tail of Gold. It was said to have Descended from the Heavens in the Sight of All the People, and to have been seen by the whole army of the Inca. Reference Note - "I have examined many Indians in reference to these details," says the narrator, and Augustin monk writing in 1554, "and they have all confirmed them as eye-witnesses". Whether it was in reference to it, or as emblems of their prowess, the Incas themselves chose as their Arms Two Serpents with their Tails Interlaced. A favorite proverb of the early missionaries was "the Gods of the Heathens are Devils" that wherever they saw a carving or picture of a Serpent they at once recognized the sign manual of the Prince of Darkness, and inscribed the fact in their note-books as proof positive of their cherished theory.

Many tribes had Myths of bisexual or Androgynous Deities, those who combine in themselves the functions of both sexes such, as the Navajos Ahsonnutli, "the Turquoise Hermaphrodite".

This is not peculiar to the New World. Many of the gods of the Orient are either Epicene, or Androgynous. Such avowedly were Mithras, Janus, Brahma, and in the Esoteric Doctrine of the Cabala, Jehovah.

The Aztec Quetzalcoatl, the Bird-Serpent, when he would promulgate his decrees, his herald proclaimed them from Tzatzitepec, the Hill of Shouting, with such a Mighty Voice that it could be heard a hundred leagues around. The Arrows which he Shot Transfixed Great Trees, the Stones he Threw Leveled Forests, and when he laid his hands on the Rocks the Mark was Indelible.

The Botocudos of Brazil attribute the Earths Destructions to the Moon Falling to the Earth from time to time.

By far the greater number represent the Last Destruction of the World to have been by Water. A few, however, the Takahlis of the North Pacific coast, the Yurucares of the Bolivian Cordilleras, and the Mbocobi of Paraguay, attribute it to a general Conflagration which Swept over the Earth, consuming every living thing except a few who took refuge in a deep cave.

One of the Mexican Traditions related by Torquemada identified this (being saved from the Deluge by a Mountain) with the Mountain of Tlaloc in the Terrestrial Paradise, and added that one of the Seven demigods who escaped commenced the Pyramid of Cholula in its memory. He intended that its summit should reach the clouds, but the Gods, Angry at his presumption, drove away the builders with Lightning. Equally fabulous was the retreat of the Araucanians. It was a three-peaked Mountain which had the property of Floating On Water, called Theg-Theg, the Thunderer. This they believed would preserve them in the next as it did in the Last Cataclysm, and as its only inconvenience was that it approached too near the Sun, they always kept on hand wooden bowls to use as parasols, umbrellas. [So they could mask the bright Sun to see the day time Comet !]

Within the Thlinkit Myths the Raven saved their ancestors from the general Flood, and in this instance it is distinctly identified with the Mighty Thunder Bird, who at the beginning ordered the Earth from the Depths and Brought Fire from the Heavens that saved them from a Second Death by Cold.

67

The Mexican Codex Vaticanus No. 3738 represents after the picture of the Deluge a Bird perched on the summit of a Tree, and at its foot Men in the act of marching. This has been interpreted to mean that after the Deluge Men were dumb until a Dove distributed to them the gift of Speech. The New Mexican tribes related that all except the leader of those who escaped to the Mountains lost the power of utterance by Terror, and the Quiches that the Antediluvian Race were "puppets, Men of wood, without Intelligence or Language."

From the Codex Chimalpopoca, a work in the Nahuatl language of ancient Mexico wherein it is written ; "Now towards the close of the year, Titlacahuan had forewarned the Man named Nata and his wife named Nena, saying, 'Make no more pulque, but straightway hollow out a large cypress, and enter it when in the month Tozoztli the Water Shall Approach the Sky.'

Often quoted in Quiches Legends ; " Then by the will of the Heart of Heaven the Waters were swollen and a Great Flood came upon the manikins of wood. For they did not think nor speak of the Creator who had created them, and who had caused their birth. They were drowned, and a Thick Resin Fell from Heaven.

A Legend of the Tupis of Brazil, their ancient songs relate that long ago, a certain very powerful Mair, that is to say a stranger, who bitterly hated their ancestors, compassed their destruction by a Violent Inundation. Only a very few succeeded in escaping – some by climbing trees, others in caves. When the Waters subsided the remnant came together, and by gradual increase populated the World. Also narrated " Monan (the Maker) seeing the ingratitude of Men, and their contempt for him who made them thus joyous, withdrew from them, and sent upon them, the Divine Fire, which Burned all that was on the Surface of the Earth. He swept about the Fire in such a way that in places he Raised Mountains, and in others Dug Valleys. Then Monan was so filled with pity that so few survived that he poured a Deluge of rain on the Earth, which Quenched the Fire, and, and flowing from all sides, formed the Ocean, which we call the Great Waters.

A refection of this Myth appears in that of the Mbocobis of Paraguay. The Destruction of the World was due to the Sun. This orb once Fell From the Sky, but Mbocobi hastened to pick it up before it did any injury, and fastened it in its place with pegs. A second time it Fell and Burnt Up the Earth. Two of the tribe, a Man and his Wife, climbed a tree and escaped

Destruction, but a Flash of Flame reached them and they fell to the ground, where they were changed into Monkeys.

The Expectation of the End of the World is a Natural Complement to the belief in Periodical Destructions of our Globe. As at certain times past the Equipoise of Nature was Lost, and the Elements Breaking the Chain of Laws that Bound them Ran Riot Over the Universe, involving All Life in One Mad Havoc and Desolation, so in the Future we have to expect that Day of Doom, when Ocean Tides shall obey no Shore, but Overwhelm the Continents with their Mountainous Billows, or the Fire, now chafing in volcanic craters and smoking springs, will leap forth on the forests and grassy meadows, Wrapping All Things in a Winding Sheet of Flame, and Melting the Very Elements with Fervid Heat. As within the Voluspa, in the language of the Norse Prophetess, " Shall the Sun grow Dark, the land sink in the Waters, the Bright Stars be quenched, and Flames climb Heaven itself."

For the heart that so constantly sympathizes with our emotions and actions, is, in most languages and most nations, regarded as the seat of Life ; and when the priests of bloody religions tore out the heart of the victim and offered it to the idol, it was an Emblem of Life that was thus torn from the field of this World and consecrated to the rules of the next. Or, offering the Life giving force toward the God (Sun) to insure more Fair Weather instead of Wrath of the Angry God who took the Life Himself. [There seems to be some confusion between the Comet, Bolide, and the Sun in their accounts.]

"This is all… The gain we reap from all the Wisdom sown… Through Ages: Nothing doubted those first sons… Of time, while we, the schooled of centuries, nothing believe." - Lytton.

The Mythology of All Races : North America, by, Hartley Burr Alexander, 1916

The Thunderer, whom the Iroquois deemed to be the guardian of the Heavens, Armed with a Mighty Bow and Flaming Arrows, Hater and Destroyer of All Things Noxious, and especially to be revered as having Slain the Great Serpent of the Waters, which was Devouring Mankind. Hino is the Thunderer's name, and his bride is the Rainbow ; he has many

69

assistants, the lesser Thunderers, and among them the boy Gunnodoyah, who was once a mortal. Hino caught this youth up into his domain, Armed him with a Celestial Bow, and sent him to encounter the Great Serpent ; but the Serpent Devoured Gunnodoyah, who communicated his plight to Hino in a dream, whereupon the Thunderer and his warriors Slew the Serpent and bore Gunnodoyah, still living, back to the Skies. The Cherokee tell a tale of "the Man who married the Thunder's sister" : lured by the maiden to the Thunder's Cave, he is there surrounded by Shape-Shifting Horrors, and when he declines to mount a Serpent-Steed saddled with a living turtle, Thunder grows Angry, Lightning Flashes from his Eye, and a Terrific Crash Stretches the young brave Senseless ; when he revives and makes his way home, though it seems to him that he has been gone but a day, he discovers that his people have long given him up for Dead ; and, indeed, after this he survives only Seven days.

To the Iroquois, the Pleiades are called the Dancing Stars. They were a group of brothers who were awakened in the night by Singing Voices, to which they began to dance. As they danced, the Voices Receded, and they, following, were led, little by little, into the Sky, where the pitying Moon transformed them into a group of fixed Stars, and bade them dance for ten days [Five] each year over the Red Man's council-house ; that being the Season of his New Year. One of the dancing brothers, however, hearing the lamentations of his mother, looked backward ; and immediately he Fell with Such Force that he was Buried in the Earth. For a year the mother mourned over his grave, when there appeared from it a tiny sprout, which grew into a Heaven-Aspiring Tree ; and so was born the Pine, tallest of Trees, the guide of the forest, the Watcher of the Skies [Persian Pleiades]. Fire-Dragon and He-Holds-the-Sky in Iroquoian cosmogony.

Mexican Holding Up the Sky

70

From The Sia by Matilda Coxe Stevenson 1894?   Hu'waka (Serpent of the Heavens) has a body like Crystal, and it is so Brilliant that One's Eyes Can Not Rest Upon Him ; he is very closely allied to the Sun.

The Cherokee Flint (Tawiskala) is obviously the evil and unsociable nature remains as a demiurgic Titan, his evil and unsociable nature remains the same. In Choctaw tales, the devil who is drowned by a maiden whom he has lured from her home, and whose body Breaks Into Stony Fragments, is apparently the same being. The Ice Man, with his Northerly Winds and Sleety Rains, who Quenched the Fire that Threatened to Consume the World.

The Thunderers, whose Steed is the great Uktena ; the Horned Snake with a Diamond in his Forehead.

The most notable instance of ritualistic sacrifice north of Mexico is that of the Skidi Pawnee, who formerly offered a virgin female captive to the Morning Star in an annual ceremony for the Fertilization of the maize fields.

Every spring, at the First Peal of Thunder, which they call the Voice of the Great Spirit Speaking from the Clouds, the Assiniboins offer it sacrifices . . .
. . . . Thunder, next to the Sun, is their great Wah-kon.

Ursa Major and the Pleiades are other Constellations Conspicuous in Indian Myth. The Assiniboin regard the Seven Stars of Ursa Major as Seven youths who were driven by poverty to transform themselves, and who rose to Heaven by means of a spiders web [There are many myths with spiders in North America, plus Gobekli Tepe, Nazca Spider ?] For the Blackfeet also these Stars are Seven brothers who have been pursued into the Heavens by a huge bear (an interesting reversal of the Eskimo story). The Mandan believed this Constellation to be an Ermine (Weasel) ; some of the Sioux held it to be a Bier , followed by mourners. The Pleiades, in Blackfoot Legend, are the "Lost Children," driven by poverty to take refuge in the Sky.

Everywhere Stars were Associated with the Dead. The Mandan considered them to be deceased Men : when a child is born, a Star Descends to Earth in human form ; at death, it appears once more in the Heavens as a Star. A Meteor was frequently regarded as a forerunner of Death ; and the Milky Way, as with the Eastern Tribes, is the Path by which Souls Ascend into Heaven.

71

The Fire-Powers, the Sun, and the Thunderers or Thunder-Birds were of first importance. The Assiniboin regard the Thunder as "the Voice of the Great Spirit Speaking from the Clouds," and the Dakota , "Thunder is an Enormous Bird." The Thunderer was pre-eminently the power of Destruction, and therefore, a tutelary of War. The Zuni, who regard the Thunder as made by the gaming Stones rolled by the Celestial Rain-Makers and the Lightning as the Arrows of Celestial Archers. It is notable that a Huge Man-Devouring Bird appears in the Mythologies of the South-Western peoples, from whose Lore the Thunderbird is absent. The belief that Stone Axes, Arrow-Heads, and "Thunderstones" or Lightning-Bolts is World-Wide.

The Omaha have a "Thunder Society" (Fletcher & Fleshe) whose Talisman is a Black Stone – suggestive enough of the Black Baetyl brought to Rome, 205 BC, as an Image of Rhea-Cybele, or of the Hoary Sanctity of the Black Stone of Mecca.

From (F & F) above : Pleiades, this Constellation bore the ancient name of Tapa, the Head of the Deer, the rites formally in charge of this generation are Lost, but they related to the Stars and the night Skies. These Rites seem to have been connected with Myths dealing with the creation. In them the Wild-Cat skin and the Fawn skin were used, there Spotted appearance having a symbolic reference to the Heavens at night.

The Magic Properties of White Stones and Crystals appear in Myths from many quarters : it is with Crystal that the Eskimo youth Slays the Tunek ; a Crystal is in the Head of the Horned Serpent ; a suggestion of Crystal-Gazing is in the Comox Myth recorded by Boas, where the Serpent gives a Transparent Stone to Man who thereupon Falls as if Dead, while the Stone Leads his Soul ; through the lands. [Bolide]

Stories of Red-Hot Rocks Hurled by Giants.

The Dakota tell the story of the Drowning of the younger brother of the First Man by Water Monsters, and of his Resuscitation after they had been Slain. He was brought to Life, they say, by means of the Sweat-Bath [Many Legends Speak of it getting Hot before the Cold], and it is not fanciful to connect the Cosmic Forces with the symbolism definite. The idea of permanence, long Life, and Wisdom they typify by the Stone ; "Man's restlessness, his questionings of fate, his destructiveness, are frequently symbolized by the Wolf" ; and in Myth the Wolf and the Stone are the two

72

demiurgic brothers – western duplicates of Flint and Sapling. One of the most interesting of Omaha rituals is the of that of the Pebble Society, sung to commemorate the Great Rock which Wakanda summoned from the Waters, at the Beginning of the World, to be a home for the animal souls that wandered about in Primitive Chaos (translated by Alice C. Fletcher) :

Toward the coming of the Sun there the people of every kind gathered, and great animals of every kind. Verily all gathered together, as well as people. Insects also of every description, verily all gather together, by what means or manner we know not. Verily, one alone of all these was greatest, inspiring to all minds, the Great White Rock, [Bolide] standing and reaching as High as the Heavens, Enwrapped in Mist [Halo], verily, as High as the Heavens. Thus my little ones shall speak of me, as long as they shall travel in Life's path, thus shall they speak of me. Such were the words, it has been said. Then next in rank thou, male of the Crane, stoodst with thy Long Beak and thy Neck, None Like to it in Length, there with thy Beak didst thou Strike the Earth. This shall be the Legend of the people of yore, the red people, thus my little ones shall speak of me. Then next in rank stood the male gray Wolf, whose cry, through Uttered without effort, verily made the Earth to Tremble, even the stable Earth to Tremble. Such shall be the Legend of the people. Then next in rank stood Hega, the Buzzard, with his Red Neck. Calmly he stood, his Great Wings Spread, letting the heat of the Sun straighten his feathers. Slowly he flapped his Wings, then floated away, as though without effort, thus displaying a power often to be spoken of by the Old Men in their Teachings.

In the Caddoan Cosmogony, the Earth was inhabited by a race of people "so Strong that they were not afraid of anybody, but they did not have good sense ; they made fun of all the Gods in Heaven." Nesaru said : 'I made them too strong. I will not keep them. They think that they are like myself. I shall Destroy them, but I shall put away my people that I like and that are smaller.'" The Giants were Killed in the Flood, while the animals and maize were preserved in a Cave. Eventually, from an ear of maize which he had raised in Heaven, Nesaru created a Woman, mother corn, whom he sent into the underworld to deliver the people imprisoned there, and to lead them once more into the Light of Day – a descent into Hell, like that of Ishtar or Persephone or many another corn Goddess.

The Pawnee of Nebraska have a Ritual of their cosmogony in which make their camp in a Circle, and range the people in Imitation of the Stations of the Stars ; and the Priests perform a drama symbolizing the creation, making movements over a Bowl of Water "to show the people how the Gods had Struck the Water when the Land was Divided from the Waters."

A very perfect Arapaho Cosmogonic Legend, begins with the Sky-World Family : "their Tipi was Formed by the daylight, and the entrance-door was the Sun." Here Lived a Man and a Woman and their two boys – Sun and Moon. In search of wives the youths go along Eagle River, which runs East and West, the older brother, Sun, travelling down Stream ; the younger, Moon, in the opposite direction. Sun takes for his wife a Water Animal, the Toad ; but Moon decides to marry a Mortal Woman, and when he sees two girls in the field, he turns himself into a Porcupine and climbs a Tree. One of the girls starts to follow the animal up the tree, but it keeps ascending, and the tree continues growing. Finally the Sky is Pierced, and Moon, resuming the form of a young man, takes the girl to wife in the Sky-World Lodge [Hall]. There a Son is Born to Her. Meanwhile the father of Sun and Moon has presented his daughter-in-law with a digging stick, but her husband forbids her to dig a certain withered plant. Out of curiosity she disobeys and uncovers a hole through which she looks down upon the camp circle of her people. She undertakes to descend by means of a sinew rope, but just before she reaches Earth with her son, Moon throws a Stone, called Heat Stone, after her, saying, "I shall have to make her return to me" – a remark which, the Indians declare, shows that there is another place for dead people, the sky-world. The Woman is killed by the Stone, but the boy is uninjured. At first he is nourished from the breasts of his Dead mother ; but afterward he is found and cared for by Old Woman Night, who had come to the spot. "Well, well!" she says to him, "Are you Little Star? I am so happy to meet you. This is the central spot which everybody comes to. It is the Terminus of All Trails from all directions. I have a little Tipi down on the North side of the River, and I want you to come with me. It is only a short distance from here. Come on, grandchild, Little Star." The Old Woman made bow and arrows for Little Star, and with these he Slew a Horned Creature with Blazing Eyes which proved to have been the husband of Night. She transformed the Bow into a Lance, and with this he began to Kill the Serpents which Infested the World. While he was sleeping on the prairie, however, a Snake entered his body and coiled itself in his skull. All the flesh fell from him, but his bones still held together, and "in this condition he gave his image to the people as a cross." Sense had not altogether deserted him ; he prayed for two days of torrential rain and two of intense heat ; and when these had passed the Serpent thrust its panting head out of his mouth, whereupon he pulled it forth, and was restored to his

74

living form. The reptile's skin he affixed to his lance, and thus equipped returned to the Black Lodge of Night, where he became the Morning Star.

Flying Snakes occur in Navaho Myth as a Genre.

The Great Mythic Serpent of Indian Lore is quite as much a Sky- as a Water-Being.

A Pawnee Myth tells of the Termination that is to come to all Earthly Life. Various portents will precede : the Moon will turn red and the Sun will Die in the Skies.

The Conception of an Abyss of Waters from which the Earth Emerges, either as a new creation or as a restoration, is found in every part of the American Continent. Not infrequently both the evocation of the World from Primeval Waters and its subsequent Destruction by Flood occur in the same Myth or Cycle, and in many instances what passes for a creation-story is clearly nothing more or less than the Post-Diluvian Renewal of the Earth.

Cheyenne drawing, representing the Medicine-Man and his wife who brought back the Sun-Dance from the Mountain of the Roaring Thunder.

Some tribes, they tell of a time when the Sun was Close to the Earth, Killing Men with its Heat. The Hare was sent to Slay it, and he Shattered the Sun into Myrid Fragments ; but these set the World Ablaze, and it was not until the Hare's Eyes Burst, and a Flood of Tears issued forth, that the Conflagration was Quenched.

Knife-Feathered Monster whom the Zuni name Achiyalatopa.

The Hopi tell of the Snake Youth and in one version the Sun-Man bears the youth on his back in his course about the Earth.

Of ceremonies proper, the most Distinctive on West Coast of America is the Annual Rite in Commemoration of the Dead, known as the "Burning" or "Cry" or the "Dance of the Dead." This is an Autumnal and chiefly Nocturnal Ceremony in which, to the dancing and wailing of the participants, various kinds of property are Burned to supply the Ghosts ; the period of Mourning is then succeeded by a Feast of Jollity.

The notion of Cataclysmic Destructions of the World by Flood or Fire, often with a Concomitant Falling of the Sky, is frequent in American-West-Coast Myth. Indeed, many of the creation-stories seem to be, in fact, Traditions of the Reforming of the Earth after the Great Annihilation, although in some Myths both the creation and the re-creation are described.

The Wintun Creation-Myth, narrated by Curtin, possesses a plot of the same type as the Kato with, Nagaitcho, the Great Traveler and Thunder. Just as he perceives that the end of the First World and of the first people is approaching, Olelbis, He-Who-Sits-Above, builds his paradisic sweat-house in the Sky-World to become a refuge for such as may attain to it. The Cataclysm is caused by the Theft of Flint from the Swift, who, for revenge, induces Shooting Star, Fire Drill, and the latter's wife, Buckeye Bush, to Set the World Afire. "Olebis looked down into the Burning World. He could see nothing but Waves of Flame ; Rocks were Burning, the Ground was Burning, Everything was Burning. great rolls and piles of smoke were rising ; Fire flew up towards the Sky in flames, in great sparks and brands. Those sparks are Sky Eyes, and all the Stars that we now see in the Sky came from that time when the First World was Burned. The sparks stuck fast in the Sky, and have remained there ever since. Quartz Rocks and Fire in the Rocks are from that time ; there was no Fire in the Rocks Before the World Fire. . . . . . . During the Fire they could see Nothing of the World below but Flames and Smoke." Olelbis did not like this ; and on the advice

76

of two old Women, his Grandmothers, as he called them, he sent the Eagle and the Hummingbird to Prop Up The Sky in the North, and to summon thence Katit, the Wind, and Men Loimis, the Waters, who lived beyond the First Sky. "The Great Fire was Blazing, Roaring All Over The Earth, Burning Rocks, Earth, Trees, People, Burning Everything. Mem Loimis started, and with her Kahit. Water rushed in through the open place made by Lutchi when he Raised the Sky. It Rushed in like a crowd of Rivers, covered the Earth, and put out the Fire as it rolled on toward the South. There was so much Water outside that could not come through that it rose to the Top of the Sky and Rushed on toward Olelpanti. . . . . . . Men Loimis went forward, and Water Rose Mountains High. Following closely after Mem Loimis came Kahit. He had a Whistle in his mouth [Pan Pipes] ; as he moved forward he Blew it with All his Might, and made a Terrible Noise. The Whistle was his own ; he had it always. He came Flying and Blowing ; he looked like an Enormous Bat with Wings Spread [Dragon]. As he Flew South toward the other side of the Sky, his Two Cheek Feathers Grew Straight Out, became Immensely Long, waved up and down [Vortices], grew till they could touch the Sky on Both Sides." Finally the Fire was Quenched, and at the request of Olelbis, Kahit drove Mem Loimis, the Waters, back to her underworld home, while beneath Olelpanti there was now nothing but naked rocks, with a single pool left by the receding Waters.

The Horned Plumed Snake of the Pueblos.

A Comox Tradition, in many ways analogous to the South-Western story of the visit of the Twin Warriors to the Sun, tell of the conquest of Tlaik, chief of the Sky, by the two sons of Fair Weather, and of the final Destruction of the Sky-Chief, who is Devoured by the Double-Headed Snake.

The most characteristic feature of the Mythology of the North-West is the cycle of Legends of which the hero is the Raven – the Yetl of the Northern tribes. Like Coyote in the tales of the interior, Raven is a Transformer and a Trickster – half Demiurge, half Clown ; and very many of the stories that are told of Coyote reappear almost unchanged with Raven as their hero ; he is in fact a literal and insular substitute for Coyote. He is greedy, selfish, and treacherous, but gluttony rather than licentiousness is his prevailing vice. He is engaged in an insatiable food-quest : "Raven never got full," says a Tlingit teller, "because he had eaten the black spots off of his own toes. In his travels from place to place, he meets animals of every description, and in contests of wit usually succeeds in destroying and eating them or in driving them off and securing their stores of food. A touch of characteristic humour is added to his portrait by the derisive "Ka, ka, ka," [Bolide popping ?] with which he calls back to his opponents as he flies away – frequently through the smoke-hole, to which he owes his blackness, having once been uncomfortably detained in this aperture. Despite all their ugliness and clownishness, the acts of Raven have a kind of fatefulness attached to them, for their consequence is the establishment of the laws that govern life, alike of Men and animals. A Haida epithet for Raven is He-Whose-Voice-is-Obeyed, because whatever he told to happen came to pass, one of his marked traits being that his bare Word or even his unexpressed Wish is a Creative act.

He is numbered among those heroes of the past about whom indecorous tales may be narrated without sullying the spirit of reverence which attaches to the regnant Gods. One of the most comprehensive of Raven stories – a Tlingit version – states that at the beginning of things there was No Daylight ; the World was in Darkness. In this period lived Raven-at-the-Head-of-Nass, who had in his house the Sun, Moon, Stars, and Daylight. Finally, in various ways he is responsible for the Flood which puts an End to the Age of Animal Beings and inaugurates the Age of Men. A Haida Legend repeats the Tlingit tale of the jealous uncle, who is here identified with the personified Raven, Nankilstlas (He-Whose-Voice-is-Obeyed). The sister gives birth to a boy, as a result of swallowing Hot Stones, but the uncle plots to Destroy the child wishing to be the only male, and puts on his huge hat [Darkness], from which a Flood of Water pours forth to Cover the Earth. One curious inversion of events, in a Kwakiut story, tells how the Antediluvian Wolves, after the subsidence of the Flood, took off their wolf-masks and became human beings.

Next Image is Norwegian, Serpent Around the Sun

78

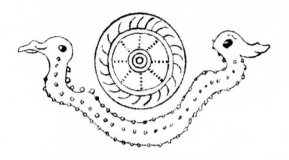

The Migration of Symbols,
by the Count Goblet D' Alviella, 1894

The Religious practices of Antiquity the Disguised or Disfigured reflection
of a Profound Primitive Wisdom.

Myth may be defined as a dramatization of Natural Phenomena.

Symbolism, the representations of the Sun by a disc or radiating face, of the
Moon by a crescent, of the air by birds, of the water by fishes, also a wavy
line. [Crow for Death, Crying Sun as Sad for being Sick, Egg for Ark, ect.]

In the Mythology of primitive nations the contest between the Sky, or the
Sun, and the clouds is frequently represented by a Fight between an Eagle
and a Serpent. This subject has been treated more than once in ancient art.
Already in the Homeric ages it had become a symbol of victory, for we are
told in the Iliad that the Trojans were on the point of abandoning the assault
on the Greek entrenchments through having seen an Eagle which held a
Serpent in its claws take flight, being wounded by its prey. Now according
to the Tradition of the Aztecs, the founding of Mexico is said to have been
resolved on owing to the apparition of an Eagle which, perched upon an
Agave [Inflorescence], and with wings outstretched towards the rising Sun,
held a Serpent in its talons. The first conquerors of Mexico saw therein an
emblem of future greatness, and to the present day this emblem figures in
the arms of the capital. Yet it is unlikely that the Aztecs had read Homer.

The Hindus and Egyptians adopted, as a symbol of the Sun, the Lotus-
Flower, which every morning opens under the first rays of that luminary to
close again at eventide, and which seems to spring up of itself on the surface
of the Placid Waters. In the Iconography of the two nations, we see this
flower serving both as a support to the Solar Gods, Horus and Vishnu.

79

R. P. Greg makes much of the fact that on many incised monuments the Gammadion [Swastika] is placed above images representing the Earth, or terrestrial creatures, and below other images symbolizing the Sky, or the Sun. Frequently the gammadion is found on the same level with Astronomical symbols ; sometimes even it occupies the upper place. Mr. Greg, it is true, gets over the difficulty by asserting that in this case it Must Represent the God of the Ether in the Capacity of Supreme God. He also contends it is especially a symbol of the Air, or rather of the God who rules the Phenomena of the Atmosphere, Indra with the Hindus, Thor with the ancient Germans and the Scandinavians, Perkun with the Slavs, Zeus with the Pelasgians and Greeks, Jupiter, Tonans, and Pluvius with the Latin race. Unfortunately, the proofs which he adduces are neither numerous nor conclusive. The fact that in India the Bull is sacred to Indra, and that on certain monetary ingots the Gammadion surmounts an image of this animal, is hardly sufficient to prove that the Swastika is a symbol of Indra.

Swastika employed as a Religious symbol amongst the Pueblo Indians.

The Legend related by Hygin, which made the Caduceus originate in Hermes Throwing his Wand between Two Serpents fighting.

The Iranian Holy Tree, whose Sap Avert Death.

The symbol of a Serpent Biting its Tail in the Cosmogony of Egypt, of Chaldea, of Greece, and of India, the Earth was believed to be Circumscribed by an Ocean or Celestial River, whose Circular Course is compared to a Serpent. [Zodiacal Light]

The transformation of the Winged Bulls which kept watch of old at the entrances to the Assyrian palaces. Their function as Gate-Keepers or guardians, in condemning them to remain immovable, imposed upon them, in spite of their Wings, rigid contours and massive forms, calculated to give at once an impression of Repose and Force.

In Chinese and, perhaps, Japanese art, the "Great Jewel" becomes a Pearl, frequently depicted Between Two Dragons facing one another, with partly-open jaws. We may, perhaps, find a curious application of this symbol in the customs of the Chinese. M. de Groodt relates that in the Festival of Lanterns they lead about a Dragon made of cloth and bamboo, before whose Mouth they wave a Round Lantern like ball or Pearl of Fire [Bolide], -

80

whether this scene represents the Conflict of the Celestial Bodies with the devouring of eclipses, or the vain effort of falsehood to Swallow up Truth.

On other seal cylinders, reproducing scenes of adoration, or of sacrifice, the rudimentary Tree sometimes accompanies and sometimes replaces the image of a naked Woman with her heels touching and hands turned towards her breasts. Now, this hieratic type is incontestably the representation of Istar, not the Chaste and Warlike Istar who was worshipped at Nineveh, but the Voluptuous and Procreative Istar venerated in particular at Babylon, and more or less related to the Goddess of the Asherim. This might justify the hypothesis of M. Francois Lenormant, who not only sought an equivalent of the Asherah in the Sacred Tree of Mesopotamia, but who also descried, - in the combination so often reproduced in Assyria of the Winged Circle suspended over the Sacred Tree, - the Old Cosmogonical pair of Assur and his companion, the Creative Heaven and the productive Earth.

The pomegranate, which contains hundreds of seeds, has at all times been considered an emblem of Fertility, of Abundance, and of Life. All Semitic nations have used it, as a symbol, on the most different kinds of religious monuments, from the pillars of Solomon's Temple to the stelai depicted amongst the bas-reliefs of the Parma baptistery bears pomegranates for its fruits, and it is also a pomegranate which, according to Tradition related by M. de Gubernatis (Mythologie des plantes), was the fruit that Eve offered Adam.

The Lotus-flower, which contrary to all the rules of botany, sometimes blossoms upon the Sacred Tree and is plucked or smelt by the two Acolytes. We have seen how this flower, which discloses itself every morning to the rays, evoked ideas of Resurrection and Immortality amongst all the ancient nations of the East. When, therefore, we find it on the Sacred Tree of the Phoenicians or the Assyrians, we have every reason to believe that it there represents a "Flower of Life." This Divine Flower, like the Fruit of the Tree of Life, will doubtlessly have figured in Myths whose Text has Not Come Down to Us, but whose Existence is sufficiently Revealed by the Monuments.

The Chaldaeo-Assyrians, in the manner of all Semitic nations, practiced phyllomancy, i.e., the Art of Divination by the Rustling of Leaves, which was Held to be the Voice of the Divinity, such as the Prophetic Trees whose office was to Reveal the Future. (The Odyssey 14.327-328 & 19.296-297 Prophecies through the Whispering of the Leaves of the Sacred Tree.)

81

Now, Endeavours to gain a Foreknowledge of the Decrees of the Divine will are often considered an Encroachment Upon the Celestial Power, a Rash Act, or even a Sacrilege, which calls for Punishment. Cuneiform Tablets, commented upon by Mr. Sayce, tell the story of a God Zu who, covetous of the supreme rank, abstracted the "Tablets of Fate" as well as the attributes of Bell, and having made good his escape in a storm, began to divulge the Knowledge of the Future. After consulting the principal Gods, Bell, to punish him, contented himself with changing him into a Bird of Prey and Exiling him, like another Prometheus, upon a Distant Mountain. According to Mr. Sayce, Zu is none other than "The Bird of the Storm," Common to so many Mythologies, which, in the Rolling of the Thunder, Discloses to Mankind the Secrets of the Future, the Knowledge of Good and Evil. It might almost be said that this Legend lies mid-way between the Scriptural account of "the original sin" and the Aryan Traditions regarding the Theft of Fire and ambrosia from the branches of the Cosmogonical Tree.

Key of Life and Star God, the oldest representation of God

The Winged Globe is a Egyptian symbol and according to an Inscription at Edfu it was Thoth himself who caused it to be placed above the entrances to all the temples in order to commemorate the Victory Won by Horus over Set, i.e., by the principle of Light and Good over that of Darkness and Evil.

The Winged Globe of the Phoenicians is found wherever their art was introduced, in Carthage, Cyprus, Sardina, Sicily, and among different peoples of Palestine. It has even been pointed out on Israelitish Seals of the Oldest Epoch, and nothing prevents us from supposing that – like the Serpent, the Golden Bull or Calf, and the idolatrous images denounced by the prophets – it served, perhaps, to furnish a Figured Representation of Yahveh.

Cuneiform Texts Elicit the Fact that these Winged Globes are No Longer Exclusively a Solar Emblem, but that we are here in the presence of a Divinity at once more Abstract and more anthropomorphic than the Sun. Perhaps this Image even served to express the general idea of Divinity, if we are to judge from its importance in the religious art of Mesopotamia. [Most Likely the Comet / Bolide and not the Sun at All.]

The researches of Assyriology have shown the commencement of intercourse between Egypt and Chaldea to belong to an Extremely Remote Period. 3800 BC   [Upper Image : Bull Horns and Vortices]

Image cut in rock at New Segovia in Central America.

83

The Seal Cylinders of Western Asia,
by Ward William Hayes, 1910

Ea Fish-Man. [Hoary Ubaid Period Tiamat/Ea had Serpents head - Wisdom]

Chaldean New Year's Day, called Zagmuku, and offering to Bau the
Goddess of fertility.

84

The original form of the Scimitar [Long Handled Sickle Type Weapon] is a
Serpent with a thick neck like the Egyptian asp. Ishtar sometimes carries the
Scimitar of Marduk, or of Perseus, her characteristic Weapon, or Emblem,
is the Caduceus. [Two Vortices around the path of a Bolide.]

The Fight between Bel and the Dragon is an early cosmogonic story of the
conflict between Order and Disorder ; of the creation of the World out of
Monstrous Chaos.

Ragnarok : The Age of Fire and Gravel,
by Ignatius Donnelly, 1883

A change came over the fair face of Nature more complete and Terrible than we have language to describe.

The Tail of the Comet seems to be perpetually in motion. It is, says one writer, "continually changing and fluctuating as vaporous masses of cloud-like structure might be conceived to do, and in some instances there has been a strong appearance even of an Undulating Movement."

The great Comet of 1858, Donnatis Comet, which many now living will remember, and which was of such size that when its head was near our horizon the extremity of the Tail reached nearly to the zenith, illustrated this continual movement of the material of the Tail ; that appendage shrank and enlarged millions of miles in length.

Mr. Lockyer believed that he saw in Coggia's Comet the evidences of a Whiling Motion.

The Legends of Mankind, in describing the Comet that Struck the Earth, represent it as partly-colored ; it is "Speckled" in one Legend ; Spotted like a Leopard in another ; sometimes it is a White Boar in the Heavens ; sometimes a Blue Snake ; sometimes it is Red with Blood of the Millions that are to Perish. Again, we shall see that the Legends represent the Monster as "Winding," Undulating, Twisting, fold over fold, Precisely as the Telescopes show us the Comets do to-day.

86

A writer, speaking of the extraordinary Comet of 1843, says : "As the Comet moves past the Great Luminary, it sweeps round its Tail as a Sword may be conceived to be held out at arm's-length, and then waved round the head, from one side to the opposite.

The Comet is obviously drawn by the influence of the Sun's mass, and is subservient to that all-pervading law of sympathetic gravitation that is the sustaining bond of the material Universe. It is ponderable substance beyond all question, and held by that chain of physical connection which it was the glory of Newton to discover. If the Comet were not a material and ponderable substance it would not gravitate round the Sun, and it would not move with increasing velocity as it neared the mighty mass until it had gathered the energy for its own escape in the enhanced and quickened momentum. In the first instance, the ready obedience to the attraction, and then the overshooting of the spot from which it is exerted, combine to establish the Comet's right to stand ranked at least among the ponderable bodies of space.

Kepler affirmed that "Comets are scattered through the Heavens with as much profusion as Fishes in the Ocean." Lalande had a list of seven hundred Comets that had been observed in his time. 1732-1807

The Earth is like a lost child in the midst of a forest full of Wild Beasts. In 1883 the Earth and Comet Biela crossed each other's orbit by one month, thus this generation missed a revelation.

The cavities in which rest the Great Lakes have been attributed to the ice-sheet, but it is difficult to comprehend how an Ice Sheet could Dig Out and Root Out a Hole, as in the case of Lake Superior, nine hundred feet deep! [Actually 1,332', Michigan 922', Huron 751', Erie 210', & Ontario 801.']

Many of the Legends tell us that, as the Comet approached the Earth, that is, as it entered our atmosphere and combined with it, it gave forth World-Appalling Noises, Thunders beyond all Earthly Thunders, Roarings, Howlings, and Hissings, that Shook the Globe.

Now reader, try to grasp the meaning of all this description. Do not merely read the words. To Read Aright, upon any subject, you must read below the words, above the words, and take in all the relations that surround the words. So read this record.

The head of the Comet sheds down Fire. Its gases have Fallen in great volumes on the Earth ; they Ignite ; amid the Whirling and Rushing of the Titanic Conflagration. The winds beat the rocks against the rocks ; they pick up sand-heaps, peat-beds, and boulders, and whirl them madly in the air.

And poor humanity ! burned, bruised, wild, crazed, stumbling, blown about like feathers in a hurricane, smitten by mighty rocks, they perish by the million ; a few only reach the shelter of the caverns ; and thence, glaring backward, look out over the ruins of a Destroyed World.

A pall of dense cloud, many miles in thickness, enfolds the Earth. No Sun, no Moon, no Stars, can be seen. "Darkness is on the face of the Deep." Day has ceased to be. Men stumble against each other. All this is depicted in the Legends.

In the midst of this Darkness and cold and snow, the remnants of poor humanity wander over the face of the Desolated World ; stumbling, awe-struck, but filled with an insatiable hunger which drives them on ; Living upon the bark of the few Trees that have escaped, or on the bodies of the animals that have perished, and even upon one another.

In the future more and more attention will be given to the Myths of Primitive races ; they will be accounted as more reliable, and as reaching farther back in time than many things which we call history. Thoughtful Men will Analyze them, Despising Nothing ; like a chemist who resolves some compound object into its original elements – the very combination constituting a history of the object.

H. H. Bancroft describes Myths as – "A mass of fragmentary Truth and Fiction, not open to rationalistic criticism ; a partition wall of Allegories built of dead Facts cemented with wild fancies ; it looms ever between the immeasurable and the measurable past."

But he adds :

"Never was a time in the history of philosophy when the character, customs, and beliefs of aboriginal Man, and everything appertaining to him, were held in such high esteem by scholars as at present."

"It is now a recognized principle of philosophy that no religious belief, however crude, nor any historical Tradition, however absurd, can be held by the majority of a people for any considerable time as true, without having had in the beginning some Foundation in Fact."

It was thought at one time that Man had made the Flying-Dragon out of his own imagination ; but we now know that the image of the Pterodactyl had simply descended from generation to generation. Sinbad's Great Bird, the Roc, was considered a flight of the Oriental fancy, until science revealed the bones of the dinosaur. All the Winged Beasts Breathing Fire are simply a recollection of the Comet.

It is Utterly Impossible that the races of the Whole World, of all the continents and islands, could have preserved Traditions from the most remote ages, of a Comet having Struck the Earth, of the Great Heat, the Conflagration, the cave-life, the Age of Darkness, and the Return of the Sun, and these things have no basis of Fact. It was not possible for the primitive mind to have Imagined these things if they had never occurred.

The second Hindoo "Avatar" gives the following description of the rapid advance of some Dreadful Object out of Space, and its Tremendous Fall upon the Earth :

"By the power of God there issued from the essence of Brahma a being in the space of an hour, grew to the size of an elephant of the largest size, and remained in the Air."

That is to say, it was an atmospheric, not a terrestrial creature.

"Brahma was astonished on beholding this figure, and discovered, by the force of internal penetration, that it could be nothing but the power of the Omnipotent which had assumed a body and become visible. He now felt that God is all in all, and all is from him ; and said to Mareechee and his sons (the attendant genii) : 'A wonderful animal has emanated from my essence ; at first of the smallest size, it has in one hour increased to this enormous bulk, and, without doubt, it is a portion of the almighty power.'"

Brahma, an earthly king, was at first frightened by the Terrible Spectacle in the Air, and then claimed that he had produced it himself !

"They were engaged in this conversation when that Vara, or 'Boar-Form,' suddenly uttered a sound like the Loudest Thunder, and the Echo Reverberated and Shook All the quarters of the Universe."

89

We shall see here, and in many other Legends, reference to the fact that there was more than one Monster in the Sky. This is in accordance with what we now know to be true of Comets. They often appear in pairs or even triplets. Within the past few years we have seen Biela's Comet divide and form two separate Comets, Pursuing their course side by side. When the Great Comet of 1811 appeared, another of almost equal magnitude followed it. Seneca informs us that Ephoras, a Greek writer of the singular fact of a Comet's separation into two parts.

There is nothing improbable in Hesiod's description of two or three Aerial Monsters appearing at or about the same time, or of one being the apparent Offspring of the other, since a large Comet may, like Biela's, have broken in two before the eyes of the people. [Androgyny]

Babylonian Seal Cylinder Art

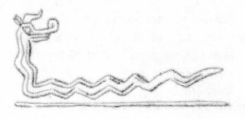

Echidna bare Chimaera, breathing resistless Fire, Fierce and Huge, fleet-footed as well as strong ; this Monster had three heads : one, indeed, of a grim-visaged Lion, one of a Goat, and another of a Serpent, a Fierce Dragon ; in front a Lion, a Dragon behind, and in the midst a Goat,

90

breathing forth the dread strength of Burning Fire. Her Pegasus slew and brave Bellerophon."

According to Hesiod, The Jove-Titans-Typhon Myth :

Born of Night a Monster appears, a Serpent, huge, terrible, speckled, flesh-devouring. With her is another Comet, Typhaon ; they the Chimaera, that breathes resistless Fire, Fierce, Huge, Swift. And Typhaon, associated with both these, is the most dreadful Monster of all, born of Hell and sensual sin, a Serpent, a Fierce Dragon, many-headed, with dusky tongues and Fire gleaming ; sending forth dreadful and Appalling Noises, while mountains and fields rock with Earthquakes ; Chaos has come ; the Earth, the Sea Boils ; there is Unceasing Tumult and Contention, and in the midst the Monster, wounded and broken up, Falls upon the Earth ; the Earth groans under his weight, and there he Blazes and Burns for a time in the Mountain fastnesses and desert places, Melting the Earth with boundless vapor and Glaring Fire. [The Egyptians and Mexicans illustrate chopped up Serpents, the Egyptian by a Cat with a knife.]

We will find Legend after Legend about this Typhon : he runs through the Mythologies of different nations. And as to his size and his terrible power, they all agree. He was No Earth-Creature. He moved in the Air ; he reached the Skies :

"According to Pindar the head of Typhon reached to the Stars, his eyes darted Fire, his hands extended from the East to the West, Terrible Serpents were Twined about the middle of his body, and one hundred Snakes took the place of fingers on his hands. Between him and the Gods there was a Dreadful War. Jupiter finally killed him with a Flash of Lightning, and buried him under Mount Etna."

But Jove, when in truth he had raised high his Wrath, and had taken his arms, his Thunder and Lightning, and Smoking Bolt, leaped up and smote him from Olympus, and Scorched all around the wondrous heads of Terrible Monster.

Ragnarok : the name is significant. According to Professor Anderson's etymology of the word, it means "the Darkness of the Gods" ; from regin, Gods, and Rokr, Darkness ; but it may, more properly, be derived from the Icelandic, Danish, and Swedish reign, a rain, and Rok, Smoke, or Dust ; and it may mean the Rain of Dust.

91

There is in the Legends of the Scandinavians a marvelous record of the coming of the Comet. It has been repeated generation after generation, translated into all languages, commented on, criticized, but Never Under Stood. It has been regarded as a wild, Unmeaning rhapsody of words, or as a premonition of some future Earth Catastrophe.

> "There saw she wade
> In the heavy Streams,
> Men – foul murderers
> And perjurers,
> And them who others' wives
> Seduce to sin.
> Brothers slay brothers ;
> Sisters' children
> Shed each other's blood.
> Hard is the World !
> Sensual sin grows huge.
> There are Sword-ages, Axes-ages ;
> Till the World falls Dead,
> And Men no longer spare
> Or pity one another."

" The Sea rushes over the Earth, for the Midgard-Serpent writhes in giant rage, and seeks to gain the land."

" The Midgard-Serpent Vomits forth Venom, Defiling All the Air and the Sea ; he is Very Terrible, and places himself side by side with the Wolf."

" In the midst of this Clash and Din the Heavens are Rent in Twain, and the sons of Muspelheim come riding through the opening."

Muspelheim according to Professor Anderson, means " the Day of Judgment." Muspel signifies an abode of Fire, peopled by fiends. So that passage means, that the Heavens Split Open, or appeared to be, by the Great Shining Comet, or Comets, Striking the Earth ; it is a word of Fire ; it is the Day of Judgment.

This next narrative is from the Younger Edda :

"The Eagle Screams,
And with pale beak tears corpses....
Mountains dash together,
Heroes go the way to Hel,
And Heaven is Rent in Twain....
All Men abandon their homesteads
When the warder or Midgard
In wrath slays the Serpent.
The Sun grows Dark,
The Earth sinks into the Sea,
The Bright Stars
From Heaven Vanish ;
Fire rages,
Heat Blazes,
And high Flames play
'Gainst Heaven itself."

The coming of the Monster, his attack upon and conquest of the Sun, his apparent Swallowing of that orb, are all found represented on both sides of the Atlantic, on the walls of the temples and in great Earth-Mounds, in the image of a Gigantic Serpent holding a Globe in its Mouth.

This Long-Trailing object in the Skies was probably the origin of that primeval Serpent-Worship found all over the World. And hence the association of the Serpent in so many religions with the Evil One. In itself, the Serpent should no more represent moral wrong than the lizard, the crocodile, or the frog ; but the heredity abhorrence with which he is regarded by Mankind extends to no other created thing. He is the image of the Great Destroyer, the wronger, the enemy.

An ancient authority (1550 M. Ferdinand Denis) gives the following Legend of the Tupi Indians of Brazil :

"Monau, without beginning or end, author of all that is, seeing the ingratitude of Men, and their contempt for him who had made them thus joyous, withdrew from them, and sent upon them Ta Ta, the Divine Fire, which Burned All that was on the surface of the Earth. He swept about the Fire in such a way that in places he raised Mountains, and in others dug valleys. Of all Men one alone, Irin Mage, was saved, whom Monau carried into the Heaven. He, seeing all things Destroyed, spoke thus to Monau : 'Wilt thou also Destroy the Heavens and their garniture ? Alas ! henceforth where will be our home ? Why should I live, since there is none other of my kind ?' Then Monau was so filled with pity that he poured a Deluging rain on Earth, which quenched the Fire, and flowed on all sides, forming the Ocean, which we call the parana, the Great Waters."

I would note a singular coincidence : The Fire that Fell from Heaven was the divine tata. In Egypt the name of deity was "ta-ta," or "pta-pta," which signified father. This became in Hebrew "ya-ya," from which we derive the root of Jah, Jehovah. And this word is found in many languages in Europe and America, and even in our own, as, "da-da," "daddy," father. The Tupi "tata" was Fire from the supreme father. [Has to be the repeated pops heard in video of Chelyabinsk Russia February 15th 2013.]

Who can doubt the oneness of the human race, when millions of threads of Tradition and language thus cross each other through it in all directions, like the web of a mighty fabric ?

If We take the ground that this Universal Tradition of a World-Conflagration was an Invention, a Falsehood, then we must conclude that this handful of Men, before they dispersed, in the very infancy of the World, shared in the propagation of a Prodigious Lie, and religiously perpetuated it for tens of thousands of years. [A believer of continental intercourse or the central propagation of Man instead of a World Wide Spectacle and its stories independently proving the testimony of the Event.]

In early ages, Mankind, all over the World, was divided into totemic septs or families, bearing animal names. It was out of this fact that the fables of animals possessing human speech arose. When we are told the Fox talked to the Crow or the Wolf, it is simply means that a Man of the Fox totem talked to a Man of the Crow or Wolf totem.

Orpheus says :

"From the beginning the Gloomy night enveloped and obscured all things
that were under the ether. The Earth was invisible on account of the
Darkness, but the Light broke through the ether and illuminated the Earth."
A great Solar-Myth underlies all the ancient Mythologies. It commemorates
the Death and Resurrection of the Sun. It signifies the Destruction of the
Light by the clouds, the Darkness, and the eventual return of the great
Luminary of the World.

The Syrian Adonis, the Sun-God, the Hebrew Tamheur, and the Assyrian
Du-Zu, all suffered a Sudden and Violent Death, disappeared for a time
from the sight of Men, and were at last Raised from the Dead.

All through the Gothic Legends runs this thought – the battle of Light and
Darkness ; the temporary Death of the Light, and its final triumph over the
grave.

All these events are perpetuated in the Sun-Worship which still exists in the
World in many forms. Even the Christian peasant of Europe still lifts his hat
to the rising Sun. [19th century]

The religion of the Hindoos was also based on the same great Cosmical
event. Indra was the great God, the Sun. He has long and dreadful contest
with Vritra, "the Throttling Snake." Indra is " the cloud-compeller"; he
"shatters the cloud with his Bolt and releases the imprisoned Waters" ; that is
to say, he slays the Snake Vritra, the Comet, and thereafter the rain pours
down and extinguishes the Flames which Consume the World. [This is a
great example of how the Myth changed into Thunder Storms over time.]

The celebration of the May-day, with its ceremonies, the May-pole, its
May-Queen, etc., is a survival of the primeval thanksgiving with which
afflicted Mankind welcomed the return of the Sun from his long sleep of
Death. In Norway, during the middle ages, the whole scene was
represented in these May-day festivals : One Man represented Summer, he
clad in green leaves ; the other represents Winter ; he is clad in straw, fit
picture of the misery of the Dark Age. They have each a large company of
attendants armed with staves ; they fight with each other until winter (the
age of Darkness and cold) is subdued. They pretend to pluck his eyes out
and throw him in the Water. Winter is slain.

95

The Russians have a Legend, they tell of Ilia, the peasant, the servant of Vladimir, Fair Sun. He meets the brigand Solovei, a Monster, a Gigantic Bird, called the Nightingale ; his Claws extend for Seven versts over the country. Like the Dragon of Hesiod, he was full of sounds - "he Roared like a wild beast, Howled like a Dog, and Whistled like a Nightingale." Ilia hits him with an Arrow in the right eye, and he tumbles headlong from his lofty nest to the Earth. The wife of the Monster follows Ilia, who has attached him to his saddle, and is dragging him away ; she offers cupfuls of Gold, Silver, and Pearls – an allusion probably to the precious metals and stones which were said to have Fallen from the Heavens. [Like the colors of the Columbia Shuttle Disintegration.] The Sun (Vladimir) welcomes Ilia, and requests the Monster to Howl, Roar, and Whistle for his entertainment ; he contemptuously refuses ; Ilia then commands him and he obeys : the Noise is so Terrible that the roof of the palace falls off, and the courtiers drop dead with fear. Ilia, indignant at such an uproar, " cuts up the Monster into little pieces, which he scatters over the fields." [Columbia Shuttle]

Subsequently Ilia hides away in a Cave, unfed by Vladimir – that is to say, without the light of the Sun. At length the Sun goes to seek him, expecting to find him Starved to Death ; but the king's daughter has sent him food everyday for Three Years, and he comes out of the Cave hale and hearty, and ready to fight again for Vladimir, the Fair Sun. These three years are the three years of the "Fimbul-Winter" of the Norse Legends.

This battle between the Sun and the Comet graduated into a contest between Light and Darkness ; and, by a natural transition, this became in time the unending struggle between the forces of Good and the powers of Evil – between God and Satan ; and the imagery associated with it has, - strange to say, - continued down into our own literature.

That great scholar and mighty poet, John Milton, had the Legends of the Greeks and Romans and the unwritten Traditions of all peoples in his mind, when he described, in the sixth book of "Paradise Lost," the tremendous conflict between the angles of God and the followers of the Fallen One, the Apostate, the Great Serpent, the Dragon, Lucifer, the bright-shining, the Star of the morning, coming, like the Comet, from the North.

The Legends of Mankind point unmistakably to the fact that the Earth, in some remote age met with a Tremendous Catastrophe ; that a Conflagration raged over parts of its surface ; that Mankind took refuge in the caves of the Earth, whence they afterward emerged to wander for a long time, in great poverty and hardships, during a period of Darkness ; and finally this Darkness dispersed, and the Sun shone again in the Heavens.

I do not see how the reader Can Avoid These Conclusions. There are but two alternatives before him : he must either suppose that all this concatenation of Legends is the outgrowth of a Prodigious Primeval Lie, or he must concede that it describes some event which Really Happened.

In some Myths the Comet Is a God ; in others a Demon ; in others a Serpent ; in others a Feathered Serpent ; in others a Dragon ; in others a Giant ; in others a Bird ; in others a Wolf ; in others a Dog ; in still others a Boar.

The Legends coincide only in these facts : - the Monster in the air ; the heat ; the Fire ; the cave-life ; the Darkness ; the return of the Sun !

If the reader takes the other alternative, that these Legends are Not Fragments of a Colossal Falsehood, then he must concede that the Earth, since Man inhabited it, encountered a Comet. No other cause or event could produce such a series of Gigantic Consequences as is Here Narrated.

As often happens, the impressive facts within Myths are Remembered, but in a Disarranged Chronological Order.

On the plateau of the Atlas, in Northern Africa, in a bare, deserted, stony place among the mountains, a collection of fifteen hundred tombs, made of rude limestone slabs, set up with one slab to form a roof, so as to make perfect Dolmens – closed chambers – where the bodies were packed in.

"Tradition says that a wicked people lived there, and for their Sins Stones were Rained Upon them from Heaven ; so they Built these Chambers to Creep Into."

Part of a great prayer of the Aztecs to Tezcalipoca, "Thine Anger and Indignation has Descended upon us in these days... coming down even as Stones, Spears, and Darts upon the wretches that inhabit the Earth ; this is the Pestilence by which we are afflicted and almost Destroyed." The children die, "broke and dashed to pieces as against stones and a wall... Thine anger and thy indignation does delight in Hurling the Stones and Arrow and Spear. The grinders of thy teeth" (the Dragon's teeth of Ovid?) "are employed, and thy bitter whips upon the miserable of thy people... Hast thou verily determined that it Utterly Perish ;... that the peopled place become a wooded hill and a wilderness of stones ?... Is there no mercy nor pity for us until the Arrows of thy Fury are spent ?... Thine Arrows and Stones have sorely hurt this poor people."

[Day Time Mexican Space Fall]

God gives over the government of the World for a time to Satan, to work his devilish will upon Job. Did not God do this very thing when he permitted the Comet to Strike Earth ? Satan in Arabic in " the heat of haste" ; Umbreit translates it, "from a Flight Over the Earth."

"Let that day be turned into Darkness ; let not God regard it from above ; and let Not the Light Shine upon it. Let Darkness and the Shadow of Death cover it ; let a Mist Overspread it, and let it be wrapped up in bitterness. Let a Darksome Whirlwind seize upon that night...Let them curse it who curse the day, who are ready to raise up a Leviathan."

This Catastrophe was indeed The Fall of Man. Think what a Fall ! From comfort to misery ; from plowed fields to the thistles and the stones ; from sunny and glorious days in a storm less land to the awful trails of the Dark Age ; the rains, the cold, the snow, the ice, the incessant tempests, the Darkness, the poverty, the coats of hides, the cave-life, the cannibalism, the Stone Age.

Here was The Fall indeed. There is nothing in antiquity that has not a meaning. The Fables of the world's childhood should be sacred from our laughter.

Our Theology, even where science has most ridiculed it, is based on a great, a Gigantic Truth. Paradise, the Summer land of Fruits, the Serpent, the Fire from Heaven, the expulsion, the Waving Sword, the "Fall of Man," the "Darkness on the face of the Deep," the age of toil and sweat – all, all, are Literal Facts.

And could we but penetrate their meanings, the Trees of Life and Knowledge and the Apples of Paradise probably represent likewise great and important facts or events in the history of our race.

And with what slow steps did Mankind struggle upward ! In some favored geographical center they recovered the arts of metallurgy, the domestication of animals, and the alphabet.

"All knowledge," says the Hindoo Krishna, "was originally bestowed on Mankind by God. They lost it. They recovered it as a recollection."

The poor barbarian Indians of American possess Traditions of this ancient civilization, Traditions in forms as rude as their own condition.

If one came and proved that at a given point he had found indications of a coal-bed or a gold-mine, he would have no difficulty in obtaining means enough to dig a shaft and excavate acres. Can not the greed for information do one tenth as much as the greed for profit ?

Great races are the weeded-out survivors of great sufferings. A Roman poet, in the Viking age : "The sea is their school of war and the storm their friend ; they are sea-wolves that prey on the pillage of the World."

The Golden Age represented in Genesis, when Adam and Eve, naked, but supremely happy, lined upon the fruits of the garden, and knew neither sorrow nor suffering, neither toil nor hunger.

But one day the Evil-One came, as in the Bible Legend ; the Prince of the Rakchasos (Raknaros-Ragnarok ?) came, and broke up this paradise.

The Dawn of Astronomy : Study of the Temple-Worship & Mythology of the Ancient Egyptians by Sir Norman Lockey, 1894

In regard to old St. Peter's at Rome, we read that "so exactly due East and West was the Basilica that, on the Vernal Equinox, the great doors of the porch of the quadriporticus were thrown open at Sunrise, and also the Eastern doors of the church itself, and as the Sun rose, its rays passed through the outer doors, then through the inner doors, and, penetrating straight through the nave, illuminated the High Altar." The present church fulfills the same conditions. [Between this Light beam are Four Serpentine Columns and on the ceiling is a single Dove, which probably represents the Four Ages caused by Serpents from the Lost Pleiad and above the High Altar where the Light shines is a Beautiful Perfect Representation of The Sun !]

The Temple of Amen-Ra at Karnak is beyond all question the most majestic ruin in the World. There is a sort of stone avenue in the center, giving a view towards the North-West, and this axis is something like five hundred yards in length. [There are really two temples in the same line on each side of the river, the chief one facing the Sunset at the Summer Solstice, the other probably the Sunrise at the Winter Solstice.]

The columns and partition walls where to limit the light which fell on their fronts and to narrow the beam into the blocked in dark sanctuary. This idea is strengthened by consideration of the astronomical telescope. Although the Egyptians knew nothing about telescopes, it would seem that they had the same problem before them which we solve by a special arrangement in the modern telescope – they wanted to keep the light pure, and to lead it into their sanctuary as we lead it to the eyepiece. To keep the light that passes into the eyepiece of a modern telescope pure, we have between the object-glass and the eyepiece a series of what are called diaphragms ; that is, a series of rings right along the tube, the inner diameters of the rings being greatest close to the object-glass, and smallest close to the eyepiece ; these diaphragms must so be made that all the light from the object-glass shall fall upon the eyepiece, without loss or reflection by the tube.

These apertures in the pylons and separating walls of Egyptian temples exactly represent the diaphragms in the modern telescope. [19th Century]

It should be noted that the Temple of Hatchepsut at Luxor is directly in line to the North-West of the Temple of Amen-Ra at Karnak and just beyond is the Valley of the Kings. Symbolically demonstrating in their architecture that the Sun is resurrected in the East and dies in the West.

If the Egyptians wished to use the light thrown for ceremonial purposes, the magnificent beam of light thrown into the temple at the Sunset (or Sunrise) hour would give them opportunities and even suggestions for so doing ; for instance, they might place an image of the God in the sanctuary and allow the light to flash upon it. We should have a "manifestation or Ra" with a vengeance during the brief time the white flood of Sunlight fell on it. [Probably a flat plane and Camera Obscura method to observe the disk, Sun spots, and Corona Mass Ejections.] [Also note : that the Seven Chambers and Corbelles of the Grand Gallery in the Great Pyramid most likely represent the Pleiades and at least one shaft should point to it.]

Star Lore of All Ages : A Collection of Myths, Legends & Facts Concerning the Constellations of the Northern Hemisphere, by William Tyler Alcott, 1911

Early in the history of Man we find the Stars all-important to his welfare. No course was pursued or plan adopted without first consulting the Heavenly bodies. They governed alike the policies of nations and the actions of individuals. They ruled absolutely over the destinies of the high and lowly, the rich and poor, and the horoscopes became a necessity of Life, and divination the highest pursuit of Man. In Sabianism, or Star Worship, we have, therefore, the earliest form of religion, and in astrology and the adoration of Stars the progenitors of the modern science of astronomy.

It is a remarkable fact that, from the earliest times, as far as we can judge from the Cuneiform Inscriptions and Hieroglyphs that have been deciphered, the sign for God was a Star.

ancient Persian Traditions are said to have considered 3,000 years ago that the whole Heavens were divided up into four great districts marking the four colures, (the meridian points of the solstices and equinoxes) each watched over by one of the "Royal Stars," Aldebaran in Taurus, Antares in Scorpio,

Regulus in Leo, and Fomalhaut in the Southern Fish. These four stars were celebrated throughout all Asia. The brilliant star in the Eagle, Altair, has been suggested as the fourth Royal Star instead of Fomalhaut. Thus, as in the vision of Ezekiel, so in the Constellation figures, the Lion, the Ox, the Man/Angel, and the Eagle stood as the upholders of the Firmament, as "the pillars of Heaven." They looked down like sentinels upon all creation, and seemed to guard the four quarters of the sky.

Leo is for many reasons significant to Masons. In the four Royal Stars, the four great Elohim, or Decans, Gods ruling the signs, were believed to dwell. The four Decans who ruled the four angles of the Heavens were the most important and most powerful. To these four Stars, the divine honours are paid of the Hebrews also of the four great Elohim and the Christians with the symbols of the four Evangelists. Astrologers distinguished Leo as "The Sole House of the Sun," and taught that the World was created when the Sun was in that sign. [Which is when the skies cleared.]

The Capricorn which appears on the Babylonian boundary stones, the most ancient of all records extant, is to all intents and purposes identical in form with the Capricorn of a modern almanac. The Greeks sometimes called the Constellation simply "Pan." From this word we get our word "Panic," which is the sort of Fear that is born of the imagination, and Pan was said to Terrorize people by the mere thought of his presence. He was also regarded as the God of rural scenery, shepherds, huntsmen, and as the God of Plenty. Caesius called it "the scapegoat." [The Comet Sinks toward this Deep Sign after the Day time Pass and the Phaethon / Icarus Strike.]

Flammarion asserts that there is a Chinese record of 2449 B.C. which locates among the stars of Capricornus a conjunction of the five planets. There was an early prediction made, that when all the planets met in this sign the World would be Destroyed by a Great Conflagration. Capricornus figures on an ancient Egyptian Mirror. The Mirror was Emblematic of Life. The Peruvians called it "the Bearded One" and during ceremonial dances wore masks with long beards. [White breaded Americans]

Mythological accounts of Draco vary considerably. By some this Serpent is the guardian of the Stars (the golden apples) which hang from the Pole Tree in the garden of Darkness, or the garden of the West.

In Greece Draco was called "Pytho"; in Anglo-Saxon chronicles he is referred to as "the Fire Drake," "the Denier of God," "the Unsleeping

Poison-Fanged Monster," and "the Terrible Enemy of Man full of subtlety and power." The same idea has come down to us in the well-known Myth of St. George and the Dragon.

There seems to have been a special effort on the part of the originators of the Constellations, at the outset almost, to symbolize by a Star group the presence of the Evil One, ever watchful, ever vigilant, gazing down upon mortals from the highest Heavens, as a perpetual menace to evil-doers and a continual reminder of original sin.

The Constellations Draco and Hercules are closely associated in ancient Mythology, and Hercules is always represented as trampling the Dragon underfoot. These two Constellations are in turn connected with Ophiuchus and Serpents, the figure of another Giant overcoming a Serpent, while he crushes the Scorpion under his feet. On the old maps the figures of these two famous Giants appear head to head.

These similar and striking groups, placed so close together in the Sky, show clearly that there was a Deliberate Intention on the part of the Inventors of the Constellations to emphasis the Great Fact of a struggle between Mankind and Serpentkind. There seems here an evident reference to God's interview with the Serpent in the Garden of Eden. "I will put enmity between thee and the Woman, and between thy Seed and her Seed. It shall bruise thy head and thou shalt bruise his heel." (Genesis 3 : 15) [The Comet or Life of Man !]

There can be little doubt that in these Star Groups we have evidence of the very earliest attempts of Man to Engrave a Record of History and Tradition for all Humanity to Read, and that in the history of these Constellations lies the Key to many of the Mooted Religious questions of the day.

The Great Pyramid was oriented to Thuban, the light from which shone down its central passage in the year 2170 B.C. At that time this Star must have seemed to all ordinary observation an absolutely fixed centre round which all the other Stars revolved, just as Polaris appears to us now. It was however much closer to the true Pole of the Heavens than Polaris is at the present time.

The Bull was an important object of worship with the Druids, and their Great Tauric Festival was held when the Sun entered this Constellation, a survival of which has come down to us in the Festival of May Day. In

104

Hebrew, Syriac, Arabic, and Coptic the word for Bull means "Coming" or "Who Cometh."

The Greeks identified Alcor of Ursa Major with the Lost Pleiad Electra, who had Wandered Away from her companions and had been changed into a Fox. This Star also marks the radiant point of the Ursid Meteor shower of November 10th.

The Great Pyramid, which was without doubt erected for Astronomical Purposes, is closely associated with the Pleiades, as Proctor has shown. In the year 2170 B.C. the date at which the Pleiades really opened the spring season by their Midnight Culmination, there could be seen through the south passageway of this gigantic mausoleum. It has been suggested that the Seven Chambers of the Great Pyramid commemorate these Seven Famous Stars. Blake says : "Either the whole of the conclusion respecting the pyramids is founded on pure imagination, or we have here another remarkable proof of the influence or the Pleiades on the reckoning of the Year."

The Egyptians called this Star group "Athur-ai" or "Atauria" meaning the Stars of Athyr (Hathor), a name also given the Seven Stars by the Chaldeans and Hebrews. From this title is derived the Latin Taurus, and the German Thier. It is possible that this title was somehow connected with the Greek letter Tau, and the sacred scarabaeus or Tau beetle of Egypt. It has been suggested that the "tors" and Arthur's seat, which were names given to British hilltops, may be connected with the "high places" of the worship of the Pleiades. Arthur's Seat at Edinburgh is a notable example of such a site.

Many of the Greek temples were orientated to the Seven Stars, notably temples erected as early as 1530 and 1150 B.C. and the noted Parthenon built in 438 B.C., and in the works of the Grecian poets we find many references to the group.

According to Lockyer, nine temples in Egypt are orientated with Draconis, the "Dragon's Head," which was the Pole Star in 3,500 BC.

Allen tells us that the Hindus pictured these Stars as a Flame typical of Agni, the God of Fire, and the regent of the Asterism. It is thought that there may be a connection between the Hindu title "Flame," and the great Feast of Lamps of the western Hindus held in the Pleiad season, October and

November, a Great Festival of the Dead which gave rise to the present Feast of Lanterns of Japan.

This closely associated Star group has from Time Immemorial impressed Mankind with a Sense of Mystery. A Great Cataclysm, possibly the Biblical Deluge, is in some way Connected with the Pleiades, and some reference to such an event can be traced in many of the Legends and Myths surrounding these Stars that have come down to us from nations far removed from each other.

Memorial services to the Dead at the season of the year when the Pleiades occupied a conspicuous position in the Heavens are found to have taken place, and to have been a feature in the history of almost Every Nation of the Earth, from remote Antiquity to the Present Day. The Universality of this Custom may be considered one of the Most Remarkable Facts that Astronomical history records, and it serves to make the study of this Group the Most Interesting chapter in All History. This Little Group of Stars, twinkling so timidly in the nights of Autumn in the Eastern Heavens, links the races of Mankind in closer relationship than any bonds save nature's. No wonder that they have inspired universal awe and admiration, that within this Group of Suns Man has sought to find the very centre of the Universe. [Figuratively, The Meaning of Our Universe, What it is All About.]

Among the Aztecs of South America we find the Pleiades the Cynosure of All Eyes, a nation Trembling at their feet. At the end of every period of fifty-two years, in the month of November when the Pleiades would culminate at Midnight, these rude people imagined the World would End. Human sacrifices were offered, while the entire population passed the night upon their knees awaiting their Doom. Far removed from the Aztecs we find the people of Japan in their great national festival, the Feast of Lanterns, a Feast that is alive to-day, commemorating at this same season of the year some Great Calamity which was supposed to have overwhelmed the race of Man, in the far distant Past, which these Seven Stars were prominent in the Heavens.

In the Talmud we find a curious Legend associating the Pleiades with an All-Destroying Flood, expressed as follows: "When the Holy One, blessed be he, wished to bring the Deluge upon the World, he took two Stars out of the Pleiades and thus let the Deluge loose, and when he wished to arrest it, he took two stars out of Arcturus and stopped it."

106

Among the ancient Egyptians the same day (November 17th) was observed, and although their calendar was subsequently changed, the occasion was not lost sight of. The date of the Pleiades at Midnight, and on this date the solemn Three Day's Festival commenced. With them, as with the three previously mentioned nations, the Festival was associated with the Tradition of the Deluge or Race-Destroying Calamity. Blake says in regard to this that "When we connect the fact that this Festival occurred on the 17th day of Athyr, with the date on which the Mosaic account of the Deluge of Noah states it to have commenced, in the second month of the Jewish year, which corresponds to November, the 17th day of the month, it must be acknowledged that this is No Chance Coincidence, and that the precise date here stated must have been regulated by the Pleiades, as was the Egyptian date." Surely this is an interesting reference to the history of these Stars.

The Persians formerly called the month of November "Mordad," meaning "the Angel of Death," and that month marked the date of their Festival of the Dead. On the day of the Midnight culmination of the Pleiades, November 17th, no petition was presented in vain to their ancient kings.

The fall of the year was especially appropriate as a season for memorial services for the Dead, as Nature's Life was then at a slow ebb and every prospect was suggestive of Death, and the preparation for the long sleep imposed by winter.

The Pleiades was a favorite Constellation of the Iroquois Indians. In all their religious festivals the calumet, pipe, was presented towards these Stars, and prayers for happiness were addressed to them.

An Onondaga Legend concerning these Stars is as follows : "A long time ago a party of Indians journeyed through the woods in search of a good hunting ground. Having found one, they proceeded to build their lodges for the winter, while the children gathered together to dance and sing. While the children were thus engaged, an old Man dressed in White Feathers, whose White Hair Shone like Silver, appeared among them and bid them cease dancing lest Evil Befall them, but the children danced on unmindful of the warning, and presently they observed that they were rising little by little into the air, and one exclaimed, 'Do not look back for something strange is taking place.' One of the children disobeyed this warning and looked back became a Falling Star. The other children reached the High Heavens safely and now we see them in their group known as the Pleiades.

Another name for the Pleiades was "the clusters," and they are frequently represented on ancient coins by a cluster of Grapes [Mistletoe]. A coin of Mallos in Cilicia shows them represented by Doves whose bodies are formed by bunches of Grapes.

The Dyaks and the Malays of Borneo imagine the Pleiades to be Six Chickens followed by their mother, who remains always invisible. At one time there were Seven Chickens, but one of them Paid a Visit to the Earth, and there received something to eat. This made the Hen Very Angry and she threatened to Destroy the Chickens, and the people on the Earth. Fortunately the latter were saved by Orion, the Mighty Hunter. At that period of the year when the Pleiades are visible the Dyaks say that "the Hen Broods her Chickens." When these Stars are to be seen they say "the Cuckoo calls."

Sun Lore of All Ages a Collection of Myths & Legends Concerning the Sun and Its Worship, by William Tyler Olcott, 1914

Solar Mythology commands attention for it is the very basis of science ; it permeates the early history of all people, its influence has made itself felt in every age, and many of the customs that govern our lives to-day are of solar origin. The Sun, above all that human eyes behold, is the chief element in Life, the Very Essence of Our Existence, and to its beneficent influence we owe all that we possess to-day, that is of worth. How few realize this fact. Our ideas concerning natural phenomena are but the result of past ages of research in the fields of science ; but when we come to a consideration of the phenomena that day and night present, in their ever-changing phases, we find it extremely difficult to clearly understand the mental viewpoint of primitive Man regarding this constant repetition of this phenomena has dulled our faculties and it escapes our attention.

In the Sun Myths of all nations we find allusions to the Capricious Nature of the Sun. Now it Smiles and Gladdens the Earth with its Golden Light, and , presently, displeased at Man, shuns his presence, and hides Sullenly for a time in Gloomy Solitude. [Cries when Sad or just one eye when Darkened.]

Plutarch, referring to the Solar Festivals of Egypt, says, that "about the Winter Solstice they lead the sacred Cow Seven times in procession around the temple, calling this the searching after Osiris [Verdure, One of the Ages.], that season of the year standing most in need of the Sun's warmth."

The great celebration of the Summer Solstice was preeminently a Fire Festival, for the ceremonies featured the lighting of huge bonfires on the hilltops, leaping through the flames, and rolling blazing wheels of Fire from the summits of the hills, indicating the Sun's descending course in the Heavens.

The Delphic Sibyl (Michelangelo) Sistine Chapel, Vatican
[Note : Four Ages Holding up the Sky.]

There was also practiced in Ireland, in connection with the Midsummer Festival which celebrated the turning-point of the Sun at the Summer Solstice, a strange dance which was religious in its character, and Solar in its origin. The Greeks called this "the Pyrrhic dance" from "pu" meaning Fire, and practiced it from the most ancient times. The feature of the dance was its Serpentine character, as the dancers circled about in a long line simulating the coils of a Serpent. In Ireland the dance had the same characteristics, and though the Esoteric Meaning of the dance had been

Lost, it was in all probability a mystic rite symbolic of the course of the Sun, for the dancers invariably circled from East to West. Sun Worship, symbolically speaking, lies at the very heart of the great festivals which the Christian Church celebrates to-day, and these relics of Heathen Religion have, through the medium of their sacred rites, curiously enough blended with practices and beliefs Utterly Antagonistic to the spirit that prompted them. The reason for the survival of many of the symbols of Sun Worship and the practice of many customs peculiar to this ancient form of idolatry, lies in the fact that the early Christian teachers found the people so wedded to their old rites and usages, that it was vain to hope for the complete abandonment of these long-cherished practices. Hence a compromise was wisely effected, and the Old Pagan Customs were deprived of the idolatry that was so Obnoxious to the Christian, and transferred as mere meaningless symbols and empty forms to the Christian festivals. Old Paganism died hard, and fought long and stubbornly in its struggle with Christianity, but time has fought for the Christian, and now even the meaning of symbols and forms that once played such an important part in Pagan Worship is lost sight of, and their former force and power is lost for evermore. [The Iron Point.]

Aztec Calendar Stone [Two Horned Serpents surrounding.]

The Greeks regarded the orb of day as an all-seeing eye, and believed that no deed escaped its detection. The Finns believed that even the abode of the dead could be reached by the blissful rays of the Sun. Because the Sun looked down on all Men, messages were given to the Sun that he might convey them to absent ones of a family, whom he beheld wherever they chanced to be.

110

Myths of China & Japan,
by Donald A. Mackenzie, 1923

The so-called "Ornaments" worn by our remote ancestors were charms against evil and ill luck. Metals were similarly supposed to have protective qualities. Iron is still regarded in the Scottish Highlands as a charm against fairy attack. In China it is protection against Dragons. Globally, Gold was the Metal of the Sun-God and Silver of the deity of the Moon. In Egypt, Horus had associations with Copper and Iron was "the Bones of Set", the Egyptian Devil. In Greece and India the Mythical ages were associated with Metals, and Iron was the Metal of the Dark Age of Evil (the Indian "Kali Yuga"). In Japan the belief prevailed that if Iron and filth were flung into ponds the Dragons raised Hurricanes that devastated the land. The Chinese roused Dragons, when they wanted rain, by making a Great Noise and by

111

Throwing Iron into Dragon Pools. The Dragon-Shaped Sea-Gods of India and the Dragon-Gods of China and Japan have close associations with Pearls. In a sixth-century Chinese work, it is stated that Pearls are Spit Out by Dragons. Dragons have Pearls "worth a hundred pieces of Gold" in their Mouths and when Dragons Fight in the Sky, Fire-Balls and Pearls Fall to the Ground, which are referred to as "Thunder-Pearls". These Illuminate a House by Night. Also known as Magic Pearls and the "Jewels of Flood and Ebb". A Mountain in Japan is called Ryushuho, which means "Dragon-Pearl Peak". It is situated in Fuwa district of Mino province, and is associated in a Legend with the Buddhist temple called Cloud-Dragon Shrine". When this temple was being erected, a Dragon, carrying a Pearl in its Mouth, appeared before one of the priests. Mountain and sanctuary were consequently given Dragon names.

Ancient Bronze Astronomical instruments adorned with Dragons, Peking and Chinese Dragon Boat Festival.

112

Sigurd Saga, Ramsund carving in Sweden

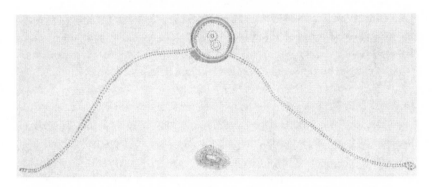

Avebury, England. A Neolithic Henge 27 miles Due North of Stonehenge.

The Mythology & Rites of the British Druids,
by Edward Davis, 1809

Ascertained by National Documents & Compared with the General Traditions & Customs of Heathenism, as illustrated by the Most Eminent Antiquaries of our Age

If ye are primitive Bards, according to the discipline of qualified instructors, relate the Great Secrets of the World which we inhabit. – There is a Formidable Animal, from the city of Satan, which has made an inroad between the Deep and the Shallows. His Mouth is as wide as the Mountain of Mynnau : neither death can vanquish him, nor hand, nor swords. There is a load of nine hundred rocks between his two paws : there is one eye in his

113

head, vivid as the blue ice. Three fountains there are, in his receptacles ; so thick about him, and flowing through him, have been the moistening horns of Deivr Donwy, the giver of waters [Triskelion]. The names of the three fountains, that spring from the middle of the Deep. – One is the increase of salt water, when it Mounts Aloft, over the fluctuating seas, to replenish the streams. The second is that which, innocently, descends upon us, when it rains without, through the boundless atmosphere. The third is that which springs through the Veins of the Mountains, as a banquet from the Flinty Rock, furnished by the King of kings. [The Comet Venting]

The smallest of the small is Hu the mighty, in the World's judgment ; yet he is the greatest, and Lord over us, we sincerely believe, and our God of Mystery. Light is his Course, and Swift : a particle of Lucid Sunshine is his car. He is great on Land and Sea – the greatest whom I shall behold – greater than the Worlds ! Let us beware of offering mean indignity to him, the great and bountiful should it be disputed, I assert – these are the Oxen of Hu the Mighty, with a part of his chain, and his five angels (or attendants) which ye now behold, with a Golden Harness of Active Flame.

Elegy of Uthr Pendragon, that is, wonderful supreme leader, or wonderful chief Dragon, this God is introduced in pageantry, and describes himself as the God of War, the Atherial, having the Rainbow for his Girdle, he is an enchanter, and the president of Haearndor, the Vessel with the Iron Door. In the second part of this poem, a sacrificing priest invokes this God for the propriety of Britain. He styles him Hu, with the Expanding Wings – father, and king of Bards – father Deon, presiding in the mundane Circle of Stones. He is again named Prydain – the glancing Hu – the sovereign of Heaven – the Gliding King – the Dragon, and the victorious Beli, Lord of the honey island, or Britain. The same personage has the name of Gwarthmor, ruler of the Sea, Menwyd the blessed, and the Dragon ruler of the World. He was the constructor of Kyd, the Ark, which passed the grievous Waters, stored with corn, and was borne aloft by Serpents.

The Circular Temple is consecrated to the Diluvian God, and his vessel ; and the season of their festive dance, is proclaimed by the Cuckoo. [The Legend of the Whorling sound of the Willamette Meteorite sailing over The Ring of Brodgar in Scotland ?]

The priest who gives the mead, beer, feast, and introduces the votaries into the temple, making proclamation in the name of the sacred edifice, and of the God himself – "I am the cell – I am the opening chasm – I am "the Bull,

114

Becr-Lled." This title has no meaning in the British language. It seems to consist of two Hebrew terms, implying the Bull of Flame. And the idea, presented by such a derivation, perfectly harmonizes with the general tenor of British Mythology. For, as those Oxen, which were merely the attendants and ministers of Hu, roared in Thunder, and Blazed in Lightning, we must suppose that the Supreme Bull himself, had an Essence Still Brighter. Hu was therefore worshipped in the form of a Bull. But this Bull, upon a great occasion, had submitted to the sacred yoke, and dragged to chain of affliction.

They knew not on what day the Stroke would be given, nor what hour of the splendid day Cwy (the Agitated person) would be born, or who prevented his going into the dales of Devwy (the possession of the Waters). They know not the Brindled Ox with the thick head-band, having Seven score [140] knobs in his collar. It was Maelgwn whom I saw, with piercing weapons : before the master of the fair Ox-Herd (Ter Y Volu), his household will not be silent. Before the two personages, the land in the Celestial Circle – before the passing form and the fixed form, over the pale white boundary. The Grey Stones they actually remove. Soon is Elgan (the Supremely Fair) and his retine discovered – for his slaughter, alas, how Great the Vengeance that ensued !

Rapidly moving, in the course of the Sky, in circles, in uneven numbers, Druids and Bards unite, in celebrating the leader.

Ner (the God of the Ocean) produced, out of the number of Vipers, one Huge Viper, with excess of windings.

May the Heavenly God protect us from a general Over-Flowing ! The first Surging Billow has Rolled Beyond the Sea Beach. A greater Tree than he, Taronwy, there has not been, to afford us a sanctuary, round the proud Celestial Circle.

Caer Ri-Gor, the gloomy enclosure – the Ark, which was closed up, so as to exclude the Light. [Atmospheric Loading Closing the World Off.]

It is perhaps worthy of remark that, as the Druid Priests of the "Gliding Hu" were called Adders or Serpents, so too the Priestess of Delphi were called the Pythia from her deity Python. [The Banishment of Snakes by Saint Patrick.]

115

New Light from the Great Pyramid, by Albert Ross, 1893

No cause acting slowly can produce sudden results.

No matter how numerous or complicated the wards of a lock may be, if but the right key is applied. The Great Pyramid proves to be the long-sought key to the Mysteries at once of Mythology and of the Great World Religions. To see it demonstrated that the Cosmic Terrors Interwoven with the very wrap and woof of All Sacred Literature, Christian and Pagan, refer to the Wrecking of the Continent of America when the Globe became involved in the consequences of the Disorder of the Skies and Buried its Civilization beneath the so-called drift deposits of the alleged glacial period.

A Pyramid is an alter signifying Death by Fire. Why was it built in a Triangular form, of cubical blocks? Because the Triangular form signified Fire, and the Cubical form the Earth visited by Fire. The Pyramid, therefore, bear witness to the "Fall of Lucifer." [Circle is the Sun.]

The Egyptian Pyramids excite in us the feeling of the sublime because, not only on account of their spatial vastness, but also of their great age, we feel ourselves dwarfed to insignificance in their presence, and revel in the pleasure of contemplating them as a Man before something Written in an Old Cipher of His Own, the Key to which He has Forgotten.

The Syrians called the Zodiac the Path of Straw ; the Chinese called it the Yellow Pathway. [Back when the Zodiacal Light was Prominent.]

"The Circle of the Heavens He walketh habitually." Job XXII. 14.

"In the house of my father are many mansions." John XIV. 2.

The Navajo Legend says the work of placing the Stars was done before the War in Heaven "scattered the pile of Stars over all the floor of Heaven just as they lie."

Alcyone is in Hebrew, the centre, foundation, base ; Arabic, Wasat, the centre ; Latin, Vergilioe, the centre, turned upon, rolled around ; the Hebrew name for the entire Pleiades group being Chima, the cumulus, in the sense of rolled around. [Chimera ?]

The gates of Eden were forever closed against Man, and the Tree of Life guarded by a Cherub (Kireb = Ox = Taurus) with a Flaming Sword. Orion was associated from earliest times with great Tempests and was Terrible to mariners. He was also Skilled in Working Iron. "Thou shalt Dash the nations to Pieces with a Rod of (meteoric) Iron." Greek : Sideros = Iron. English : Sidereal = affecting Unfavorably by the Influence of the Stars, Baleful ; "Sidereal Blasts" (Milton) : Siderated = Blasted by Stars, Planet-Struck : Siderite = Magnetic Iron or lodestone : Sidereal = relating to the Stars.

The month of the Gemini was called by the Chaldeans, Sivan, or the month of bricklaying, which circumstance, in connection with the wide-spread custom of laying the foundations of cities in human blood, speaks eloquently and tragically of the period of Rebuilding among the Survivors of some Appalling Destruction. When, further, we find Sivan present among the Hindus as Siva, the Destroyer, corresponding to our Satan, we are impelled to exclaim with William Hazlitt, "Words are the Only Things that Last Forever !"

The eternal ethical Truths deduced by the grandest minds, from the Astronomical Events connected with the history of the Planetary Fratricide were communicated to the common people in the nave of the church in Allegories. Thus the initiates sought to bring within the reach of the humblest minds, the fruits of the most difficult sciences and the most ancient learning. The Secret (i.e., "Sacred") Religion arose from the natural insuperable difficulty of communicating the Great Truths of Astronomy to the Ignorant, and of Preserving Records of the Great Phenomena of Nature. Without Universal relations no ethic, but only

117

expediency, is possible. All the Mystery and Allegory grew upon the necessity of using symbols and characters by which the Skilled might Communicate with Each Other, but which the Ignorant ran away with. And as they were Infinitely in the Majority, the Learned found their symbols taken out of their own hands, and they were Not Allowed to Rectify the Errors of General Ignorance, Nor to Explain their own Meaning.

Our Sun is known to be moving through space from the direction of Argo towards Hercules (as if on a Ferris Wheel Gondola of an arm of the Milky Way). Sidereal religion prevailed in Mesopotamia before the invention of writing, since the earliest symbol of a Deity known to us is a Star. Thus the deity Sibut, probably connected with the Pleiades, is determined by a Star with the Number 7 by its side. . . . . . . Thus in the Old Testament Abram lifted his hand, and did 'Seven' (swear) by Eljun (El-On, El-Star) [God Star], God the highest. Osiris means Elevated One or The Highest, like Zeus of Homer, Hyperion of Hesiodus, and he was originally God in the Pleiades. All the names of divinities can be connected, like Sibut, Seboot, with the Pleiades, so that the 'Sevenning' of Abraham may be referred to the God dwelling in this Constellation of Seven Stars. The Hebrew word for Pleiades, Kihmah, means the Associates. [Host, Watchers, Brood, ect.]

Bel's Flaming Sword of the Cherub, Kireb or Bull, according to the language of the Cuneiform Inscriptions, originally referred to the Pleiades in Taurus, whence Fire was supposed first to have Descended Upon Earth. According to Phoenician Tradition the Seven sons of Zeus-Chronos and of Rhea were connected with the Pleiades, the Constellation inhabited, according to old Babylonian and Hebrew Tradition, by the God Sibut-Sebaot. Pherecydes says Zeus-Chronos, the Creator of Fire, was Throned in the Pleiades where Fire Originated. Matarisvan, the messenger of Indras, was sent from the Matarii or Pleiades to the Earth, and Agni, whose secret name was Matarisvan, brought the Fire to Earth. The Pleid Alcyone and her husband perished by Water (Deluge), they were turned into halcyons (Kingfisher).

Pythagoras may be assumed to have known the reason why the Sun took the place of the Fire as symbol of divinity, and could assign to the Sun the central position in the Universe without giving up the Oriental Connection of Fire with the Pleiades, as the Throne of the God by whom the Fire had been Sent. From this would arise the conception of the Pleiades group as center of the Universe. [Sagittarius is and Opposite, must be Figuratively.] In the most ancient parts of the Zend-Avesta, the one God Ormuzd, is designated as the first of Seven angles or Watchers in conjunction with whom he created the World by his word. In Genesis Jehovah says, 'Let us create Man in our image.' Later passages attribute the honor of the first Seven angles to a vicar of God, a mediator, Sraosha. This Messiah of the Iranians was originally connected with Fire and with the Pleiades. A mediatorial position similar to that assigned to Seroah or Sraosha was held by Mithras, who was first connected with Fire and then with the Sun. Like Ormuzd, Mithras is represented riding on the Bull, and Jehovah is described as riding on the Cherub, [Kireb or Bull]. This Bull is the Constellation Taurus with the Pleiades Birds on its Back. [Dove]

In the Book of Enoch, Messiah is described as Coming Down in the Form of a White Bull with Large Horns. Thus also in Enoch LXXXIX. The first Adam is described as a White Cow sprung from the Earth. With the Seven Stars of the Pleiades in the Constellation of the Bull are Connected the Seven Amshaspands and Seven Buddhas. The Seven lamps of Moses' candlesticks, like the Seven elevations of the tower of Bable, and the Seven steps or altars of the Great Pyramid, referred to the Seven Stars, later planets of the solar system.

The divine enlightenment coming from above, and of which Men are allowed to partake, has for its source the Seven eyes of the Lord of Sabaoth, which run to and fro through the Whole Earth. Zech 4:10 Upon one Stone shall be Seven eyes : behold, I will engrave the graving thereof, saith the Lord of Hosts, and I will remove the iniquity of that land in one day. Zech 3 : 9. The child sneezed Seven times, and the child opened his eyes. [Haliburton global sneeze blessing.] And I beheld, and, lo, in the midst of the throne and of the four beasts [Ages], and in the midst of the elders, stood a Lamb as it had been slain, having Seven horns and Seven eyes, which are the Seven Spirits of God sent forth into all the Earth. Rev. 5 : 6.

A scriptural reference to the Pleiades as the source of Fire is found in Isaiah LIX., 5 ; "Eggs of a Cockatrice have they hatched. Who so is eating their eggs doth die." The Hebrew word translated Cockatrice (Tsiphoni) is from the same root as the Egyptian Typhon, or the Destructive Element in Nature

119

(modern Typhoon) represented as a Monstrous Fiery Serpent which Fell like Lightning from the Skies. The Cockatrice was a fabulous Serpent said to have been produced by a Cock's egg (Hen and Chickens, the Egyptian symbol for the Pleiades, whence Fire first Fell to the Earth), which had been brooded by a Serpent. Its breath (the Noisome Pestilence) and even its look (the Gorgon's head) were Fatal.

The Commemoration of the Dead was Connected among the Egyptians with a Deluge, which was typified by the priest placing the image of Osiris in a sacred Coffer or Ark, and launching it out into the Sea, where it was borne out of site. This Celebration took place on the 17th day of Athyr, the date on which the Mosaic account of the Deluge of Noah states it to have commenced, in the second month (of the Jewish year, which corresponds to November) and on the 17th day of the month. Here is No Chance of Coincidence. Both the Egyptian and the Mosaic date was fixed by the Pleiades.

This explains the rites of the Druids. The 1st of November was with the Druids a Night full of Mystery, in which they Celebrated the Reconstruction of the World. A Terrible rite was connected with this ; the Druidess nuns were obliged to pull down and rebuild each year at this time the roof of their temple as a symbol of the Destruction and Renovation of the World. If one of them in bringing the materials for the new roof let fall her sacred burden she was lost. Her companions seized with a fanatic transport, rushed upon her, and tore her to pieces. On the same night the Druids Extinguished the Sacred Fire which was kept continually burning in the sacred precincts, and at that signal all the Fires in the island were one by one put out, and Primitive Darkness reigned throughout the land. [simulating the Gloom...]

In our calendar November 1st is still marked All Saints' Day, and in the pre-Reformation calendars the last day of October was marked All Hallow Eve, and the 2nd of November All Souls', clearly marking a Three-Days' Festival of the Dead, commencing in the evening and regulated by the Pleiades. Hence also the Hallowe'en torches of the Irish, the Bonfires of the Scotch, the coel-coeth Fires of the Welsh, and the tindle Fire of Cornwall, all lighted in Hallowe'en. To this day, in France, the people repair to the cemeteries and lunch at the graves of their ancestors.

The Great Festival of the Mexican Cycle was held in November at the time of the Midnight Culmination of the Pleiades. It began at Sunset, and at Midnight, as the Constellation approached the Zenith, a human victim was offered up to Avert the Calamity impending over the human race. They had a Tradition that the World had been Destroyed at the time. They had a superstition that the World was in Danger of Destruction at the End of the 'Age' or cycle of fifty-two years ; and all the people prepared themselves for that Dreadful and Ultimate Calamity. They took leave of the Light with tears, and expected Death without any previous sickness. They Broke their Household Vessels as unnecessary lumber [New and Old World Legends mention the Earth being shattered like pottery.], Extinguished their Fires, and walked about like disturbed people, without daring to take any rest, till they knew whether they were to be forever consigned to the regions of Darkness. On the Dawning of day they began to recover their spirits, with their eyes fixed toward the East ; and at the first appearance of the Sun, they saluted him with all their musical instruments, and congratulated each other upon their security for the duration of another age. They immediately crowded to their temples to render thanks to their Gods, and to receive from the priests New Fire, which had been preserved for them throughout the night [The Image Pg. 167 shows they hand made the New Fire.]. Next they made new provision for their necessary subsistence, and this day was spent in public rejoicings ; the diversions being dedicated to the renewal of time, much after the manner of the secular games among the Romans.

We are told by Hyginus, a contemporary of Ovid, that on the Fall of Troy (which happens, according to Virgil, at every renovation of the Earth and

Skies) "Electra, one of the Pleiades, quitted the company of her six sisters, and passed along the Heavens toward the Arctic Pole, where she remained visible in tears and with Disheveled Hair, to which the name Comet is applied." Chambers thinks this means that "a Comet" proceeded from Taurus towards the North Pole. [The Great Lakes]

Hebrew Traditions state that in the Great Catastrophe the Fires of Justice (Lucifer, Levi-a-than, the Old Serpent) were assuaged by the Waters of Mercy (Deluge, glacial epoch which was produced by an extraordinary and "unaccountable influx of heat" !). The Sabians, whose name, though seemingly derived from Hebrew Saba (the Host of Heaven), the Sabians themselves derive from Sabi, the son of Seth, the reputed author of Astronomy, we read that they sacrifice at the Pyramids a black Calf (Taurus) and a Cock (Pleiades-poultry). The Hindu Tarika is a Demon Destroyed by Kartiykeya, called the Pleiades, also the general of the Celestial Armies, who is depicted as mounted upon a Peacock instead of upon the Pleiades Hen and Chickens of the Egyptian Planisphere.

A custom, still extant in the sacred dances of the American Pueblo Indians, of including in the carefully rehearsed dance around the sacred Fires (representing the circling course of the planets around the central Sun) the Lawless Pranks of a Clown, who runs amuck amongst the dancers, as if seeking to involve everything in Satanic Confusion. [Like Loke in Norse Myth] [The Comet Running Chaotically Through the Inner Solar System.]

Arabian Astronomers say that when the Sun reappeared after the Great Catastrophe it was by the Star Denebola in the tale of the Zodiacal Lion. This Astronomical fact is commemorated in an ancient standard of British India. [Cat – Astro – Phe]

Leo represents the Nemean Lion, which Leaped Down from the Skies, and was slain by Hercules. Leo is an emblem of Violence and Fury in the Hieroglyphical writings. He is represented by the Hindus as rending a Stone Asunder, as Samson (Samson = the Sun in Leo) Pulling Down the Temple of Baal. [The previously blinded Sun and his hair grown back.]

The stately palaces, august temples, and stupendous edifices of Maha Balipore in India are universally believed by every Hinhu, whether learned or unlearned, to have been Destroyed by a General Deluge, brought upon the Earth by the immediate mandate of the supreme God.

122

Virgo ruled during the Golden Age, when the Earth brought forth fruits in abundance without the labor of Man. The Constellation of Virgo, bearing the sheaf, whence her Zodiacal Mansion was called the house of corn. [After the climate change, Man had to learn agriculture to survive.]

The Constellation Leo and Virgo explains the meaning of The Sphinx, uniting the head of Virgo and the body of the Lion, the offspring of Chimera, a Monster of Fire and Water, and thus affords a clue to that Disaster after which the Sun of Righteousness arose with healing in his wings (as we see in Egyptian emblems), close by the Star Denebola at the overlapping of Virgo. [The Sphinx is the Virgin and Lion Composite Commemorating the Resurrection of the Sun after the Catastrophe.]

According to Plato, the priests of Sais told Solon, the Greek Lawgiver, when he visited Egypt, 600 BC, that the story of Phaeton was "a Myth which really signified a Declination of the Bodies moving around the Earth and in the Heavens, and a Great Conflagration of things upon the Earth."

The prayer of the Aztec priests to the supreme invisible God Tezcatlipoca : "Thine Anger has Descended upon us as Stones, Spears, and Arrows upon the wretches that inhabit the Earth. O valiant and all-powerful Lord, the common people are almost made an End of and Destroyed. And what is most pitiful of all, the little children, that are innocent and understand nothing, only to play with pebbles and to heap up little mounds of Earth, they too die, broken and dashed to pieces, - a thing very pitiful and grievous to be seen, for there remain of them not even those in cradles, nor those that could not walk or speak. Is there to be no mercy nor pity for us until the Arrows of thy Fury are spent to our utter Perdition and Destruction ? Shall the Sun nevermore Shine upon us ? Must we remain in perpetual Darkness ? We are all as Drunken and Without Understanding. Already the little children Perish of Hunger, for there is none to give them food nor drink nor consolation nor caress ; none to give the breast to them that suck, for their fathers and mothers have Died and left them orphans, suffering for the sins of their fathers."

The description of the next coming of the Son of Man in the clouds of Heaven : "As the Lightning comes out of the East, and shines to the West, so shall be also the presence of the Son of Man. Wherever may be the carcass, there will the eagles be gathered. And speedily after the affliction of those days, the Sun shall be Darkened, and the Moon shall not give her Light, and the Stars shall Fall from Heaven, and the powers of the Heavens shall be Shaken. And there will be signs in the Sun and Moon and Stars ; and on the Earth anguish of nations in perplexity of a Roaring and Tossing of the Sea. Men fainting from fear and expectation of the things coming on their habitations ; for the Powers of the Heavens will be Shaken. And the sign of the Son of Man shall then appear in the Heavens ; and then All the tribes of the Earth shall Lament, and they shall see the Son of Man coming upon the clouds of Heaven with Great Majesty and Power. And he will send his angels with a Great Sound of a Trumpet, and they shall gather his chosen ones from the four winds and from one extremity of the Heavens to the other. And he will place the sheep [Aries] at his right hand, but the goats [Capricornus] at his left. Then he will also say to those at his left hand, 'Depart from me ye cursed into aionian Fire.'" [Where the Taurid Stream Vanishes into Capricorn.]

"Therefore hath the Anger of Jehovah Burned among his people, and he stretched out his Hand against it, and Smiteth it, and the Mountains Tremble, and their carcass is as filth in the midst of the out places. With all his Anger did not turn back, and still his Hand is Stretched Out ! And he lifted up an ensign to nations afar off, and Hissed [Ophidian] to it from the Ends of the Earth, an Lo ! Swift with Haste It Cometh, there is none weary or stumbling in it, it doth not slumber nor sleep, whose Arrows are Sharp and all its Bows Bent. Hoofs of its Horses as Flint have been reckoned, and its wheels as a Hurricane." Isaiah 5 : 25-28

"And it Howleth against it in that day as the Howling of a Sea, and it hath looked attentively to the land, and Lo ! Darkness – Distress, and Light hath been Darkened by its abundance. Howl ye, for near is the day of Jehovah, as Destruction from the Mighty it Cometh. Therefore all hands do fail, and every heart of Man doth fail, and every heart of Han doth melt, a friend at his friend they marvel, their faces – the appearance of Flame ! Lo ! the day

124

of Jehovah doth come, Fierce, with Wrath and Heat of Anger, to make the land become a Desolation, yea, its sinning ones he Destroyeth from it. For the Stars of the Heavens and their Constellations cause not their Light to Shine, Darkened hath been the Sun in its going out, and the Moon causeth Not its Light to come forth. And I have appointed on the World Evil, and have Caused to Cease the Excellency of the World and the Excellency of the Terrible I make low. Everyone who is found is Thrust Through, and their sucklings are Dashed to Pieces before their eyes. How hast thou Fallen from the Heavens, Lucifer, son of the Dawn ! Thou hast been cut Down to Earth, O weakener of nations ! Lo, Jehovah is Emptying the Land and is Making it Waste, and hath overturned it on its face, and hath scattered its inhabitants. Mourned, faded, hath the World ; languished, faded, hath the World. Fear and a snare and a trap are on ye, O inhabitants of the land ! And it hath come to pass he who is fleeing from the Noise of the fear doth fall into the snare ; and he who is coming up from the midst of the snare is captured by the trap. For windows on high have been opened, and Shaken are the Foundations of the land. Utterly Broken Down hath been the land, utterly Broken hath been the land, utterly moved hath been the land. Stagger Greatly doth the land as a drunkard. An Overflowing Scourge, when It Passeth Over, ye have been to it for a treading place. From the fullness of Its Passing Over It taketh you, by day and by night, and It hath been only a Trembling to consider the Report, and It hath been at an instant suddenly, by Jehovah of Hosts thou art inspected, with Thunder and with an Earthquake, and Great Noise, Hurricane, and Whirlwind, and Flame of Devouring Fire. And as a dream, a vision of the night, hath been the multitude of all the nations who are warring against Ariel."   Isaiah 13

The power of the prophetic language is Not the product of Art but of Appalling Experience Instead. [Also, seems to be only a Single Causation.] Mankind has Regained the Key to the Scientific Basis of all the Mythologies of the past and of all true religion in the present.

With these preliminary considerations it becomes possible to extract from the incantations of the venerable Babylonian Tablets details of human suffering at the time of the Great Catastrophe even more vivid than those already cited from Isaiah.   [Below, from Cuneiform Texts]

"The Wicked God, the Wicked Demon, the Demon of the Desert, the Demon of the Mountain, the Demon of the Sea, the Noxious Cherub [Kireb, Taurus], the enormous Uruku the Bad Wind itself, the Wicked Demon which seizes the body, which disturbs the body. Cruel Agony

125

which never ceases, nightmare, unremitting fever, unremitting Plague, food which reduces the body of Man to a skeleton' food which eaten is returned again, liquids which make the drinker swell, fatal poison the Pestilential wind which comes from the desert and returns not. The frost which makes the Earth to shiver, the excess of heat which makes the skin to crack, evil destiny which unexpectedly cuts off a Man's career, parching thirst which aids the Spirit of the Plague. He who being hungry in a pit beseeching is therefore reduced to eat dust. The day of mourning, the wind which brings misfortune, the day of misfortune, the fatal wind which makes itself felt, the day of misfortune, the fatal wind precedes It, the messengers of loss, the ravagers of Earth, the Lightning which ravages the country, the Seven Gods of the Vast Heavens, the Seven Gods of the great Earth, the Seven Gods of the igneous spheres, the Seven Gods, these are the Seven Gods, the Seven Gods malevolent Gods, the Seven malevolent phantoms, the Seven malevolent Phantoms of the Flames, in the Heavens Seven, on the Earth Seven, Spirit of the Heavens, conjure ! Spirit of the Earth, conjure ! Devastator of Heaven and Earth, Devastator of Earth, the genius who Devastates countries, the genus who Devastates the countries and whose power is very great, whose power is very great, whose Trampling is Formidable, Telal, the Bull which Pierces, the very strong Bull, the Bull which passes through the dwellings, the indomitable Telal, there are Seven of them. They obey no commands, they Devastate the country. They know no order, they Watch Men, they devour flesh ; they make blood flow ; they drink blood. On high they bring trouble, and below they bring confusion. Falling in rain from the sky, issuing from Earth, they penetrate the strong timbers, the thick timbers ; they pass from house to house. [Meteoric showers that is why they built huge Stone Dolmens / Temples !] Doors do not stop them, bolts do not stop them, they glide in at the doors like Serpents, they enter by the windows like the wind. They hinder the wife from conceiving by her husband ; they take the child from the knees of the Man ; they make the free Woman leave the house where she has borne a child, they, they are the voices which cry and which pursue Mankind, they assail country after country, they take away the slave from his place. They make free Woman to leave her house and her child. They make the son quit his father's house. They make the Dove from his Dove-Cote to fly away ; the force the Bird to lift himself up on his wings ; they make the Swallow fly from his nest into space ; they cause the Ox to run away ; and the Lamb to escape. The wicked Demons, who lay snares. From the four cardinal points the impetuosity of their Invasion Burns like Fire. They violently attack the dwellings of Man, they wither everything in the town or in the country. They oppress the freeman and the slave, they Pour Down like a

126

Violet Tempest in Heaven and Earth. They shall precipitate this Man into the Water ; they shall Bury him in the ground ; they shall cause him to be overwhelmed with Stones ; they shall Burn him with Fire ; they shall drive him into exile into places where he Cannot Live. May the great Gods cover him with Absolute Confusion, may they Root Up his Stability, may they Efface his Posterity. May the Sun, the Great Judge of Heaven and Earth, pronounce his Condemnation, and take him in his snares ! May Gula, the great lady. The spouse of the Winter Sun, pour inside him a deadly Poison ; may she cause his blood and sweat to flow like water ! Mat Bin, the captain of Heaven and Earth, the son of Anu, the hero, Inundate his fields ! May Serakh Destroy the first of his harvest...may he Enervate his animals ! May Nebo, the supreme intelligence, overwhelm him with Affliction and Terror, and lastly, may he hurry him into Incurable Despair ! I will cause the Earth to Fall into the Water, putting the South in place of the North.

Hurukan in the Popul Vuh of the ancient American Quiches : "Then the Waters were agitated by the will of Hurakan (Heart of Heaven) and a Great Inundation came upon the heads of these creatures ... they were Engulfed, and a Resinous Thickness Descended from Heaven ... the face of the Earth was obscured, and a heavy Darkening rain commenced, rain by day and rain by night ... There was heard a Great Noise Above their heads, as if produced by Fire. Then were Men seen running, pushing each other, Filled with Despair ; they wished to climb upon their houses, and the houses, tumbling down, fell to the ground. They wished to climb upon the trees, and the trees Shook them off ; they wished to enter the Caves and the Caves Closed themselves before them ...Water and Fire contributed to the Universal Ruin." [Doesn't sound like a Lightning Storm or Volcano.]

The Pima Indians say that the son of the Creator was called Szeuka. An Eagle prophesied the Deluge, but his warning was despised. "Then in the twinkling of an eye there came a Peal of Thunder, and an Awful Crash, and a Green Mound of Water Reared Itself Over the Plain. It seemed to stand upright for a second, then, cut Incessantly by the Lightning, goaded on like a Great Beast, it flung itself upon the prophet's hut. When the morning broke there was nothing to be seen alive but one Man – if indeed he were a Man : Szeuka, son of the creator. He killed the Eagle, restored its victims to life and repeopled the Earth with them."   (Atlantis-Donnelly)

Job's description of the Leviathan, with his Teeth and Jaws of Fire. "But wilt thou catch the Serpent with a hook, and put a halter about his nose ? Or wilt thou fasten a ring in his nostril, and bore his lip with a

127

clasp ? Will he address thee with a petition softly, with the voice of a suppliant ? And will he make a covenant with thee ? And wilt thou take him for a perpetual servant ? And wilt thou play with him as a bird, or bind him as a sparrow for a child ? And do the nations feed upon him, and the nations of the Phoenicians share him ? And all the ships come together would not be able to bear the mere skin of his Tail. Neither shall they carry his head in fishing vessels. But thou shalt lay thy hand upon him once, remembering the War that is Waged by his Mouth ; and let it not be done any more. Hast thou not seen him, and hast thou not wondered at the things said of him ? Dost Thou Not Fear because Preparation has been Made by Me ? For who is there that resists Me ? Or who will resist Me, and abide, since the Whole World under Heaven is Mine ?

"I will not be silent because of him, though because of his power one shall pity his antagonist. Who will open the face of his garment, and who can enter within the fold of his breastplate ? Who will open the doors of his face ? Terror is round about his Teeth. His inwards are as brazen plates, and the texture of his skin as a smyrite Stone. One part cleaves fast to another, and the air cannot come between them. They will remain united each to the other ; they are closely joined and cannot be separated. At his Sneezing a Light Shines, and his Eyes are as the appearance of the morning Star. Out of his mouth proceed as it were burning lamps, and as it were hearths of Fire are cast abroad. Out of his nostrils proceeds Smoke of the furnace burning with Fire of coal. His breath is as live coals, and a Flame goes out of his mouth. And power is lodged in his neck, before him Destruction runs. The flesh also of his body is joined together ; if one pours violence upon him, he shall not be moved. His heart is firm as a Stone. And it stands like an unyielding Anvil. And when he turns, he is a terror to the four-footed wild beasts which leap upon the Earth. If spears should come against him, Men will effect nothing, either with spears or the breast-plate. For he considers Iron as chaff, and brass as rotten wood. The bow of brass shall not wound him, he deems a slinger as grass. Mauls are counted as stubble ; and he laughs to scorn the waving of the firebrand. His lair is formed of sharp points : and all the Gold of the Sea under him is as an immense quantity of clay. He makes the deep boil like a brazen Caldron ; and he regards the Sea as a pot of ointment, and the lowest part of the deep as a captive ; he reckons the Deep as his range. There is Nothing Upon the Earth like him, formed to be sported with by My Angels. He beholds every high thing ; and he is King of All that are in the Waters."

(Job XL 20, XLI Septuagint Version)

Near the Pipe Stone Quarry, Minn., on a high mound, is the Thunder's Nest (nid-du- Tonnere), where a very Small Bird sits upon her Eggs during fair weather, and the Skies are Rent with Bolts of Thunder at the approach of a Storm, which is occasioned by the hatching of her Brood. (Pleiades' Hen.) This Bird is eternal, and incapable of reproducing her own species : she has often been seen by the medicine-men, and is about as large as the end of the little finger. Her mate is a Serpent, whose Fiery Tongue Destroys the young ones as soon as they are hatched, and the Fiery Noise Darts through the Skies.

The quartz-rock at the Pipestone Quarry is of close grain and exceedingly hard, eliciting the most brilliant sparks from steel ; and in most places, where exposed to the Sun and the air, has a high polish on its surface, entirely beyond any results which could have been produced by Diluvial action, being perfectly glazed as if by Ignition. (Ignatius Donnelly 1880's)

Ormuzd, the God of Light and the Good Principle, informed Zoroaster that he had once given to Man a place of delight and abundance, called Eiren, Which at the beginning was more beautiful than all the World which his power had called into existence. Nothing could equal the beauty of this delightful place which Ormuzd Created, but afterwards the Serpent introduced Winter, which congealed the Water, the Earth, and the Trees. No mention is made in Genesis of the Serpent having introduced winter, but it is said that after The Fall, Jehovah God made to the Man and to his wife coats of skin to clothe them, hence it is evident that Winter was upon them. The connection of the Fall of Lucifer with the change of seasons from summer to winter, both annually and in the Great Year of the Earth.

"And the word of the Lord came unto me the second time, saying, What seest thou ? And I said, A Seething Pot do I see ; and the front thereof is turned from the North. And the Lord said unto me, Out of the North shall evil break forth over All the inhabitants of the land.

At that time shall be announced to this people and to Jerusalem, a Dry Wind from the Mountain-peaks in the wilderness, coming on the road to the daughter of my people ; not to winnow, nor to cleanse the corn ; A Strong Wind from these places shall come unto Me : now also will Myself pronounce judgment against them. Behold, like clouds shall he come up, and like a Whirlwind shall be his Chariots ; Swifter than Eagles are his Horses. Woe unto us ! for we are Wasted.

129

For a voice declareth from Dan, and publisheth unhappiness from the Mountain of Ephraim.

I am Shaken at the very chambers of my heart ; I cannot remain silent ; because at the Sound of the Cornet, hast thou heard, O my soul, the Alarm of War. Ruin upon Ruin is called out ; for the Whole Land is Wasted ; suddenly are my tents Wasted ; and in a moment my curtains. How long shall I see the standard, hear the Sound of the Cornet ? I look at the Earth, and, lo, it is without form and void ; and toward the Heavens, and their Light is gone. I look at the Mountains, and, lo they tremble, and all the hills are moved. I look, and, lo, there is no Man, and all the Birds of the Heavens are fled. I look, and, lo, the fruitful country is a Wilderness, and all its cities are Laid Waste at the Presence of the Lord, because of the Fierceness of his Anger.

And thou, O waste one, what wilt thou do ? Though thou clothe thyself with scarlet, though thou adorn thyself with Gold, in vain shalt thou make thyself beautiful." (Jeremiah I., IV)

In the mysteries of Egypt, while Light ruled, the pure soul was in no danger, but when the Darkness came ("In one dreadful night," says Solon to Plato), when the eternal Waters which Flow along the Vaulted Heavens Fall in gigantic cascades adown the West, the soul followed the Sun and the other luminaries into Darkness. At intervals Gigantic Serpents barred the way, which led through regions full of Flame and Fire, peopled by hideous Monsters whose office was to torture the damned. Here the sound was as an Immense Humming of Wasps [Scorpion Men] ; yonder it was as the Howling of the Beasts for their mates ; elsewhere it was as the Rolling of the Thunder.

On the so-called "battle-field of ages" in Peru, where thousands of skeletons were found, it was remarked with astonishment that every skull had been wounded by a flint driven down through it from the top. Elsewhere we are told that a Peruvian king was reviewing his troops, when suddenly a Star Increased Prodigiously in size and Fell to Earth before the very eyes of his whole army.

Much of the scoffing and hopeless skepticism of the day the responsibility rests with the unreasoning defense of faulty and inadequate views of religion and scripture by individuals and churches, which show forth a zeal for truth but without knowledge.

130

"The book of concealed mystery of the Qabbalah is the book of equilibrium of balance. Equilibrium is the harmony which results from the analogy of contraries, it is the dead centre where, the opposing forces being equal in strength, rest succeeds motion. It is the living synthesis of counterbalancing power. The book teaches that the creator, the one and only substance, exists in the ten numerical emanations (the ancient ten Zodiacal Signs). Of these the first is Kether, or the Crown, otherwise known as the ancient of days, the Great Father of All. The second emanation is Chokmah, or Wisdom. The third is Binah, the Understanding, the All-Mother, otherwise called the Great Sea (or the Ring of Waters above the Firmament). The offspring of Wisdom and Understanding is the fourth emanation, Gedulah, Greatness or Magnificence, Scintilling Flames (the Meteoric Ring beyond the Over Sea). Behind the shoulders of the Bride (Binah, the Great Sea or aqueous ring) the Serpent (or Meteoric Ring) rears his head. The Serpent is centripetal force, ever seeking to penetrate into Paradise ; but his Head is Broken by the Waters of the Over Sea (Binah). The Serpent is the executor of judgment. The Water symbolizeth that measure of mercy by which judgments and punishments are mitigated. The Serpent holdeth his Tail in his Mouth that he may form a Circle [Circuit around the Sun]. If a defect occurreth in only one numeration of the system through the fault of the inferiors, he is immediately manifest, and commenceth his accusations before the throne of glory. There is in the Destroyer no hastening to the outer, because he is centripetal and not centrifugal. But his Head is Broken by the Waters of the Great Sea (Wisdom, the fountain of mercy and loving kindness)." - (Compare Maters : "Qabbalah Unveiled.")

"Blow ye the Cornet in Zion, and Sound an Alarm on my holy Mount ; let all the inhabitants of the land Tremble ; for the day of the Lord Cometh, for it is nigh. It is a day of Darkness and of Gloom, a day of clouds and of Tempestuous Obscurity, like the morning Dawn spread out upon the Mountains : a people numerous and strong, the like of which hath never been and after it there will be none any more, even to the years of all coming generations. Before it Devoureth a Fire ; and behind it Singeth a Flame : like the garden of Eden was the land before it, and after is a Desolate Wilderness."

In establishing the identity of Bacchus and Osiris certain facts, of great interest to every intelligent and educated Christian are brought out, namely, Bacchus was overtaken by Fire Falling from Heaven, and the Lord Jesus Christ saw Satan Falling like Lightning from the Heavens.

131

The Hindu Avatars or Saving Incarnations of the deity, always accompany Gigantic Catastrophes, such as will attend the coming of the Lord at the last day.

True religion, in which the Cosmical is forever the symbol of the ethical, preserve through times of ignorance the priceless clews to a recovery of the knowledge of our remote ancestors, their experiences, and their lofty representative genius ! The fall of Water from the Skies was commemorated in trials by Water and in baptism ; the Fall of Stones from the Skies suggested the custom of Stoning blasphemers ; the Fall of Fire gave rise, not only to trials by Fire, and burning on altars and at the stake, but also to Fireworks, which are always used in religious ceremonies in China, the land where they were invented. Chinese boys and girls are not allowed to touch fire-crackers, these implements of religious warfare being used only to drive out devils. Similarly, children are not allowed to fly kites, nor do their fathers fly them save on the ninth day of the ninth month, when Dragons, Fishes, and Animals, as Astronomical Emblems, are sent up into the air, together with sacred texts. These practices, particularly that of sending up texts, seems naïve to the point of absurdity, if regarded to Convey Information to Omniscient Deity ; but as means of impressing ideas upon the minds of the people, they are not only legitimate, but also ingenious and effective.

In Greek Theion (Sulphur, Brimstone) is derived from Theios (Divine). The ancients called Brimstone eminently the Divine thing, because, among other things, God made it an instrument of his Vengeance on the Heathen and other Delinquents, condemning their land to Brimstone and Fire Forever. The English Brimstone means Burning Stone. Hence the use of Sulphur and Brimstone by the idolators of various nations in their purifications (Pure = Fiery).

Religion has long been Mistrusted by Men of Science, as the Daughter of Astrology ; and the planetary candelabra of Moses and of Revelation have frequently been adduced in proof of a presumedly Fatal Connection between religion and the absurdities of popular astrology. Indications are multiplying, in these later days, that the absurd elements of ancient astrology are merely corruptions of primitive Traditions which survived the general wreck in the Great Catastrophe. Upon the broken fragments of the former Wisdom, ethical and intellectual Man has had to subsist from that era to the present time, when at last modern science is Recovering a Knowledge of the Universe which enables us to infer something of the Nature of the

132

primeval Wisdom of which post-diluvian relics, outside of Holy Writ, are generally but the most grotesque caricatures. Soon religion may once more gain the courage to heed the command of Isaiah, to "look unto the rock whence it was hewn, and to the Hole of the Pit whence it was Dug up."

Prophecy is based upon the idea of the reign of law, and the consequent conviction that the thing which is, is the offspring of the thing that has been, and the parent of the thing which shall be. Prophecy assumes that what has been (Experience) is the Key to the right Understanding of the Present, and a barometer of the Future. In order for the Past to predict the Future, from the known to prognosticate the unknown, prophecy must be the issue of the union of Knowledge and Intuition. The method of prophecy is to realize the idea of the future by means of images Drawn from the Past as it is Known to All, or at least to the prophet himself. In other words, prophecy declares what shall be, what necessarily must be, in a World where law reigns, on the basis not of what might have occurred in the past, but of what Did Occur.

Let us imagine, if we can, the tiny human race, on this tiny planet in the Solar system, over taken by Instant Ruin form the Skies. Then let us read in Isaiah and in the minor prophets the graphic details of what we passed through ; and then let us try to rise to a faint conception of the grandeur of the intuitions and the indestructibility of the hope that could inspire us to say, "Though he slay me, yet will I trust him." [This is difficult to Understand, yet Existence is so Profound and Real that We must forgive It. Mirror]

"Near is the great day of Jehovah, bitterly shriek there doth a mighty one, a day of Wrath is the day, a day of Adversity and Distress, a day of Waste and Desolation, a day of Darkness and Gloominess, a day of Cloud and Thick Darkness, a day of Trumpets and Shouting. And in the Fire of his Jealousy [Of Whom? The Sun?] consumed is the Whole Land." – (Zephaniah I. 14-18.) "The Lord Jehovah with a Trumpet Bloweth, and he hath gone with Whirlwinds." – (Zechariah IX. 14.) "For ye came not near to the Mount touched and Scorched with Fire, and to Blackness and Darkness and Tempest and a Sound of a Trumpet... and (so terrible was the sight) Moses said, I am fearful exceedingly and tremble." – (Hebrews XII. 18-19, 21.) "The Lord himself, in a Shout, in the voice of a chief messenger, and in the Trump of God, shall Come Down from Heaven." – (1 Thessalonians IV. 16.) "I was in the spirit on the Lord's Day, and I heard behind me a Great Voice, as of a Trumpet, saying, I am Alpha and Omega, the First and the Last." – (Revelation I. 10, 11.)

133

"And Jesus having been born in Bethlehem of Judea... lo, MAJI from the East came to Jerusalem, saying : 'Where is he who was born king of the Jews ? For we saw his Star in the East, and we came to worship him". (Matt. II. 1,2.)

Ignorance is Bliss, tis Folly [Foolishness] to be Wise.

Astrology originated in the custom of methodically Watching the Heavens, and taking note of certain quarters for signs of either Present Safety or Impending Evil. The ancient bishop was an Astronomical Seer and dwelt in a See-House. The Pueblo Indians still keep Watchmen on the ramparts of their stone dwellings and safe retreats to tell them of the Night, what its Signs of Promise are ; and they rejoice at the reappearance, night after night, of Stars whose visibility indicates continued Freedom from Peril.

In the Book of Enoch, Chapters LXXXVII. and LXXXVIII., is a very clear Allegorical description of the Deluge ; and a Star is said to have Fallen from Heaven. The Allegory is carried on through several chapters till it comes to a being called a White Cow (Taurus), who is said to have brought forth a Black Wild Sow (Typhon) and a white sheep (Aries). With the production of the white sheep (the change point of the Vernal Equinox from Taurus to Aries, approx. 2123 BC) [One of the Ages most think of the Deluge] the Allegory of the Bull (Taurus) ends ; and although many other animals are named continually, the Beeve is never once named afterward till the conclusion, when the Bull is said to return (25,827 years, or a grand zodiacal year later), takes the lead. The distinction between the Beeve and the sheep is marked in a way that is most extraordinary, and the change from the Bull Taurus to the ram Aries is so clear that it cannot be mistaken.

The birth of the Black Wild Sow simultaneously with the white sheep (Aries) reminds us that Typhon, the Great Boar, was the emblem of the Terror-Striking, Paroxysmal Frenzy and Lunacy-producing power of Destruction and Disorder. Hence the beauty of the symbolism in Mathew VIII. 28-34 ; Mark V. 1-20 ; and Luke VIII. 26-39, where the demons are commanded to return to the Swine (the Boar Typhon) whence they originally issued. Thus, as the Great Fiery Dragon, or Leviathan, was once Cast Out of Heaven, and Fell into the Sea, causing it to Boil like a pot, so these demons-infested Swine are now cast into the Sea, whereupon the victims of nervous shock and mental disorder are seen sitting, clothed and of sound mind once more.

134

In the Veda we find the Maruts, literally the Smashers. The Vedic poet Sees them approach with Golden Helmets, with Spotted Skins on their shoulders, Brandishing Golden Spears, Whirling their Axes, Shooting Fiery Arrows, and Cracking their whips amid Thunder and Lightning.

"Son of Man, take up a lamentation upon the king of Tyrus, and say unto him, Thus saith the Lord God ; thou sealest up the sum, full of Wisdom, and perfect in Beauty. Thou hast been in Eden the garden of God ; every precious Stone was thy covering, the sardius, topaz, and the diamond, the beryl, the onyx, and the jasper, the sapphire, the emerald, and the carbuncle, and gold : the workmanship of thy tablets and thy pipes was prepared in thee in the day that thou wast created. Thou art the Anointed Cherub that Covereth ; and I have set thee so ; thou wast upon the Holy Mountain of God ; thou hast walked up and down in the midst of the Stones of Fire. Thou wast perfect in thy ways from the day that thou wast Created, till Iniquity was found in thee... I will cast thee as profane out of the Mountain of God : and I will destroy thee, O covering Cherub, from the Midst of the Stones of Fire." Ezekiel XXVIII. 12-19. [One and the Same.]

The Chaldean "Incantation of the Seven Maskim" [Cuneiform Text]

"Seven are they, they are Seven ; in the caverns of the Ocean they dwell, they are clothed in the Lightnings of Heaven, of their Growth the Deep Waters can tell. Seven are they, they are Seven. Broad is their way and their Course is Wide, when the seeds of Destruction they sow, o'er the top of the hills where they Stride to lay Waste the smooth highways below, Broad is their way and their Course is Wide. Fear is Not in them, Nor Awe, Supplication they heed not Nor Prayer ; for they know No Compassion nor law, and are Deaf to the Cries of Despair, - fear is not in them nor awe. Cured are they, they are cursed, they are foes to Wise Ea's great name ; by Whirlwind are all things dispersed on the paths of the Flash of their Flame, - cursed are they, they are cursed. Spirit of Heaven, oh, help ! Help, O Spirit of Earth ! They are Seven, thrice said, they are Seven. For the Men they are Bearers of Thrones, but for Men they are Breeders of Death, and the authors of Sorrows and Moans. They are Seven, thrice said, they are Seven. Spirit of Heaven, Oh, Help ! Help, O Spirit of God !"

Epicurus [300 BC] describes the Deposers :
"They lie beside their nectar, and the Bolts are Hurled far below them in the valleys, and the clouds are lightly curled round their golden houses Girdled with the Gleaming World, where they smile in secret, looking over Wasted lands, Blight and Famine, Plague and Earthquake, Roaring Deeps and Fiery Sands, Clanging Fights and Flaming Towns, and Sinking Ship and Praying Hands."

The religion of the Roman Catholic Church retains in its theological system a survival of the ancient Solar Cult. It is thus the legatee of the surviving, almost extinct, properties of those proud old faiths in which Men drew inspiring vitalities from the diffusion of the Solar essence. In the coal formations we see blocks of anthracite, in which are impressed the leaves of vegetable growth from which that drew its origin. The Solar religion is thus imprinted into the fossilized strata of the faiths that have hardened in the lapse and pressure of ages. But the human constitution, also impressed with lines of immemorial heredities, bears stamped within it the final and obscure remains of the Same Creative Splendor. Rome is a coal-bed, alike in its theology, its art, custom, pageant, and ritual ; it holds the woven-in lines of the cult in which Greece, Persia, and more ancient Chaldea, and still more ancient cultured and heroic peoples, lived, flourished, and passed away.

To this complexion must we come at last. As the spirit dies out of its body to find the freedom of the new existence beyond the grave, so the ripening, quickening, reasoning Man must die out of the body of ecclesiasticism, out of its ligatures, out of its alluring promises or threatening of peril ; must look to it with neither fear nor hope ; and look upon it simply as a nonentity, which, from the absolute ground it is.

For the Christian denominations the Hebrew Bible is the language of their forefathers. It contains survivals of previous Babylonian and Egyptian forms of religion, but it represents the monotheistic section, rather than the whole range of Babylonian religion. Gentile religion is not the language of the forefathers of historic Christianity, but it is that which, added to Jewish religion, made historic Christianity possible.

"Joseph. According to Traditions, Taurus was the emblem of Ephraim, who assumed the standard of his father Joseph, whom Moses compares to a young Bull. 'Joseph is a fruitful bough by a well, whose branches run over a wall.' The Hebrew words 'fruitful bough' are 'Son of a Cow.' The word

136

translated wee, means 'eye,' and the great Star Aldebaran in Taurus is called by the Arabians the Bull's eye. It is Very Strange to translate the Hebrew 'benoth' branches, since it really signifies Daughters.' The Pleiades were called Daughters by the Chaldeans, and the word for wall is really Bull, and since they are above Taurus, the literal translation 'whose daughters run over a Bull' (instead of branches run over a wall) is perfectly intelligible. 'From thence is the shepherd, the Stone of Israel.' The Arabians call one of the Stars of Orion by the name of Al Rai – the Shepherd." (Drummond makes no allusion to the facts that 1, It was from the Pleiades, directly above Orion, that Fire and Stones Fell from the Heavens ; 2, that the brilliant pageant of Stars from Orion up to the Pleiades was anciently known as Jacob's ladder, which reached up to the Heavens. In Jacob's dream, his head rested on a Stone which doubtless had Fallen from thence when the angels or ministers of Fire Descended to Earth.)

In the worship of the present day we find multitudes of words and expressions employed without any definite or rational meaning, simply because around them cluster associations hallowed by the memory of unnumbered generations of devout souls of whom the World was not worthy. Thus, for instance, to thee Cherubim (Taurids) and Seraphim (Burning Ones) continually do cry, Holy (Healing), Holy, Holy, Lord God of the Sabaoth (Pleiades) !" suggest the remotest semblance of objective Astronomical Fact ? Yet it is now admitted that no religion was ever founded on Fable for the Express Purpose of Deceiving. Religion was at first the highest expression of the Facts of Life and the Universe as those Facts appeared to the worshipper, and when religion ceases to correspond to Facts as they Honestly Appear to the worshipper, Its Days are Numbered with All Candid Men.

Plainly, the continued use of words to which a definite and rational meaning is no longer attached is a cause of stumbling to the non-worshipper, while to the worshipper they are the merest fetishes, however great their devotional power may seem to be. Whenever Understanding and Reverent Emotion are Separated, religion must inevitably work mischief by breeding Superstition, which, instead of uniting Men in bonds of Mutual Helpfulness, tends to Array them Against each Other in Antagonisms that are Bitter and Irreconcilable precisely in proportion as they are Senseless and Unnecessary.

Given an hypothesis, it is easy to collect apparent "proofs" in any desired quantity. Such, however, is not the process by which the present work has taken shape. Learned geologists had studied California long before the eventual days of 1849, yet it was not a geologist who discovered stores of Gold in California soil. So, too, scholars and theologians have worked for ages over the very ground containing the important discoveries made in the present work, yet these discoveries have at last been made unexpectedly and as it were by Accident. The evidence not having been sought with a direct view to establish a preconceived result, but instead having accumulated while the author was Actually in Search of Something Else, we have here to deal, not with an hypothesis, but with seemingly Unavoidable Conclusions.

As also with the Present Author, contemporary religion wasn't even considered to be in the scope of inquiry until searching for Horary Myths and then it became an Obstacle in which I Struggled to Avoid.

In conducting an investigation such as the present one, there was but one course to pursue. All obtainable witnesses, regardless of nationality or creed, had to be summoned, and their testimony taken in full and examined at length. The verdict must accord, not necessarily with the individual opinions of the various witnesses as to the meaning of their testimony, but with the indications of the testimony of All the witnesses taken as a Whole.

All Mythology and all religion have one and the same origin ; but that the One story of which the various religions and Mythologies are only different versions had its origin not in the impressions produced upon the minds of primitive savages by the orderly course of terrestrial phenomena, but instead in a Stupendous Catastrophe which underlies the entire Bible from Genesis to Revelations, as the Fall of Lucifer, The Morning Star, The Devil, The Old Dragon, or Satan, as he is variously termed ; and that the sacred books, emblems, rites, and ceremonies of all faiths and ages, instead of prophesying exclusively salvation to come, also point back, as the ground for individual faith and hope, to the Great Cosmic Salvation whose eternal memorial was fixed in the Zodiacal Signs and ancient Constellations before it was embodied in any sacred books known to us.

The Golden Age was not a Tradition but a Distinct Recollection ; the goodness of the Creator had been manifested to their abundant satisfaction by Past Ages of happiness and prosperity ; and since the Dread Catastrophe which had threatened the Ruin of the Heavens and the Earth, Disorder had been put down and a new order initiated which promised the attainment of other goods in the place of what had been lost. Thus, to Prehistoric Man after the Great Catastrophe, the beauty in the World proclaimed the goodness of God, and the Restoration of Order after the inroad of Chaos,

138

his power. The only question was why Infinite Goodness and Infinite Power had permitted the Great Disaster to Occur. [Very Good Question !]

Those who Reason Without Astronomical Knowledge will Never reach the Truth.

The creed of Plutarch : "I believe," says Plutarch ("On Isis and Osiris"), "that the happiness of the eternal Life which is the attribute of Deity, consists in his Knowledge of all things ; for without Knowledge and Understanding immorality would be Not Life, but only duration. Therefore, the pursuit of Truth, especially with reference to the being of Deity, is the pursuit of holiness ; it is a desire which, in learning and inquiring, becomes as it were an adoration of Deity ; it is a service which is Far Holier than any form of abstinence or temple worship, and is particularly pleasing to Deity because he himself is Wisdom and Philosophy."

Passing through sufferings inconceivable to our boldest flights of imagination, the memory of which it was long sought to preserve to all time by means of the Sacred Mysteries Anciently Celebrated Everywhere. Impressed and instructed in the school of bitter experience, their precise observations of the Phenomena of the Universe.

The Golden Bough, a Study in Comparative Religion, by J. G. Frazer, Volumes 1 & 2, 1894

Roman and Sabine priests might not be shaved with Iron but only with bronze razors or shears ; and whenever an Iron graving-tool was brought into the sacred grove of the Arval Brothers at Rome for the purpose of cutting an inscription in stone, an expiatory sacrifice of a lamb and a pig was offered, which was repeated when the graving-tool was removed from the grove. In Crete sacrifices were offered to Menedemus without the use of Iron, because it was said, Menedemus had been killed by an Iron Weapon in the Trojan War. The Archon of Plataeae might not touch Iron ; but once a year, at the annual commemoration of the Men who fell at the battle of Plataeae, he was allowed to carry a sword wherewith to sacrifice a Bull. To this day a Hottentot, Black, priest never uses an Iron knife, but always a sharp splint of quartz in sacrificing an animal or circumcising a lad. Amongst the Moquis of Arizona stone knives, hatchets, ect., have passed out of common use, but are retained in religious ceremonies. Negroes of the Gold Coast remove

139

all Iron or steel from their person when they consult their Fetish. The Men
who made the Need-Fire in Scotland had to divest themselves of All Metal.
In making the clavier (a kind of Yule-Tide Fire-Wheel) at Burghead, no
Hammer may be used ; the Hammering must be done with a Stone.
Amongst the Jews no Iron tool was used in building the temple at Jerusalem
or in making an altar.

For the house, when it was in building, was built of stone made ready at the
quarry ; and there was neither Hammer nor Axe nor any tool of Iron heard in
the house, while it was in building.   I Kings 6 : 7. 1917

And if thou wilt make an altar of stone unto me, thou shalt not build it of
hewn stones : for if thou lift up a tool upon it, it shall be defiled.
                                                    Exodus 20 : 25   1906

The gilded plough with which the Siamese mock king opens the ploughing
may be compared with the bronze ploughs which the Etrucans employed at
the ceremony of founding cities ; in both cases the use of Iron was probably
forbidden on superstitious grounds. [Read somewhere wherein they plough
the gates when founding of a city. The Threshold Covenant ?]

The story of Adonis spent half, or according to others a third, of the year in
the lower World and the rest of it in the upper World, is explained most
simply and naturally by supposing that he represented Vegetation,
especially the corn, which lies buried in the earth half the year and reappears
above ground the other half. Certainly of the annual phenomena of nature
there is none which suggests so obviously the idea of a yearly Death and
Resurrection as the disappearance and reappearance of Vegetation in autumn
and spring. [A connection to the Pleiades and Adonis as in 3/3 year of the
rising, setting, and below Pleiades.]

The next of those Gods, whose supposed Death and Resurrection struck
such deep roots into the religious faith and ritual of Western Asia, is Attis.
He was to Phrygia what Adonis was to Syria. Like Adonis, he appears to
have been a God of Vegetation, and his Death and Resurrection were
annually mourned and rejoiced over at a Festival in Spring. The Legends
and Rites of the two Gods were so much alike that the ancients themselves
sometimes identified them. Attis was said to have been a fair youth who was
beloved by the Great Phrygian Goddess Cybele. Two different accounts of
his Death were current. According to the one, he was killed by a Boar, like
Adonis. According to the other, he mutilated himself under a pine-tree, and

140

died from the effusion of blood. The latter is said to have been the local story told by the people of Pessinus, a great centre of Cybele worship, and the whole Legend of which it forms a part is stamped with a character of rudeness and savagery that speaks Strongly for its Antiquity. But the genuineness of the other story seems also vouched for by the fact that his worshipper, especially the people of Pessinus, abstained from eating swine. After his death Attis is said to have been changed into a Pine-Tree. The ceremonies observed at his Festival are not very fully known, but their general order appears to have been as follows. At the Spring Equinox (22d March) a Pine-Tree was cut in the woods and brought into the sanctuary of Cybele, where it was treated as a divinity. It was adorned with woolen bands and wreaths of violets, for violets were said to have sprung from the blood of Attis, as anemones from the blood of Adonis ; and the effigy of a young Man was attached to the middle of the Tree. On the second day (23 March) the chief ceremony seems to have been a blowing of Trumpets. The third day (24th March) was known as the Day of Blood : the high priest drew blood from his arms and presented it as an offering. It was perhaps on this day or night that the mourning for Attis [Tammuz] took place over an effigy, which was afterwards solemnly buried. The fourth day (25th March) was the Festival of Joy (Hilaria), at which the Resurrection of Attis was probably celebrated – at least the celebration of his Resurrection seems to have followed closely upon that of his Death.

A late explanation of the first beginnings of religion after the True Meaning was Lost in the Horary Neolithic Causation.

"Woe to Us" the cry, weep for Tammuz, Adonis, Attis, Dionysus, ect.

Once a year the Egyptians sacrificed Pigs to the Moon and to Osiris, and not only sacrificed them, but ate of their flesh, though on any other day of the year they would neither sacrifice them nor taste of their flesh. Those who were too poor to offer a Pig on this day baked cakes of dough, and offered them instead. The fate of the Pig in Egypt became fear and horror and outweighed the reverence and worship and became to be looked on as an embodiment of Set or Typhon, the Egyptian Devil and enemy of Osiris. For it was in the shape of a Boar that Typhon menaced the Eye of the God Horus, who burned him and instituted the sacrifice of the Pig, the Sun-God Ra having declared the Pig Abominable.

Bonfires are most commonly lit on the Winter and Summer Solstices and Hallow E'en and Spring [Spring Equinox].

141

One of the occasions on which these Fire-Festivals are held is Easter Eve, the Saturday before Easter Sunday. On that day it has been customary in Catholic countries to Extinguish All the Lights in the Churches, and Then to Make a New Fire, sometimes with Flint and Steel, sometimes with a Burning-Glass. At this fire is lit the Easter candle, which is then used to rekindle all the extinguished lights in the church. In many parts of Germany a bonfire is also kindled, by means of the New Fire, on some open space near the church. It is consecrated, and the people bring sticks of Oak, Walnut, and Beech, which they char in the Fire, and then take home with them. Some of these charred sticks are thereupon burned at home in a Newly-Kindled Fire, with a prayer that God will preserve the homestead from Fire, Lightning, and Hail. Thus every house receives "New Fire." Some of the sticks are placed in the fields, gardens, and meadows, with a prayer that God will keep them from Blight and Hail.

The Zonal-Belt Hypothesis : A New Explanation of The Causes of the Ice Ages, by Joseph T. Wheeler, 1908

Primitive Man saw the last remnants of these strange sights in the Sky, and the echo of his thought in the form of Mythology has sounded down through the lapse of centuries. Furthermore, it was visible to him, for he has recorded the Fact on his Monuments, and many of the roots from which his archaic languages are derived have their origin in Sky Scenes. He Worshipped the Phenomena which He Saw, making Gods and Devils of the various features, handing down to us the substance of his impressions in that form of Mythology which portrays the Nature Myth.

The pillars of Heaven Tremble, and Dread at his beck. By his power the Seas are suddenly gathered together, and his Wisdom has Struck the Proud One. His spirit hath adorned the Heavens, and his Obstetric hand brought forth the Winding Serpent.   Job 26 : 11-13 1906

Ubiquitous Sky-Serpent :
The Toltecs called their Sky-God, Quetzalcoatl. "The Popol Vuh, the great collection of quiche Myths, presents Gukumatz as one of the four principal Gods who Created the World. Gukumatz means Shining or Brilliant Snake, and hence seems to be the same character as known to the Nahuatls, or Aztecs, as Quetzalcoatl, whose name means the Bright or Shining Snake."

Quetzalcoatl was reputed to be a very good vapor spirit, a kind of Coverer. He was the son of Camaxtli, the Shiner of Yesterday, He fought the enemies that had risen against his father, and attacked the Temple of the Cloud-Snakes' Mountain. He was tall, of white complexion. His reign was the Golden Age of the Toltecs. He was pursued by enemies and obliged to Fly. One of these was a near kinsman, a splendid youth, named Tezcatlipoca, The Smoking Mirror. This kinsman was his bitter enemy. Quetzalcoatl was pressed from land to land. By some accounts he disappeared in a boat on the Sea ; by others he perished on the snow-covered peak of Orizaba (the Olympian Cloud-Mountain of the Aztecs), mounting to Heaven on the smoke of the funeral pile. When he vanished the Sun withdrew his Shining. In the museum down at Mexico an image of Quetzalcoatl is on exhibition which is girt about with Snakes of very savage mien. Their peculiarity is that they are both Bird and Reptile, a kind of Feathered Flying Serpent, indicating Rapid Flight. This idea of Rapid Flight is frequently associated with the White One. [Bolide]

The Arabian Legend, Abou Mohammed the Lazy, who is a very great magician, with power over the forces of the air and the Afrites (Winged Creature of Fire), beholds a Battle between two Great Snakes, one tawny-colored, the other white. The tawny Serpent is overcoming the white one ; but Abou Mohammed kills it with a Rock. The white Serpent departed, and was absent for a while, but returned ; and the tawny Serpent was torn to pieces and scattered over the land, and nothing remained of her but her head.

143

Adonis over Typhon, Indra over Vritra, of Dimiriat over Dahish, of
Timadonar over Ariconte, of Hercules over the two Serpents strangled while
he was an infant, of Osiris over Set, etc., etc.

Canst, thou with Him spread out the Sky, which is strong as a Molten
Mirror ?   Job 37 : 18 1917

To place on the altar that which was seen in the Sky was a natural sequence.
Fire Worship is the logical result of seeing Fire in Heaven.

The Maoris of New Zealand have a story entitled 'The Legend of the
Children of Heaven and Earth.' Men had but one pair of primitive ancestors ;
they sprang from vast Heaven that exists above us, and from the Earth
which lies beneath us. According to the Traditions of our race, Rangi and
Papa, or Heaven and Earth, were the source from which, in the beginning,
all things originated. Darkness then rested upon the Heaven and upon the
Earth, and they still both clave together, for they had not yet been Rent
Apart ; and the children they had begotten were ever thinking amongst
themselves what might be the difference between Darkness and Light ; they
knew that beings had multiplied and increased, and yet Light had Never
broken upon them, but it ever continued Dark. At last the beings who had
been begotten by Heaven and the Earth, worn out by the continued
Darkness, consulted amongst themselves, saying, Let us now determine
what we should do with Rangi and Papa, whether it would be better to slay
them, or to rend them apart. Then spoke Tu-ma-tauenga, the fiercest of the
children of Heaven and Earth, 'It is well, let us slay them.' Then spake
Tane-mahuta, the father of forests and of all things that inhabit them or that
are constructed from Trees, 'Nay, not so. It is better to rend them apart,
and to let the heaven stand far above us, and the Earth lie under our feet.
Let the Sky become as a stranger to us, but the Earth remain close to us as
our nourishing mother.' The brothers all consented to this proposal, with
the exception of Tawhiri-ma-tea, the father of winds and storms, and he,
fearing that his kingdom was about to be overthrown, grieved greatly at the
thought of his parents' being torn apart. Five of the brothers willingly
consented to the separation of their parents, but one of them would not agree
to it. The brothers all tried, in vain. The God and father of Fish and
Reptiles, ect. – everyone failed. Then at last slowly uprises Tane-mahuta,
the God and father of forests, of birds, and of insects, and he struggles with
his parents ; in vain he strives to rend them apart with his hands and arms.
Lo, he pauses, his head is now firmly planted on his mother, the Earth, his
feet he raises up and rests against his father, the Skies ; He strains his back

144

and limbs with mighty effort. Now are rent apart Rangi and Papa, and with cries and groans of woe they shriek aloud. 'Wherefore slay you thus your parents? Why commit you so dreadful a crime as to slay us, as to rend your parents apart?' But Tane-mahuta pauses not, he regards not their shrieks and cries ; far beneath him he presses down the Earth, far, far above him he thrusts up the Sky. No sooner was Heaven rent from Earth than the multitude of human beings were discovered whom they had begotten, and who had hitherto lain concealed between the bodies of Rangi and Papa. Fierce desire came to Tawhiri-ma-tea, God and father of the winds and storms, to wage war against his brethren who had done such unhandsome deed to their parents. Then came forth his progeny, the mighty winds, the fierce squalls, the clouds, dense, dark, fiery, wildly bursting ; and in their midst their father rushed upon his foe. Tane-mahuta and his giant forests were taken unawares, unsuspecting, when the raging hurricane burst upon them, the mighty trees were snapped in twain, prostrated, trunks and branches left torn upon the ground for insect and grub to prey on. The sea was swept and tossed with surgings and mountain waves till Tangaroa, God of the Ocean and father of all that dwell therein, became affrighted and fled. The Storm-God attacked his brothers, the Gods and progenitors of the tilled food and the wild, but Papa, the Earth, caught them up and hid them, and he searched and swept to find them, in vain. It was in one of these attacks that dry land was made to disappear beneath the waters. He fell upon the last of his brothers, the father of fierce Men, but him he could not even move. Man stood erect, unshaken upon the bosom of his mother Earth. At last the hearts of the Heaven and the storm became tranquil, and their passion was assuaged. From that time clear light increased upon the Earth, and all the beings which were hidden between Rangi and Papa before they were separate now multiplied upon the Earth.

The Four Horses of Revelation are another instance of the Fourfold Division of early time. In All parts of the World the same divisions seem to have been observed, and the inference is that there actually was something in the Sky which caused these Ages to be noted.

The Popul Vuh, the national book of the Quiches, tells us of Four Ages of the World. The Man of the first Age was made of clay ; he was strengthless, inept, watery ; he could not move his head, his face looked but one way ; his sight was restricted, he could not look behind him (that is, he had no knowledge of the past) ; he had been endowed with language, but he had no intelligence, so he was consumed in the water. Then followed a higher race of Men ; they filled the World with their progeny ; they had intelligence but

145

no moral sense ; they forgot the heart of Heaven. They were destroyed by
Fire and Pitch from Heaven, accompanied by Tremendous Earthquakes,
from which only a few escaped. Then followed a period when all was Dark,
save the White Light as yet of the primeval World. Once more are the Gods
in council, in the Darkness, in the night of a Desolated Universe. Then the
people prayed to God for Light, evidently for the return of the Sun. Hail ! O
Creator ! They cried. O Former ! Thou that hearest and understandest us !
abandon us not ! forsake us not ! O God, thou art in Heaven and on Earth ;
O Heart of Heaven ! O Heart of Earth ! give us descendants, and a
posterity as long as the Light endure. It was thus they spake, living
tranquilly, invoking the return of the Light ; waiting the rising of the Sun.
But no Sun came, and the four Men and their descendents grew uneasy. We
have no person to watch over us, they said ; nothing to guard our Symbols !
Then they adopted Gods of their own, and waited. They kindled fires for
the climate was colder ; then there fell great rains and hailstorms, and put
out their fires. Seveal times they made fires, and several times the rains and
storms extinguished them. Many other trials also they underwent in Tulan,
famines and such things, and a general dampness and cold – for the Earth
was moist, there being no Sun. Many generations seem to have grown up
and perished under the Sunless Skies, waiting for the return of the Light ;
for the Popul Vuh tells us that here also the language of all the families was
confused, so that no one of the first four Men could any longer understand
the speech of the others. This shows that many, many years – it may be
centuries – must have elapsed before that vast volume of moisture, carried
up by evaporation, was able to fall back in snow and rain to the land and
sea, and allow the Sun to shine through the Blanket of the Dark. Starvation
encountered the scattered fragments of Mankind. There were Four of these
Cycles and at the end of each, by the agency of one of the elements, the
human family was swept from the Earth, and the Sun blotted out from the
Heavens, to be again Rekindled.

By the power of God there issued from the essence of Brahma a being
shaped like a boar, white and exceedingly small ; this being, in the space of
an hour, grew to the size of an elephant of the largest size, and remained in
the air. Brahma was astonished on beholding this figure, and discovered,
by the force of internal penetration, that it could be nothing but the power of
the Omnipotent which had assumed a body and become visible. He now felt
that God is all in all, and all is from him, and all in him ; and said to
Mareechee and his sons (the attendant genni) : 'A wonderful animal has
emanated from my essence ; at first of the smallest size, it has in one hour
increased to this enormous bulk, and, without doubt, it is a portion of the

146

almighty power.' They were engaged in this conversation when that Vara, or 'Boar-Form,' suddenly uttered a sound like the Loudest Thunder, and the echo reverberated and Shook All the quarters of the Universe. But still, under this dreadful awe of Heaven, a certain wonderful divine confidence secretly animated the Hearts of Brahma, Mareechee, and the other genii, who immediately began praises and thanksgiving. That Vara (Boar-Form) figure, hearing the power of the Vedas and Mantras from their mouths, again made a Loud Noise, and became a Dreadful Spectacle. Shaking the Full Flowing Mane which hung down his neck on both sides, and erecting the humid hairs of his body, he proudly displayed his two most Exceedingly White Tusks ; then, rolling about his wine-colored (red) eyes and erecting his Tail, he descended from the region of the air, and plunged headforemost into the Water. The whole body of Water was convulsed by the motion, and began to rise in Waves, while the guardian spirit of the Sea, being terrified, began to tremble for his domain and cry for mercy.

We must not omit mentioning the Seven Headed Vasuki, the King of Serpents, who was made into a rope to twirl the churn of Heaven. It is said that he churned the foaming Waters of the Sea until the milky waves arose, lashed to whiteness, and in the midst of these mighty convulsions he caused the storm to bring the things of beauty out from the Heaving bosom of the Deep to their birth. The fourth avatar of Vishnu was that of The Great Mountain, Mandara the Lofty, which acted as a churning stick to stir the foaming Waters, the King Snake being used as a rope to twirl the stick around. Now, the Cloud Mountain always was the Home of the Gods. The Greeks had their Olympia, the North American Indians had their Sky-Mountain, and the Mohammedan Mythology records the Fact that Mount Caf, which Encircled the Earth, was the home of Giants. It was said to rest upon the sacred Emerald-colored Stone, sakhral, whose reflected light was the cause of the tints of the Sky. The Scandinavians Myths also mention the Mountain Giants, and the Egyptians had their Pyramids. That the Babylonian Gods lived above or on top [In the Crags] of the World-Mountain [Sky Mountain] therefore seems quite natural. The Mountain of the World is also called the Mountain of the Neither World (Shad Aralu) in the Cuneiform Inscriptions. The Gods Ea, Sin, Shamash, Nebo, Adad, Ninib, and their sublime consorts, were All born in a House [Hut/Pie Sign] situated on top of this Mountain. In some form or other, Nearly All the Peoples of Antiquity have left a record of this Sky-Mountain Phenomena, but perhaps the Babylonians and Assyrians have excelled them all. Their Ziggurats, or staged towers, were Imitations of this Mountain, and they were the temples of their Gods. The temple in so far as it was erected to

147

serve as a habitation for the God, says Jastrow, was to be the reproduction of the Cosmic E-Kur – a Mountain House on a small scale, a miniature Kharsag-Kurkura. In Assyria we find one of the oldest temples bearing the name E-Kharsag-Kurkura, that stamps the edifice as the reproduction of the Mountain of All Lands. Some of the Mountain titles of these deities and their temples were as follows : The name Zikkurat itself means Mountain Peak. Bel's temple at Nippur was E-Kur, the Mountain House of Bel. Belit, his consort, was called Nin-Khar-Sag, or the Lady of the Great High Mountain. Bel was often addressed as if he himself Were the Mountain : the Great Mountain, the Lofty Bel, the Mighty Bel. Originally he was the Mountain Mass In The Sky. In Ur was the House of the Great Mountain, the Glorious Mountain House, the Lofty House, the Heavenly House, the link of Heaven and Earth, the Summit House.

Ishtar was originally good, personified, she was known as 'the Mother,' for the reason that she seemed to give birth to All the Sky Phenomena. She was also known as the Brilliant Goddess, and as the Mistress of the Mountains. Afterwards she became Violent, and the Verdant Earth under her greenhouse roof trembled. Thus she lost her good character, and the Assyrians, seeing her Transformation, henceforth considered her the Goddess of Battle and war. Her character is like that of the good Cherub of Ezekiel, who afterwards became a menace and terror. Thou art the anointed Cherub that Covereth ; and I have set thee so : thou wast upon the Holy Mountain of God ; thou hast walked up and down in the midst of the Stones of Fire. Thou wast perfect in thy ways from the day that thou wast Created, till iniquity was found in thee. By the multitude of thy merchandise they have filled the midst of thee with Violence, and thou hast sinned : therefore I will cast thee as profane out of the Mountain of God : and I will destroy thee, O covering Cherub, from the midst of the Stones of Fire.

Ezekiel 28 : 14-16

Omoroka was the name of the Woman which Bel cleft in twain, from one half of which he made the dome of Heaven, and from the other half the Earth. In Chaldea her name is Thamte, i.e., Tamtu, the Babylonian for Sea or Ocean, which in the Greek is Thalassa. This Tiamat or Sea, according to the Myth, took the form of a Huge Serpent, she and Apsu, her consort, revolted against the Gods, that is against the Sun, Moon, and Stars, by creating a brood of Monsters which Destroyed them. In other words, the Serpent belt became a Sun-obscuring, Star-Devouring Pall, a Spreading Canopy. [Atmospheric Loading] [The book proposes a Saturn type ring(s) around the Earth, I contend that it is the Circuit of Comet 2p/Encke.]

They have joined their forces and are making War, Ummu-Khubur (i.e., Tiamat), who formed all things, has made in addition weapons invincible, she has spawned Monster-Serpents, sharp of tooth and cruel of fang ; with poison instead of blood she has filled their bodies. Fierce Monster-Vipers she has clothed with terror, with splendor she has decked them, and she has caused them to mount on high. Whoever behold them is overcome by dread. Their bodies rear up and none can withstand their attack. She has set up the Viper, and the Dragon, and the Monster Lakkamu. It will be noted, Tiamat is said to have Created All things in the Cuneiform Text, hence this revolt against the Gods was against her own offspring, which fact is sustained by various other Babylonian Texts as well as by the Myths of other lands. The interpretation is clear. When the First Canopy [Atmospheric Loading] known by Tradition to the Babylonians became thin it gave birth to the Gods ; in other words, the Sun, Moon, and Stars were seen through it.

It is said of Solon the Greek law-giver, that when he visited Egypt, six hundred years before Christ, he had a talk with the priest of Sais about the Deluge of Deucalion. The following is Plato's account : "Thereupon, one of the priests, who was of very great age, said, 'O Solon, Solon, you Hellene.' Solon, hearing this, said, 'What do you mean?' 'I mean to say,' he replied, 'that in mind you are all young ; there is no old opinion handed down among you by ancient Tradition, nor any Science which is Hoary with Age. And I will tell you the reason of this : there have been, and There Will Be Again, many Destructions of Mankind arising out of many causes. There is a story which even you have preserved, that once upon a time Phaeton, the son of Helios, having yoked the steeds in his father's chariot, because he was not able to drive them in the path of his father, burnt up all that was upon the Earth and was himself destroyed by a Thunderbolt. Now, this has the form of a Myth, but really signifies a declination of the bodies moving around the Earth and in the Heavens, and a Great Conflagration of things upon the Earth recurring at long intervals of time." "Dialogues," XI, 517, Timaeus.

Rawlinson says : "Other feasts were held in honour of Osiris on the seventeenth day of Athyr and the nineteenth of Pashons ; in the former of which the 'Loss of Osiris,' and in the latter his recovery, were commemorated. A Cow, emblematic of Isis, was Veiled in Black and led about for four successive days, accompanied by a crowd of Men and Women, who beat their breasts in memory of the supposed disappearance of Osiris from Earth and his sister's search for him ; while, in memory of his recovery, a procession was made to the seaside, the priests carrying a

149

sacred chest, and, an image or emblem of Osiris fashioned out of Earth and Water having been placed in it, the declaration was made, 'Osiris is found ! Osiris is found !' amid general festivity and rejoicing."

The Abbe Brasseur de Bourbourg gives a Legend from the Quiche Indians of Central America which depicts this same scene: "Now, behold, our ancients and our fathers were made lords, and had their dawn. Behold, we will relate also the rising of the Sun, the Moon, and the Stars ! Great was their joy when they saw the Morning-Star, which came out first, with its resplendent face before the Sun. At last the Sun itself began to come forth ; the animals, small and great, were in joy ; they rose from the water-courses and ravines, and stood on the mountain-tops, with their heads toward where the Sun was coming. An innumerable crowd of people were there, and the Dawn cast Light on all these people at once. At last the face of the ground was dried by the Sun ; like a Man the Sun showed himself, and his presence warmed and dried the surface of the ground. Before the Sun appeared, muddy and wet was the surface of the ground, and it was before the Sun appeared, and then only the Sun rose like a Man. But his heat had no strength, and he did but show himself when he rose ; he only remained like a Mirror ; and it is not, indeed, the same Sun that appears now, they say, in the stories." [Early History of Mankind   Edward B. Tylor 1878]

Heaped were the Mountains in heaps. The Serpents began to twine – there were Seven of these 'Fiery Phantoms,' that twirled away at the Line, over them rushed Heaven's Ocean, - Anu a River Broad which Flowed Round this World of Ours, Around where the Monster clawed. Ea, alias the 'House of the Waters,' lived in this Ocean Vast, an 'Exalted Fish' they called him, in the story of Vishu cast. The ancient Britons tell us that : The profligacy of Mankind provoked the great Supreme to send a pestilential wind upon the Earth. A pure poison descended, every Blast was Death. At this time the patriarch, distinguished for his integrity, was shut up, together with his select company, in the enclosure with the strong door. [Dolmen] Here the just ones were safe from injury. Presently a Tempest of Fire arose. It split the Earth asunder to the Great Deep. The lake Llion burst its bounds, and the waves of the sea lifted themselves on High Around the borders of Britain, the rain poured down from Heaven, and the waters covered the Earth. [Mythology of the British Druids]

The Aztecs prayed to Tezcatlipoca, who was represented as a Flying Serpent – that their cry was : "Is it possible that this lash and chastisement are not given for out Correction and Amendment, but only for our Total

Destruction and overthrow ; that the Sun will never more shine upon us, but that we must remain in Perpetual Darkness ? . . . . It is a sore thing to tell how we are all in darkness. . . . . . . O Lord, ... make an end of this smoke and fog. Quench also the burning and destroying fire of thine anger ; let serenity come and clearness, let the small birds of the people begin to sing and approach the Sun." [Native Races Bancroft]

Connected with the thought that the Old Sky was a Labyrinth, or Puzzle, which the clearing away of the 'templum,' or wide expanse, solved to the satisfaction of the early inquirer into the Ways of Nature, is the Great Labyrinth which was constructed by Daedalus. It was like The Lost Sky River, Maeander, for which the Grecian River is named, which Flows Back On Its Course, Returning To Itself. [Serpent Eating its Tail] It was a Ring or spiral vapor-belt, and Daedalus built it for a certain king named Minos, a sky-king, though called a Creton. Somehow the builder lost the king's esteem, and the evil monarch forth with imprisoned him in a high tower. From this he escaped, only to find that he could not leave the island, as Minos was keeping a strict watch on all departing vessels. Now, Daedalus said of the king that though he might control the land and sea, yet he could not rule the regions of the crystal air. With that he set himself to fabricate wings for himself and his son, Icarus, that they might fly away. When these contrivances were finished, he said unto his son ; "Now follow me, my Icarus, and you will be quite safe. I warn thee, fly along the middle track ; nor low, nor high ; if low thy plumes may flag with Ocean's spray ; if high the Sun may dart his fiery ray." But Icarus, like All the Old Sky Phenomena, Fell. It is recorded that he flew overly high, and that the Sun melted the wax which attached his wings to his body.

Minos confined in his Labyrinth a fearful Sky-Monster which was reputed to be half a Bull and half a Man. This bloody creature, known as the Minotaur, as the story goes, was fed by his master with human victims. For this purpose Minos made the Athenians furnish him each year with Seven youths and Seven maids. The poor Athenians submitted to this yearly tribute for a long time, until Theseus, a Sky-Revolving hero of the vapors, decided to put an end to the infamous practice. He sailed away, promising to return with white sails set in token of victory. Arrived at his journey's end, he killed the Bull and found his way back again through the Labyrinthian mists by means of a thread given him by the good Ariadne, the daughter of the old king. This child of Minos was the Light, and when once outside the walls of the Great Sky Prison or Labyrinth he took her with him. Landing on an isle, he abandoned her, and in doing so made a great mistake. He had promised to return with white sails set, but when he left the Light behind, all was Darkness. Seeing this blackness while the ship was yet afar, his father, thinking him dead, killed himself.

Pegasus, the Winged Horse, was one of the most Beautiful and Bright of the racing steeds. We can picture him in our minds as he stood with nostrils smoking in distain of Man, for, be it remembered, he never allowed any but the Gods to ride on his back. Yet because Pallas Athene commanded him so to do, he departed from his custom and allowed Bellerophon to mount. Forthwith they went to Battle with the Bloody Dragon of the Fiery tale, known as Chimaera. From her Pitchy Throat issued Flame Smoke and Sulphurous Mist. Pegasus seemed willing to enter this Battle for Athene's sake, for these Mists were working Havoc with her Sky. It will be recalled that she was the Blue-Eyed Goddess of the free breeze, the air of Heaven itself, and naturally she could not endure this Polluting Chimaera any longer. Chimaera was nothing but a Vial, Fire-Breathing Lion, Dragon, or Goat, anyway. Bellerophon and the Bright Sun-Horse of course conquered her.

The expectation of the End of The World is a Natural complement to the belief in Periodical Destructions of Our Globe. As at certain times past the Equipoise of Nature was lost, and the elements breaking the chain of laws that bound them ran Riot over the Universe, involving All Life in one Mad Havoc and Desolation, so in the future we have to expect that day of Doom.

Within a Russian Legend, Baba Yaga waking up in the morning and seeing that her colt was stolen, set off in pursuit of the thief, Prince Ivan, at full speed did she fly up the Fiery River in her Iron Mortar, urging it on with the Pestle, sweeping away her traces with the broom. [There is another story with a Mortar and Pestle, which would describe a high speed Bolide with a shockwave ahead of the elongated Meteor.]

The great Krakatoa Eruption in July and August, 1883, and see the lesson that it has taught us on the constitution of our atmosphere. Before the occurrence, but few had the slightest suspicion that twenty miles over our heads a mighty tempest is incessantly hurling with speed much greater than the most awful hurricane. All that Krakatoa did was simply to provide the charges of dust by which for one brief period this wind was made visible. In the autumn of 1883 the newspapers were full of accounts of strange appearances in the Heavens. These came from Ceylon, the West Indies, and other tropical places. All had the same tale to tell. All these phenomena were due to Krakatoa. It was in the late autumn that the marvelous series of

Celestial Phenomena connected with the great eruption began to be displayed in our country. [printed in PA. USA 1908] Then it was that the glory of the ordinary Sunsets enhanced by a splendor which has dwelt in the memory of all those who were permitted to see it. The dust from Krakatoa produced this. Three times round went the glorified dust-cloud, and then drifted towards the poles. What would it have done if it had been elevated to yet greater heights ? [How close the Erudites of the past have come to solving the Mysteries, yet it is interesting to hear from eyewitnesses of the jet stream being discovered and the effects of such an eruption on our atmosphere !]

After the (Zonal-Belts), [the Serpent Eating his Tail ; Zodiacal Light Stream], passed away [Dissipated by the Solar Wind] Bifrost became associated with the Rainbow. We may infer from this that the original structure had a very delicate appearance. The Japanese speak of 'The Floating Region.' In their Myth of creation the story runs that, "The Sun, Earth, and Moon were still attached to each other like a head to the neck, or arms to the body. They were little by little separated, the parts joined them growing thinner and thinner. This part, like an isthmus, was called 'Heaven's Floating Bridge.'" This was the first World of the Scandinavians, Asgard, the land of the AEsir. It is a matter of record that the Celestial Bridge touched the outer edge of the home of the Gods. Sleipnir, Odin's marvelous Sun-Horse, used to rush unhesitatingly upon the Bridge, which trembled beneath his weight. In other words, its flimsy material was seen to vibrate and quiver in the strong Light of the Sun. Other Scandinavian Sun-Horses were Glad (Bright), Gyller (Gilder or Golden), Gler (the Glassy, the Shining One), Skeidbrimer (Fleet-Foot), Silfrintop (Silver Top), Gisl (the Sunbeam), and Goldtop, Heimdall's steed of beauty, whose Mane Shone like the Sun. Along with these Rapid Ones may be mentioned Frey's Boar, which like the Boar of Ermanthus, which Hercules brought to his master, was a Vapor-Form [From the Sky]. His Golden Bristles Flashed in the Sunlight, and he is said to have so Swift that Sleipnir with his eight legs could not out stride him. The second World [layers of the Heavens] of the Scandinavians was Midgard, the World of Men. The Midgard Serpent ran within it, East and West wardly. It is recorded that the River Ocean flowed around the World of Men. In the original conception this Ocean River was the Midgard Serpent, it was supposed to be united with the Terrestrial Ocean. Thus when Thor the storm or 'Thunder God' was in the Hall of the Giant Utgard-Loki, he was obliged to drink from a horn, large at the top, but exceedingly long, winding coil after coil to such a distance that the end could not be distinguished. Indeed, says the record, "the end of the horn

153

which could not be seen reached to the Great River." Thor drank so deeply that Men thereafter called it the ebb of the tide.

Loki comes from the word Lukos, Bright. [Lucifer means "Light Bringer."]

What more is needed to prove that the Nature Marvels of the one land were the Wonder Talk of the other, and that both originated from the Same Sky Scenes?

Weeping for Baldur and weeping for Tammuz are one and the same thing. Baldur's body was placed in a ship and set afire and they desired to set it adrift, but it was so large that they were unable to move it. In this predicament they called upon the Giantess, Hyrroken (the Smoking Fire), who came riding on a Wolf, using Twisted Serpents for her reins and with a single push set the burning funeral Pire adrift. A survival of the custom is found in the Chinese day of weeping, which comes in mid-summer and is called the 'Dragon Boat Festival.' The bewailing of Adonis was in memory of the same phenomenon.

Bulfinch says that Jupiter summoned the Gods to council. They obeyed the call, and took the Road to the palace of Heaven. The Road, which any one may see in a clear night, Stretches Across the Face of the Sky. Along the Road stand the Palaces of the Illustrious Gods. Jupiter addresses the assembly. He set forth the frightful condition of things on the Earth, and closed by announcing his intension to Destroy the Whole of its inhabitants, and provide a new race, unlike the first, who would be more worthy of Life, and much better worshipers of the Gods. So saying, he took a Thunderbolt, and was about to launch it at the World, and Destroy it by Burning ; but, recollecting the danger that such a Conflagration might set Heaven itself on Fire, he changed his plan, and resolved to Drown it.

The demon Fudo-mio-o

The Hymns of the Rigveda, by T. H. Griffth, 1890

Your chariot yoked for both alike, immortal, ye of Mighty Acts, Travels, O Asvins, in the Sea. High on the forehead of the Bull on chariot wheel ye ever kept ; the Other round the Sky Revolves. (1 : 30 : 18,19) [Two Suns]

I will declare the Manly deeds of Indra, the first that he achieved, the Thunder-Wielder. He Slew the Dragon, then disclosed the Waters, and cleft the channels of the Mountain torrents. He Slew the Dragon Lying on the Mountain : his Heavenly Bolt of Thunder Twashtar fashioned. Like the lowing Kine in rapid flow descending Waters glided downward to the Ocean. Impetuous as a Bull, he chose the Soma, and quaffed in threefold sacrifice the juices. Maghavan grasped the Thunder for his Weapon, and Smote to Death this firstborn of the Dragons. [REV.] When Indra, thou hadst Slain the Dragons' firstborn, and overcome the charms of the enchanters, then giving Life to Sun and Dawn and Heaven, thou foundest not one foe to stand against thee. Indra with his own great and deadly Thunder smote into pieces Vritra worst of Vritras. As Trunks of Trees,

155

what time the Axe hath Felled Them [Tunguska], low on the Earth so lies
the Prostrate Dragon. He, like a mad weak warrior, challenged Indra, the
great impetuous many-slaying hero. He brooking not the Clashing of the
Weapons, Crushed-Indra's foe- the Shattering Forts in Falling. Footless and
Handless still he challenged Indra, who Smote him with his Bolt between
the shoulders. Emasculate yet claiming manly vigour, thus Vritra lay with
Scattered Limbs Dissevered. There as he lies like a bank-bursting River, the
Waters taking courage flow above him. The Dragon lies beneath the feet of
torrents which Vritra with his greatness had encompassed. Then humbled
was the strength of Vritra's mother : Indra hath Cast his Deadly Bolt against
her. The mother was above, the son was under, and like a Cow beside her
Calf lay Danu. Rolled in the midst of never-ceasing currents flowing
without a rest for ever onward, the Waters bear off Vritra's nameless body :
the foe of Indra sank to during Darkness. Guarded by Ahi stood the thralls
of Dasas, the Waters stayed like Kine held by the robber. But when he had
smitten Vritra, opened the Cave wherein the Floods had been imprisoned.
A Horse's Tail wast thou when he, O Indra, smote on thy Bolt ; thou, God
without a second, thou hast won back the Kine, hast won the Soma ; thou
hast let loose to flow the Seven Rivers. Nothing availed him Lightning,
nothing Thunder, Hailstorm or Mist which he had Spread Around him :
when Indra and the Dragon strove in battle, Maghavan gained the victory
for ever. Whom sawest thou to avenge the Dragon, Indra, that fear
possessed thy heart when thou hadst Slain him ; that, like a Hawk affrighted
Through the Regions, thou crossedst nine-and-ninety flowing rivers ? Indra
is king of all that moves and moves not, of creatures tame and Horned, the
Thunder-Wielder. Over all living Men he rules as Sovran, containing all as
spokes within the felly.   (1 : 32 : 1-15)

Thou hast unclosed the prisons of the Waters ; thou hast in the Mountain
seized the Treasure rich in gifts. When thou hadst Slain with might the
Dragon Vritra, thou, Indra, didst raise the Sun in Heaven for all to see.
                                                        (1 : 51 : 4)

Then Heaven Himself the Mighty, at that Dragon's Roar Reeled back in
Terror when, Indra, thy Thunderbolt, in the wild joy of Soma had Struck
Off with Might the Head of Vritra, Tyrant of the Earth and Heaven.
                                                        (1 : 52 : 10)

So with my tongue I deck, to please that Indra, my hymn, as 'twere a
Horse, through love of glory, to reverence the hero, bounteous giver,
famed far and wide, Destroyer of Castles. Even for him hath Twashtar

forged the Thunder, most deftly wrought, Celestial, for the Battle, wherewith he reached the vital parts of Vritra, striking-the vast, the mighty-with the Striker. At the libations to this mighty maker, Vishnu swift swallowing drink and pleasant dainties stole the dress viands ; but the stronger hero Pierced the Wild-Boar while he Shot through the Mountain. To him, to Indra, when he Slew the Dragon, the dames, too, consorts of the Gods, Wove praises. The Mighty Heaven and Earth hath he Encompassed : thy greatness Heaven and Earth, combined, exceed not. Yea, of a Truth, his Magnitude Surpasseth the Magnitude of Earth Mid-Air, and Heaven. Indra, approved by all Men, self-resplendent, Waxed in his home , Loud-Voiced and Strong for Battle.   (1 : 61 : 5-9)

A White Horse, asuins, ye bestowed on Pedu, a Dragon-Slaying Steed sent down by Indra, Loud- Neighing, [Ta-Ta-Ta Sound] conquering the foe, high-metted, firm-limbered and vigorous, winning thousand treasures.
                                                        (1 : 118 : 9)

Floods great and many, Compassed by the Dragon, thou badest swell and settest free, O hero. Strengthened by songs of praise thou Rentest piecemeal the Dasa, him who deemed himself immortal. For, hero, in the lands wherein thou joyedst, in hymns of praise, O Indra, songs of Rudras, these Streams in which is thy delight approach thee, even as the Brilliant Ones draw near to Vayu. We who add strength to thine own splendid vigor, laying within thine Arms the Splendid Thunder – with us mayest thou, O Indra, Waxen Splendid, with Surya overcome the Dasa races. Hero, thou slowest in thy valor Ahi concealed in Depths, Mysterious, Great Enchanter, dwelling, enveloped Deep within the Waters, him who checked Heaven and stayed the Floods from flowing. Indra, we laud thy great deeds wrought aforetime, we laud thine exploits later of achievement ; we laud the Bolt that in thine Arms lies eager ; we laud thy two bay Steeds, heralds of Surya. Indra, thy bay Steeds showing forth their vigour have sent a Loud Cry Out that Droppeth Fatness. The Earth hath spread herself in all her fullness : the cloud that was about to move hath rested. Down, never ceasing, hath the rain-cloud settled : Bellowing, it hath wandered with the Mothers. Swelling the Roar in the far distant limits, they have Spread Wide the Blast sent forth by Indra. Indra hath Hurled Down the Magician Vritra who lay beleaguering the Mighty River. Then both the Heaven and Earth Trembled in Terror at the strong hero's Thunder when he Bellowed. Loud Roared the mighty hero's Bolt of Thunder, when he the friend of Man Burnt up the Monster, and, having drunk his full of flowing Soma, baffled the guileful Danava'a devices.   (2 : 11 : 2-10)

He who fixed fast and firm the Earth that Staggered, and set at rest the Agitated Mountains, who measured out the air's wide middle region and gave the Heaven Support, He, Men, is Indra. Who Slew the Dragon, freed the Seven rivers, and drove the Kine forth from the Cave of Vala, begat the Fire between Two Stones, the spoiler in warriors battle, He, O Me, is Indra. He who created all these things that perish, who chased away the humbled race of Dasas, who like a hunter conquering takes booty the foeman's treasure, He, O Men, is Indra. (2 : 12 : 1-4)

He who discovered in the fortieth autumn Sambara as he dwelt among the Mountains ; who Slew the Dragon putting forth his vigour, the Demon lying there, He, Men, is Indra. Who with his Seven Bright Rays, the Bull the Mighty, set free the Seven Great Floods to flow at pleasure : who, Thunder-Armed, Rent Rauhina in pieces when Scaling Heaven, He O ye Men, is Indra. Even the Heaven and Earth bow down before him, before his strength the Very Mountains Tremble. (2 : 12 : 11-13) (Translator's note : Seven bright rays : said to mean Seven forms of Indra. Rauhina is said to be name of a Demon.)

Now, Verily, will I declare the exploits, mighty and true, of him the true and mighty. In the Trikadrukas he drank the Soma : then in its rapture Indra Slew the Dragon. High Heaven in Unsupported Space he stablished : he filled the two Worlds and the Air's mid-region. Earth he upheld, and gave it wide expansion. These things did Indra in the Soma's rapture. (2 : 15 : 1,2)

Great art thou, Indra ; yea, the Earth, with gladness, and Heaven confess to thee thine high dominion. Thou in thy vigor having Slaughtered Vrtra didst free the Floods arrested by the Dragon. Heaven Trembled at the birth of thine effulgence ; Earth Trembled at the fear of thy displeasure. The steadfast Mountains Shook in agitation : the Waters flowed, and desert spots were Flooded. (4 : 17 : 1, 2)

Moreover, when thou wast first born, O Indra, thou Struckest Terror into all the people. Thou, Maghavan, Rentest with thy Bolt the Dragon who lay against the downward slopes of Heaven. (4 : 17 : 7)

The Dragon stretched against the Seven prone rivers, where no joint was, thou Rentest with thy Thunder. (4 : 19 : 3)

Agree, through these our Watery oblations, Goddesses, Heaven and Earth, with Ahibudhnya. As if to win the Sea, the Gharma-heaters have opened, as they come anear, the Rivers. (4 : 55 : 6)
(This stanza is difficult and its meaning is obscure, the last part rendered : the Dragon of the Deep, is a Divine Being who Presides Over the Firmament. Ahirbudhnya : the Dragon of the Deep, or 'Leviathan of the Sea of Heaven,' the distant, invisible and deified being who Presides Over the Firmament.)

Thou for the people who oppress hast kindled the Earthly Firmament and that of Heaven. With heat, O Bull, on every side consume them : heat Earth and Flood for him who hates devotion. (6 : 22 : 8)

Impetuous as a bear, O Maruts, is your Rush Terrible as a Dreadful Bull. They who with mighty strength o'erthrow like Oxen difficult to yoke, Hurl Downward e'en the Heavenly Stone, Cast Down the Hill, the Mountain as they Race Along. (5 : 56 ; 3, 4)

All the Gods raised as 'twere a Shout of Triumph, a laud to Indra that Slew the Dragon. (5 : 29 : 8)

One car-wheel of the Sun thou rollest forward, and One thou Settest Free to Move for Kutsa. [Two Suns] (5 : 29 : 10)

Let not the Dragon of the Deep annoy us, and gladly may he welcome our addresses. (5 : 41: 16)

Yea, Indra, all the deities installed their one strong champion in the van for battle. What time the Godless was the God's assailant, Indra they chose to win the Light of Heaven. Yea, e'en that Heaven itself of Old Bent Backward before thy Bolt, in Terror of its Anger, when Indra, life of every living creature, Smote Down within his lair the Assailing Dragon. Yea, strong one ! Twashtar turned for thee, the Mighty, the Bolt with thousand spikes and hundred edges, eager and prompt at will, wherewith thou Crushedst the Boasting Dragon, impetuous hero. (6 : 17 : 8-10)

159

The Thunder Weapon in Religion & Folklore :
A Study in Comparative Archaeology,
by Christopher Blinkenberg, 1911

In the Orestes Legend it is said that he sat upon the Thunder Stone (Zeus Fallen from the Heavens) and thus purified from the consequences of his matricide. It had more probably been a Meteor[ite], for in modern times Meteor[ite]s have in several places been looked upon as Thunderstones.

Even if these Customs were not in historical times associated with a Stone Fallen from the Sky, still the idea evidently preserved in them is that a God Descends to the Earth in the form of Lightning.

A Stroke of Lightning is in modern Greek called astropeleki (Sky-Axe).

In Greek literature it may be show that popular belief in ancient Greece associated the Stone Axe with the idea of the Descent of a Stone from the Sky accompanied by Lightning. [Thunder of similar accord.]

Supernatural beings, Fire Demons, or Dwarfs Cast or Forged and endowed the Thunder-Axe with supernatural power for the Gods who Welded it. Indra's Vajra was made by Tvshtar.

The Lightning is produced by a Stone which Shoots Down from Heaven to Earth. It splits trees, Kills Men and Beasts, and Penetrates Deep into the Ground. Then in course of time [Seven years] it moves upwards, and will eventually be found lying on the Ground. Further, the Thunderstone in Descending Produces the Violent Clap and the Devouring Fire. So far the ideas are of a physical rather than of a religious nature. But physics and theology were not clearly differentiated in the mind of Primitive Man, and with these physical ideas others, which we should call religious, were closely linked. The Stone which Descends from the Sky is a Powerful God. Nor is it regarded as lifeless after the Fall ; the Divine Power is still alive within it. Thus the Thunderstone is placed on an altar and worshipped with sacrifices, or at any rate is kept in a safe and secret place. The spot on which it has Fallen is regarded as having been chosen by the God for his abode, and therefore as being holy ground is not to be violated by the foot of Man or beast. [It is said that conical Meteorites of Cybil are stored in ancient catacombs under the Vatican before it was built to hide the old religion.]

The Thundergod is moreover regarded as the Most Powerful of all the Gods of Heaven and Earth, since the effects of his Anger are so Terrible and so Evident. [Originally Meteoric and evolved into Lightning and Thunder.]

The nature of the ideas themselves gives strong support to the view that they originated at a Very Early Period ; it is natural therefore that in historical times only scattered survivals should be found presenting a derived and remodeled form of the Thunderstone belief.

In eastern Asia, the Malay Archipelago and other places, the Thunderstone belief meets and combines with native ideas : the Thunder is produced by an Enormous Dragon, and the Thunderstones (i.e. the Stone Axes) are the Dragons Teeth.

In Babylonian art and throughout the whole region, the Lightning was depicted as the Heavenly Fire, a conception which also appears in Inscriptions. Thus Assurnasirpal says : "For two days I Thundered over them like the Thundergod Adad ; I made Flames of Fire to Rain Down Upon Them."

161

On the boundary-stones the Lightning is usually seen behind the Bull, which is the animal sacred to Adad. [Adad Bolt, Left and Dorje Bolt Right]

The priest of Tibet in certain religious ceremonies holds a bronze bell in his left and a bronze Dorje in his right hand. These instruments are employed in incantations, and a ritual representation of the act of coition is also performed. Several of the deities of Tibetan religious art carry the Dorje as an attribute. A Legend from Nepal relates how Buddha wrested the Thunderbolt from Indra in Battle ; the Weapon of Indra then reappears, on Tibetan soil, as the Dorje. The word Dorje etymologically means "the King of Stones," and There Can Hardly Be Any Doubt that the Thunderweapon of Metal in the Lamaistic cult is the successor of the Thunderstone, just as was probably the case in the cults of Hellenized Asia of the Keraunos. In Japan the Buddhist priests employ a very similar instrument, called the Ko.

In Homer, Poseidon the Earthshaker has recourse to his Trident when he Stirs Up All Nature : a Hurricane rages on All Sides ; land and sea are Hidden by Clouds ; the Gloom of Night Covers the Sky (Odyssey, V. 291) ;- when he Shivers the Rock (Odyssey, IV. 506) ; or when, with Apollo, he makes the Waterbrooks of Mount Ida Swell, and Scatters the Stones and Tree-Trunks which the Achaeans have laboriously joined to a wall round their camp (Illiad, XII. 27). Poseidon's conduct here is reminiscent of the Assyrian Storm-God "Adad the Mighty, who Overwhelmeth the regions of the Foe, Lands and Houses alike" (Tiglathpileser I.'s cylinder-inscription from Assur, about 1100 BC). If the Trident was originally a fishing spear it is remarkable that every trace of it as such has Disappeared so completely from ancient Epic poetry. The poet may indeed describe Men as "Speared like fishes" by beings of gigantic strength (Odyssey, X. 124) ; but neither fishes nor foes are anywhere Speared by Poseidon's Trident. The fact that

162

the Homeric poems never give us any really clear picture of the Trident and its use seems to prove that in the region to which the poems belonged it was Little Known or already Half Forgotten.

Thor's Hammer, the word Mjolnir means "Crusher."

It has long been said that the hiding of Mjolnir eight miles under the ground is a reminiscence of the idea associated with the Thunderstone belief that the Stone sank Deep into the Earth. [Hammers aren't thrown.]

The Thunderstones, according to popular belief, were Hurled from the Sky with the Lightning. [19th Century]

As to the Use made of Mjolnir in Making Compacts, it is still seen in the "Knocking Down" of Lots at Actions. [Judge's Gavel]

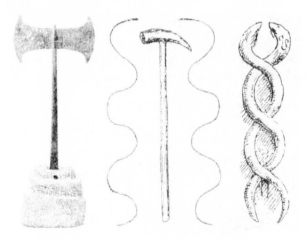

In the remote past the idea arose amongst the peoples of the old hemisphere that Lightning and Thunder were produced by the Descent of a Stone from Heaven to Earth. The Stone which Shot Down from the Heavens contained in itself the superhuman power manifested in the effect of the Lightning ; the Thunderstone in Fact was a Divine Being, Dangerous and Terrible, the object of Worship and of Fear.

In old Babylonian art and Picture-Writing Fire was represented by zigzag lines. [more like wavy] Hence arose a conventional representation of the Lightning in the form of two or three wavy lines joined together at the bottom. [Lightning is just the Opposite.] In this shape the Lightning became an object of worship and was placed as a Weapon in the hand of Adad, the

Babylonian Thundergod. As a cult-object the Lightning was made of some Hard Material, generally No Doubt of Metal, and in this form was carried East and West to those nations which came under the influence of the Babylonian civilization.

We have a number of communications to the effect that Stone Axes and other antiquities of the stone age have been found in graves together with burnt bones. This, if true, would serve as an illustration of the statement in the later Edda that Thor Consecrates Balder's Funeral Pyre with Mjolnir. [The Meteor/Comet Killed the Sun]

The popular belief is that whenever "the Thunder Strikes," a Thunderstone comes Down with the Lightning, Buries itself Seven fathoms Deep in the Earth, and gradually rises until it comes to the surface again in the Seventh year.

According to the Rig-Veda the Thunderbolt (Vajra) is Indra's usual Weapon in the Battle against his enemies ; he fashioned it himself or it was made by Tvashtar ; it has 1000 points, 100 edges, etc. Depending on the interpretation it is made of Iron, Copper, or Stone and the root of the name Vajra means Hard, Strong.

On Java "Thunder Teeth." [Dragon Teeth from Jason and the Argonauts.]

Gold Coast where the Akra Negros call them God-Axe or Axe-God.

Bronze Vortices Goat

164

The Serpent Symbol & the Worship of the Reciprocal Principle of Nature in America, by R. G. Squier, 1851

The Great annual festival, preceded by purifications, fastings, and the ceremonial of lighting the New Fire. The Festival of the First New Moon of Spring, in acknowledgment of the return of the reproductive influence, was attended by very rigorous rites. The participants bathed formally in some adjacent stream, and mortified themselves in various ways, drinking only of a certain bitter concoction designated the "black drink." In some instances they cut long gashes up and down their limbs with flints or fish-bones, a process which they call "scratching." The altar in the center of the national heptagon was constructed of a Conical Shape of fresh Earth. A circle was drawn around the top to receive the Fire of Sacrifice. Upon this was laid, ready for use, the inner bark of Seven different kinds of Trees. This bark was carefully chosen from the East side of the trees, and was clear and free from blemish. Near the close of the festival the sacrifices were made, with great solemnity. The day was devoted to fasting, even the infants were denied nourishment until afternoon ; adults until night. A short time before Sunset the people again assembled in the national heptagon. Near the altar, where the Fire had been kept burning all day, the white dressed buck, doe, and fawn skins had been replaced. The priest and his assistant now took their position to the Eastward of the Fire, facing East. Behind and about them stood the Seven prime counselors, in a semicircle. The priest raised the flowers of the old, wild tobacco from the buckskin, and flung them on the Fire. They emitted a very singular odor. After this, the priest having cut off the end of the tongue of the buck which had been brought in, put it into the Fire. Whilst burning it was eyed with intense attention, as everything relative thereto was deemed significant of Life or Death. The sacrifice being offered, the buck, which had been dressed whole, was cooked and placed

165

by itself. A kind of thick mush was made of newly pounded meal, to be eaten with it, and no other accompaniment was permitted. The meat was required to be so distributed as to give each person present some portion of it ; not a particle must be suffered to see the next morning ; all must be consumed. Other meat cooked for the occasion might be kept, but none of this. The night, only infants were allowed to sleep. The women passed most of it in the friendship dance. On the following morning the festival was considered at an end.

The kindling of the New Fire took place not long after the above Festival. The ceremonies were as follows. The day being fixed upon, early in the morning the Seven persons who were commissioned to kindle the Fire commenced their operations. One was the official Fire-Maker ; the remaining Six his assistants. A hearth was carefully cleared and prepared. A round hole being made in a block of wood, a small quantity of the dry Golden-Rod weed was placed in it. A stick, the end of which just fitted the opening, was whirled rapidly, until the weed took Fire. The Flame was then kindled on the hearth, and thence taken to every house, by the Women, who collectively waited for that purpose. The Old Fires having been everywhere extinguished, and the hearths cleansed, New Fires were Lighted throughout the country, and a sacrifice was made in each one of them of the First Meat Killed afterwards by those to whom they respectively belonged. The corresponding Festival of the Aztecs was celebrated in honor of Xiuhteuctli, God of Fire, "Master of the Year," whose wife or companion, Xochitli, was, as her name signifies, Goddess of the Earth and Corn, "she who supports us." To this deity were offered the First Fruits of the year ; and when they dined, the Mexicans made an offering to him of the first morsel of their food and the first draught of their drink, by throwing them into the Fire. This custom was also common amongst the North American tribes. The first festival in honor of Xiuteuctli was held in August ; on this occasion a large Tree was brought from the forest, and planted in the center of the area or court of the temple, which was regarded as the image of the God. The succeeding night was spent in dancing and singing about the Tree ; and next day the sacrifices, some of which were of human victims, were performed. The second festival in honor of Xiuhteuctli was in February ; the hunters then went out and brought in game, which was presented to the priests. Part was used in burnt offerings to the God, and the rest consumed by the people on this occasion the Fires in the temple and in all the private habitations were Extinguished and afterwards Rekindled by Friction, before the Image of the God. The accompanying engraving of the mode of lighting the New fire, amongst the Mexican, is copied from one of the ancient Mexican rituals.

The great Hermaphrodite first principle, in its character of unity, the supreme Monad, or Cnuphis, among the Egyptians. According to Plutarch, this God was without beginning and without end, the One, uncreated and eternal, above all, and comprehending all. And as Brahm, "the Self-existent Incorruptible" Unity of the Hindus, by the direction of His energetic will upon the Expanse of Chaos, "with a thought" (says Menu) produced a "Golden Egg, Blazing like a Thousand Stars," from which spring Brahma, the Creator ; so, according to the mystagogues, Kneph, the Unity of Egypt, was represented as a Serpent thrusting from his mouth an Egg, from which proceeds the divinity Phtha, the active, creative power, - equivalent, in all his attributes, to the Indian Brahma. In the Orphic Theogony a similar origin is ascribed to the Egg, from which springs the "Egg-born Protogones," the Greek counterpart of the Egyptian Phtha. The Egg in this instance also proceeds from the pre-eminent Unity, the Serpent God, the "Incomparable Cronus," or Hercules.

According to Maurice's Indostan and other authorities, the vivification of the Mundane Egg is allegorically represented in the Temple of Daibod, in Japan, by a vast Egg, which is shown floating in an expanse of Waters against which a Bull is Striking with his Horns. Near Lemisso, in the island of Cyprus, is still to be seen a gigantic Egg-shaped vase, which is supposed to represent the Mundane or Orphic Egg. It is of Stone, and measures thirty feet in circumference upon on side, in a semicircular niche, is sculpted a

167

Bull. According to Cory, the Egyptians symbolized one who governs all things by a Serpent ; for amongst them it is the spirit which Pervades the Universe.

Assuming for the entire structure a religious origin, it can be regarded only as the recognized symbol of some grand Mythological idea. What abstract conception was thus typically commemorated, we have no certain means of knowing.

The principle God of the Aztec pantheon was Tezcatlipoca, Tonacatlecoatl, or Tonacateuctli. If we consult the etymology of these names, we shall find ample confirmation of the correctness of the deductions already drawn from the Mythologies of the East. Thus, Tonacateuctli, embodied Lord Sun, from Tonatiuh, Sun, Nacayo, or Catl, body or person, and Teuctli, Master or Lord. When words are compounded, in the Mexican language, they first lose their final syllable or syllables. Thus, from Tepuztli, Iron, and Mecatl, Chain, we have Tepuzmecatl, Iron Chain, instead of Tepuztlimecatl. Again, Tonacatlcoatl, the Serpent Sun, from Tonatiah and Catl, as above, and Coatl, Serpent. If we adopt another etymology for the names we shall have Tonacateuctli, Lord of our Flesh, from To, the possessive pronoun plural, Nactl, flesh or body, and Teutli, Master or Lord. We shall also have Tonacatlecoatl, Serpent of our Flesh, from To and Nacatl, and Coatl, Serpent.

Like the other deities of Mexico, he bore a multitude of names, allusive to his various attributes. The name by which he was best known was Tezcatlipoca, which he is said first to have manifested himself to Man, Tlil, Dark, and Poca, Smoke. The explanation of this designation is best given in the accompanying engraving and explanation from the Codex Vaticanus.

"Tezcatlipoca, here represented, was one of their most potent deities ; they say he once appeared on the top of a Mountain called Tezcatepec, which signifies the Mountain of Mirrors. They paid him great reverence and adoration, and addressed him, in their prayers, with the appellation of Titlalahuan, which means, 'Lord whose servants we are.' They paint in his hands a sort of Weapon (the Xiuatlatli), together with a shield and quiver of arrows, and at his feet a Serpent and a heap of Fire, denoting that he is the creator of the elements. They believe him likewise to be the Originator of Wars. The old people say that those who entered where his idol stood, fell on their faces, and thus adored him ; and that they took a little Earth from the ground, which they swallowed with the greatest reverence, and

168

addressed him, 'Lord, since we are thy servants, grant us that which we may need.'"

The small curved outlines surrounding the central figure are the signs or Hieroglyphics of Smoke. From the left foot proceeds a Serpent, and also the signs of Fire and Water. The face is represented covered with a mask of itzli, Obsidian, or, as it was called in Mexico, Teoitzli, "Divine Stone." No Man ever saw the face of Tezcatlipoca, for, says Sahagun, he appeared only "as a Shade." Indeed the Mexican idea of the Godhead was similar to that of the Jews. Like Jehovah, Tezcatlipoca dwelt in the "midst of Thick Darkness." This idea gave rise to his name, "Yoalliehecatl," "obscurity and air," or wind. Thus the first prayer in the sixth book of Sahagun commences, "O valiant Lord, beneath whose Wings we shelter and defend ourselves, and find protection, thou art invisible and impalpable, even as night and air." When he Descended upon the mount of Tezcatepec, Darkness Overshadowed the Earth, while Fire and Water, in mingled Streams, flowed from beneath his feet, from its summit. The accessories of his descent combined all the elements of the Grand and Terrible. "Before him went the Pestilence, and Burning Coals went forth at his feet." "He made Darkness his secret place ; his pavilion round about him were Dark Waters and Thick Clouds passed, Hail Stones and Coals of Fire."

They believed Tezcatlipoca to possess every perfection with which human imagination could invest the Deity ; they represented him as 'merciful and long-suffering,' and yet the 'Stirrer Up of Strife,' and the 'Giver of Life,' yet he required the blood of sacrifices to flow for ever on his altars ; he pardoned the guilty only in consideration of the blood of the innocent ; he was the Supreme Unity, yet he had associates in the government of the Universe. That the unity of Tezcatlipoca formed an essential article in the Mexican creed, is undoubted ; yet their belief in that unity was not inconsistent, it would appear, with their acknowledging, like the Jews, a plurality of Gods, and sinking into the grossest excesses of idolatry. The above unity is unequivocally declared in the following passage of the third chapter and sixth book of Sahagun, when the Mexican high priest addressed Tezcatlipoca as the God of Armies or of Hosts ; 'I entreat of thy majesty, who art our invincible emperor, that it may be thy good pleasure that those who die in this War may be received with compassion and with love by our father the Sun and our mother the Earth, for thou alone reignest and art our God.'

We have seen that the Stone Itzli, or Obsidian, was sacred to Tezcatlipoca, and was thence called "Divine Stone." The true image of this God was made of this Stone, and the respect in which it was held recalls to the mind of the inquirer the veneration with which the Assyrians regarded the God Baal, or Helagabal (the Sun), whose image was a Conical Black Stone, (Lingham?) which it was believed had Fallen from Heaven into the sanctuary of the Temple at Emesa, the ancient Hamath. It was afterwards taken to Rome by the Emperor, Marcus Aurelius Antoninus II., who devoted himself to its worship. The Black Stone in the sanctuary of the Caaba, will occur to the intelligent reader in this connection.

It is a plan of the Temple of the Great Serpent of Avebury, England. This temple is situated upon the downs of Wiltshire, twenty-six miles northward from the celebrated ruins of Stonehenge, and is one of the most imposing, as it certainly is one the most interesting, monuments of the British Islands. The temple of Avebury consisted originally of a Grand Circumvallation of Earth, 1400 feet in diameter, enclosing an area of upwards of twenty-two acres. It has an inner ditch, and the height of the embankment, measuring from the bottom of the ditch, is seventeen feet. It is quite regular, though not an exact circle in form, and has four entrances placed at unequal distances apart, though nearly at right angles to each other. Within this grand circle were originally two double or concentric circles, composed of massive upright Stones : a row of large Stones, one hundred in number, was placed upon the inner brow of the ditch. Extending upon either hand from this grand central structure, were parallel lines of huge upright Stones, constituting, upon each side, avenues upwards of a mile in length. These formed the body of the Serpent. Each avenue consisted of two hundred Stones. The Head of the Serpent was represented by an oval structure, consisting of two concentric lines of upright Stones ; the outer line containing forty, the inner eighteen stones. This head rests on an eminence known as Overton or Hakpen Hill, from which is commanded a view of the entire structure, winding back for more than two miles to the point of the Tail, towards Bekhampton. [Today Obscurely Known and half the Stones.]

It is said that in the ritual of Zoroaster, not only were Serpents esteemed the first Gods and the superintendents of the World, but the great expanse of Heaven and even nature itself were described under the symbol of a Serpent. Certain it is that in the earlier monuments of Assyria, antedating the Persian empire, we find evidences of the adoration paid to the Serpent. But perhaps the most remarkable application of the Serpent symbol, in that quarter of the world, and which has its counterpart in Egypt, is its combination with the

170

Circle, Egg, or Globe, and Wings. This Hierogram seems to have been Allusive to the loftiest religious conceptions of the nations by whom it was adopted. This compound symbol demonstrates the high position which the Serpent symbol occupied in the symbolical systems of the earliest historical ages of the World. In Egypt it appears upon every temple, and upon almost every monument, and has generally been regarded as an emblem of consecration. The monuments of Nineveh are also fruitful in representations of this symbol, which is regarded by Mr. Layard as, in some way, allusive to the Sun, and its powers. [The Bolide / Comet.]

I am convinced that there is a Deeper Significance concealed beneath it than has yet been explained ; and that a further study of the primitive religions of the East will yet throw much new light upon its meaning. The fact that the crux ansata, the Taautic sign of Life, is sometimes dependent from the Necks of the Serpents, should not be overlooked in attempting its solution. [The Serpent can Strike or Pass Over , Life or Death, Sun or Darkness]

The Evolution of the Dragon, by G. Elliot Smith, 1919

Frankincense and other Spices were Indispensable in temples where Bloody Sacrifices form part of the religion. The atmosphere of Solomon's Temple must have been that of a sickening slaughter-house, and the fumes of incense could alone enable the priests and worshippers to support it. This would apply to thousands of other temples through Asia, and doubtless the places of kings and nobles suffered from uncleanliness and insanitary arrangements and required an antidote to evil smells to make them endurable.

171

Neither the ethnologist nor the priestly apologist will, as a rule, admit that he does not know why such ritual acts as pouring out water or burning incense are performed, and that they are wholly Inexplicable and Meaningless to him. Nor will they confess that the real inspiration to perform such rites is the fact of their predecessors having handed them down as sacred acts of devotion, the meaning of which has been Entirely Forgotten during the process of Transmission from Antiquity. Instead of this they simply pretend that the significance of such acts is obvious. Stripped of the glamour which religious emotion and sophistry have woven around them, such pretend explanations become transparent subterfuges, none the less real because the apologist are quite innocent of any conscious intention to deceive either themselves or their disciples. It should be sufficient for them that such ritual acts have been handed down by Tradition as right and proper things to do. But in response to the instinctive impulse of all human beings, the Mind Seeks for Reasons in justification of actions of which the real inspiration is Unknown.

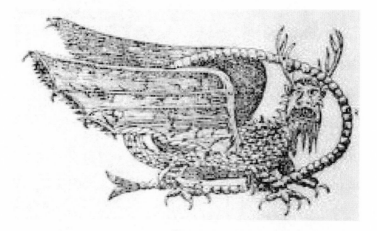

The 'Piasa' Rock, as is generally designated, was referred to by the missionary explorer Marquette in 1675. Its situation was immediately above the city of Alton, Illinois. On the flat face of a high rock were painted, in red, black, and green, a Pair of Monsters, each as large as a calf, with Horns like a Deer, Red eyes, a Beard like a Tiger, and a frightful expression of countenance. The face is something like a Man, the body covered with Scales ; and the Tail so long that it passes entirely round the body, over the head, and between the legs, ending like that of a Fish. Mr. Mc Adams, of Alton, Illinois, says, "The name Piasa is Indian and signifies, in the Illini, "The Bird Which Devours Men.""

172

The Dragon in China "is the Heavenly giver of fertilizing rain." In the Shu King "the emblematic figures of the ancients are given as the Sun, the Moon, the Stars, The Mountain, the Dragon, and the variegated animals (Pheasants) which are depicted on the upper sacrificial garment of the Emperor."

The Dragon sheds a Brilliant Light at night, usually from his Glittering Eyes. He is the giver of omens, good and bad, rains and Floods. The Dragon-Horse is a vital spirit of Heaven and Earth and also of River Water.

The ecclesiastical vestments of the Wu-ist priests are endowed with magical properties which are considered to enable the wearer to control the order of the World, to avert unseasonable and calamitous events, such as drought, untimely and superabundant rainfall, and eclipses. These powers are conferred by the decoration upon the dress. Upon the back of the chief vestment the representation of a range of Mountains is embroidered as a symbol of the World : on each (the right and left) of it a large Dragon arises above the billows to represent the fertilizing rain. They are surrounded by Gold-Thread figures representing clouds and Spirals typifying Rolling Thunder. A Ball, sometimes with a Spiral decoration, is commonly represented in Front of the Chinese Dragon. The Chinese writer Koh Hung tells us that "a Spiral denotes the Rolling of Thunder from which issues a Flash of Lightning. The Chinese Triquetrum, i.e., the well-known three-comma shaped figure, the Japanese Luitsu-Tonioe, the ancient spiral, represents Thunder also. Which involves the consideration of the almost World-Wide belief in a Thunder-Weapon and its relationship to the Spiral ornament, the Octopus.

It is still the custom in many places, and among them especially the religion near the headwaters of the Nile itself, to regard the king or rain-maker as the impersonation of the life-giving properties of water and the source of all fertility. When his own vitality shows signs of failing he is killed, so as not to endanger the fruitfulness of the community by allowing one who is weak in life-giving powers to control its destinies. Much of the evidence relating to these matters has been collected by Sir James Frazer in "The Dying God," 1911, who quotes from Dr. Seligman the following account of the Dinka "Osiris" : "While the mighty spirit Lerpiu is supposed to be embodied in the rain-maker, it is also thought to inhabit a certain hut which serves as a shine. In front of the hut stands a post to which are fastened the Horns of many Bullocks that have been sacrificed to Lerpiu ; and in the hut is kept a very Sacred Spear which bears the name of Lerpiu ; and is said to

173

have Fallen from Heaven Six generations ago. As fallen Stars are also called Lerpiu, we may suspect that an Intimate Connexion is supposed to exist between Meteorites and the Spirit which animates the Rain-Maker" (Frazer). Here then we have a house of the Dead inhabited by Lerpiu, who can also enter the body of the ram-maker and animate him, as well as the ancient Spear and the Falling Stars, which are also animate forms of the same God, who obviously is the homologue of Osiris, and is identified with the Spear and the Falling Stars. In spring when the April Moon is a few days old Bullocks are sacrificed to Lerpiu. "Two Bullocks are led twice [Seven times] round the shrine and after wards tied by the ram-maker to the post in front of it. Then the Drums beat and the people, old and young, Men and Women, dance round the shrine and sing, while the beasts are being sacrificed. 'Lerpiu, our ancestor, we have brought you a sacrifice. Be pleased to cause rain to fall.'

Note: They don't want Hathor to Fall.

The Egyptians entertained the belief that the Sun-God was born of the Celestial Cow Mehetweret, a name which means "Great Flood," and is equivalent of the primeval Ocean Nun. In other words the Celestial Cow Hathor, the embodiment of the Life-Giving Waters of Heaven and Earth, is the mother of Horus. So also Aphrodite was born of the "Great Flood" which is the Ocean.

174

The story of the "Destruction of Mankind" was re-edited, and Hathor was called the "Eye of Ra." In the earlier versions she was called into consultation solely as the giver of Life and, to obtain the Life-Blood, she cut Men's throats with a knife. But as the Eye of Ra she was identified with the Fire-Spitting Uraeus – Serpent which the king or God wore on his forehead. She was both the Moon and the Fiery Bolt which Shot Down from, the Sky to Slay the enemies of Ra. For the Men who were originally slaughtered to provide the blood for the elixir now became the enemies of Ra. The reason for this was that, human sacrifice having been abandoned and substitutes provided to replace the human blood, the story-teller was at a loss to know why the Goddess killed Mankind. A reason had to be found – and the rationalization adopted was that Men had to be against the Gods and had to be killed. This interpretation was probably the result of a Confusion with the Old Legend of the Fight between Horus and Set, the rulers of the two kingdom of Egypt. The possibility also suggests itself that a pun made by some priestly jester may have been the real factor that led to this mingling of two originally separate stories.

In the "Destruction of Mankind" the story runs, according to Budge, that Ra, referring to his enemies, said : ma-ten set udr er set, "Behold ye them (Set) fleeing into the Mountain (Set)." The enemies were thus identified with the Mountain or Stone and with Set, the enemy of the Gods." In Egyptian Hieroglyphics the symbol for Stone is used as the determinative for Set. When the "Eye of Ra" Destroyed Mankind and the rebels were thus identified with the followers of Set, they were regarded as creatures of "Stone." In other words the Medusa-Eye petrified the enemies. From this feeble pun on the part of some ancient Egyptian scribe has arisen the World-Wide stories of the influence of the "Evil Eye" and the petrifaction of the enemies of the Gods." As the name for Isis in Egyptian is "Set" it is possible that the confusion of the Power of Evil with the Great Mother may also have been facilitated by an extension of the same pun. It is important to recognize that the Legend of Hathor descending from the Moon or the Sky in the form of Destroying Fire had nothing whatever to do with the first instance, with the phenomena of Lightning and Meteorites. It was the result of verbal quibbling after the Destructive Goddess came to be identified with the Moon, the Sky and the "Eye of Ra." But once the Evolution of the story on these lines prepared the way, it was inevitable that in later times the powers of Destruction exerted by the Fire Horn the Sky should have been identified with the Lightning and Meteorites. When the Destructive Force of the Heavens was attributed to the "Eye of Ra" and the God's enemies were identified with the followers of Set, it was natural that the Traditional enemy of Set who was also The More Potent Other "EYE OF RA" should assume his mother's role of Punishing Rebellious Mankind. That Horus did in fact take the place at first occupied by Hathor in the story is revealed by the series of trivial episodes from the "Destruction of Mankind" that reappear in the "Saga of the Winged Disk." The Winged Disk was at once the Instrument of Destruction and the God Himself. It Swooped (or Flew) Down from Heaven like a Bolt of Destroying Fire and Killed the enemies of Ra.

The original "Boat of the Sky" was the crescent Moon, which, from its likeness to the earliest form of Nile Boat, was regarded as the vessel in which the Moon (seen as a faint object upon the crescent), or the Goddess who was supposed to be personified in the Moon, travelled across the Waters of the Heavens. [More likely the Vehicle of the Waters above.]

The history of the Thunder-Weapon cannot wholly be ignored in discussing the Dragon –Myth because it forms an integral part of the story. It was Animated Both by the Dragon and the Dragon-Slayer.

Thus we have arrived at the stage where, by a distortion of a series of Phases, the new incident emerges that by means of a human sacrifice the Nile Flood can be produced. By a further confusion the Goddess, who originally did the slaughter, becomes the victim. Hence the story assumed the form that by means of the sacrifice of a beautiful and attractive maiden the animal of Inundation can be produced. As the most potent symbol of Life-Giving it is essential that the victim should be sexually attractive, i.e. that she should be a virgin and the most beautiful and desirable in the land. "When the practice of human sacrifice was abandoned a figure or an animal was substituted for the maiden in ritual practice, and in Legends the hero rescued the maiden, as Andromeda was saved from the Dragon. The Dragon is the personification of the Monsters that Dwell in the Waters as well as the Destructive Forces of the Flood Itself. But the Monsters were no other than the followers of Set ; they were the victims of the slaughter who became identified with the God's other Traditional enemies, the followers of Set. Thus the Monster from whom Andromeda is rescued is merely another representative of herself ! But the Destructive Forces of the Flood now enter into the programme. In the phases we have so far discussed it was the slaughter of Mankind which Caused the Inundation : but in the next phase it is the Flood itself which Causes the Destruction, as in the later Egyptian and the Borrowed Sumerian, Babylonian, Hebrew – and in fact the World-Wide-Versions. [Most Probable a Global Event Seen By All] Ra's boat becomes the ark ; the winged disk which was dispatched by Ra from the boat becomes the Dove and the other Birds sent out to spy the land, as the Winged Horus spied the enemies of Ra. Thus the new Weapon of the Gods – we have already noted Hathor's knife and Horus's Winged Disk, which is The Fire from Heaven, the Lightning and the Thunderbolt – is the Flood. Like the others it can be either a beneficent giver of Life or a Force of Destruction. But the Flood also becomes a weapon of another kind. One of the earlier incidents of the story represents Hathor in opposition to Ra. The Goddess becomes so Madden with the Zest of Killing that the God becomes alarmed and asks her to desist and spare some representatives of the Race. But she is deaf to entreaties. Hence the God is said to have sent to Elephantine for the Red Ochre to make a Sedative draught to overcome her destructive zeal.

In China the Dragon was sometimes called "The Celestial Stag." The composite animal of Ea-Marduk, the "Sea-Goat" (the Capricornus of the Zodiac), was also the vehicle of Varuna in India, whose relationship to Indra was in some respects analogous to that of Ea to Marduk in Babylon. The Indian "Sea-Goat" or Makara was in fact intimately associated both with Varuna and with Indra. This Monster assumed a great variety of forms [Shapeshifters], such as the crocodile, the dolphin, the Sea-Serpent or Dragon, or combinations of the heads of different animals with a Fish's body.

In his Hibbert Lectures Professor Sayce claimed that the name of Ea was expressed by an Ideograph which signifies literally 'the Antelope.'

In Africa the Dragon role of the female Antelope may be assumed by the Cow or Buffalo. In the case of the Gods Soma and Dionysus their association with the Antelope or Deer may be extended to the Bull. Miss Davis states that in the Homa Yasht the Deer-headed lunar mansion over which the God Pleiades is spoken of as "leading the Paurvas," i.e. Pleiades : "Mazda brought to thee (Homa) the Star-Studded Spirit-Fashioned Girdle (the Belt of Orin) leading the Paurvas. Now the Bull-Dionysus was

177

especially Associated with the Pleiades on ancient gems and in classical Mythology – which form part of the sign Taurus." The Bull is a sign of Haoma (Homa) or Soma. The Belt of the Thunder-God Thor corroborates the fact of the diffusion of these Babylonian Ideas as far as Northern Europe.

Having invested the numbers four and twenty-eight with special sanctity and brought them into association with the measurement of four parts and so being the number Seven in to the Sacred Scheme. Once this was done the Moon's phases were used to justify and rationalize this procedure, and the length of the week was incidentally brought into association with the Moon-Goddess, who had Seven avatars, perhaps originally one for each day of the week. At a later period the number Seven was arbitrarily brought into relationship with the Pleiades. [Inverse]

The Seven Hathors were not only mothers but fates also. Aphrodite was chief of the fates. The number Seven is associated with the pots used by Hathor's priestesses at the celebration inaugurated the New Year ; and it plays a prominent part in the story of the Flood. In Babylonia the sanctity of the number received special recognition. When the Goddess became the Destroyer of Mankind, the device seems to have been adopted of intensifying her powers of Destruction by representing her at times as Seven Demons.

Aphrodite as the Thunder-Stone. As a surrogate of the Great Mother, the Eye of Ra, the Thunder-Weapon was also identified with any of her varied manifestations. The Thunderbolt is one of the manifestation of the Life-Giving and Death-Dealing Divine Cow, and therefore is able specially to protect mundane Cows."

There are numerous hints in the ancient literature of other countries in confirmation of the association of the Great Mother with "Falling Stars." In a Fragment of Sanchoniathon, Astarte, travelling about the habitable World, is said to have found a Star Falling through the air which she took up and consecrated. Aphrodite also was looked upon as a Meteoritic Stone that Fell from the Moon. In the "Iliad," Zeus is said to have sent Athena as a Meteorite from Heaven to Earth.

The close association of the Ram with the Thunder-God is probably related with the fact that the Sun-God Amon in Egypt was represented by the Ram with a distinctive Spiral Horn. This Spiral became a distinctive feature of the God of Thunder throughout the Hellenic and Phoenician Worlds and in

178

those parts of Africa which were affected by their influence or directly by Egypt. But the Ram also became associated with Agni, the Indian Fire-God, and the Spiral as a head-appendage became the symbol of Thunder throughout China and Japan. The Myth of the Celestial drink Soma, brought down from Heaven by a Bird ordinarily called Cyetta, "Eagle," is parallel to that of Agni, the Celestial Fire brought by Mataricvan. This parallelism is even expressly stated in the Rig Veda, verse 6 of hymn 1 to Agni and Soma. Mataricvan brought the one from Heaven, the Eagle brought the other from the Celestial Mountain. The octopus as a surrogate of the Great Mother was primarily responsible for the development of the life-giving attributes of the Spiral motif. But the close Connexion of the Great Mother with the Dragon and the Thunder-Weapon prepared the way for the special association of the Spiral with Thunder, which was confirmed when the Ram with its Spiral Horn became the God of Thunder.

Set, the enemy of Osiris, who is the real prototype of the Evil Dragon, was the antithesis of the God of Justice : he was the father of Falsehood and the symbol of Chaos. He was the Prototype of Satan, as Osiris was the first definite representative of the Deity of which any record has been preserved. The history of the Evil Dragon is not merely the Evolution of the Devil. But it also affords the explanation of his Traditional peculiarities, his Bird-like features, his Horns, his Red Colour, his Wings and Cloven Hoofs, and his Tail. They are All of Them the Dragon's Distinctive features ; and from time to time in history of past ages we catch glimpses of the reality of these identifications. In one of the earliest woodcuts found in a printed book Satan is depicted as a monk with the Bird's Feet of the Dragon.

A most interesting intermediate phase is seen in a Chinese water-colour in the John Rylands Library, in which the Thunder-Dragon is represented in a form Almost Exactly reproducing that of the Devil of European Tradition. Early in the Christian era, when ancient beliefs in Egypt became disguised under a thin veneer of Christianity, the story of the conflict between Horus and Set was Converted into a conflict between Christ and Satan. But the Biblical references to Satan leave no doubt as to his identity with the Dragon, who is specifically mentioned in the book of Revelations as "the Old Serpent, which is the Devil and Satan." (XX : 2) The Devil Set was symbolic of Disorder and Darkness, while the God Osiris was the Maintainer of Order and the giver of Light alike Shamash as the All Seeing Judge of the Sun. The creation of a beneficent deity of such moral grandeur inevitably emphasized the baseness and the malevolence of the "Power of Evil." No longer are the Gods merely glorified human beings who can work good or evil as they will ; but there is now an All-Powerful God Controlling the Morals of the Universe, and in Opposition to Him "the Dragon, the Old Serpent, which is the Devil and Satan."

As the Great Mother became confused with the pestle, so, the Soma-plant, whose stalks are Crushed by the priests to make the Soma-libation, becomes in the Vedas itself the Crusher or Smiter, by a very characteristic and frequent Oriental conceit in accordance with which the agent and the person or thing acted on are identified. The Pressing-Stones by means of which Soma is Crushed typify Thunderbolts. In the Egyptian story the God Ra instructed the Sekti of Heliopolis to pound the materials for the food of immortality. In the Indian version, the Gods aware of their mortality, desired to discover some elixir which would make them immortal. To this end, Mount Meru (the Great Mother) was cast into the Sea (of milk), Vishnu, in his second avatar as a tortoise, supported the Mountain on his back ; and the Naga Serpent Vasuki was then Twisted Around the Mountain until they had churned the amrita or Water of life, Wilfrid Jackson has called attention to the fact that this scene has been depicted, not only in India and Japan, but also in the Pre-Columbian Codex Cortes drawn by some Maya artist in Central America.

The mystical potency attaching to certain numbers doubtless originated in associations of thought that to us are obscure. The number Seven, in Egyptian magic, was regarded as particularly efficacious. Thus we find references to the Seven Hathors, the Seven daughters of Ra, who stand and weep and make Seven knots in their Seven tunics, and similarly, the Seven hawks who are in front of the barque of Ra.

The Star Sothis rose helically on the first day of the Egyptian New Year. Hence it became "the Second Sun in Heaven," and was identified with the Goddess of the New Year's Day [Pleiades]. The identification of Hathor with this "Second Sun," may explain why the Goddess is said to have entered Ra's Boat. She took her place as a crown upon his forehead, which afterwards was assumed by her surrogate, the Fire-Spitting Uraneus-Serpent. When Horus took his mother's place in the Myth, he also entered the Sun-God's boat, and became the prototype of Noah seeking refuge from the Flood in the ship the Almighty instructed him to make. In memory of the beer-drinking episode in the Destruction of Mankind, New Year's Day was celebrated by Hathor's priestesses in wild orgies of beer drinking. This event was necessarily the earliest celebration of an anniversary, and the prototype of all the incidents associated with some special day in the year which have been so many milestones in the historical progress of civilization. The first measurement of the year also naturally forms the starting point in the farming of a calendar.

181

The Babylonian Tiamat was originally as a Huge Serpent and throughout the World the Serpent is pre-eminently a symbol of the Evil Dragon and the Powers of Evil. The Serpent that tempted Eve was the homologue both of the mother of Mankind herself and also of the Tree of Paradise. It was the representative of the Dragon-protector of Pearls and of other kinds of treasure : it was also the Goddess who animated the Sacred Tree as well as the protector who attacked all who approached it. It was the Evil Dragon that tempted Eve to eat of the forbidden fruit which brought her Mortality.

The question naturally arises : what is a Myth ? The Dragon-Myth of the West is the religion of China. The Literature of Every Religion is Saturated with the Influence of the Myth. In what respect does Religion differ from Myth ? Originally Science and Religion were Not Differentiated. Both were the outcome of Man's attempt to peer into the meaning of Natural Phenomena, and to extract from such Knowledge Practical Measures for Circumventing Fate. His ever-insistent aim was to Combat Danger to Life. Religion was differentiated from Science when the measures for controlling Fate became invested with the assurance of Supernatural Help, for which the growth of a knowledge of natural phenomena made it impossible for the mere scientist to be the sponsor. It became a question of Faith rather than Knowledge ; and Man's instinctive struggle against the risk of Extinction impelled him to cling to this larger hope of salvation, and to embellish it with an ethical and moral significance which at first was lacking in the eternal search for the elixir of Life. If religion can be regarded as archaic science enriched with the belief in supernatural control, the Myth can be regarded as effete religion which has been superseded by the growth of a loftier ethical purpose. The Myth is to Religion what Alchemy is to Chemistry or Astrology is to Astronomy. Like these sciences, religion retains much of the material of the cruder phase of thought that is displayed in Myth, alchemy, and astrology, but it has been refined and elaborated. The dross has been to a large extent eliminated, and the pure metal has been molded into a more beautiful and attractive form. In searching for the elixir of Life, the makers of religion have discovered the Philosophers Stone, and with its aid have transmitted the base materials of Myth into the Gold of Religion. If we seek for the Deep motives which have prompted Men in all ages so persistently to search for the elixir of Life, for some means of Averting the Dangers to which their Existence is Exposed, it will be found in the instinct of Self-Preservation, which is the fundamental factor in the behavior of all living beings, the means of preservation of the Life which is their distinctive attribute and the very essence of their being. The Dragon was originally a concrete expression of the Divine Powers of Life-Giving ; but with the development of a higher conception of religious ideals it became relegated to a baser role, and eventually became the symbol of the Powers of Evil. [Spaces Falls are Spectacular and also Dangerous.]

The Mysteries of Mithra, by Franz Cumont, 1900

Sacrifices to Mithra were Bovines and Flying Birds and performed in a Cave [Dark]. According to the Mithraic theory, Wheat and Vine sprang from the spinal cord and the blood of the Sacrificed Bull. [Kill the Meteor Stream and Verdure Returns.] Mithraic Kronos Representing Boundless Time. 190 AD The figure is entirely nude, the body being entwined six times by a Serpent, the head of which rests on the skull of the God. Four Wings decorated with the symbols of the Seasons issue from the back. Each hand holds a Key, and the right in addition a Long Scepter, the symbol of authority. A Thunderbolt is on the breast and on the base of the statue may be seen the Hammer and Tongs of Vulcan, the Cock and the pine-cone. The keys symbolize the monarch of the Heavens whose Portals he Opens. Head of a Lion. [Also the Caduceus Representing the Bolide.]

The clergy reserved for the Elite Exclusively the Revelation of the Original Mazdean Doctrines concerning the Origin and Destiny of Man and the World, whilst the multitude were forced to remain content with the Brilliant and Superficial Symbolism Inspired by the Speculations of the Chaldeans. The Astronomical Allegories Concealed from the Curiosity of the Vulgar the Real Scope of the Hieratic Representations, and the promise of complete illumination, long withheld, fed the ardor of faith with the Fascinating Allurements of Mystery.

Each of the planetary bodies presided over a day of the week, to each someone metal was consecrated, each was associated with someone degree in the initiation, and their number has caused a special religious potency to be attributed to the number Seven. [Pleiades forgotten and planets usurped.]

The planets and the Signs of the Zodiac never ceased to preserve their Icon Testable Primacy, for It Was They above all others, According to the Astrologers, that Controlled the Existence of Men and Guided the Course of Things. Mythology and Erudition were everywhere mingled. This was the capital doctrine that Babylon introduced into Mazdaism : belief in Fatality, the conception of an Inevitable Destiny controlling the events of this World and Inseparably Conjoined with the Revolution of the Starry Heavens.

The ancient Iranian Legend is lost, but the bas-relief recount certain episodes of it, and its contents appear to have been somewhat as follows : The Light Bursting from the Heavens, which were conceived as a solid vault, became, in the Mythology of the Magi, Mithra born from the Rock. The Tradition ran that the "Generative Rock," of which a standing image was worshipped in the temples, had given birth to Mithra on the banks of a River, under the Shade of a Sacred Tree, and that shepherds alone, ensconced in a neighboring Mountain, had Witnessed the Miracle of his Entrance onto the World. They had seen him Issue Forth from the Rocky Mass, his head adorned with a Phrygian cap, Armed with a Knife, and carrying a Torch that had Illuminated the Somber Depth Below.

Worshipfully the shepherds drew near, offering the divine infant the first fruits of their flock and their harvests. But the young hero was naked and exposed to the Winds that Blew with Violence : he had concealed himself in the branches of a fig-Tree, and detaching the fruit from the tree with the aid of his Knife, he ate of it, and stripping it of its leaves he made himself garments. Thus equipped for Battle, he was able henceforward to measure his strength with the other powers that peopled the Marvelous World into

184

which he had entered. For although the shepherds were pasturing their flocks when he was born, all these things came to pass before there were Men on Earth. The God with whom Mithra first measured his strength was the Sun. The latter was compelled to render homage to the superiority of his rival and to receive from him his investiture. His conqueror placed upon his head the Radiant Crown that he has borne in his Daily course ever since his Downfall. Then he caused him to Rise Again, and extending to him his right hand concluded with him a solemn covenant of friendship. And ever after, the two allied heroes faithfully supported each other in all their enterprises.

The most extraordinary of these epic adventures was Mithra's combat with the Bull, the first living creature created by Ormazd. This ingenious fable carries us back to the Very Beginning of Civilization. . . . The redoubtable Bull was grazing in a pasture on the Mountain-side ; the hero, resorting to a bold stratagem, seized it by the Horns and succeeded in mounting it. The infuriated quadruped, breaking into a gallop, struggled in vain to free itself from its rider ; the latter, although unseated by the Bull's Mad Rush, never for a moment relaxed his hold ; he suffered himself to be dragged along, suspended from the Horns of the animal, which, finally exhausted by its efforts, was forced to surrender. Its conqueror then seized it by its hind hoofs, dragged it backwards over a road strewn with obstacles into the Cave which served as his home.

This painful Journey (Transitus) of Mithra became the symbol of human sufferings. But the Bull, it would appear, succeeded in making its escape from its prison, and Roaming Again at large over the Mountain Pastures. The Sun then sent the Raven [death], his messenger, to carry to his ally the command to Slay the fugitive. Mithra received this cruel mission much against his will, but submitting to the decree of Heaven he pursued the Truant Beast with his agile dog, succeeded in overtaking it just at the moment when it was taking refuge in the Cave which it had quitted, and seizing it by the nostrils with one hand, with the other he plunged deep into its flank his hunting-knife.

Then came an extraordinary prodigy to pass. From the body of the moribund victim sprang all the useful herbs and plants that cover the Earth with their Verdure. From the spinal cord of the animal sprang the wheat that gives us our bread, and from its blood the vine that produces the sacred drink of the Mysteries. In vain did the Evil Spirit launch forth his unclean demons against the anguish-wrung animal, in order to Poison in it the very sources

185

of Life ; the scorpion, the ant, the Serpent, strove in vain to consume the genital parts and to drink the blood of the prolific quadruped ; but they were powerless to impede the Bull, gathered and purified by the Moon, produced all the different species of useful animals, and its soul, under the protection of the dog, the faithful companion of Mithra, ascended into the Celestial spheres above, where, receiving the honors of divinity, it became under the name of Silvanus the guardian of herds. Thus, through the sacrifice which he had so resignedly undertaken, the Tauroctonous hero became the Creator of all the beneficent beings on Earth ; and, from the Death which he had Caused, was born a New Life, more rich and more Fecund than the old. [Orion fighting Taurus with his Dog Sirius.]

Meanwhile, the first human couple had been called into Existence, and Mithra was charged with keeping a watchful eye over this privileged race. It was in vain the Spirit of Darkness invoked his Pestilential scourges to Destroy it ; the God always knew how to balk his mortiferous designs. Ahriman first desolated the land by causing a protracted Drought, and its inhabitants, Tortured by Thirst, implored the aid of his ever-victorious adversary. The divine archer discharged his Arrows against a Precipitous Rock, and there Gushed forth from it a Spring of Living Water [Spewing Geyser from the Sky Mountain] to which the suppliants thronged to cool their parched palates. But still more Terrible Cataclysm followed, which menaced All Nature. A Universal Deluge depopulated the Earth, which was overwhelmed by Waters of the Rivers and the Seas. One Man alone, secretly advised by the Gods, had constructed a Boat and had saved himself, together with his Cattle, in an Ark which floated on the broad expanse of Waters. Then a Great Conflagration Ravaged the World and consumed utterly both the habitations of Men and of Beasts. But the creatures of Ormazd also ultimately escaped this new peril, thanks to Celestial protection, and henceforward the human race was permitted to wax great and multiply in peace.

The Angel-Messiah of Buddhists, Essences & Christians, by Ernest Von Bunsen, 1880

Sidereal Religion prevailed in Mesopotamia before the invention of writing, since the earliest symbol of a deity known to us was a Star. Thus the deity Sibut, probably connected with the Pleiades, is determined by a Star with the number Seven by its side. The name Osiris, derived from Wasar, means the elevated one or 'the Highest,' like the name Zeus of Homer and

186

Hyperion of Hesiodus. All the names of divinities can be connected, like Sibut-Sebaot, with the Pleiades, so that the 'Sevening' of Abram may be referred to the God dwelling in this Constellation of Seven Stars. The comparison of the most ancient calendars known to us has led Mr. E. G. Haliburton, of Nova Scotia, to prove, that a New Year's Festival connected with and determined by the Pleiades was, by almost universal custom, and partly in times called Pre-Historic, connected with a three days' Festival of the Dead. It corresponded with the Christian festivals of All Saints and All Souls, at the beginning of November, and was preceded in some countries by a Holy Evening or Halloween. At first it was the appearance of the Pleiades at Sunset, later their culmination at Midnight, which determined the commencement of the year. According to the calendar of the Brahmans of Tirvalore the year began in November, and the First Month was called after the Pleiades Cartiguey or Krittikas. The later name Weber has shown to mean 'the Associates,' those who are Bound Together, the Heap, whilst the Hebrew word for the Pleiades, Kimah, has exactly the same meaning.

Also, the first of the Naxatras, of the stellar houses or stations of the Moon, was marked by the Pleiades. This Indian year, determined by the Pleiades, began with the 17th of November, approximative at the time of the Pleiades culminating at Midnight, and this commencement of the year was celebrated by the Hindu Durga, a Festival of the Dead. Mr. Haliburton has shown that on the 17th of November, or Atliyr – the Athyr of the Egyptians and Atauria of the Arabs – the Three Days Feast of the Isia took place, which culminated in the finding of Osiris, the Lord of Tombs, evidently contemporaneously with the Culmination of the Pleiades, at Midnight. It was on that same day, in the second month of the Jewish year, which corresponds with our November, that Noah shut himself up in the Ark, according to Genesis ; that is, on the same day when the image of Osiris was by the priests shut up in a sacred Coffer or Ark. According to Greswell, this New Year's Commemoration on the 17th of November obtained among the Indians in the earliest times to which Indian calendars can be tracked back. It is sufficient for our argument, that its commencement can be proved long before the birth of Gautama-Buddaha.

If the 17th of November was New Year's-Day, the second month commenced on the 17th of December, and 'the eighth day,' Buddha's birthday, when the power of the Sun ceases to decrease and again begins to increase. The text in Buddhistic writings we are considering presupposes the commencement of the year on the 17th of November, and thus points to the 25th of December. This is confirmed by another statement in the same

187

scripture. At the time of Buddha's birth, 'The asterism Chin was passing and the asterism Koh was coining on.' Evidently this refers to the contemporaneous rising and setting of certain Stars on opposite side of the horizon. According to the Christian calendar the birthday of John the Baptist is on the day of the Summer Solstice, when the Sun begins to decrease. The words attributed to him in the Forth Gospel, that he must decrease and Jesus increase, may be referred to this connection of the respective birth-days of John and of Jesus with the Summer Solstice. As there are six months between this change in the Sun's position, so according to the Gospel after Luke, the Baptist was exactly six months younger than Jesus. (Luke 1 :24)

The basis of the symbolism about Crossing a Stream which leads to the Tree of Life and immortality, seems to have been the Egyptian Tradition, of Eastern origin, about Osiris, who is represented with the Tree of Life before him, and whose body had been Cut Up into fourteen parts. The Lord of the Tombs was symbolized by the setting Sun, but previously by the Mysterious Pleiades, passing through the Stream of the Lower World. Thus he passed by the fourteen invisible lunar asterisms in order to rise again in the East, at the end of the supposed Stream of Death, or the Lethe-River of later Traditions, the Water of which are drunk by the souls of the departed before entering Elysium. Mr. Haliburton is prepared to prove that Paradise was supposed to be in the 'Land of the Pleiades,' in which was supposed to grow 'the Tree of Life.' Since the Solar symbolism took the place of that of the Pleiades, our interpretation of Nirvana with its Tree of Life, as the Sun, is thus confirmed. The most ancient (Egyptian) representation of the Tree of Life (about 1,400 BC), is a palm, in Greek Phoinix (Job XXIX : 18 ; Ps. XCII : 13), and Herodotus called the Egyptian pi-enech, which means aeon, the Phoenix, which he described as like an Eagle. It is, we suggest, the Eagle on the back of the Apis, that is, of Taurus with the Pleiades from whence, that is from the Matarii, the Matarisvan or messenger of Agni brought Down the Fire, according to Mr. Haliburton's discovery. The symbol of the Spirit of God was the Dove, in Greek Peleia, and the Samaritans had a Brazen Fiery Dove, instead of the Brazen Fiery Serpent. Both referred to Fire, the symbol of the Holy Ghost, and later is referred to Christ. Birds are connected with the Egyptian representations of the Tree of Life, and thus with Fire, a very ancient symbolism.

According to Pherecydes (about544 BC), or rather according to the 'Phoenician' Tradition to which he referred, the fundamental cause of all phenomena in nature is Zeus or Chronos, whom he also calls, but distinguishes in a certain sense from Chthon, that is, the material substances

188

of the Earth, including the sea. He designates Chronos as a deity, dwelling in that part of Heaven which is nearest to the Earth. We know that Chronos is the Seb [Set] of the Egyptians, and with Ehea-Netpe he gave birth to the five planets, in honour of which, five additional days were added to the calendar of 360 days, after that Thoth, the God of history and Astronomy, who is represented as riding on the Moon, and whose Mystical numbers was 72, had played at dice with the Moon, and gained for each planet the 72nd part of 360 days. This Egyptian Legend seems to have been framed after the Phoenician Legend or Myth of the Seven children of Chronos and Ehea, of which the youngest had been translated to the Gods. Movers has explained these Seven children of Zeus-Chronos by the Pleiades, one of which Seven Stars had disappeared in course of time. Since Pherecydes admits to have drawn from a Phoenician source, he must have known this Phoenician Legend, and he may be assumed to have connected with the Seven sons of Zeus-Chronos the Seven Patasci of the Phoenicians, and the Cabiri of Egyptians and Greeks, whom some identified with the sons of Ehea. Zeus-Chronos thus seems to have been by Pherecydes connected with the Pleiades in Taurus, as the divinity dwelling in these Seven Stars, like the Sibut of the ancient Babylonians, the Sebaot or Zabaot of the Hebrews, and other deities about the theogony of the tutor of Pythagoras.

The first creation Zeus-Chronos was Fire. According to the Indian Myth on the Descent of Fire, the same was brought to Earth from Heaven by a messenger of Indra, by Agni, called Matarisvan. This name, Mr. Haliburton has connected with the Matarii, as the Pleiades are still called by islanders in the pacific. We have pointed out in another places, that the Fire-Sticks or Arani of the Indians, which were a sacred symbol to the ancient Babylonians, point to the origin of the cross as connected with the symbolism of Fire. It can be shown that Bel's Flaming Sword which turned every way, and the Flaming Sword of the Cherub, that is, Kirub or Bull, according to the language of Cuneiform Inscriptions, Originally Referred to the Pleiades in Taurus, from whence Fire was supposed to have First Descended upon the Earth. This symbolism enables us to suggest that Pherecydes may have regarded as dwelling-place of Zeus-Chronos the Eastern determining Star of aboriginal times, Aldebaran in Taurus, or Pleiades in the same Constellation. Since the Seven sons of Zeus-Chronos and of Khea, according to Phoenician Legend were, as we showed, Connected with the Pleiades, this Constellation, inhabited according to Old Babylonian and to Hebrew Tradition, by the God Sibut-Sebaot, appears indeed to have designated the part of the Earth which was conceived to be nearest to Heaven and the dwelling-place of Zeus. For the Pleiades stood

189

once nearest to the most ancient Equinoctial points observed, and the parts of the sphere determined by the latter mark those points on the horizon where the path of the Sun appears to touch the path of the fixed Stars, and at the same time the equator, and thus the Earth. This explanation is finally confirmed by the fact to which Pherecydes refers, that Zeus-Chronos was the Creator of Fire and then of the Earth, as if the Creator of Heaven and Earth, whilst the Pleiades, as already said, were regarded as the locality where Fire originates.

In order to frame the World, Zeus transforms himself into Eros, the God of love, not mentioned in the Homeric Poems, but whom the Orphics before Pherecydes explain to have been the son of Chronos, and the first who issued forth from the mundane Egg. Eros was thus Connected with Castor, the first-born of the Dioscuri, who were called sons of Zeus and Leda. Since the Dioscuri can be Connected with the Aswin, or two Bulls of Indian Tradition, with the rising and setting-Tarus, to which also Osiris and the Cherbum and Seraphin were referred, the argument gains in force, that Zeus, who was called the highest, like Osiris-Wasar, according to the most ancient Greek theogony known to us, was supposed to be the God Inhabiting the Pleiades in Taurus. Eros became the vicar of Zeus and the framer of the World, and so Serosh took the place of Ormuzd as first of the Seven Amshaspancls, which referred to the Pleiades.

Like Eros, Serosh was considered as the framer of the World. Again, as Serosh-Sraosha was Connected with the Celestial Watchers, and thus with the Pleiades, being therefore opposed by the ideal hero in the opposite Constellations of Scorpio or the Serpent, the adversary of Eros is the Serpent-Deity Ophioneus. Eros must therefore be regarded as one of the ideal heroes of Light, who were connected with the Constellation of the Spring-Equinox, originally with Taurus and the Pleiades, and opposed by Serpent-Deities. Eros was contrasted to Ophioneus as Ormuzd was to Ahriman, Indra to Ahi, Osiris to Typhon, Dionysos to the Serpent-footed Titans, Apollos to Python, Buddha to Mara (Naga), Christ to Antichrist, the Satan, Devil, or Old Serpent. The localization of these Eastern and Western symbols enables us to assert that the Theogony of Pherecydes, and therefore also of Pythagoras, was inseparably Connected with Astrological Observations of the East. It is certainly not only the Myth of Demeter and of Dionysos, the Indian Bacchus, which can be proved to have been introduced into Greece from without.

Pythagoras could assign to the Sun the central position in the Solar System, without giving up the Oriental Connection of the Fire with the Pleiades, the latter as the Throne of the God by whom Fire had been Sent. From this the conception would arise of the Pleiades, or a Star in this Constellation, as the Throne of Hestia and as centre of the universe. In the most ancient parts of the Zendavesta the one God Ahura Mazda or Ormzd is designated as the first of Seven angles or Watchers, in conjunction with whom he Created the World by his Word. But by later passages in the Holy Book of the Iranians the honour of the first of Seven angles is attributed to vicar of God, to a mediator, to a divine messenger or angel, to Sraosha. This ideal hero and Messiah of Iranian Tradition was originally Connected with Fire, and thus, with the Seven Stars of the Pleiades, from which a divine messenger, the Matarisvan, according to Indian Tradition, brought Down Fire, as already pointed out. Fire was the symbol of the spiritual power, the Hegh or Meh of the Zendavesta, the Mah or Maha in Sanscrit, and the Maya of Buddism. This divine messenger and importer of Fire, and of the spirit symbolized by Fire, was called Agni, whose secret name was Matarisvan, the Heavenly Man from the Pleiades in Taurus, the Throne of the God of Seven Stars, of Indra, the Celestial Bull, as of Osiris, of Zeus-Chronos, of the Sibut of the ancient Babylonians, the Seaot or Sabaoth of the Hebrews, and so also of other deities.

It thus becomes probable that the West-Iranians, the Chaldeans, Casdim, or conquerors of Mesopotamia, in 2,450 BC, the year of shem's birth, that those whom Berosus calls Medes – and all events not long after, if not ever since this Median conquest by the Casdim or Chaldeans, whom we regard as the Shemites of Genesis, the ancient Babylonians knew of such a Celestial Being who distributed good among Men, as his name, Silik-mulu-dug (khi?) implies. He is said to walk before or to be the forerunner, the messenger, of Hea, who is Provably the God in the Pleiades, like the Sibut of the Babylonians. As was done by the Agni of the Indians, this the Arani-Messiah of Mesopotamia was Connected with the Arani or Fire-Sticks. A mediatorial position similar to that assigned to Serosh was held by Mithras, who was first connected with Fire and then with the Sun. Like Ormuzd, Mithras is represented Riding on the Bull, and Jehovah is described as Riding on the Cherub, Kirub or Bull. This Bull is certainly the Constellation of Taurus ; and the same Mithraic representation Connects with the Bull a scorpion, evidently the Opposite Constellation. Also the Hebrews knew Traditions according to which the Memra or Word of God, the Messiah, was symbolized first by Fire, that is, by the Fiery or Brazen Serpent, which probably pointed to Lightning, [Meteor] and later the

191

Hebrews symbolized the word by the Sun. The transition from Fire-symbolism to Sun-symbolism took place in early historical times. The Seven stages of the tower of Babel or Bab-Il were probably commenced by the first king of the Median dynasty.

In harmony with Buddhistic conceptions, the Angel-Messiah is described as coming to Earth in order to dwell among Men, but not having found a dwelling place he returned to the angles. We saw Buddha's descent is figuratively described as that of an Elephant, and so here Messiah is described as coming down in the form of a White Bull with large horns. In the book of Daniel the two-horned he-goat refers, not to Cyrus the Messiah, but to Alexander, whom the Koran designates as Dulkarnaim or the two-horned One. According to the Book of Enoch, already Adam had come to Earth as a White Bull. We have interpreted the Bull-symbol as referring to the Celestial Bull, to the Constellation of Taurus with the Pleiades, and have connected with these Seven Stars the Seven Amshaspands and Seven Buddas. Here Enoch, 'the Seventh from Adam,' as if the Seventh Buddha, is indentified with the Angel-Messiah, that is with the One like a Son of Man in the Danielic vision. Enoch's terrestrial body is described as melting away, and his spirit was transformed into a Heavenly body, 'the second body,' expected after the coming of Serosh. This is a parallel to Buddha's transformation on the mount. Enoch, whose translation is referred to in Genesis, was regarded as the Seventh incarnation of the Angel of God.

Ancient Calendars & Constellations,
by Emmeline Plunket, 1903

The importance and trustworthiness of the Babylonian Cuneiform Inscriptions can scarcely be over-rated. They were inscribed on soft clay which was afterwards baked either by the Sun or fire and No Correction or Erasure can have been made in them since that date.

The Origin of All Religious Worship,
by Charles-Francois Dupuis, 1790

The attentive reader will admire the prophetic words of Mr. Dupuis, his profound erudition and his exuberant store of historical knowledge of antiquity, exhibited in his explanations of all religious systems, but especially of that of the Christian dogma in the shape of Catholicity. Stripping it of all its ancient drapery and finery, he fearlessly plants the torchlight of Reason and history into the midst of the Dome of St. Peter, and from its glare all the phantoms of superstition and Traditional imposition seems to vanish like the shades of night before the rising Sun. If the foundations of the whole edifice of this dogma are thereby materially impaired, it is that Science and Truth are no respector of creeds or persons, and like the Sun will shine on the just and the unjust.

Isis and Nephthys in the Zodiacal Sanctuary of Dendera, Egypt.

Inscription of the Temple of Sais, Egypt : I am all that has been, all that is, and all that shall be, and no mortal has lifted yet the veil, that covers me.

Although this God was everywhere and was all, which bears a character of Grandeur and Perpetuity in this Eternal World, yet did Man prefer to look for him in those Elevated Regions, where that mighty and radiant luminary seems to Travel Through Space, overflowing the Universe with waves of its Light, and through which the most beautiful as well as the most beneficent action of the Deity is enacted of Earth.

In the Apocalypse these same Pleiads are called the Seven Angels, which Smite the World with Seven last Plagues.

The Scandinavians have their God Locke, who makes war to the Gods and chiefly to Thor ; he slanders the Gods, says the Edda, and is the great artificer of frauds. He has a wicked spirit ; of him are born three Monsters, the Wolf Feuris, the Serpent Midgard, and Hela or Death.

The tomb of Osiris, hidden under those enormous masses, known by the name of Pyramids, erected by the Egyptians in honor of that luminary, which distributes the Light. One of them has its four faces regarding the

193

four cardinal points of the World. From the dimensions and from the latitude under which this Pyramid had been constructed, it followed, that a fortnight before the Equinox of Spring, which is the exact epoch, at which the Persians celebrated the renewal of Nature, it had to cease to throw shadow at noon, and that it continued so, until a fortnight after the Equinox of Autumn. It should seem as if the Egyptians, always grand in their conceptions, had the boldest project ever imagined, a Pyramid which separates the boreal from the austral hemisphere, the reign of Goodness from that of Evil, that of Light from that of Darkness. They wanted the shadow to disappear at noon from all faces of the pyramid, during all the time, that the Sun would remain in the luminous hemisphere, and that the boreal face should be covered with shadow, when night should begin to resume its sway in our hemisphere, in other words, at the time when Osiris would descend to the tomb and to the infernal regions. The tomb of Osiris was covered with shadow for nearly six months ; afterwards light invested it entirely at noon, as soon as Osiris on his return from Hell, resumed his reign by passing into the luminous hemisphere.

The first basis is the existence of a Great Disorder having been introduced in to the World by a Serpent, which had tempted a Woman, to pluck forbidden Fruits ; a Trespass, which had for consequence, the Knowledge of Evil, until then Unknown to Man, and which could only be redeemed by a God conqueror of Death and of the Prince of Darkness. This is the fundamental dogma of the Christian religion ; because in the opinion of the Christians, the incarnation of Christ had become necessary, merely, because he had to Redeem the Evil introduced into the Universe by the Serpent, which had seduced the first Woman and the first Man. These two dogmas cannot be separated from each other : if there is no sin, there is no atonement ; if there is no trespasser, then no redeemer is required.

The Boundesh of the Persians holds the following language : "Ahriman , or the principle of Evil and of Darkness, he from whom all the Evil in this World is proceeding, Penetrated into Heaven under the form of a Serpent, accompanied by Dews or bad Genii, whose only business was to Destroy." And in another place he says : "When the bad Genii Desolated the World, and when the Star Serpent made Itself a Road between Heaven and Earth : this Petiare Arriman, full of Death and Corruption, Made in The River the Great Adder [Zodiacal Stream], the mother of winter, which congealed the Water, the Earth and the Trees. Thus Destroying Ormuzd's Eiren, the Delightful Place of Abundance that he had made for Man.

194

The following is a quote from "Maimonides," the wisest of the Rabbis :

"We must not understand or take in a literal sense, what is written in the book on the creation, nor form of it the same ideas, which are participated by the generality of Mankind, otherwise our ancient Sages would not have so much recommended to us, to Hide the Real Meaning of It, and Not to Lift the Veil, which Covers the Truth contained therein. When taken in its literal sense, that work gives the most absurd and most extravagant ideas of the Deity. Whosoever should divine its True Meaning, Ought to Take Great Care in Not Divulging It. This is a maxim, repeated to us all our Sages, principally concerning the Understanding of the work of the six days. It is possible, that somebody, either Through Himself, or by means of the Light Obtained from Others, may Succeed to Divine its Meaning ; then let him be Silent, or if he speaks of it, let it be done only in as veiled a manner as I do, leaving the remainder to be Guessed, by those who can hear me."

Allegory was the Veil with which Sacred Science Enveloped Itself and that they have acknowledged to contain a Hidden and Allegorical Sense, of which they say we must carefully Abstain from Giving the Interpretation to the Vulgar.

The thread of the Astronomical Science had been Lost, ancient Legends which are No Longer Understood.

The Christians are incontestably either Sectarians or Plagiarists of the Religion of the Magi. Many people, who will not admit our explanations, either through Ignorance, or Being Inclined, to Slander what they Do Not Comprehend, as all the Fathers of the Church used to do in their Criticisms on Paganism.

Without fearing in the least the criticism of a sect, where Credulity is a Sacred Duty. Illiterate Men, Degrade his Reason, Infecting Reason and causing it to Wither. There is very little hope of curing our species of this general Delirium.

Religion interferes with everything ; it lays hold of Man at the moment, when he issues from the womb of his mother ; it presides over his education ; it puts its seal on the most important engagements, which he may contract during His Life ; it surrounds the bed of the dying ; it conducts him to the grave, and it follows him still beyond that, by the Illusion of Hope and Fear.

195

Stolid credulity Poisoning the Reason of so many millions of people by religious errors.

Verities – the Light of Reason is made to Shine in all its Brightness, without mixing with it the Shades of Mystery. When the errors are entirely ignored, the soul remains in all its freshness and purity, such as it came from the hands of Nature, and in this state it is far more able to Reason about its duties, than when it is already Corrupted by education and a false science. Alas ! How few Men have been so happy as to be able to destroy the prejudices of their first education, fortified by example and by custom, and who with the aid of philosophy have succeeded to efface the remembrance of what they had Learned at Great Expense.

The Egyptians were celebrating the Mysteries of the Passion of Osiris at Night in the Middle of a Lake, by the name of vigils and holy nights, Easter is one of them...

The Chaldeans called the Heaven of the fixed Stars, the Heaven of the Cherubims, above which they placed the Great Sea or the Upper Waters.

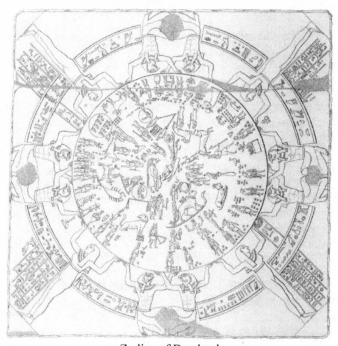

Zodiac of Denderah

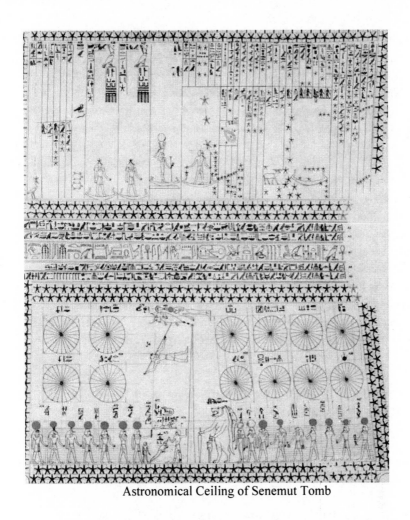
Astronomical Ceiling of Senemut Tomb

Development of Religion & Thought in Ancient Egypt, by James Henry Breasted, 1912

It was Horus who saved them from every ill which Set did to them. Excerpt from hymn called "Horus-eye" or the Sun-God's eye.

The Pyramid Texts, the oldest source, indicates assassination : "his brother Set felled him to the Earth in Nedyt" ; or "his brother Set overthrew him upon his side, on the further side of the land Gehesti" ; but another document of the Pyramid Age, and possibly quite as old as the passage quoted from the Pyramid Texts, says : "Osiris was drowned in his New Water (The Inundation)."

197

Even in death the life-giving power of Osiris did not cease. The faithful Isis drew near her dead Lord, "making a shadow with her pinions and causing a wind with her wings . . . raising the weary limbs of the silent-hearted (dead), receiving his seed, bringing forth an heir, nursing the child in solitude, whose place is not known, introducing him when his arm grew strong in the Great Hall" [The Norse refer to the Great Hall also.]

"O Osiris, ... Horus hath avenged thee. Horus hath come that he may recognize thee. He hath smitten Set for thee, bound."

"Though thou Departest, thou Comest again ; though thou Sleepest, thou Wakest again ; though thou Diest, thou Livest again. Stand up, that thou mayest see what thy Son has done for thee. Awake, that thou mayest hear what Horus has done for thee. He has Smitten for thee the One that Smote thee, as an Ox ; he has Slain for thee the One that slew thee, as a Bull. He has bound for thee the one that bound thee. . . . . . . How beautiful are they who saw, how satisfied are they who beheld, who saw Horus when he gave Life to his father, when he offered satisfaction to Osiris before the Western Gods."

There is possibly another connection in which the Pyramid form may be discerned as belonging to the Sun-God. The triangle of Zodiacal Light which some have claimed to be able to discover in the East at Sunrise at certain times, and the writing of the Solar God, Soped's name with a Triangle or Pyramid after it, may have some connection with the use of the Pyramid as a Solar symbol.

"The Sky Weeps for thee, the Earth Trembles for thee" say the ancient mourners for the King (Osiris)." "Clouds Darken the Sky, the Stars Rain Down, the bows (a Constellation) stagger, the bones of the Hells-Hounds Tremble, the Porters are silent, when they see king Unis, dawning as a soul." Pyramid Texts

The Gods of the Egyptians or Studies in Egyptian Mythology, by E. A. Wallis Budge, 1904

A solar character was introduced into Egypt by the "Followers of Horus," or the "Blacksmiths," who invaded the country, and conquered the natives, and settling down there, built up the great dynastic civilization which we call the Egyptian.

Apep, the Great Serpent-Devil of Mist, Darkness, Storm, and Night, and his Fiends, the "Children of Rebellion," where indeed a formidable opponent of the Sun-God, induced Terror in the Minds and were hostile to Man, within the Egyptian Mythology.

The Bull and Cow were the principal objects of worship and they were regarded as deities in Predynastic Times. The Great Strength of the Bull, and his almost Irresistible Attack in Fighting and Headlong Rush, excited the Fear and admiration of Primitive Man. For thousands of years the kings of Egypt delighted to call themselves "Mighty Bull".

Sacrificed Bulls eaten to incarnate the deity within the body of participants.

"Unas is the Bull of Heaven which overcometh by his will, and which feedeth upon that which cometh into being from every God, and he eateth of the provender of those who fill themselves with words of power and come from the Lake of Flame."

The food of the Bull Unas is also said to be those who came from the Lake of Fire, or the city of She-Sasa, from the Book of the Dead chapter CVIII, we learn that She-Sasa was situated in Sekhet-Sasa [Pleiades], i. e., a district in Heaven, where the beatified dead obtain food. Also same as field of fire. Poureth down Water from Heaven, Tremble the Stars. . . . . . .

In the Book of the Dead the throne of God is made of Iron, that its legs terminate in Hoofs like those of Bulls, and that its sides are ornamented with faces of Lions. [Where and When, From Taurus when the Sun was in Leo.]

Neter is the word for God with an Axe and sometimes the determinative of the word (Neterta) is a Woman, and at other times a Serpent. Neter – divine arm. Means mighty, strong, strength, power, same as the Hebrew El. [The ideograph is similar to a flag on a standard, a hatchet with a long handle.] [The Thunder Axe.]

It is Surprising to find so much Similarity existing Between the Primeval Gods of Sumer and those of Egypt, especially as the resemblance Cannot be the result of Borrowing. It is out of the question to assume that Ashur-bani-pal's editors borrowed the system from Egypt, or that the Literary Men of the time of Seti I. borrowed their ideas from the Literati of Babylonia or Assyria, and we are Therefore Driven to the Conclusion that Both the

199

Sumerians and the early Egyptians Derived their Primeval Gods from Some Common but Exceedingly Ancient Source. [The Whole World Saw It !]

From the papyrus of Nes-Amsu, a passage contains a very interesting addition and variant reading, which makes "father" Nu declare that his eye, i.e., the Sun, was covered over with large numbers of "bushes" for an indefinite number of periods, each containing sixty years ; now "bushes," otherwise called "hair," is the name given to the clouds which hang round the Sun at Sunrise, obscure his rays, and it seems as if the God intends to complain that his Sight was impeded by them for Centuries. The words following seem to indicate that Vegetation and reptile, including worms or Serpents, proceeded from the God Rem, and that they were the product of the Tears which fell from Khepera, but this rendering is not wholly certain. The Vegetation and worms here mentioned are forms of Mist and Cloud which Wholly or Partially Hide the Sun, and the line is probably added to the text to account for the "bushes" of which "father" Nu spoke above. Of the God Rem, we know nothing, but as the word rem means "to Weep," and an allusion to "Crying or Weeping," is contained in the line in which the name of the God occurs, we may assume that he was the personification of Ra's tears. [One cries when Sad. Sad Sun no Bright Shine.]

THE HISTORY OF THE CREATION OF THE GODS
AND OF THE WORLD.

The Book of Knowing the Evolutions of Ra and of Overthrowing Apep (Serpent). The words of Neb-er-tcher. He says : - "I was (or, the Creator became) of what came into being. I came into being in the forms of Khepera coming into being in Primeval Time. I came into being in the forms of Khepera. I was (or, became) the Creator of what came into being, that is to say, I produced myself from the primeval matter which I made. I produced myself from primeval matter. My name is Osiris, the primeval matter of primeval matter. I have done my will all in Earth this, and I have spread abroad in it ; I raised up my hand. I was alone ; not born were they. Not had I spit in the form of Shu, not had I emitted Tefnut I brought into my mouth my own my name, that is to say, a Word of Power, and I, even I, came into being in the form of things which came into being, and I came into being in the forms of Khepera. I came into being from the primeval matter, coming into being in multitudes of forms from the beginning. Not existed created things any in land this ; I made whatsoever was made everything. I was alone, not existed any other who worked with me in place that ; I made what I made therein by means of divine soul that which I raised

200

up therein out of Nu (i.e., the Primeval Abyss of Water) from a state of inertness, not found I a place whereon I could stand. I worked with the spirit which was in my heart, I laid a foundation before me, I made whatsoever was made all. I was alone, I laid a foundation in my heart, I made other things which came into being, and manifold were the things which came into being of Khepera came into being what they gave birth to out of creations of their offspring. I, even I, spat in the form of Shu, and I emitted Tefnut, and I became from God one Gods Three, that is to say, from myself Two Gods came into being on Earth this. Were raised up therefore Shu and Tefnut in Nu (the Primeval Watery Abyss) wherein they were. Behold, my eye brought to me they in the Train of a henti period, they proceeded from me. I collected my members, they came forth from myself after I had union with my clenched hand, came to me my heart (or, will) out of my hand. The seed which fell into my mouth, I spat in the form of Shu, I emitted water in the form of Tefnut, I became from being God one Gods Three, that is to say, from myself Two Gods came into being on Earth this. Were raised up therefore Shu and Tefnut from out of Nu wherein they were. Saith my father Nu, "They Covered up my Eye [or made weak] after them with Bushes, Twice, for Hen Periods. Vegetation and reptiles came from the God Rem, from the Tears falling from me. Cried my eye, came into being Mankind. I endowed it with will power. It raged at me after it came finding another growth within its place. Fell its vigorous power upon its bushes, upon the bushes which I placed there to make adornment in it. Ruling therefore on its seat in my face it ruleth the Whole Earth. Gave birth Shu and Tefnut to Nut, Osiris, Heru-khenti-an-maati, Set, Isis, Nephthys, and behold, their children they create beings manifold in Earth this from the beings of children, from the beings of their children. They invoke my name, they overthrow their enemies, they create words of power for the overthrow a Apep (Serpent), who is to be bound by the two hands of Aker, not may be his two hands, not may be his two feet, may he be Chained to One Place even as Inflicteth Ra his Blows decreed for him. He is Overthrown On His Back Wicked, Slit is his Face for what he Hath Done, and he remaineth upon his back Evil. [Bad Comet Beat Up the Sun.]

In dynastic times Apep was a personification of the Darkness of the darkest hour of the night, against which Ra must not only fight, but fight successfully before he could rise in the East in the morning ; But Originally he was the Thick Darkness which Enveloped the Watery Abyss of Nu, and which formed such a Serious Obstacle to the Sun when he was making his way out of the Inert Mass which he proceeded to Rise The First Time. [After the Deluge.]

201

In the Egyptian Texts we have at present no account of the First Fight which took place between Ra and Apep, but it is clear from several passages in the "Books of Overcoming Apep" that such a thing must have Occurred, and that the means employed by the Sun-God for Destroying his Foe resembled those made use of by Marduk in slaying Tiamat. The original of the Assyrian story is undoubtedly of Sumerian origin, and must be Very Old, and it is probable that both the Egyptians and the Sumerians Derived their Versions from a Common Source. [Progenitor of Encke the Double Sexed Being.]

In the Assyrian version Marduk is armed with the invincible Club which the Gods gave him, and with a Bow, Spear, Net, and Dagger ; the Lightning was before him, and Fierce Fire filled his body, and the four-fold wind and the Seven-Fold Wind [Shock Wave] went with him. Marduk grasped the Thunderbolt and then mounted his Chariot, drawn by four Swift and Fiery horses which had been trained to beat down under their feet Everything which came in their way.

The divine one (Ra) had Gown Old, he dribbled at the mouth, his spittle fell upon the Earth, and his slobbering dropped upon the ground. And Isis kneaded some thereof with Earth in her hand, and formed therewith a Sacred Serpent in the form of a Dart ; she did not set it upright before her face, but let it lie upon the ground in the Path whereby the great God went forth, according to his heart's desire, into his double kingdom. Now the Holy God arose, and the Gods who Followed Him as though he were Pharaoh went with him ; and he came forth according to his daily wont ; and the Sacred Serpent Bit Him. The Flame of his Life Departed from him ; and he who dwelt among the Cedars was overcome. The Holy God opened his Mouth, and the Cry of his Majesty Reached unto Heaven ; his Company of Gods said, 'What hath happened?' and his Gods exclaimed, "What is it?' But Ra could not answer, for his jaws Trembled and all his members Quaked, the Poison Spread Swiftly through his flesh just as the Nile rusheth through all his land. . . . . . . I was Bitten by a Serpent which I saw not. Is it Fire [Conflagration]? Is it Water [Deluge]? I am Colder than Water, I am Hotter than Fire. All my flesh Sweateth, I Quake, mine Eye Hath No Strength, I Cannot See the Sky, and the sweat rusheth to my face even as in the time of summer [Deathly Snake Bite Sick!]. The above text was to be recited over figures of Temu, "the Bull of his mother," and Horus, and Isis. [In the extracts of a Myth of Ra, Isis is trying to obtain the Sun-God's true name to legitimize her son Horus as the New Sun after the Atmospheric Loading Dissipated.] [Osiris after the -13K and Horus after the 2,300 B.C.]

202

Another Myth of Ra of considerable interest is that which describes the destruction of mankind, and tells how Men scorned the great Sun-God because he had become old ; the test of this, in a mutilated condition, is found inscribed upon the walls of the tombs of Seti I. and Rameses IV. at Thebes, and from it the following is clear. "Ra is the God who created himself after he, had risen in sovereignty over Men, and Gods, as well as over things, the One. And Mankind was uttering words of complaint, saying, 'Behold now, his Majesty, life, strength, and health to him ! hath become old, his bones are like Silver, his limbs are like Gold, and his hair is like unto real Lapis-Lazuli.' Now his Majesty heard the words which Mankind spake concerning him, and he said unto those who were following him, 'Cry out, and bring ye unto me mine Eye, and Shu, and Tefnut, and Seb, and Nut, and the fathers and the mothers who were with me when I was in Nu, together with my God Nu. Let him bring his ministers with him, and let them be brought silently, so that Mankind may not perceive it and take to Flight with their Hearts [Kill Them.]. Come thou with them to the Great House, and let them declare their plans, for I will go forth from Nu unto the place wherein I performed creations, and let those Gods be brought unto me there.' Now the Gods were on both sides of Ra and they bowed down even to the ground in presence of his Majesty, and he spake his words in the presence of the father of the firstborn Gods, the maker of Men, and the king of those who have knowledge. And they spake before his Majesty, saying, 'Speak unto us, for we are listening' ; an Ra spake unto Nu, saying, 'O thou firstborn God, from whom I came into being, O ye Gods my ancestors, behold ye what Mankind is doing, they who were created by mine Eye are uttering murmurs against me. Give me your attention, and seek ye out a plan for me, and I will Not Slay them Until ye shall say what I am to do concerning it.'

Then the Majesty of the God Nu, the son of Ra, spake saying, 'Thou art the God who art greater than he that made thee, and who art the sovereign of those who were created by him, thy throne is set, and the Fear of Thee is Great ; let then thine Eye be upon those who of Ra spake saying, 'Behold ye how they have taken Flight into the Mountains ! Their hearts are Afraid because of what they have said.' Then the Gods spake before the Majesty, saying 'Make thine Eye to Go Forth [Bolide], and let it Destroy for thee those who utter evil words of blasphemy against thee. There is Not an Eye upon All this Earth which can resist thine when it Descendeth in the Form of Hathor [Bull].' And the Goddess Hathor went forth and Slew the people on the Mountain, and the Majesty of this God spake, saying. 'Come, come in peace, Hathor, the work is accomplished.' And the Goddess said, 'Thou livest for me. When I had gained the Mastery over Men it was well pleasing to my heart.' And the Majesty of Ra spake, saying, 'I will gain the mastery over them as king, and I will Destroy them' ; and it came to pass that Sekhet waded about in the night season in the blood, beginning at Suten-henen (Herakleopolis Magna). Then the Majesty of Ra spake, saying, 'Cry out and fetch me swift and speedy messengers who can run like the wind' ; and straightway one brought these messengers. And the Majesty of this God spake, saying, 'Let them go to Abu (Elephantine), and bring me mandrakes in great number' ; and one brought to him these mandrakes, and the Majesty of this God gave them to Sekhet who dwelleth in Annu (Heliopolis) to Crush. And behold, when the Women were Crushing the Barley to make Beer, he placed these mandrakes in the vessels which were to hold the Beer, and some of the Blood of the Men who had been Slain. Now they made Seven thousand vessels of Beer. [Soma][Get the God's Drunk and they will Stop Killing.]

Now when the king of the South and North, Ra, had come with the Gods to look at the Beer, and the Daylight appeared after the Goddess had slaughtered Mankind in their season as she Sailed up The River, the Majesty of Ra said, 'It is doubly good, but I must protect Mankind against Her.' And Ra spake, saying, 'Let them take up the Vases and carry them to the place where Men and Women are being Slaughtered.' Then the Majesty of the king of the South and North, Ra, commanded them to Pour out from the Vessels during the time of the beauty of Night [Night Time Space Fall] the Beer which made Men wish to lie down, and the regions of the four Heavens were therewith even according to the Will of the Majesty of this God. Now when the Goddess Sekhet came in the morning and found the regions Flooded, her face beamed with joy, and she drank of the Beer and Blood, and her Heart was Glad, and she became Drunk, and she took No further heed of Mankind. And the Majesty of Ra spake unto this Goddess, saying 'Come, come in peace, O fair and gracious Goddess ;' and henceforth there were young and beautiful Women in the city of Amen (also called "City of Apis"). Then the Majesty of Ra said unto this Goddess, 'There shall be prepared for thee vases of drink which shall make thee Wish to Sleep at every Festival of The New Year, and the number thereof shall be in proportion to the number of my handmaidens '; and from that day until this present Men have been wont to make on the occasions of the Festival of Hathor Vases of Beer which will make them Sleep, in number according to the number of the handmaidens of Ra. And the Majesty of Ra spake unto this Goddess, saying, 'Behold, the pain of the burning heat of sickness hath come upon me ; whence cometh this pain ?' Then the Majesty of Ra said, 'I am alone, but my Heart hath become Exceedingly Weary of being with Them (i.e., with Men) ; I have slain Some of Them, but there is a remnant of Worthless Ones, and the Destruction which I Wrought among them was not Commensurate with my Power [KT Boundary].' And the Gods who were in His Train said unto him, 'Tarry not in thy weariness, for thy might is in proportion to thine own will.' Then the Majesty of this God said unto the Majesty of Nu, 'For the First Time my Limbs Have Lost Their Power, and I will never permit this thing to happen a second time.'" [the Promise not to do it again.] [Isis Rainbow alike Ishstar Necklace] [That much H2O in the Atmosphere and when the Sun gained would be Spectacular !]

When Ra had described his weariness to Nu, this God commanded Shu to perform the work of Ra and to take the place of his Eye, and directed the Sky Goddess Nut to help Ra. Nut asked Nu how this was to be done, and he told her to take Ra upon her back ; thereupon Nut took the form of a Cow, and Ra seated himself upon her back. In due course Mankind saw Ra on the back of Nut, and they were filled with remorse at their former behavior towards him, and they wished to see slain their enemies who had blasphemed him, but his Majesty did not tary, and he went on into the temple. On the following day as soon as the morning had come, Men went forth armed with bows and spears in order to do battle with the enemies of Ra, and as soon as the God saw this he said to them, "Your Sins are Forgiven you, for the sacrificial slaughters which ye have made have done away with the murders." Then Ra raised himself from the back of the Goddess Nut into the sky, where he made for himself a kingdom in which all people were to be assembled. Finally he ordered a Field to come into being, and straightway the Field of Hetep ("Peace"), came into being, and the Majesty of the God said, "I will make grow Green Herbs therein," and straightway there came into being Sekhet, "and I will plenish it with objects which sparkle, that is to say with Stars." Thereupon the Goddess Nut Quaked in all her members, and Ra declared that he would make supports to come into existence to strengthen her, and straightway supports appeared [Hold Up the Sky - Return of Blue Sky.]. Ra next ordered his son Shu to place himself beneath the Goddess Nut, who was Trembling, in such a way as to Support her body, and he ordered him to take heed to the Supports, or Pillars, whereon the Goddess rested [Holding up the Cow! - Stop the Space Fall], and to protect them, and to keep Nut stayed upon his head.

The Majesty of the God Ra commanded Thoth to give the order that the God Seb [Set], should come into his presence forthwith, and when he had done so, and Seb had appeared before him, Ra told him that Strife had Arisen by Reason of the Snakes, which were In his (Seb's) Territory, and, he added, "May they Fear Me as long as I am Alive." Ra also told him to find out what their plans were, and then to go to the place wherein was his father Nu, and to warn him to be Careful about what was on the Earth and in the Water [NEO's !]. Then the text become difficult to read. [The Serpents Should be Watched and Spells (Spacecraft) Made to Control Them.]

A very early Egyptian Tradition made a Great Fight to take place between the God of Light and the God of Darkness, and in later days Ra himself, or some form of him [Bolides or Sun Ages], generally one of the Horus Gods, was identified with the God of Light, and Set, in one form or other, was identified with the God of Darkness [Yet He was Light and produced Darkness.]. Thus the fights of Ra and Apep (Serpent), and Heru-Behutet and Set, and Horus, son of Isis, and Set, are in reality only different versions of one and the same story, though Belonging to Different Periods. In all these fights Thoth [The Recorder] played a prominent part, for when the Eye of Ra, i.e., the Sun [Or Bolide], was doing battle with Set [Set is the Boilde/Comet mix up], this Evil Power managed to Cast Clouds over it, and it was Thoth who swept them away, and brought the Eye Alive, and Whole, and Sound, and Without Defect "to its Lord" (Book of the Dead, XVII 71 ff) ; he seems also to have performed the same office for Ra after his combat with Apep. At the contest between Horus, son of Isis, who fought with Set in order to avenge the Murder of His Father Osiris, Thoth was present, and when Horus had Cut Off his Mother's [Isis's] Head because of Her Interference in the fight at the moment when victory was inclining to him, it was Thoth who gave her a Cow's Head in place of her own. In all these fights Thoth was the arbiter [And Scribe.].

Thoth is called the "Great God in Het-Abtit," meaning "House of the Net."

In a prayer we read : "Hail, thou 'God who lookest behind thee,' thou 'God who hast gained the mastery over thine heart,' I go a-fishing with the Cord of the 'Untier of the Earth,' and of him that maketh a way through the Earth. Hail, ye fishers who have given birth to your own fathers, who lay Snares with your Nets, and who Go Round about in the Chambers of the Waters, take ye not me in the Net wherewith ye Ensnared the helpless Fiends, and Rope me not in with the Rope wherewith ye Roped in the Abominable Fiends of Earth, which had a frame which reached unto Heaven, and weighted Parts that Rested Upon the Earth." From this passage it is clear that the Egyptians possessed a Legend in which one power or the other in the Mythological combats was armed with a Net wherein he tried to Ensnare his adversary. In the Book of the Dead the deceased says, "Lift thyself up, O thou Ra, who dwellest in thy divine shrine, draw thou into thyself the Winds, inhale the North wind, and swallow thou the beqesu (?) of thy Net on the day wherein thou breathest Maat." It is evident from its context that Ra possessed a Net, and we are certain from the former extract that is was one of the Weapons which he employed in his war against the God and Fiends of Darkness. [Casting Net an Illusion when a Bolide Explodes Showering Smoking Fragments as in the Tiamat story, ahead , mentioning weights to pull it down to Earth.] [A Snare looks just like the Snake eating his Tail, used more often in Babylonian stories.]

The story of the defeat of Set (Serpent) by Heru-Behutet is told in the texts on the walls of the temple of Edfu substantially as follows : - In the year 363, of Ra-Heru-khuti, the king of the South and North who Liveth for Ever and Ever, his Majesty found himself in the country of Ta-kens, for he had gone to the district of Uauat, because certain folk had Conspired Against their Lord. Having Suppressed the Rebellion [Calm vs.Chaos] he returned to Edfu, and deputed his son Heru-behutet to continue the War on his behalf ; this God had observed how Men had conspired against his father, and he was ready to carry out his behests. Thereupon Heru-behutet Flew Up to Heaven In The Form Of A Winged Disk, and ever after he was called "Great God, Lord of Heaven." From the Height of Heaven he was Able to See his father's enemies, and he Chased them in the form of a Great Winged Disk ; he attacked them with such Wrath and Vigour, <u>that They Lost their Senses and Could See Neither with Their Eyes Nor Hear with their Ears</u> <u>[Blinded and Deafened by the Monster Bolide !]</u>, and Every Man fell Upon His Neighbor and Slew Him, and in a moment All were Dead. And straightway Horus, with Many-Coloured Shapes and Feathers, returned to his form as a Winged Disk and took up his position in the boat of Ra. . . . . . . [Alike the Colorful Feathered Serpent of Mexico.]

207

Later on he (Horus) came along with his "Blacksmiths," each having a Spear made of Divine Iron and a Chain.

Horus's Talisman

Later on in the same story : Heru-behutet and Horus together pursued the foe Set, and both Gods were of the same form and appearance. They had the bodies of Men, and the heads of hawks, and they wore the White and Red Crowns, with plumes, and Uraei (Serpents). All these events took place on the Seventh day of the month Tybi and the place wherein they happened was called Aat-shatet. After these things Set changed himself into a Serpent which Hissed Loudly, and he Sought Out a Hole for Himself in the Ground [Crater] wherein he Hid himself and lived, whereupon Ra said, "The Monster Ba hath turned himself into a Hissing Serpent, let Horus, the son of Isis, set himself above his hole in the Form of a Pole on the top of which is the of Horus so that he may never again come forth therefrom."

In the original fight between Ra and Apep, or Horus and Set, the Sun-God was Accompanied by his Followers, whose duties, apparently, consisted in watching the Combat, and who were, like Ra himself, Unconnected with the Earth. But in the Fight of Heru-Behutet with Set, the Companions of the Gods were Beings in the Forms of Men who were Armed with Spears and Chains for Fettering purposes, and they were rewarded by him after the manner of Men. The God himself was Armed with a Very Long Spear made of "Iron of the God" or "Divine Iron," and with a Chain of Unusual Length [Vortices Contrail Across the Sky.].

The Facts Indicate That We Are Not Dealing Entirely With Mythological Events, and it is nearly certain that the triumphant progress ascribed to Heru-Behutet is based upon the exploits of some victorious invader who established himself at Edfu in very early times, and then made his way with his followers Northwards, beating down all opposition as he went. It is pretty clear that he owed his success chiefly to the superiority of the weapons with which he and his Men were armed, and to the material of which they were made ; given equality of bravery in two bodies of Men opposed each other, troops armed with weapons or flint would not long oppose successfully those armed with weapons of Iron. In other words, the followers of Horus, who are called Mesniti in the texts were actually Workers In Metal, or, "Blacksmiths," and Men who knew how to Smelt Iron Ore and to Forge the Metal into Weapons of offence and defense. These Men Called their Workshop of Foundry Mesnet of Mesnit, and later, when their leader and themselves had become deified, and priests had been appointed to perform the worship of the Gods, the portion of the Temple which was set apart for them was also called Mesnet or Mesnit, and when the Metal Statue of the God of the rising Sun, Heru-Behutet, was brought out by them from their chamber the God was said to issue from the Foundry wherein he had been Cast, and the Mesnet was identified with that Portion of the Sky from which the Sun-God Appeared. [Or was it the God who Shone Bright Like the Sun?]

It Is Of Course, Impossible to say who were the Blacksmiths that swept over Egypt from South to North, Or Where They Came From, but the writer (Budge) believes that they represent the Invaders in Predynastic Times, who made their way into Egypt, from a country in the East, by Way of the Red Sea [Maybe the ones who lived in the Valley of the Red Sea], and by some road across the Eastern desert, e.g., that through the Wadi Hammamat, or that which touches the Nile, a little to the South of Thebes. They brought with them the Knowledge of Working in Metals and of Brick-Making, and having conquered the indigenous peoples in the South, i.e., those round about Edfu, they made that city the centre of their civilization, and then proceeded to conquer and occupy other sites, and to establish sanctuaries for their God or Gods. In later times the indigenous priesthoods merged the Legendary history of the deified king of the Blacksmiths in that of Horus, the God of Heaven in the Earliest Times, and in that of Ra, which belonged to a later period. The priests of Edfu found many parts of this mixed history very difficult to explain, and they endeavored to get of their difficulties by the fabrication of foolish etymologies and puns, whereby they sought to elucidate events and names. These, however, have a certain importance, for they at least Prove that Parts of the Legends were not understood when the puns or plays on words were made, and that the Legends Themselves Are Of Great Antiquity [-13K BP] ; another point is also made clear by them, i.e., that the Egyptians themselves were not better informed on such subjects than we are.

Heru-Thema, "Horus the Piercer." is a form of Horus that attacked Set, the Murderer of His Father Osiris, with his Long Spear with a Sharp-Pointed

Iron Head ; he is represented in the form of a Hawk-Headed Man in the Act of Driving his Long Spear into some Unseen Foe on or below the ground. [He's Stabbing the Bull in Astronomical Chart – page 197.]

Soon after the birth of her child she [Isis] was persecuted by Set, who kept herself and Horus prisoners in a house, but by the help of Thoth she escaped with her child one evening, and set out on her way under the protection of Seven Scorpions called Tefen, Befen, Mestet, Mestetef, Petet, Thetet, and Matet. These Scorpions probably represent the Seven stars of the Constellation Canis Major [The Pleiades !], in which the Stars of Isis and Sothis were situated. The last Three Scorpions showed Isis the way and led her to the town of Per-Sui or Crocodilopolis, and then on to the city of Thebti, the city of the Two Sandals-Goddess where the swamp country begins. Whilst Isis was Absent one day Horus was Stung by a Scorpion, and when she came home she found him lying on the ground, and the foam was on his lips, and his heart was still, and there was not a muscle or limb of him which was not rigid ; she had protected him against Set, and against the possibility of attack by any being in the Papyrus Swamps, but a Scorpion had Stung the Child, and he was Dead. Whilst Isis was Lamenting his Death her sister Nephthys came with Serqet, the Scorpion Goddess, and advised her to Cry Out To Heaven for help, and She Did So, and her Cry Penetrated to Ra in his "Boat of Millions of Years." The Great God Stopped His Boat, and Thoth Came Down With Words Of Power, and by means of these things had taken place Horus set to work to avenge the Death of his father Osiris, and it was under his form of "Horus, the Avenger of his Father," that he appealed so strongly to the imagination of the Egyptians.

According to a notice in the Calendar given in the Fourth Sallier Papyrus, Horus began his Fight with Set, which Lasted Three Days, on the 26th day of the month of Thoth, and the Two Gods Fought in the Form of Two Men. Isis was present at the Fight and, because she in some way supported Set against Horus, her son turned upon her with the fury of a "Panther of the South," and cut off her head. Thoth, however, seeing what had been done, took the head of the Goddess, and by means of his Words of Power transformed it into the Head of a Cow, and then fixed it upon the body of Isis. According to Plutarch, Isis found that her son Horus had succeeded in Fettering Set and in Binding him in Chains, but Not Wishing that he should Perish she loosed his Fetters and set him at liberty ; then which were upon it. We have no means of assigning a date to the composition of the above Legend, But It Must Be Very Old, and it is easy to see that it is only a Version of the Older Legend of the Combat between Ra and Apep, and

Heru-ur and Set, and Heru-Behutet and Set, and it is, of Course, one of the Sources of All the Post-Christian Legends of the overthrow of Dragons by kings and heroes, e.g., Alexander the Great and Saint George. When Horus had overcome Set he succeeded to the inheritance of his father, and took his seat upon the throne of Osiris, and Reigned In His Stead ; and in the words addressed to Osiris by the official Hunefer, "Horus is triumphant in the presence of the Whole Company of the Gods, the Sovereignty Over The World hath been given unto him, and his dominion is in the Uttermost parts of the Earth. The throne of the God Seb hath been adjudged unto him, along with the rank which hath been founded by the God Temu, and which hath been stablished by decrees in the Chamber of Books, and hath been inscribed upon an Iron Tablet according to the command of thy father Ptah-Tanen, on the great throne. . . . . . . Gods Celestial and Gods Terrestrial transfer themselves to the service of thy son Horus, and they follow him into his Hall, where a decree is passed that he shall be Lord over them, and they perform the decree straightway."

Thou art the beautiful Prince, who risest like the Sun with the White Crown, and thou art the Lord of Radiant Light and the Creator of Brilliant Rays. The Gods ascribe praises unto thee, and he who loveth thee stretcheth out his hands to thee. Thy Flame Maketh Thine Enemies to Fall, and Thine Eye Overthroweth the Sebau Fiends, and it Driveth its Spear Through the Sky into the Serpent-Fiend Nak and Maketh it to Vomit that which it hath swallowed. [Explode]

Set persuaded Seventy-Two [A Number dealing with Precession.] persons to join with him in a conspiracy to Kill Osiris [The Verdure and Golden Age before the -13K BP Event] and he contrived a proper stratagem to execute his base designs. Then privily taken the measure of Osiris's body, he caused a Chest [Ark] to be made exactly of the same size with it, as beautiful as might be, and set off with all the ornaments of art. This Chest he brought into his banqueting Hall ; where, after it had been much admired by all who were present, Set, as it were in jest, promised to give it to any one of them, whose body upon trial it might fit. Upon this the whole company, one after another, go into it, but as it did not fit any of them, last of all Osiris lays himself down in it, upon which the conspirators immediately ran together, clapped the cover upon it, and then fastened it down the outside with nails, pouring likewise melted lead over it. After this, they carried it away to the river side, and conveyed it to the sea by the Tanaitic mouth of the Nile ; which for this reason is still held in the utmost abomination by the Egyptians, and never named by them but with proper marks of detestation. These things, say they, were thus executed upon the 17th day of the month Athyr, when the Sun was in Scorpio [Halloween], in the 28th year of Osiris's reign ; though there are others who tell us that he was no more than 28 years old at this time.

Set is said "to depart, having the Harpoon of Iron in him," and to have Thrown Up Everything which he had Eaten and to have been put in a Place of Restraint. [Same as Satan.]

A statement in Plutarch's De Iside et Osiride (62), informs us that Typhon was called Seth, and Bebo, and Smy, "all of them words of common import, and expressing certain violent and forcible restraint and withholding, as likewise contrariety and subversion ; we are, moreover, informed by Manetho that the Load-Stone is by the Egyptians called the 'Bone of Horus,' as Iron is, the 'Bone of Typho." This Information is of Considerable Interest, for it makes the Identity of Set and Typhon Certain, and it is, moreover, supported by the Evidence of the Inscriptions. That Iron was Connected with Set or Typhon Is Quite Clear from the passage quoted by Dr. Brugsch in which Thoth is said to have obtained from Set the Knife with which he cut up the Bull.

Egyptian Literature Comprising Egyptian Tales, Hymns, Invocations ; The Book of the Dead ; and Cuneiform Writings, by E. A. Wallis Budge, 1901

Homage to thee, O Ra , thou stridest over the Heaven, being glad of heart, and the Lake of Testes is content. The Sebau Fiend hath Fallen to the Ground ; his arms and his hands have been hacked off, and the knife hath severed the joints of his body. Ra hath a fair wind ; the Seket boat goeth forth and sailing along it cometh into port.

Homage to thee, O Lord of the Acacia Tree, the Seker boat is set upon its sledge ; thou turnest back the Fiend, the worker of Evil, and thou causest the Utchat to rest upon its seat.

Grant thou that I may come unto the Heaven which is everlasting, and unto the Mountain where dwell thy favored ones. May I be joined unto those Shinning Beings, Holy and perfect, who are in the underworld ; and may I come forth with them to behold thy beauties when thou Shinest at eventide and goest to thy mother Nu.

It shall come to pass that the Evil One shall Fall when he Layeth a Snare to Destroy Thee, and the joints of his neck and of his back shall be hacked asunder.

Hail, O ye Gods of the land of Amentet who make offerings and oblations unto Ra-Tem, ascribe ye glory unto him when ye meet him. Grasp ye your weapons and overthrow ye the Fiend Seba on behalf of Ra, and repulse the Fiend Nebt on Behalf of Osiris.

. . . . on the day of making him to triumph over Set and his Fiends in the presence of the great sovereign chiefs who are in Annu ; on the Night of the Battle and overthrow of the Seba-Fiend in the presence of the great sovereign princes who are in Abtu . . . .

According to the desire of my (Osiris) heart, I Have Come From the Pool of Fire, and I have quenched the Fire. . . . . . . Sailest up the Pool of Fire in the Underworld.

. . . . bandages of Set which Fetter My Mouth ; and may the God Tem hurl them at those who would fetter me with them, and drive them back. May my Mouth be Opened, May My Mouth be Unclosed by Shu with his Iron Knife wherewith he Opened the Mouths of the Gods. I am the Goddess Sekhet, and I sit upon my place in the Great Wind of Heaven. . . . . . .

. . . . those Gods who dwell in their companies and who go round about the Turquoise Pool . . . . [Must be Day time Comet !]

I am the Bull enveloped in Turquoise, the Lord of the Field of the Bull, the Lord of The Divine Speech of the Goddess Septet (Sothis) at her hours.

. . . . I have driven back those who would come to the Turquoise sky. . . .

A Flame of Fire and a Scepter of Crystal. I Buried Them by the Furrow of Manaat as 'things for the night." A Scepter of Flint, the Name of Which is 'Giver of Winds.' . . . [Bolide and Concussion]

The Lake of a Million Years ; the Whole Company of the Gods move about among those who are at the side of him who is the Lord of divisions of places. And I say, 'On every road and among these millions of years is Ra the Lord, and his Path is in the Fire, and They Go Round About Him.'

Religion of the Ancient Egyptians, by Alfred Wiedemann, 1897

Hymn to the Aten :

Eyes Shine Brightly until thou settest ; ceaseth all labour when thou settest in the West . . . . . . .Thou ordainest since thou Createdst the Earth, and raisedst them up (i.e. its inhabitants), For thy son who came forth from thy body, the King of Upper and Lower Egypt, who liveth by Truth, the Lord of the two lands . . . .

The expressions "Lord of Heaven," "Lord of Earth," "He who giveth Life For Ever," "He who Illuminateth the Earth," "He who Reigneth in Truth," frequently appear among his titles.

I go forth unto the Heaven, I traverse the Iron sky, my body is in the Midst of the Stars.

From The Destruction of Mankind : There is No Eye Among Mankind Which Can Withstand Thine Eye when it Descendeth in the Form of the Goddess Hathor. [Arc Welding Bright Light]

Therein do I gather as its inhabitants Things which Hang from Heaven, even the Stars. Then Nut Trembled Exceedingly (i.e. the Vault of Heaven Shook so that the Stars were Dislodged and Fell, as Ra had Commanded, into the Land which He Made). [Holding up the Cow.]

From The Legend of the Winged Disk : Behold, Set Went Forth And Cried Out Horribly (neha) as he Flung Forth Curses for that which Horbehudti had done when he Slew the Foes. Then spake Ra to Thoth : 'The Horrible One (nehaha) Cries Out Loud at that which Horbehudti hath done against him.' Then Spake Thoth to Ra : 'Therefore such Cries shall be called Horrible (nehaha) from this day forth.' [South America ta-ta-ta]

Set changes into a Black Hog and Takes Out an Eye of Horus. [Boar Kills Adonis i.e., Verdure]

The chief function of Shu was to Separate the Heavens from the Earth (Nut from Seb), in order to provide the Path for the Sun (Ra).

A Greek papyrus addresses Seth as "Hill – Shaker," "Thunderer'" "Hurricane – Raiser," "Rock – Shaker," ; "The Destroyer, who disturbs the Sea Itself."

Apop is Thrown Into the Ocean at the New Year's Day Festival.

Harris Magic Papyrus : "The God of Ombos Sharpeneth his Arrows in him ; he Shaketh Sky and Earth by his Thunder – Storms ; his magic powers are Mighty, conquering his enemy ; his Battle-Axe cutteth up the Wide – Mouthed Dragon."

From Plutarch : The death of Osiris is first announced by the Pans and Satyrs of Chemmis, i.e., from the Spirits who Accompanied the Birth of the Sun.

Hu the God of Wisdom and The Divine Word holds the Mundane Egg.

215

From the Book of the Dead : "Furthermore I shall Ruin all that I have Made. This Earth will appear as an Abyss, in (or, as) a Flood as in its Primeval Condition. I am the one remaining from it together with Osiris. My forming is then made to me among other Serpents which Men Never Knew, which the Gods Never Saw."

The Annual Festival of Osiris's Death is Inscribed within the Temple of Denderah.

Plutarch says the Deluge happened between the 17th and 20th of Athyr while the Sun was in Scorpio.

In Abydos Seker, the God of Death was before Osiris.

The Three Day Fight Festival were represented by the words "Great Coming Forth"

Egyptian Year was divided into Three Seasons. Orion held the soul of Horus. There are Seven forms of Osiris. The kingdom of Seker was the Tuat, or the Other World. It was shrouded in Thick Darkness, and was formed by bare, sandy deserts, which were full of terrifying Monsters, some winged, and some many headed.

Priest wore Leopard's skin. [Spotted as many World Wide Traditions]

The Pyramid Texts : Translated by Samuel A. B. Mercer 1952 Would have gone here, notes lost in computer crash, maybe in the next version.

Isis Serpent Ra
from numerous translations of hieroglyphs

"Isis was a woman, more knowing in her malice than millions of Men, clever among millions of the Gods, equal to millions of spirits, to whom as unto Ra nothing was unknown either in heaven or upon Earth. The God Ra came each day to sit upon his throne ; he had grown old, his mouth trembled, his saliva dropped upon the ground. Isis kneaded it with her hand along with the dust that had adhered to it ; she moulded there form a Sacred Serpent, to which she gave the form of a Spear Shaft. She wound it not about her face, but flung it on the road along which the great God walked, as often as he wished, in his twofold kingdom. The venerable God went forth, the other Gods accompanied him, he walked along as on other days. Then the Sacred Serpent bit him. The divine God opened his mouth, and his Cry Rang Out to Heaven. His Ennead of Gods called: 'What is it ?' and the Gods cried, 'Look there !' He could make no answer, his jaws chattered, his limbs shook, the venom took hold of his flesh as the Nile covers its banks with water. When the heart of the great God was quieted, he called to his followers: 'Come to me, ye children of my limbs, ye Gods who have emanated from me ! Something painful hath hurt me ; my heart perceiveth it, yet my eyes see not ; my hand hath not wrought it, nothing that I have made knoweth what it is, yet have I never tasted suffering like unto it, and there is no pain which is worse.......I went forth to see what I had created, I was walking in the two lands which I have made, when something stung me which I knew not. Was it fire, was it water ? My heart is in flames, my limbs tremble, all my members shiver. Let there be brought unto me the children of the Gods of beneficent words, who have understanding mouths, and whose power reaches unto Heaven.' The children of the Gods came, full of woe ; Isis came with her magic ; with her mouth full of the breath of life, whose recipes destroy pain, whose word gives life to the dead. She said: 'What is it, what is it O father of the Gods ? A Serpent hath wrought this suffering in thee, one of thy creatures hath lifted up his head against thee. Surely he shall be overthrown by beneficent incantations ; I will make him retreat at the sight of thy rays.' The Holy God opened his mouth : 'I walked along the road, traveling through the two lands of the Earth, after the desire of my heart, that I might see what I had created ; then was I bitten by a Serpent that I saw not. Is it Fire, is it Water ? I am colder than Water, I am hotter than Fire, all my limbs sweat, I tremble, my eye is unsteady, I see not the shy, drops roll from my face as in the Season of Summer.' Isis replied to Ra: 'O tell me thy name, father of the Gods, then he live who is released from pain by thy name.' But Ra answers: 'I have created Heaven and Earth, I have set the hills in order, and made all beings that are thereon. I am he who created the Water, and caused the Primeval Ocean to issue forth. I created the spouse of his divine mother. I created the Heavens and the secrets of the two horizons, and have ordered the souls of the Gods. I am he who illuminates all things at the opening of his eyes ; if he Closes his Eyes, All is Dark. The water of the Nile rises when he bids it ; the Gods know not his name. I make the hours and create the days, I send the year and Create the Inundation, I make the Fire that lives, I purify the house. I am Khepera in the morning, Ra at noon, and Tum at evening.' The venom departed not, it advanced further, the great God became no better. Then Isis said to Ra: 'Thy name was not pronounced in the words thou hast repeated. Tell it to me and the poison will depart ; then shall he live whose

217

name is thus named.' The poison glowed like Fire ; it was hotter than the flame of Fire. The majesty of Ra said : 'I grant thee leave that thou shouldest search within me, O mother Isis ! And that my name pass from my bosom into thine.' So the God hid himself from the other Gods ; his everlasting bark was empty. When the moment arrived for extracting the heart whereon the name was written, Isis said to her son Horus: 'He must yield up unto thee his Two Eyes the Sun and Moon.' So the name of the great God was taken from him, and Isis, the great enchantress, said : 'Depart, O poison, leave Ra : let the eye of Horus go forth from the God and Shine out of his Mouth. I, I have done it ; I throw on the Earth the victorious poison, for the name of the great God is extracted from him. Let Ra live and the poison die !' So spake Isis, the great one, the regent of the Gods, who knows Ra and his true name."

The Threshold Covenant or the Beginning of Religious Rite, by H. Clay Trumbull, 1896

In Northwestern India at early harvest time the first fruits of the grain-field are not taken to the threshing-floor, but are brought home to be presented to the Gods at the household altar, and afterwards eaten by the family, with a portion given to the Brahmans. The first bundle of corn is deposited at the threshold of the home, and a libation of water is made a completion of its offering. The grain being taken from the ear, of a portion of this first-fruits, is mixed with milk and sugar, and every member of the family tastes it Seven times.

Among the Prabhus of Bombay, at the time of the birth of a child, an Iron crowbar is placed "along the threshold of the room of confinement, as a check against the crossing of any evil spirit." This is in accordance with a Hindoo belief that evil spirits keep aloof from Iron, "and even nowadays pieces of Horseshoe can be seen nailed to the bottom sill of door of native houses." Iron seems, in various lands, to be deemed of peculiar value as a guard against evil spirits, and the threshold to be the place for its efficacious fixing. Similarly, "in East Bothnia, when the Cows are taken out of their winter quarters for the first time, an Iron bar is laid before the threshold, over which all the Cows must pass ; for, if they do not, there will be nothing but trouble with them all the following summer."

Of portions of Ireland, it was said, early in this century : "On the 11th of November, every family of a village kills an animal of some kind or other ; those who are rich kill a Cow or sheep, others a goose or a turkey ; while

218

those who are poor . . . kill a Hen or a Cock, and sprinkle the threshold with the blood, and do the same in the four corners of the house ; . . . to exclude every kind of evil spirit from the dwelling,"

The foundation-stone of a new building is, in a sense, the threshold of that structure. Hence to lay the foundations in blood is to proffer blood at the threshold. Traces of this custom are to be found in the practices of the Legends of peoples well-nigh all the World over. Apparently the earlier sacrifices were of human beings. Later they were of animals substituted for persons. The idea seems to have been that he who covenanted by blood with God, or with the Gods, when his house, or his city, was builded, was guarded, together with his household, while he and they were dwellers there ; but, if he failed to proffer a threshold sacrifice, his first-born, or the first person who crossed the bloodless threshold, would be claimed by the ignored or defied deity.

There is, indeed, a suggestion of this idea in the curse by Joshua, when he destroyed the doomed city of Jericho, against him who should rebuild its walls, he not being in covenant with and obedient to the Lord. "Cursed be the Man before the Lord, that riseth up and buildeth this city Jericho : with the loss of his firstborn shall he lay the foundation thereof, and with the loss of his youngest son shall he set up the gates of it." (Josh. 6 : 26) A later record tells of the fulfillment of this curse. It says of the reign of Ahab : "In his days did Hiel the Bethel-ite build Jericho : he laid the foundation thereof with the loss of Abiram his firstborn, and set up the gates thereof with the loss of his youngest son Segub ; according to the word of the Lord, which he spake by the hand of Joshua the son of Nun." (1 Kings 16 : 34)

Describing a ceremony on a large Chinese junk when starting out on a long voyage, an observer tells of the sacrifice of a Fowl in honor of the divinity called Loong-moo, or the Dragon's Mother. A temporary altar was erected at the bow of the vessel, as its beginning, or threshold, and the blood of the sacrificed Fowl was shed there. Pieces of silver paper were "sprinkled with blood (of the fowl), and then fastened to the door-posts and lintels of the cabin." The cabin door is the home door of the voyager.

It would seem that, in primitive practice, the hand of the covenanter dipped in the sacrificial blood on the threshold, and stamped on the door-posts and lintel, was the sign-manual of the covenant between the contracting party or parties, and God, or this custom, as still surviving in the East, have been given, from Constantinople, Jerusalem, and Morocco. Naturally, therefore, the sign-manual by itself came to stand for, or to symbolize, the covenant of the threshold altar ; and the stamp of the red hand became a token of trust in God or the Gods covenanted with in sacrifice, and of power or might resulting from this covenant relation. Wherever the red hand was shown, or found, it was a symbol of covenant favor with Deity, and it came to be known, accordingly, as the "Hand of Might." In the region of ancient Babylonia, also, the red-hand stamp is still to be seen on houses and on animals, apparently as the symbol of their covenant consecration by their owner. Dr. Hilprecht says : "Over all the doors of the rooms in the large khan of Hillah, on the Euphrates, partly built upon the ruins of ancient Babylon, I noticed the red impression of an outspread hand, when I was there in January, 1889. Several white horses in our caravan from on their haunches." This symbol is much used in Jerusalem. Referring to its frequency, Major Conder says : "The 'Hand of Might' is another Jewish belief which may be supposed to have an Aryan origin. This hand is drawn on the lintel or above the arch of the door. Sometimes it is carved in relief, and before one house in the Jew's quarter, in Jerusalem, there is an elaborate specimen, carefully sculptured and colored with vermilion. The Jewish and Arab masons paint the same mark on houses in course of construction ; and, next to the Seven-branched candlestick, it is probably the commonest house-mark in Jerusalem." [Arm of God / Lud Northmen]

In all stages of the transition from house to temple, the sacredness of the threshold, of the door, of the entrance-way, of the gate, was recognized in architecture and in ceremonial. Often the door, or the gate, stood for the temple, and frequently the threshold was an altar, or an altar was at the threshold. There are, indeed, reasons for supposing that the very earliest form of a primitive temple, or sanctuary, or place of worship, was a rude doorway, as covering or as localizing the threshold altar. This would seem to be indicated by Prehistoric remains in different parts of the World, as well as in the later development of the idea in the earlier historic ages. Two Upright Stone Posts, with or without an overlaying stone across them, and with or without an altar stone between or before them, are among the most ancient remains of primitive Man's handiwork ; and a similar design is to be recognized, all the way along in the course of history, down to the elaborate doorway standing by itself as a memorial of the revered dead, or to the monumental triumphal arch as an accompaniment of the highest civilization. And the very name of door, or gate, attaches persistently to the loftiest temple and to the most exalted personage. As the earliest altar was the threshold, the earliest temple was a doorway above the altar at the threshold. When the first dwellers on the plains of Chaldea, after the Deluge, gathered themselves for the building of a common structure reaching God-Ward, they, in their phraseology, called that structure Bab-el, or Bab-ilu, or Babi-ilu, the Door of God. ancient Egyptians called the sovereign head of their national family "Per-ao" (Pharaoh), the exalted House, or Gate, or Door .

Jesus Christ did not hesitate to say of himself as the Way to God : 'I am the Door : by me if any Man enter in he shall be saved.'

In China, Japan, Korea, Siam, and India, a gate, or doorway, usually stands before Confucian and Buddhist and Shinto temples, but apart from the temple, and always recognized as of peculiar sacredness. These doorways, in many places, are painted blood-colored. They stand "at the entrance of temple grounds, in front of shrines and sacred Trees, and in every place associated with the native Kami" – or Gods. Yet, again, in all these countries, the temple gateway is a main feature, or a prominent one, in the chief sanctuaries.

Swinging doors, or gates, are represented, in the religious symbolism of ancient Babylonia, as opening to permit the God Shamash, or the Sun, to start out on his daily circuit of the heavens. A door, or a doorway, appears as a shrine for a God in various cylinders from this region ; and the God is shown standing within it, just beyond the threshold. Indeed, the doorway shrine is a common form on the Babylonian and the Assyrian monuments, as a standing-place for the Gods, and for the kings as representative of the Gods. In ancient Egypt the doorway shrine of the Gods was prominent, as in Babylonia. Moreover, a false door was represented in the earlier mastabahs, or tombs, of the Old Empire of Egypt. This representation of a door was toward the West, in which direction Osiris, the God of the under-world, was supposed to enter his realm as the Sun went down. Gradually this false door came to be recognized as the monumental slab, tablet, or

221

stele, on which were inscribed the memorials of the deceased. As a doorway or a niche, square-topped, or arched, it was the shrine of the one worshipped ; and as a panel, or independent stele, it was the place of record of the object of reverence. [Tombstones]

In Phenicia, Carthage, Cyprus, Cyprus, Sardinia, Sicily, and in Abyssinia, a like prominence was given to the door as a door, in temple and in tomb, and as a niche for the figure of a deity or for the representation of one who had crossed the threshold of the new life.

It is obvious that the idea of the sacredness of the threshold, in the home, in the temple, or in sanctuary, is not of any one time or of any one people, but is of human nature everywhere. It shows itself all the World over, and always. And it has to do with Life, and its Perpetuation or reproduction.

A temple has added sacredness in China according as its foundation is on a spot originally chosen or honored by a representative of Heaven as a threshold of a place of worship. Thus Tai Shan, or the "Great Mount," in the province of Shantung, China, is mentioned in the Shoo King, or Book of Records, as the site of the great Emperor Shun's altar of sacrifice to Heaven, 2254 B.C., or, say, three centuries before the time of Abraham. On this Holy Mountain, as the earliest historic foundation of Chinese worship, "is the great rendezvous of devotees, every sect has there its temples and idols, scattered up and down its sides ; " and great multitudes come thither to worship from near and far.

Among the early Babylonians and Egyptians, as among other primitive peoples, the twofold symbols of sex are counted the sacred emblem of life, and as such are borne by the Gods of Life, and by those who have the power of Life and Death from those Gods. The Circle and Rod, or Ring and Bolt, conjoined, are in the right hand of the Babylonian Sun-God Shamash ; as, in the Ankh, or Crux Ansata, they are in the right hand of every principal deity of ancient Egypt. It is much the same with the Phoenicians and others. In the innermost shrine of the most sacred Shinto temples of Japan, the Circular Mirror, and the Straight Dagger, with the same meaning as the Circle and Rod in Babylonia and Egypt and Phoenicia, are the only indications of the presence of deity ; and the worshipers in those temples can come no farther than the threshold of the shrine containing these emblems. It seems clear that the Egyptian Passover rite was a rite of threshold covenanting, as ordered of God and as understood by the Israelites. Its sacrifice was on the threshold of the homes of the Hebrews on the threshold of a New Year, and on the threshold of a new nationality.

Survivals of the primitive Threshold Covenant are found in various customs among Oriental Christians, and Christians the World over. Thus Easter is still looked at in some regions as the continuance of Passover, and the blood on the threshold is an accompaniment of the feast. Among the modern Greeks, each family, as a rule, buys a lamb, kills it, and eats it on Easter Sunday. "In some country districts the blood (of the lamb) is sometimes smeared on the threshold of the house." Easter, like the Jewish Passover, is the threshold of the new ecclesiastical year. At the church of the Holy Sepulcher, in Jerusalem, a principal incident in the Easter Festivities is the Bringing Down of Fire from Heaven at the Opening of the New Ecclesiastical Year. This ceremony seems to be a survival of the Primitive Custom of Seeking New Life, in its symbol of Fire, at the threshold of the home and of the New Year, in the East and in the West.

Saint George and the Dragon

A terrible Dragon had ravaged all the country round a city of Libya, called Selena, making its lair in a marshy swamp. Its breath caused pestilence whenever it approached the town, so the people gave the Monster two sheep every day to satisfy its hunger, but, when the sheep failed, a human victim was necessary and lots were drawn to determine the victim. On one occasion the lot fell to the king's little daughter. The king offered all his wealth to purchase a substitute, but the people had pledged themselves that no substitutes should be allowed, and so the maiden, dressed as a bride,

223

was led to the marsh. There St. George chanced to ride by, and asked the maiden what she did, but she bade him leave her lest he also might perish. The good knight stayed, however, and, when the Dragon appeared, St. George, making the Sign of the Cross, bravely attacked it and transfixed it with his Lance. Then asked the maiden for her Girdle, he bound it round the neck of the Monster, and thereupon the princess was able to lead it like a lamb. They then returned to the city, where St. George bade the people have no fear but only be Baptized, after which he cut off the Dragon's head and the townsfolk were all Converted. The king would have given George half his kingdom, but the Saint replied that he must ride on, bidding the king meanwhile take good care of God's Churches, honour the Clergy, and have pity on the poor.

The Seven Tablets of the History of Creation
from Numerous Translations of Cuneiform Text

There was a time in the height Heaven was not named. Below, the Earth bore no name, and the Primeval Apsu who begat them was there from the first, the source of both. And Raging Chaos, Tiamat, the Mother of All. Where Aspu and Tiamat their Waters mingled together. No field was formed, no marsh was seen. When of the Gods none had been called into being, and no destinies were ordained. Then were the Gods, their totality, Created in the Midst of Heaven. Lakhmu and Lakhamu, emerged, periods elapsed . . . . Anu, Bel, and Ea were Created and order prevailed. Ummu-Khubur (Tiamat), Mother of the Hollow, the Creator of Everything, not being able to rest added strong warriors, Created Great Serpents, sharp of tooth, merciless in attack. With poison in place of blood, she filled their bodies. Furious Vipers she clothed with Terror, fitted them out with Awful Splendor, made them high of stature, that their countenance might inspire Terror and arouse Horror, their Bodies Inflated, their Attack Irresistible. She set up Basilisks (Cockatrices or other type), Great Serpents and Lakhami, a Great Monster, a Mad Dog, a Scorpion-Man, a Goat-Fish, a Great Bull, and other Raging Creatures of the River carrying Merciless Weapons not dreading battle. She raised and exalted Kingu among them to be their chief. To march at the head of the forces, to lead the Host. To command the Weapons to Strike, to give the orders for the fray. To be the first in battle was, supreme in triumph. She ordained him and clothed him with authority. Tiamat then addresses Kingu directly : 'Through my word to thee, I have made thee the greatest among the Gods. The rule over all the Gods I have placed in thy hand. The greatest shalt thou be, thou, my consort, my only one.' Tiamat thereupon gives him the tablets of fate,

224

hangs them on his breasts, and dismisses him. 'Thy command be invincible, thy order authoritative, go Quench the Illuminating-God.' [Kill the Sun.] Anshar sends his son Anu with a message to Tiamat : Go and step before Tiamat. May her liver be pacified, her heart softened. Anu obeys, but at the sight of Tiamat's awful visage takes flight. Then Ea is sent and also returns unsuccessful. Anshar decides to send his son Marduk against Tiamat : Marduk heard the word of his father. His heart rejoiced and to his father he spoke. 'When I shall have become your avenger, binding Tiamat and saving your life, then come in a body, in Ubshu-kenna ("the chamber of fates" where Marduk sits on New Year's Day and decides the fate of mankind for the ensuing year.), let yourselves down joyfully, my authority instead of yours will assume control, unchangeable shall be whatever I do, irrevocable and irresistible, be the command of my lips.' Go Gaga, messenger joy of my liver, to Lakhmu and Lakamu I will send thee. Anshar your son has sent me, the desire of his heart he has entrusted to me. Tiamat, our mother is full of Hate towards us, with all her might she is Bitterly Enraged. I sent Anu, he could not endure her presence. Ea was afraid and took to flight. Marduk has stepped forward, the chief of the Gods, your son, to proceed against Tiamat, he has set his mind. Marduk's declaration is then repeated. Upon hearing the message Lakhmu and Lakamu and "all the Iggi." They ate bread, they drank wine. The sweet wine took away their senses. They became drunk, and their bodies swelled up. Thou art honored among the great Gods, thy destiny is unique, thy command is Anu. Marduk, thou art chiefest among the Great Gods, thy fate is unequalled, thy word is Anu ! Henceforth not without avail shall be thy command, in thy Power shall be the Word of thy Mouth, irresistible shall be thy command ; none among the Gods shall transgress thy boundary. Abundance, the desire of the Shrines of the Gods, shall be established in thy sanctuary, even though they lack offerings. O Marduk, thou art our avenger ! We give thee sovereignty over the Whole World. Thy Weapon shall never lose its power, it shall Crush thy foe O Lord, Spare the Life of him that putteth his Trust in thee, but as for the God who began the rebellion, pour out its Life. Command that the cloak disappear ! Then command that the cloak return ! Marduk proceeds to the test. As he gave command, the cloak disappeared. He spoke again and the cloak was there. Now go against Tiamat, cut off her life, let the winds carry her blood to hidden regions. The Four Winds he grasped so that she could not escape. The South and North winds, the East and West winds, he brought to the Net, which was the gift of his father Anu. He creates the Evil Wind [Shockwave], the Whirlwind, the Hurricane, making of the Four Winds he created, the Sevenfold Winds, to destroy the life of Tiamat, they followed

225

after him. Marduk, taking his most powerful weapon, the Thunderbolt, in his hand and mounts his chariot, which is driven by Fiery Steeds. He set the Lightning in front of him, with Burning Flame he Filled his Body and made straight for the hostile camp. The sight of the God inspires Terror on all sides. The Lord clothed in Terror of <u>Overpowering Brightness,</u> which <u>All Beheld,</u> came nearer with his eye fixed upon Tiamat, piercing with his glance at Kingu her consort. Kingu starts back in alarm. He cannot endure the, Majestic Halo, which surrounds Marduk. Kingu's associates – the monsters – are terrified at their leader's discomfiture. Tiamat alone does not lose her courage. Marduk, brandishing his great Thunderstone Weapon, addresses Tiamat : Why hast thou set thy mind upon Stirring Up Destructive Contest ? He reproaches her for the hatred she has shown towards the Gods, and Boldly Calls her out to the contest : Stand Up ! I and Thou, come let us Fight. When Tiamat heard these words she acted as possessed, her senses left her ; Tiamat Shrieked Wild and Loud, trembling and shaking, her whole frame shook down to its very foundations. She pronounced an incantation, uttering her sacred formula. Then Tiamat and Marduk, Chief of the Gods, advanced towards one another. They advanced to the contest, drew nigh for fight and the Gods of Battle Cried Out for their Weapons. The Lord spread out his Net in order to enclose her. The Destructive Wind, which was behind him, he sent forth into her face. As Tiamat opened her mouth full wide, he drove in the Evil Destructive Winds, so that she could not close her lips. The Terrible Winds inflated her stomach exceedingly. Her heart was beset, she lost her reason, she opened still wider her mouth, he seized the spear and plunged it into her stomach, he Pierced her entrails, he tore through her heart, he seized hold of her and put an end to her life, he Cast Down her carcass and Stood Upon her and smashed her skull. [Explosion and towering mushroom Cloud.] After having vanquished Tiamat, her Host were scattered the Gods her helpers, who marched by her side, trembled and afraid. In the Net the valiant Marduk caught her Associates. They try to flee, but he captures them all – including Kingu – without much difficulty and puts them into his great net. Most important of all , he tears the Tablets of Fate from Kingu and places them on his breast. This act marks the final victory. Henceforth, the Gods with Marduk – and no longer Tiamat and her Brood – Decree the Fate of the Universe. There is great rejoicing among the Gods, who heap presents and offerings upon Marduk. As the vanquisher of Chaos, Marduk is naturally singled out to be the establisher of the Fixed Form and Order of the Universe. He cut through the channels of her blood like one does a flat fish into two halves and made the North Wind bear the life giving fluid away into secret places and for Three Years and Three Months, one Day and one night the Blood of the

226

Dragon flowed [Encke Orbit !]. The one half he fashioned as a covering for the Heavens, attaching a bolt and placing there a guardian, with orders not to permit the Waters to come out. He passed through the Heavens, he inspected the expanse. Next, Marduk sets the regulation of the course of the Subterranean Sea [The Night Sky]. The name given to this Sea was Apsu. In front of Apsu, he prepared the dwelling of Nu-dimmud (Ea). The Lord measured out the structure of Apsu. Corresponding to it, he fashioned a great structure Esharra, out of the other half of Tiamat. Esharra is a poetical designation of the Earth and signifies, "House of Fertility." He established the districts of Anu, Bel, and Ea. He established the Stations for the Great Gods ; the Stars, their likeness, he set up as Constellations. He fixed the year and marked the divisions. The Twelve months he divided among Three Stars. From the beginning of the year till the close he established the station of Nibir to indicate their boundary. So that there might be no deviation nor wandering away from the course he established with him, the stations of Bel and Ea. He attached large gates to both sides, made the bolts secure to the left and right. In the midst he made the zenith Nannar, the Moon God, he caused to go forth and handed over to him the night. He fixed him as the luminary of the night to mark off the days, saying : At the beginning of the month, when thou shinest upon the land, Thou commandest the horns to determine six days, and on the Seventh day to divide the crown. Marduk's heart prompted him and he devised a cunning plan. He opened his mouth and unto Ea he spake, that which he had conceived in his heart he imparted unto him : my blood will I take and bone will I fashion, I will make Man, that Man may worship Us. I will Create Man who shall inhabit the Earth, that the Sevices of the Gods may be established, and that their Shrines may be Built. But I will alter the ways of the Gods, and I will change their paths ; together shall they be oppressed, and unto evil shall they. . . . . . O Asari, bestower of planting, Creator of Grain and Plants, who caused the Green Herb to grow up ! O Asaru-alim, who is revered in the house of council, whose provision is Abundance, he who created them Anew. Should their wants be Pure, then are they satisfied. Should he make an Incantation, then are the Gods Appeased. Should they attack him in anger, he shall withstandeth their onslaught ! None among the Gods can rival him ! Tutu is Zi-ukkina, the Life of the Host of the Gods, who establish for the Gods the Bright Heavens. He set them on their way, and ordained their path ; never shall his great deeds be forgotten among Men. Tutu as Zi-azag thirdly they named, the bringer of purification, the God of the favouring breeze, the Lord of hearing and mercy, the Creator of fullness and Abundance, the founder of Plenteousness, who increaseth all that is Small. In sore distress we felt his favoring breeze, let them say, let them Pay Reverence, let them

227

Bow in Humility before him ! Tutu as Aga-azag may Mankind fourthly
magnify ! The Lord of the pure Incantation, the Quickener of the Dead,
who had mercy upon the captive Gods, who removed the yoke from the
Gods his enemies, for their Forgiveness did he Create Mankind, the
Merciful one, with whom it is to bestow Life ! May his deeds endure, may
they never be forgotten in the mouth of Mankind whom his hands have
made ! Tutu as Mu-azag, fifthly, his pure incantation may their mouth
proclaim, who through his pure incantation hath destroyed all the evil ones !
Sag-zu, who knoweth the heart of the Gods, who seeth through the
innermost part ! The evil-doer he hath not caused to go forth with him !
Founder of the assembly of the Gods, subdue of the disobedient, director of
righteousness, who destroyed all the wicked, who exalted in a royal
habitation, who among the Gods is gloriously supreme ! Adu-nuna, the
counselor of Ea, who created the Gods his fathers, unto the path of whose
majesty no God can ever attain ! The Star, which shineth in the Heavens.
May he hold the Beginning and the Future, may they pay homage unto him,
saying, he who forced his way through the midst of Tiamat without resting,
let his name be Nibiru, the Seizer of the Midst ! For the Stars of Heaven he
upheld the paths, he Shepherded all the Gods like Sheep ! He conquered
Tiamat, he troubled and ended her life, in the future of Mankind, when the
days grow old, may this be heard without ceasing, may hold sway forever !
Since he Created the realm of Heaven and fashioned the firm Earth, the
Lord of the World, the father Bel hath called his name. This title, which all
the spirits of Heaven proclaimed, did Ea hear, and his spirit was rejoiced,
and he said : he whose name his fathers have made glorious, shall be even
as I, his name shall be Ea ! The binding of all my decrees shall be control,
all my commands shall he make known ! By the name of "Fifty" did the
great Gods proclaim his fifty names, they made path pre-eminent. Let them
be held in remembrance, and let the First Man proclaim them ; let the Wise
and the Understanding consider them together ! Let the father repeat them
and teach them to his son ; let them be in the ears of the pastor and the
shepherd ! Let a Man rejoice in Marduk, the Lord of the Gods, that he may
cause his land to be Fruitful, and that he himself may have prosperity ! His
Word Standeth Fast, his command is unaltered ; the utterance of his mouth
hath no God ever annulled. He gazed in his anger, he turned not his neck ;
when he is Wroth, no God can withstand his Indignation. Wide is his heart,
broad is his compassion. The Sinner and evil-doer in his presence . . . .

Tammuz and Istar
From Numerous Translations of Cuneiform Texts

"To Hades the land whence none return, the region of Darkness, Istar, the
daughter of Sin (the Moon), inclined her ear, Yea, Istar herself, the
daughter of Sin, inclined her ear to the house of Darkness, the dwelling of
the God Irkalla, to the house from whose entrance there is no exit, to the
road from whose passage there is no return, to the house from whose
visitors the Light is excluded, the place where dust is their bread and their
food is mud. The Light they behold not, in Darkness they dwell, they are
clad like birds in a garment of feathers. Over the door and the bolt is
scattered dust. Istar, on arriving at the Gate of Hades, to the opener of the
gate addresses the word : 'Opener of the Waters, open thy gate ! Open thy
gate that I may enter ! If thou openest not the gate that I may enter, I will
smite the door, the bolt I will shatter, I will smite the threshold and pass
through the portals. I will raise up the dead to devour the living, above the
living the dead shall exceed in number.' The keeper opened his mouth and
speaks ; he says to the princess Istar : 'Stay, O lady, thou must not break it
down ! Let me go and declare thy name to Nin-ki-gal, the queen of Hades.'
The opener descended and declares her name to Nin-ki-gal Allat : 'O
Goddess, the Water of Life thy sister Istar is come to seek ; trying the
mighty bars she has threatened to break open the doors.' When Allat heard
this she opened her mouth and says : 'Like a cut-off Herb has Istar
descended into Hades ; like the lip of a drooping reed she has prayed for the
Waters of Life. What has her heart brought me ? What has her liver brought
me ? When she says : this Water with my bridegroom, like food would I
eat, like beer would I drink : let me weep for the heroes who have left their
wives ; let me weep for the handmaids whom from the bosom of their
husbands thou hast taken ; for the little child let me weep whom thou hast
taken ere his days are come is taken away. Go, keeper nevertheless, open
for her thy gate ; strip her also according to the ancient rules.' The keeper
went, he opened for her his gate : 'Enter, O lady, let the city of Cutha
receive thee ; let the palace of Hades rejoice at thy presence.' The first gate
he caused her enter, and touched her ; he threw down the mighty crown of
her head. 'Why, O keeper, hast thou thrown down the mighty crown of my
head ?' 'Enter, O lady, for thus are the orders of Allat.' The second gate he
caused her enter and touched her ; he threw away the earrings of her ears.
'Wherefore, O keeper, hast thou thrown away the earrings of my ears ?'
'Enter, O lady, for thus are the orders of Allat.' The third gate he caused
her enter and touched her ; he threw away the precious stones of her
necklace. 'Wherefore, O keeper, hast thou thrown away the precious stones

229

of my necklace ?' 'Enter, O lady, for thus are the orders of Allat.' The fourth gate he caused her enter and touched her ; he threw away the ornaments of her breasts. 'Wherefore, O keeper, hast thou thrown away the ornaments of my breasts ?' 'Enter, O lady, for thus are the orders of Allat.' The fifth gate he caused her enter and touched her ; he threw away the gemmed girdle of her waist. 'Wherefore, O keeper, hast thou thrown away the gemmed girdle of my waist ?' 'Enter, O lady, for thus are the orders of Allat.' The sixth gate caused he enter and touched her ; he threw away the bracelets of her hands and feet. 'Wherefore, O keeper, hast thou thrown away the bracelets of my hands and my feet ?' 'Enter, O lady, for thus are the orders of Allat.' The Seventh Gate he caused her enter and touched her ; he threw away the cincture of her body. 'Wherefore, O keeper, hast thou thrown away the covering robe of my body ?' 'Enter, O lady, for thus are the orders of Allat.' When for a long time Istar descended into the region of Hades, Allat beheld her and was haughty before her. Istar took not counsel, she besought her with oaths. Allat her mouth opened and speaks, to Namtar, the plague-demon, her messenger, the word she utters : 'Go, Namtar, take Istar from me, and lead her out ; sixty times strike Istar with disease : the disease of the eyes strike into her eyes ; the disease of the side strike into her side ; the disease of the feet strike into her feet ; the disease of the heart strike into her heart ; the disease of the head strike into her head ; into her, even the whole of her, and into each limb strike disease.' After that the lady Istar into Hades had descended, with the cow the bull would not unite, and the ass the female would not approach, the handmaid in the street would not approach the freeman, the freeman ceased to give his order, the handmaid ceased to give her gift. Pap-sukal, the messenger of the mighty Gods, bowed his face before the Sun-God, Shamash : 'There is woe below, for All Things are Full of Destruction.' Shamash went ; in the presence of Sin his father he stood, in the presence of Ea the king his tears flowed down : 'Istar into the lower regions has descended, she has not ascended back ; for a long time Istar into Hades has descended, with the cow the bull will not unite, the ass the female ass will not approach ; the handmaid in the street will not approach the freeman, the freeman has ceased to give his order, the handmaid has ceased to give her gift.' Ea in the wisdom of his heart formed a resolution ; he created Atsu-su-namir, the Sphinx, the Androgyny ; 'Go Atsu-su-namir, towards the Gate of Hades set thy face ; let the Seven gates of Hades be opened at thy presence ; let Allat see thee and rejoice at thy presence, when her heart is at rest and her liver is appeased. Conjure her also by the names of the great Gods. Raise thy heads, to the roaring Stream set thy ear ; may the lady Istar overmaster the roaring Stream, the Waters in the midst of it may she drink. Allat on

230

hearing this, she struck her girdle, she bit her thumb : 'Thou hast asked of me a request none should request ! Go, Atsu-su-namir, let me injure thee with a great injury ! May the garbage of the sewers of the city be thy food ! May the vessels of the daughters of the city be thy drink ! May the Darkness of the dungeon be thy habitation ! May the threshold be thy seat ! May drought and famine strike thine offspring !' Allat opened her mouth and says, to Namtar, 'Strike open the firmly-built palace, the Asherim (Stone stakes or cones) adorn with Stones of the Dawn ; bid the springs of Earth come forth and seat them on a throne of Gold ; over Istar pour the Waters of Life and bring her before me.' Namtar went and smote the firmly-built palace, he shattered the thresholds which bear up the Stones of Light, he bade the springs of the Earth come forth, on a throne of Gold did he seat them, over Istar he poured the Waters of Life and brought her along. The first gate he passed her out of and restored to her the cincture of her body ; the second gate he made her pass, and restored to her the bracelets of her hands and her feet. The third gate he passed her out, and restored to her the gemmed girdle of her waist. The fourth gate made her pass, and restored to her the ornaments of her breasts. The fifth gate he passed her out, and restored to her the jewels of her necklace. The sixth gate he made her pass, and restored to her the earrings of her ears. The Seventh gate he passed her out, and restored to her the mighty crown of her head. 'If she (Allat) has not given thee that for which the ransom is paid her, turn back to her again for Tammuz the bridegroom of thy youth. Pour over him the Pure Waters, anoint him with precious oil. Clothe him with a purple robe ; a Ring of Crystal let him strike upon the hand. Let Samkhat the Goddess of joy enter the liver of Istar.' Before this the Goddess Tillili had taken her jewels, the Eye-Stones also which were unbroken ; the Goddess Tillili had heard of the death of her brother Tammuz ; she broke the Jeweled Circlet which she had taken, even the Eye-Stones which were full of the face of Light, crying 'O my brother, the only one, do not destroy me.' ' In the day that Tammuz bound on me a Ring of Crystal and a Bracelet of Turquoise, at that time he bound them on me, at that time he bound them on me. Let the wailing Men and wailing Women bind them on the funeral pyre, and smell the sweet savour.'

Istar Pleads for the Love of Gilgamesh
From Numerous Translations of Cuneiform Text

To secure the grace of Gilgamesh, the exalted Ishtar raises her eyes. Come, Gilgamesh, be my spouse. Give, O give unto me thy manly strength, be thou my husband and I will be thy wife. I will place thee on a chariot of Lapis Lazuli and Gold [Sunny Blue Skies], with wheels of Gold and horns of Sapphire, drawn by great steeds. Large kudanu-lions thou shalt harness to it. With sweet odor of cedars enter our house. Upon entering our house thou shalt sit upon a lofty throne, and people will kiss thy feet. Kings, lords, and princes will be submissive to thee, products of mountain and land, they will bring as tribute to thee. Gilgamesh retorts : Tammuz, the consort of thy youth, thou didst cause weeping and didst bring grief upon him every year. The bright-colored allallu bird thou didst love. Thou didst crush him and break his pinions. In the woods he stands and laments, O my pinions ! Thou didst love a lion of perfect strength, Seven and Seven times didst thou dig a snaring pit for him, thou didst love a stallion superior in the fray, with whip and spur thou didst urge him on. Thou didst force him on for Seven double hours, thou didst force him on when wearied and thirsty ; his mother Silili thou madst weep. Thou didst love a shepherd of the flock who continually poured out incense before thee, and, for thy pleasure, slaughtered lambs day by day. Thou didst smite him, and turn him into a tiger, so that his own sheep-boys drove him away, and his own dogs tore him to pieces. When Ishtar heard such words she became enraged, and went up into Heaven, and came unto her father Anu, and to her mother Antum, the sovereigns of the Skies, and thus spoke unto them : O, this king my beauty doth despise, my sweetest charms beholds not with his eyes. And Anu to his daughter thus replied : My daughter, thou must subdue his vaunting pride, and he will claim thy beauty and thy charms, and gladly lie within thy glorious arms. My father, Gilgamesh has insulted me ; Gilgamesh has upbraided me with my evil deeds, my capricious love and of violence, I hate him now, daddy, as I did love ! And Anu opened his mouth and spoke – said unto her, the mighty Goddess Ishtar : Thou shalt not remain so disconsolate, even though Gilgamesh has upbraided thee with thy deeds of evil and of violence. And Ishtar opened her mouth and said, she spoke unto Anu : My father, send your Fierce Winged Heaven-Bull Full of Fury to Crush Gilgamesh, and I will aid the Beast to strike him prone, till in death shall breathe his dying groan ! For answering my love for him with scorn and insults, proud monarch, from his throne he shalt be torn ! The Bull will bring about Seven years of famine, Anu said, Are you

232

prepared for such devastation ? Er, Yes ! Out of Anu's realm a Shining
Monster, Body Filled with Flame, thick brazen plates and horns of
adamant ; now it Flies toward the palace, Roaring from the Skies. The Gods
appear above to watch the fight, and a Loud Roar Echoes from the Skies,
and Uruk's three hundred warriors barrage the Great Bull and Burning
bloody gore they are all dashed to pieces. Eabani then leapt to his hoofs and
cinched his own flank strap and with Gilgamesh leaped headlong into the all-
out tumid and both are thrown aback. Now with Spreading Wings and
Breast of Scales it comes again, with maddened fury a Flash with Fire along
the Roaring Skies ; Fierce its Eyeballs Glare, in Swiftest Flight o'er them
Drops from the Skies. As Gilgamesh raised his Enormous Gleaming Sword
the Beast turned in fear and caught Eabani in his chest with its diamond hard
horns, in mortal pain Eabani by thickness of Tail caught with his Iron grasp
and cried : Quick ! Strike at its head ! Thus following his dear friend's
commands he swung and triumphantly ended the combat by severing head
from carcass ! And Gilgamesh now turned his furious face toward the Gods,
and on the Beast doth place his foot ; he raised his gory Sword on high, and
sent his Shout Defiant to the Sky : Tis thus, ye foes divine ! The king
proclaims his war against your power, and highest names! Hurl ! Hurl !
your Darts of Fire, ye vile Kal-bi (dogs) ! My challenge hear ! ye Cravens
of the Sky ! The monarch and his wounded Seer have cleft the head from
Anu's Bull prone lying they drag it in from the plain within the city where
all can view the slain. The heart they brought to Shamash's holy shrine,
before him laid the offering divine. Ishtar mounts the high walls of Uruk
and in violent rage she pronounces a curse : Cursed be Gilgamesh, who has
enraged me, who has killed the Divine Bull ! Eabani, upon hearing these
words of Ishtar, ripped out the privy member of the Kine and throws it into
her face and says : Here, you and your harlots know what to do with that !
Upon the spectacle she and her maids sped off to the Skies Loudly Cooing
with joy and seduction.

The Deluge
From Numerous Translations of Cuneiform Texts

Tsit-napishtim tells his story :
I will reveal to thee, O Gilgamesh, the hidden word, and the decision of the
Gods to my preservation will I declare the secret to thee. Shurippak, a city
which thou knowest, which lieth on the bank of the Euphrates, that city is
ancient and the Gods were within it, to make a Deluge and Whirlwind the
Great Gods have brought their heart. There was even their father Anu, and
their counselor the warrior Bel, and their messenger Ninib, and their

233

governor Ennugi. The Lord of Wisdom, Ea, sat also with them, and he repeated their purpose to the hut of reeds, saying : O reed-hut, reed-hut ! O wall, wall ! O reed-hut, hear ! O wall, understand ! Thou Man of Shurippak, i.e., Tsit-napishtim, son of Ubara-Tutu, pull down thy house, build a ship, forsake thy possessions, take heed for thy Life ! Abandon thy goods, save thy Life, and bring up living Seed of every kind into the ship to preserve the sleep of Plants and Living Beings. As for the ship, which thou shalt build, well planned must be its length shall bear proportion each to each, and thou shalt launch it in the Ocean ! I took heed, and spake unto Ea, my Lord, saying : The command, O my Lord, which thou hast given ; I will honour, and will fulfill. But how shall I make answer unto the city, the people and the elders thereof ? Ea opened his mouth and spake, and he said unto me, his servant, Thus shalt thou answer and say unto them : Bel hath cast me forth, for he hateth me, and I can no longer live in your city ; nor on Bel's Earth can I any longer lay my head. I will therefore go down to the Deep and dwell with my Lord Ea, will I Live. On the fifth day I constructed its frame ; its sides were 140 cubits high ; its deck was likewise 140. I laid down its form, I fashioned it ; I divided its hull into six sections, I divided its upper deck into Seven compartments ; its main deck I divided into nine chambers. With water-pegs on the inside I caulked it. I selected a mast; and added all that was necessary. Six sars of bitumen I smeared over the outside. Three sars of bitumen I smeared over the inside. With all that I possessed I loaded it ; with all the Silver I had I filled it ; with all the Gold I had I loaded it ; with all that I had of the Seed of Life of every kind I loaded it ; I put into the ship all my family and my dependents ; the cattle of the field, the wild animal of the field, the progeny of the people, craftsmen, all of them I brought up. A fixed time Shamash had appointed, saying : the Lord of Darkness will at eventide send a heavy rain ; then go enter into the ship, and shut thy door. The appointed season arrived, and the ruler of the Darkness sent at eventide a Destructive Rain. Of the storm I saw the beginning ; to look upon the storm I was in Terror ; I entered into the ship and closed the door. To the pilot of the ship, to Puzur-Bel the sailor, I committed the great ship, and the contents thereof. When the Break Dawn appeared, there arose up from the horizon on the Firmament of Heaven Black Clouds. Which Ramman in the midst thereof Roared the Thunder, and Nabu and Marduk went before, the throne-bearers Passed like Messengers over the Mountain and plain, in their Terror they Shake the Earth. Like a Combat over Men it came on. Uragal parted the anchor-cable. There went Ninib, and he made the storm to burst. Ira, God of Pestilence, tore down the ship's mast. The Anunnaki carried Flaming Touches, and with the Brightness thereof their Sheen the Lit Up the Earth. The Whirlwind

234

of Ramman mounted up into the Heavens and all Light turned into Darkness.
The Tempest Raged for a whole day. The Flood Reached to Heaven, and all
was Confusion ; Men by reason of the Darkness could see nothing, and they
perished miserably. No Man beheld his fellow, no longer could Men know
each other. In Heaven the Gods were afraid of the Deluge, they retreated,
they ascended up into Heaven of Anu. The Gods lay down like hounds, in
the enclosure of Heaven they lay cowering. Then Istar Screamed Aloud like
a Woman in travail, wailing : The race of Man hath been turned back into
clay, because I assented to an evil thing in the council of the Gods ! Alas : I
have assented to an evil thing in the council of the Gods, and agreed to a
storm which hath destroyed my people ! That which I brought forth – where
is it ? I will truly give birth to my people again, and like the spawn of fish
will filleth the sea ! The Gods of the Anunnaki wept with her, the Gods
were bowed down, they sat down weeping, their lips were pressed together
for six days and six nights the wind blew, and the Deluge and the Tempest
Overwhelmed the Land. When the Seventh day drew nigh, then ceased the
Raging Tempest and the Deluge, and the storm, which had fought like a
Host. Then the sea, its voice was fixed silent and it went down ; and the
hurricane and the Deluge ceased. I looked upon the sea and cried aloud, for
all Mankind like reeds the corpses floated. In place of the fields a swamp lay
before me. I opened the window and the Light fell upon my cheek ; I bowed
myself down, I sat down, I wept praying ; over my cheeks and nose flowed
my tears. I looked upon all the quarters of the expanse, and behold all was
Sea. After Twelve days the land appeared, to the land Nitsir the ship took
its course. The mountain of the land of Nitsir held the ship fast and did not
let it slip. The first day, the second day, the mountain Nitsir held the ship
fast. The third day, the fourth day, the mountain Nitsir held the ship fast.
The fifth day, the sixth day, the mountain Nitsir held the ship fast. When
the Seventh day drew nigh, I sent out a Dove, and let her go forth. The
Dove flew hither and thither, but there was no resting-place for her and she
returned. Then I sent out a swallow, and let her go forth. The swallow flew
hither and thither, but there was no resting-place for her and she returned.
Then I sent out a raven and let her go forth. The raven flew away and beheld
the abatement of the waters, and she came near, wading and cawing, but did
not return. Then I brought all out unto the four winds, offered a sacrifice, I
made a libation on the peak of the Mountain. By Sevens I set out the vases,
around them I heaped up reed, and cedar-wood, and incense. The Gods
smelt the savour, the Gods smelt the sweet savour, the Gods gathered like
flies about him that offered up the sacrifice. Then the Lady of the Gods
drew nigh, and she Raised on High the Great Jewels, which Anu had made
according to her wish, and said : What Gods these are ! Verily, by the

235

jewels [Rainbow] of Lapis Lazuli [the Blue Sky] which are upon my neck, I
Will Not Forget ! These days I have set in my Memory, and Truly Never
Will I Forget Them ! Let the Gods come to the offering, but Bel shall not
come to the offering, since he refused to ask counsel and sent the Deluge,
and handed over my people unto Destruction. Now when Bel drew nigh, he
saw the ship, and was very wroth ; he was filled with anger like that of the
Gods, - the Igigi [the Pleiades], saying : Who then hath escaped with his
Life ? No Man was to survive the Destruction ! Then Ninib opened his
mouth and spake, and said to the warrior Bel, Who but Ea could have
planned this thing ? For the Sage Ea knoweth all arts ! Then Ea opened his
mouth and spake, and said to the warrior Bel, Thou art the governor of the
Gods, O warrior, how, why, without taking counsel, didst thou cause the
Deluge ! On the Sinner visit his Sin, and on the Transgressor visit his
Transgression ; but hold thy hand, that All be Not Destroyed ! And forbear,
that All be Not Confounded ! Instead of sending a Deluge, let lions come
and minish Mankind ! Instead of sending a Deluge, let hyenas come and
minish Mankind ! Instead of sending a Deluge, let a famine come and waste
the land ! Instead of sending a Deluge, let the Plague-God come and slay
Mankind ! And Ea said ; I did not reveal the purpose of the Great Gods. I
caused Atrakhasis to see a dream, and thus he heard the purpose of the
Gods. Thereupon Bel arrived at a decision, and he went up into the ship.
He took my hand and brought me forth, he brought my wife forth, he made
her to kneel at my side, he turned towards us, he stood between us, he
blessed us, saying : Hitherto hath Tsit-napishtim been of Mankind, but now
let Tsit-napishtim and his wife be like unto the Gods, even us, and let Tsit-
napishtim dwell afar off at the Confluence of the Streams ! Then they took
me, and afar off, at the Mouth of the Rivers, they made me to dwell.

The Adapa Legend
cuneiform inscription
by Morris Jastrow, 1898

The beginning of the story is missing, but the general context can be
restored. Adapa of Eridu was famed in Legend as a Sage, and his ordinary
title Apqallu indicates that he was one of the pre-diluvian wise Men. He is
said to have written a work on Astronomy, and, like the Seven Sages, he
was patron of the priesthood of incantations. To Adapa the God Ea gave
vast understanding, "that he might give names to all concepts in the Earth."
A fisherman, Adapa, is engaged in plying his trade when a storm arises.
Adapa is designated as the son of Ea. The place where he is fishing is
spoken of as 'The Sea' and this body of Water as the beginning of the great
Okeanos, being sacred to Ea. The story assumes a period of close
intercourse between Gods and Men, a time when the relationship involved

236

in being 'a son of a God' had a literal force which was lost to a more advanced generation. Yet, he was of "Human offspring," that is one descended from the Human Race, and mortal leader of Men. Adapa, accordingly, is portrayed as fishing for the 'House of his Lord,' i.e., for Ea. When a storm breaks loose from the South under the form of a Bird. The South Wind, the winged female monster Shutu, blew and drove him under the Water. Into the dwelling-place (of the Fish) it engulfs him. 'O South Wind, thou hast overwhelmed me with thy cruelty (?). Thy wings I will break.' Even as he spoke the wings of the South Wind were broken. For Seven days the South Wind did not blow across the land. Anu, the God of Heaven, is astonished at this long-continued disappearance of the South Wind, and asks a messenger of his, who is called the god Ilabrat, for the cause. Anu inquires : "Why has the South Wind not blown for Seven days across the land ?" His messenger Ilabrat answers him : "My lord ! Adapa, the son of Ea, has broken the wings of the South Wind." Anu, upon hearing the news, is enraged, and cries for 'help' against an interference in his domain. He denounces Adapa in solumn assembly, and demands his presence of Ea, in whose domain Adapa has taken refuge. The text at this point is defective, but one can gather that Ea, who constitutes himself Adapa's protector, warns the latter, as he warned Parnapishtim (of the Deluge). He advises him to present himself at the throne of Anu for trial, and to secure the intervention of the two Gods, Tammuz and Gishzida (the Trees of Life and Knowledge), who are stationed at the gate of Heaven, Anu's dwelling-place. To accomplish this, Adapa is to clothe himself in garments of morning (sackcloth), and when the doorkeepers ask him the reason for his mourning, he is to answer : . . . Two Gods have disappeared from our Earth, therefore I have been brought to this plight. And when he is asked : "Who are the two Gods who have disappeared from Earth ?" Tammuz and Gishzida will look at one another ; they will sigh and speak a favorable word before Anu, and the glorious countenance of Anu they will show thee. Tammuz and Gishzida will know that they are meant. The mourning of Adapa will be regarded as a sign of reverence for the two Gods, whose sympathy will good-will will thus be secured. Further advice that Ea offers to Adapa : When thou comest before Anu they will offer thee food of death. Do not eat. They will offer thee waters of death. Do not drink. They will offer these a garment. Put it on. They will offer thee oil. Anoint thyself. The order that I give thee do not neglect. The word that I speak to thee take to heart. The messenger of Anu approached Ea. 'Adapa has broken the wings of the South Wind. Deliver him into my hands . . .' Ea obeys the order, delivers up Adapa, and everything happens as was foretold. Upon mounting to Heaven and on his approach to the gate of Anu, Tammuz and Gishzida were stationed at the gate of Anu. They saw Adapa and cried 'Help, Lord (Anu, it will be recalled, utters the same cry.) ! Why art thou thus attired ? For whom hast thou put on garments of Mourning ?' Adapa replies : 'Two Gods have disappeared from Earth, therefore do I wear a mourning garment.' 'Who are the two Gods who have disappeared from the Earth ?' Tammuz and Gishzida looked at one another,

237

broke out in lament. 'O Adapa ! Step before King Anu.' As he approached, Anu saw him and cried out to him : 'Come Adapa, why hast thou broken the wings of the South Wind ?' Adapa answered Anu : 'My lord ! For the house of my lord I was fishing in the midst of the Sea. The Waters lay still around me like a Mirror, when the South Wind began to blow and forced me underneath. Into the dwelling of the Fish it drove me. In the anger of my heart I broke the wings of the South Wind.' Tammuz and Gishzida thereupon intercede with Anu on behalf of Adapa, and succeed in appeasing the God's wrath. Anu is appeased, but he is astonished at Ea's patronage of Adapa, as a result of which a mortal has actually appeared in a place set aside for the Gods. Why did Ea permit Man, the unclean mortal, to see the interior of Heaven and Earth ? A mind cunning has he bestowed upon him and created him unto fame. 'Now what shall we grant him ? Offer him bread of Life, that he may eat of it.' They brought it to him, but he did not eat. Waters of Life they brought him, but he did not drink. A garment they brought him. He put it on. Oil they brought him. He anointed himself. Anu looked at him and lamented over him. 'Come, Adapa, why didst thou not eat and not drink ? Now thou canst not live.' Adapa replies, unconscious of the deception practiced on him : 'Ea, my Lord, commanded me not to eat and not to drink.' Whereupon, Anu ordered his messenger to take Adapa back to the Earth. "In the days when Adapa, the offspring of Man, With his . . . cruelly broke the wings of the South Wind, and ascended to Heaven, so verily did this come to pass, and whatsoever he brought about evilly for Men, and disease which he brought about in the bodies of Men, this will the Goddess Ninkarrak allay. May the sickness depart, the disease turn aside. Upon that Man may his crime fall and . . . may he rest not in sweet sleep."

What his subsequent fate is we do not know, for the tablet here comes to an end. [There is a complete (?) version easily found online if interested.]

Enuma Elish : The Seven Tablets of Creation, or the Babylonian and Assyrian Legends Concerning the Creation of the World and of Mankind. Vols. 1 & 2 by L. W. King 1902

The Cuthaean Legend line 10. A people who had the bodies of Birds of the Hollow, Men who had the faces of Ravens, had the Great Gods Created, and in the ground the Gods created a dwelling-place for them. Tiamat gave them suck, the Lady of Gods brought them into the World. In the Midst of the Mountain they became strong, they waxed great, they multiplied exceedingly. Seven kings, brethren, fair and comely, Three hundred and sixty thousand in number were their forces. line 17.

On some traces of the history of creation in religion and astrological literature.

line 7 The . . . ., of war and battle is in the hand of Marduk, the director of the Gods, at whose battle Heaven Quaked, at whose Wrath the Deep is troubled ! At the point of his Weapon the Gods turned back ! To his furious attack there was no opponent ! O Mighty Lord, to whom there is no rival in the assembly of the Great Gods ! In the bright firmament of Heaven his course is supreme ! In E-kur, the temple of true worship, exalted is his decree ! With the Evil Wind his Weapons Blaze Forth, with his Flame steep Mountains are Destroyed ! He Overwhelmeth the expanse of the Billowing Ocean ! The son of E-sara is his name, the Hero of the Gods is his title ! From the Depth is he Lord of the Gods of human habitations ! Before his Terrible Bow the Heavens stand fast ! . . . . Plague and Destruction, and Tempest, ... line 21.

In a fragment there is a reference to Marduk's drawing forth of the mulmullu, or the Spear-Star of Marduk, which we know from Tablet IV of the Creation Series, l. 101, he plunged into the belly of Tiamat, after he had filled her with the Evil Wind.

The Religion of Babylonia and Assyria,
by Morris Jastrow, 1898

As long as activity prevails in any branch of Science, all results are provisional. Increasing knowledge leads necessarily to change of perspective and to a readjustment of views. The chief reason for writing a book is to prepare the way for the next one on the subject. The time has come for focusing the results reached, for sifting the certain from the uncertain, and the uncertain from the False.

Accepting a view or a Tradition from one's Teacher does not constitute a person an Authority.

Ea the God of the Waters of the Deep. 'God of Humanity' par excellence Oannes, and also the Culture-God of primitive Babylonia, the God of Wisdom, the instructor of his worshippers in Arts and Science. "the Antelope of the Deep" "the Ship of the Divine Antelope of the Deep"

Nin-a-gal 'God of great strength' and patron of the [Black] Smiths art.

Nergal "the mighty one of the great dwelling-place" Jensen "the God of the region of the Dead." 'king of the Nether World.' "the great dwelling place" He is the personification of some of the Evils that bring Death to Mankind, particularly Pestilence and War. The Death that follows in his path is a Violent One, and his Destructive Force is one that Acts upon Large Masses rather than upon the Individual. Hence, one of the most common ideographs used to express his name is that which signifies 'Sword.' War and Pestilence are intimately associated in the mind of the Babylonians. Among other nations, the Sword is, similarly, the symbol of the Deity, as the Plague-Bringer as well as the warrior. Different from Nin-ib, who is also a God of War, Nergal symbolizes more particularly the destruction which accompanies war, and not the strong champion who aids his subjects in the fight. Nergal is essentially a Destroyer, and the various epithets applied to him in the religious texts, show that he was viewed in this light. He is at times the 'God of Fire,' again 'the raging king,' 'the Violent one' 'the one who Burns' ; and finally identified with the glowing heat of Flame.

Bel, as the God of Earth, was associated with Anu, as the God of Heaven, and Ea, as the God of the Deep, to form a triad that embraced the entire Universe. It is tempting to suppose that the first command of the Decalogue (Exodus, XX) contains and implied reference to the Babylonian triad. And God spake all these words, saying, I am the Lord thy God, which have brought thee out of the land of Egypt, out of the house of bondage. Thou shalt have no other Gods before me. Thou shalt not make unto thee any graven image, or any likeness of anything that is in Heaven Above, or that is in the Earth Beneath, or that is in the Water under Earth : Thou shalt not bow down thyself to them, nor serve them : for I the Lord thy God am a Jealous God, visiting the inequity of the fathers upon the children unto the

240

third and fourth generation of them that hate me ; And shewing mercy unto thousands of them that love me, and keep my commandments.

Sennacherib calls Ashur the Great Mountain or Rock, - a phrase that recalls a biblical metaphor applied to the deity. He is 'the guide of the Gods.'

Ishtar was invoked as the great Goddess of battle and war. She appears at times in the role of a Violent Destroyer. Her appearance is that of a being clothed with Fiery Flames, and streams of Fire are sent down by her upon the enemies of Ashurbanabal. Also as Goddess of fertility, who gradually brings Vegetation, strength, and productivity back again.

A hymn to the Storm-God, Ramman, enables us to specify the Great Terror that the God, as the general source of disturbances in the Heavenly Phenomena, inspired. The God is addressed as The Lord who in his Anger holds the Heavens in his control, Ramman in his Wrath the Earth has Shaken. The Mighty Mountain – thou dost overturn it. At his anger, at his Wrath, the Gods of Heaven mount up to Heaven [Fly to a safe place.], the Gods of Earth enter the Earth. Into the foundation of Heaven Shamash enters. [The Sun is obscured.]

The illustrations adduced will suffice to show the manner in which the Babylonians conceived the relationship between Mankind and the Gods. His divine associates are no less anxious than human subjects to Pacify the might of God. The element of Fear Alternated with that of Love, and no matter how near the Gods were felt to be, one was never certain of their good will.

Ishtar, the Goddess of the morning am I, Ishtar, the Goddess of the evening am I, Ishtar, - to open the Lock of Heaven belongs to my supremacy. Heaven I Destroy, Earth I Devastate, - such is my supremacy. . . . . . . The Mountain I sweep away altogether, - such is my supremacy. The Destroyer of the Mountain wall am I, their foundation am I, - such is my supremacy. May thy heart be at rest, thy liver (the seat of emotions) be Pacified. By the great Lord Anu, may thy heart be at rest. By the Lord, the Great Mountain Bel, may thy liver be Pacified. O supreme mistress of The Mountain of the Universe , may thy liver be Pacified. . . . . . . [NEO, be nice to us.]

How long, O mistress, will the mighty foe Oppress thy land, in thy great city Erech Famine has settled, in E-ulbar, the house of thy oracle, blood is poured out like water, throughout thy districts he has kindled Conflagrations, and poured [Fire] over them in columns. O my mistress, I

241

am abundantly yoked to misfortune, O my mistress, thou hast encompassed me, thou hast brought me into pain, the mighty foe has Trodden me down as a Reed, I have no judgment, I have no wisdom, like a 'dry field' I am Desolate night and day, I thy servant beseech thee, May thy heart be at rest, thy liver be Pacified.

This text is in the form of a communication made to the king. Ashur has given him the four ends of the Earth. In the house where he shines and is the greatest scion of the reigning dynasty, the king has no rival. Like the rising Sun he shines. This is the greeting from Bel Tarbasi 'Lord of the court' and the assembled Gods.

The God Ashur himself now addresses the king :
As for those enemies that plot against thee, that force thee to march out, thou didst open thy mouth, "Verily I implore Ashur." I have heard thy cry. Out of the Gate of Heaven I proclaim Aloud, 'Surely I will hasten to let Fire Devour them. Thou shalt stand among them. In front of thee I shall rise up. Up onto the Mountain I bring them, there to rain down upon them Destructive Stones. Thine enemies I hew down, with their blood I fill the River. Let them behold and glorify me, for Ashur, the Lord of Gods, am I.'

This important and striking message, coming direct from Ashur we are told, is to be formally presented and read in the presence of the king. Instructions are added to the priests to pour out a libation of precious oil. Sacrifices of animals and waving of incense are to accompany the presentation. The oracle, as the God's answer to the king's questions, thus gave rise to ritual as elaborate as the rites connected with the preparation for the answer.

The Assyrians could not cut themselves loose from Ancient Traditions, and continued to erect huge piles of brick, as the homage most pleasing in the eyes of their Gods. The book of Genesis characterized the central idea of the Babylonian and Assyrian temples when it represented the people gathered in the valley of Shinar – that is, Babylonia – as saying : 'Come, let us build a city and a tower that shall reach up to Heaven.' (Gen. XI 4.) The Babylonian and Assyrian kings pride themselves upon the height of their temples. Employing, indeed, almost the very same phrase that we find in the Old Testament, they boast of having made the tops of their sacred edifices as high as 'Heaven.' The temple was to be in the literal since of the word a 'high place.' But, apart from the factor of natural growth, there was a special reason why the Babylonians aimed to make their sacred edifices high. The oldest temple of Babylonia at the present time known to us, the temple of Bel at Nippur, bears the characteristic name of E-Kur, 'Mountain House.' The name is more than a Metaphor. The sacred edifices of Babylonia were intended as a matter of fact to be Imitations of Mountains. It is Jensen's merit to have suggested the explanation for this rather surprising ideal of the Babylonian temple. According to Babylonian notions, it will be recalled, the Earth is pictured as a Huge Mountain [In all the Cuneiform Texts I have read this is never mentioned, yet the Sky Mountain is many times.]. Among other names, the Earth is called E-Kur, 'Mountain House.' The popular and early theology conceived the Gods as sprung from the Earth. They are born in Kharsag-kurkura, 'the Mountain of all lands,' which is again naught but a designation for the Earth, though at a later period some particular part of the Earth, some Mountain peak, may have been pictured as the Birthplace of the Gods, much as among the Indians, Persians, and Greeks we find a particular Mountain singled out as the one on which the Gods dwell. The transfer of the Gods or of some of them to places in the Heavens was a scholastic theory, and not a popular belief. It was a natural association of ideas, accordingly, that led the Babylonians to give to their temples the form of the dwelling which they ascribed to their Gods. The temple, in so far as it was erected to serve as a habitation for the God and an homage to him, was to be the Reproduction of the Cosmic E-Kur, - 'a Mountain House' on a small scale, a miniature Kharsag-kurkura. In confirmation of this view, it is sufficient to point out that E-Kur is not merely the name of the temple to Bel at Nippur, but is frequently used as a designation for temple in general ; and, moreover, a plural is formed of the word which is used for divinities. In Assyria we find one of the oldest temples bearing the name E-kharsag-kurkura, that stamps the edifice as the reproduction of the 'Mountain of all Lands' ; and there are other temples that likewise bear names in which the idea of a Mountain is introduced.

The name E-Kur, 'Mountain House,' though evidently an appropriate designation for the Ziggurat, becomes the term for the sacred area which included in the time a large series of buildings used for the cult, whereas the Ziggurat itself receives the special name of 'House of Oracle,' another name or perhaps the name of a second Ziggurat at Nippur is Im-kharsag 'Mountain of Awe,' and similarly in the case of the Ziggurat is distinct from that of the sacred quarter – the temple in the broader sense.

The two large brick columns at the entrance to the Nippur court may have well been erected in honor of some deity and are paralleled in the case of the Solomonic Temple by the two large columns, known as Yakhin and Boaz, that stood at the gateway. These names are yet unexplained. Their symbolic character, apart from other evidence, may be concluded from the circumstance that, as Schick has shown, the columns stood free, and did not serve as a support for any part of the gateway. There is no need, therefore, for any hesitation in comparing these two columns, whose presence in the Solomonic structure is certainly due to foreign influence, to those found at Nippur.

That the columns at Nippur were erected in accordance with recognized custom follows from De Sarzec's discovery of two enormous round columns within the sacred quarter of Lagash. In the light of Peter's excavations, the significance of the columns at Lagash becomes clear. Unfortunately, De Sarzec's excavations at Lagash at the point of the mound in question were interrupted, but he gives reason for believing that other columns existed near the two large ones found by him.

E-dur-an-ki, 'the link of Heaven and Earth,' the name of a Ziggurat at Larsa. The above name approaches closely to the conception of a Ziggurat in the book of Genesis, as a 'ladder' connecting Heaven and Earth. Gen. XXVIII. 12.

E-temen-an-ki, 'the foundation Stone of Heaven and Earth,' assigned to the Ziggurat to Marduk in Babylonia. E-Babbara, 'the Brilliant House,' which, as the name of the temples to Shamash at Sippar and Larsa, recalls at once the character of the Sun-God. E-kharsag-ella, or 'House of the Glorious Mountain,' the name of a temple to Gula in Babylon.

In the Babylonian temples a piece of furniture to which great religious importance was attached was a Great Basin known as 'Apsu,' – the name, it will be recalled, for 'The Deep.' The name indicates that it was a symbolical representation of the domain of Ea. The comparison with the Great 'Sea' that stood in the court of Solon's Temple naturally suggests itself, and there can be little doubt that the latter is an Imitation of a Babylonian model. The Ziggurat itself being an attempt to reproduce the shape of the Earth, the representation of the 'Apsu' would suggest itself as a natural accessory to the temple. The Ziggurat and the Basin together would thus become living symbols of the current Cosmological Conceptions. The 'Sea' was cut of large blocks of Stone and was elaborately decorated. One of the oldest has a frieze of female figures on it, holding in their outstretched hands flagons from which they pour Water.

244

Another sacred object in the construction of which much care was taken was the Ship in which the deity was carried in solemn procession. The ruler Gudea tells us that he built the 'beloved Ship' for Nin-girsu, and gave it the name Kar-numa-ta-uddua, the Ship of 'the one that Rises Up Out of the Dam of the Deep.' Through Nebuchadnezzar we learn that these Ships were Brilliantly Studded with Precious Stones, their compartments handsomely fitted out, and that in them the Gods were carried in solemn procession on the Festivals celebrated in their honor. It is likely that this excursion of the Gods symbolized some homage to the chief Water-deity, Ea. Bau's Ship was described by an epithet of the Goddess as 'the Ship of the Brilliant Offspring,' the reference being to the Descent of the Goddess from father Anu [Sky / Space].

Note : Two Equal Sized Suns

245

The Origin and Growth of Religion as Illustrated by the
Religion of the ancient Babylonians, by A. H. Sayce
The Hibbert Lectures, 1887

Religion has always loved to Cloak itself in Mystery, and a priesthood is
notoriously averse from revealing in plain language the Secrets of which it
Believes itself the possessor. To the Exoteric World it speaks in parables ;
the people that knoweth not the law is Accursed.

The Annalistic Tablet takes us back reign by reign, dynasty by dynasty, to
about the year 2400 BC. [2,300 B.C. strike ?]

"Sargon, the mighty king, the king of Accad am I, my mother was a
princess ; my father I knew not ; the brother of my father dwells in the
Mountain.   In the city of Azupiranu, which is built on the bank of the
Euphrates, my mother, the princess, conceived me ; in a secret place she
brought me forth ; she placed me in a basket of reeds ; with bitumen my exit
gate she closed ; she gave me to the river, which drowned me not. The river
carried me along ; to Akki the irrigator it brought me ; Akki the Irrigator in
the goodness of his heart lifted me up ; Akki the Irrigator reared me as his
own son ; Akki the Irrigator made me his, and in my Gardenership did Istar
love me. For 45 years I ruled the kingdom. The Men of the black-headed
race I governed, I organized. Over rugged Mountains in chariots of bronze
I rode. I governed the Upper Mountains ; I ruled the rulers of the Lower
Mountains. To the Sea-Coast three times did I advance ; Dilmun submitted ;

the fortress of the Goddess of Hades (Dur-an-Kigal) bowed . . . . I destroyed . . . . When the king who comes after me in future days shall govern the Men of the black-headed race ; shall ride over the rugged Mountains in chariots of bronze, shall govern the Upper Mountains and rule the kings of the Lower Mountains ; to the Sea-Coast shall advance three times ; shall cause Dilmun to submit ; when the fortress of the Goddess of Hades shall bow ; from my city of Accad . . . ."

The Sea-Coast seems to mean The Mediterranean and Dhi-dhi – Phoenicia.

The earlier Sumerian pronunciation tal-tal or tatal is a title of Ea as the God of "Wisdom." One of the earliest of the monarchs whose names are found at Tel-loh is called Taltal-kur-galla, "the Wise One of the Great Mountain."

Asipu or "Diviner" plays a considerable part in the religious literature of the Babylonia, and the very phrase bit assaputi, "the house of the oracle," is actually met with. A God who seems to be Bel in his character of delivering oracles through the Voice of the Thunder is called "the hero who prophesies" or "divines uprightly."

"The Abysses" or "Deeps" of the great Gods is an expression which requires explanation. The temples of Babylonia were provided with large Basins Filled of Water and used for purificatory purposes, which resembled "The Sea" made by Solomon for his temple at Jerusalem, and were called Apsi, "Deeps" or "Abysses." The ceremonies attending the construction of a Bronze Bull intended to support one of these Seas, are described in W.A.I. iv. 23, No.1. The "Sea" is stated to have been placed "between the Ears of the Bull" (line 17). It was with these "Deeps" that the pasisu or "anointing priest," whose office it was to purify and cleanse, was specially concerned. The Basins doubtless stood in the Open Air, in the great court within which the temple itself was erected. [Image Pg. 59. Note : 7 Bulls]

The little chapel of Makhir, "the God of Dreams," discovered by Mr. Hormuzd Rassam at Balawat, near Mosul, gives us further information about the internal arrangement of the shrine. In this, Mr. Rassam found a marble coffer containing Two Stone Tablets which recorded Assur-natsir-pal's victories and the erection of the chapel. The coffer and its contents remind us Forcibly of the Israelitish Ark with its "Two Tables of Stone" (1 Kings VIII. 9) [Also the Two Tablets of Destiny]. The Coffer of the little temple of Imgur-Bel, or Balawat, resembled in form the Arks, or "Ships" as they were termed, in which the Gods and their symbols were carried in

247

religious processions. It thus gives us a fair idea of what the Israelitish Ark of the Covenant must have been like. It, too, was a small shrine of rectangular shape, carried by means of staves passed through rings at its four corners. It is somewhat curious that the Assyrian Ark should have assumed this shape. The name by which it went to the last was that of a "Ship," a proof that it was originally in the form, not of an Ark, but of a Ship. The same transformation is observable in the Biblical account of the Deluge as compared with that of the Cuneiform Inscriptions ; here also "the Ship" of the Babylonian version has become "an Ark." But the fact that the Arks of the Babylonian Gods were once Ships points to a period when the first who made use of them were dwellers by the Sea-Shore [And access to Iraq Bitumen]. We are referred back to the ancient Chaldean city of Eridu, on the shores of the Persian Gulf, from whence, as we shall see hereafter, the religion and religious ceremonies of pre-Semitic Babylonia had once spread. The Gods of Eridu were Water-Gods, and, like the deities of Egypt, had each his Sacred Ship. These Ships occupied an important place in the Babylonian ritual ; they had special names, and were the visible abodes of the divinities to whom they belonged. Let us listen, for instance, to an old hymn that was recited when a new image of the God was made in honour of "the Ship of Enthronement," the Papakh or "Ark" of Merodach (Marduk) :

"Its helm is of cedar (?) wood . . . . Its Serpent-like Oar has a handle of Gold. Its mast is pointed with Turquoise. Seven times Seven Lions of the field (Eden) occupy its deck. The God Adar fills its cabin built within. Its side is of cedar from its forest. Its awning is the palm (?) wood of Dilvum. Carrying away (its) heart is the canal. Making glad its heart is the Sunrise. Its house, its ascent, is a Mountain that gives rest to the heart. The ship of Ea is Destiny. Nin-gal, the princess (Dav-kina), is the Goddess whose word is Life. Merodach is the God who pronounces the good name. The Goddess who benefits the house, the messenger of Ea the ruler of the Earth, even Nan-gar (the lady of work), the Bright One, the mighty workwoman of Heaven, with pure (and) blissful hand has uttered the word of Life : 'May the Ship before the Canal ! May the Ship behind thee sail over its mouth ! Within thee may the heart rejoicing make holiday !'"

The hymn was an heirloom from Sumerian Eridu. It had come down from the days when Merodach was not as yet the God of Babylon, but was the son of Ea, the Water-God of Eridu. It is written in Accadian, and no Semitic Translation is attached to it.

Circumcision was known to the Babylonians as it was to the Jews. In a magical text (W.A.I. ii. 17, 63) it was termed arlu, the Hebrew arel, which is used in Hebrew and Arabic in a precisely opposite sense ; but the ideographic equivalents of the Babylonian word ("the shaping of the phallus") show what its signification in Assyrian must be.

Merodach was the intercessor between the Gods and Men, and the interpreter of the will of Ea, the God of Wisdom. In an old bilingual hymn he is thus addressed : "Thou art Merodach, the merciful Lord who loves to raise the Dead to Life." (W.A.I. iv. 19. 1. 11.) The expression is a remarkable one, and indicates that the Babylonians were already acquainted with a doctrine of the Resurrection at an early period.

A hymn to Samas (Shamash) the Sun-God begins with the following words :

"O Sun-God, king of Heaven and Earth, director of things above and below, O Sun-God, thou that clothest the Dead with Life, deliver by thy hands, Judge unbrided, director of Mankind, Supreme is the mercy of him who is the Lord over difficulty, bidding the child and offspring come forth, Light of the World, Creator of all thy Universe, the Sun-God art thou."

The best idea of what a Babylonian religious service was like, may be gathered from the instructions given to the priest who watched in the Temple of Bel-Merodach at Babylon on the Night of the First Day of the New Year.

"In the month Nisan, on the second day (The Babylonians, like the Jews, reckoned the day from evening to evening.) and the first hour (kasbu) of the night, the priest (Uru-gal, "the Chief Watcher") must go and take the Waters of the River in his hand ; he must enter into the presence of Bel, and, putting on a robe in the presence of Bel, shall address to Bel this hymn :

'O Bel, who in his strength has no rival, O Bel, king of blessedness, Bel (the Lord) of the World, Seeking after the favour of the great Gods, Bel, who in his glance has Destroyed the strong, Bel (the Lord) of kings, Light of Mankind, establisher of Trust ; O Bel, thy sceptre is Babylon, Borsippa is thy crown ! The Wide Heaven is the habitation of thy liver ! O Lord, thine is the habitation, (and) the interpretations of visions ; O father (?) of Lords, thee they behold the father of Lords ; thine is the glance, (and) the seeing of Wisdom ; they Magnify (?) thee, O master of the strong ; they adore (?) thee, O king (and) mighty prince ; they Look Up to thee, show unto them Mercy ; cause them to behold the Light that they may tell of thy righteousness. O Bel (Lord) of the World, Light of the spirits of Heaven,

Utterer of blessings, who is there whose Mouth Murmurs not of thy righteousness or speaks not of thine exaltation and celebrates not thy glory ? O Bel (Lord) of the World, who dwellest in the Temple of the Sun, reject not the Hands that are raised to thee ; Show mercy to thy city Babylon, To E-Saggil thy temple incline thy face, Grant the prayers of thy people the sons of Babylon !"

Nothing can be more explicit than the statement that E-Sagila, the temple of Merodach, was also the Temple of the Sun. We thus come to Understand the attributes that are ascribed to Merodach and the language that is used of him. He is "the Light of the spirits of Heaven," as the Sun-God, the wide Heaven is naturally his dwelling-place, and he raises the Dead to Life as the Sun of Spring Revivifies the Dead Vegetation of Winter.

The part that he plays in the old Mythological poems, in the poems, that is, which embody the ancient Myths and Legends of Babylonia, is now fully explained. One of the most famous of these was the story of the combat between Merodach and Tiamat, the Dragon of Darkness and Chaos. Merodach advances to the fight armed with a Club and Bow which Anu had placed in his hand and which subsequently became a Constellation [Orion], as well as with his own peculiar weapon which hung behind his back. It was shaped like a Sickle, and is the Khereb with which Greek Mythology armed the Asiatic hero Perseus. When we remember the close parallelism that exists between this conflict of Merodach with Tiamat and the war recorded in the Apocalypse between Michael and "The Great Dragon," it is Difficult Not to Trace in the lineaments of Tiamat the Earliest Portraiture of the Mediaeval Devil.

There are traces of an old Accadian notion of the Universe according to which "The Deep" was a Flowing Stream which Surrounded the Earth like the Okeanos of Homer. It was sometimes compared to a Snake, sometimes to a Rope, and was called "the Rope of the Great God," "the River Rope of the Great God," "the River of the Snake," "the River of the Great Deep," "the River of the sheepcote of the ghost-world," "The Ocean Stream," and "the River of Innina." [The Zodiacal Stream] The spirit of deity who personified it was Innina. (In)nina seems to be the divinity who in later days was assumed to have given the name to Nineveh, and the name is explained as meaning "the God Nin," or "the divine Lord," just as Innana means "the Goddess Nana," "the divine lady," and the daughter of Ea [Tiamat]. This has a curious parallelism to "the Golden Cord" of Homer (Iliad

250

VIII.19), which Zeus offered to let the other Gods Hang from Heaven to Earth, in the vain endeavor to drag him down from the upper end of it.

In the cosmology of Eridu, therefore, the origin of the Universe was the Watery Abyss. The Earth lay upon this like a wife in the arms of her husband, and Dav-kina accordingly was adored as the wife of Ea. It was through her that the oracles of Ea, heard in the Voice of the Waves, were communicated to Man. Dav-kina is entitled "the Mistress of the Oracular Voice of the Deep," and also "the lady who creates the Oracular Voice of Heaven." Perhaps the latter title should rather be rendered "the Lady of Heaven whence the Oracular Voice is Created." The Oracles delivered by the Thunder, the Voice of Heaven, thus because the reflex of the Oracles delivered through the Roaring Sea. We may see here an allusion to the doctrine of a Watery Abyss Above The Sky, of "the Waters Above the Firmament," that is, of which we read in Genesis.

Originally, like Merodach, Adar had been a Solar deity. We are distinctly told that he was "the Meridian Sun," whose scorching heats represented the fiercer side of Ball-Worship. But whereas Merodach was the Sun conceived of as Rising from the Ocean-Stream, Adar was the Sun who issues forth from the shades of Night [Halloween]. One of his titles was "the Voice" or "Oracle Supreme" and another curious title "Lord of the Pig." This latter title connects Adar with the Ares of Greek Mythology, who in the form of the Wild Boar Slew the Sun-God Tammuz. Under the name of Baru, Adar was identified with Iron, since the name of "Iron" was denoted in Accadian by Bar, "The Shining," which was written with the Determinative of Divinity, indicative of the Meteoric Origin of the First Iron worked in Babylonia. [!]

Adar bears the same relation to Mul-lil that Merodach bears to Ea. Each alike is the Son and messenger of the Older God. But whereas the errands upon which Merodach is sent are errands of mercy and benevolence, the errands of Adar are those that befit an implacable warrior. He contends not against the powers of Darkness, like Merodach, for the father whose orders be obeys is himself the ruler of the powers of Darkness ; it is Against Mankind, as in the story of the Deluge, that his Arms are directed. He is a Solar hero who belongs to the Darkness and not to the Light in which Mythologist identify as the "God of Glowing Fire."

It is thus that one of his brothers is "the first-born" of Mul-lil, Mul-nugi, "the Lord from whom there is no return." He is called "the throne-bearers"

251

of the Deluge-Tablet who "Went Over Mountain and Plain" carrying Destruction with Them. Mul-nugi is the Lord of Hades, the God who is called Irkalla in the Legend of the Descent of Istar, and out of whose Hands there is no escape.

Nin, signifies "Lord" and "lady" its primary meaning being "The Great One." [Tiamat]

Oannes, or Ea, had the body of a Fish, and, like a Fish, he sank each night into the Waters of the Persian Gulf when the day was closed which he had spent among his favorite disciples of Eridu. The Culture-God himself had once been a Totem, from which we may infer how long it was before Totemism disappeared, at all events from southern Babylonia, where the contact with Semitic thought was less strong and abiding than was the case further North.

We can learn a good deal about this totemism from the old ideographic representations of the names of the chief deities. They are like fossils, embodying the beliefs of a period which had long passed away at the date of the earliest monuments that have come down to us. The name of Ea himself affords us an example of what we may find. It is sometimes expressed by an Ideograph which signifies literally "an Antelope," thus we are told that Ea was called "the Antelope of the Deep," "the Antelope the Creator," "the Antelope the prince," "the lusty Antelope;" and the "Ship" or Ark of Ea in which his image was carried at Festivals was entitled "the Ship of the Divine Antelope of the Deep." We should, indeed, have expected that the animal of Ea would have been the Fish rather than the Antelope, and the fact that it is not so points to the conclusion that the Culture-God of southern Babylonia was an Amalgamation of two earlier deities, one the divine Antelope, and the other the divine fish. Perhaps it was originally as the God of the River that Ea had been adored under the form of the wild beast of the Eden or Desert. [Comet Encke sinks off into the Ocean at Capricorn]

252

There was yet another animal with which the name of Ea had been associated. This was the Serpent. The Euphrates in its southern course bore names in the early inscriptions which distinctly connect the Serpent with Ea on the other hand, and the Goddess Innina on the other. It was not only called "the River of the Great Deep" – a term which implied that it was a prolongation of the Persian Gulf and the Encircling Ocean ; it was further named the River of the Subur Lilli, "the Shepherd's Hut of the Lillu" or "Spirit," "the River of Innina," "the River of the Snake," and "the River of the Girdle of the Great God." In-nina is but another form of Innana or Nana, and we may see it in her at once the Istar of Eridu and the Female correlative of Anuna. Among the chief deities reverenced by the ideographs of "Fish" and "enclosure," which served in later days to denote the name of Nina or Nineveh. It seems clear, therefore, that the pronunciation of Nina was attached to it ; and Dr. Oppert may accordingly be right in thus reading the name of the Goddess as she appears on the monuments of Tel-loh. Nina, consequently, is both the Fish-Goddess and the divinity whose name is interchangeable with that of the Snake. Now Nina was the daughter of Ea, her eldest daughter being described in a text of Tel-loh as "the Lady of the city of Mar," [Sea] the modern Tel Id, according to Hommel, where Dungi built her a temple which he called "the House of the Jeweled Circlet" (Sutartu). This latter epithet recalls to us the Tillili of the Tammuz Legend as well as the Istar of later Babylonia. In fact, it is pretty clear that Nina, "the Lady," must have been that Primitive Istar of Eridu and its neighborhood who mourned like Tillili the death of Tammuz, and whose title was but a dialectic variation of that of Nina given to her at Erech.

It is now possible to explain the Allusions in an old Accadian poem, in which Merodach is made to describe his Weapon of War. After comparing it with "the Fish of Seven fins," he goes on to say : "The tempest (matu) of battle, my Weapon of fifty heads (I bear), which like the Great Serpent of Seven heads is yoked with Seven heads, which like the strong Serpent of the Sea (sweeps away) the foe." Here the Serpent is regarded as essentially a Serpent of the Sea [Space], and in its Seven [From the Pleiades] heads we may see the Primitive Conception of its Divine Power. The "Evil Spirits" were Seven in number also, like the spirits of the Earth ; and the Mythical Fish which may be the Totem of the Fish-God is provided with Seven Fins. The Destructive Character of the Great Serpent is naturally Insisted On. Doubtless the Serpent-God of the Primitive Sumerian was Morally of a Negative Nature, or else regarded as injuring only his enemies, while he did good to those who Propitiated him [Her]. But this early Serpent-Worship faded away with the transformation of the Totem into an Anthropomorphic

253

Deity. The Goddess Nina ceased to retain her Serpentile Attributes, and after the era of the monuments of Tel-loh passed almost entirely out of memory ; while the Serpent became, what indeed he always seems to have been in genuine Semitic belief, the incarnation of wickedness and guile. We read in the bilingual lists of "the Evil Serpent," "the Serpent of Darkness;" and it is probable that the imagination of a later time confounded this Serpent of Darkness with the Dragon of Tiamat, the leader of the powers of Night and Chaos. It was a curious process of development which eventually transformed the Old Serpent-Goddess, "the lady Nina," into the embodiment of all that was hostile to the powers of Heaven ; but, after all, Nina had sprung from the Fish-God of the Deep, and Tiamat is Herself "The Deep" in a Semitic Dress.

The Bull of Light, the Bull who Ploughed the Great Furrow of the Sky.

A Horary Pseudo-Science was the belief that in the Thunder Men heard the Voice of the Gods. The old belief marked its impress upon Hebrew as well as upon Assyro-Babylonian thought. "The Voice of thy Thunder was in the Whirlwind," (Ps. LXXVII. 18.) says the Psalmist ; and nothing can show more clearly what must once have been the Canaanitish faith than the poetic imagery of another Psalm (XXIX.): "The Voice of the Lord is upon the Waters ; the God of glory Thundereth ; the Lord is upon many Waters. The Voice of the Lord is Powerful ; the Voice of the Lord is full of majesty. The Voice of the Lord Breaketh the Cedars [Tunguska]; yea, the Lord breaketh the Cedars of Lebanon... The Voice of the Lord Shaketh the Wilderness ; the Lord Shaketh the Wilderness of Kadesh. The Voice of the Lord maketh the Hinds to Calve [Also in Cuneiform Text], and Discovereth the Forests." In the Talmud, "the Voice of the Lord" has become the bath qol, or "daughter of the Voice," a supernatural message from Heaven which sometimes proceeds from the Holy of Holies, sometimes as Socrates assumed, a form of intuition directing the recipient as to his course in Life.

This prophetic Voice of Heaven was heard in the Thunder by the Accadians as well as by the Semites. I have already noticed that the Accadians believed the Sounds of Nature [Including Bolide Blasts] to be Divine Voices, from which the initiated could Derive a Knowledge of the Future [NEO's]. At Eridu it was more especially the Roar of the Sea in which the Sumerian priest listened to the revelations of his deities, and this perhaps was the Oracle through which Oannes had spoken to Men. In the rival city of northern Babylonia, where the supreme God presided over the realm of the Dead, and not over the Waters of the Sea, the Divine Voice came to Men in the Thunder. By the side of Mul-lil, the Lord of the Ghost-World, stood Mul-me-sarra, "the Lord of the Voice of the Firmament." Mul-me-sarra, in Fact, was but Mul-lil himself in another form, and hence, as Lord of Hades, was the author, not only of the Thunder, but of Subterranean Noises As Well. "A Darkness came from the middle of the Deep, the Doom Descended from the Midst of the Heaven, the Sword Mowed Down the Earth like Grass ; towards the four winds the Flash went Overthrowing like Fire. It Sickened the Men of the city, it Tortured their bodies. In city and land it caused Lamentation ; small and great alike it Smote. Freeman and handmaid it bound ; with wailing it filled them. In Heaven and Earth like a storm-cloud it rained ; it made prey. To the place of supplication of their God they hastened and Raised High the Voice. They received his mighty aid and like a Garment it Concealed them. They . . . . him and the poison was expelled . . . . they embraced his feet . . . . his body was tired. In lamentation he smites his breast." The Dazzling Fiend, the Evil Wind, the Assaulting Wind which Strips Off the Clothing of the Body like an Evil Demon, ... [Shock Wave !]

The Evil South-West Wind

"O Mighty Mountain of Mul-lil, Im-kharsag whose head rivals the Heavens ; the pure Deep has been laid as its foundation. Among the Mountains it lies like a Strong Wild Bull. Its Horns Glisten like the Splendor of the Sun-God. Like the Star of Heaven that proclaims the day it is full of Glittering Rays. The mighty mother Nin-lilli (the lady of the Ghost-World), the reverence of E-Sara (the Temple of the Hosts of Heaven), the glory of E-Kura (the Temple of the Hosts of Earth), the adornment of E-Giguna (the Temple of the City of Darkness), the heart of E-Ki-gusura (the temple of the land of light)."

255

In this hymn the World-Tree of Eridu, whose roots were planted in the Deep, has made way for a World-Mountain, with its head reaching unto Heaven like the tower of Babel, and its feet planted upon the Deep. As the conception of the World-Tree belonged to Sumir or southern Babylonia, so the conception of the World-Mountain belongs to Accad or northern Babylonia ; it is expressly termed the Mountain of Mul-lil, and is identified with Nin-lil, the "reverence of E-Sara," whose son was the Sun-God Adar. It is at least noticeable that one of the hymns to the Sun-God which originated at Sippara begins by declaring that he "Rose from the Mighty Mountain," "from the Mountain of the Stream," "the place of the destinies."

Little by little, as the conception of the Gods and their dwelling-place became spiritualized, "the Mountain of the World" passed first into the Sky and then into the Invisible "Heaven of Anu," the conception of the future condition of Mankind became spiritualized also. [Will the next pass or hit ?]

The Babylonian of the historical period was firmly persuaded that in the Ocean-Stream that Encircled the World lay the Germs of the Whole Universe. This belief stands in marked contrast to that prehistoric belief in a "Mountain of the World" which survived only in Mythology. No doubt the two conceptions could be reconciled by those who Undertook the trouble ; it was possible to hold that this Mountain of the World was not the central shaft around which the Earth and Heavens were built, but merely the centre of the existing World. [The Center of What Matters, the NEO's.]

God is compared to a Rock in the Old Testament (Deut. XXXII. 15, Ps. XVIII. 2), and the worship of Sacred Stones was widely spread through the Semitic World. The Sacred Stone was a Beth-el, or "House of God;" no habitation of a mere spirit, but the dwelling-place of deity itself. Its sanctity was not inherent ; it was sacred because it had been transformed into an altar by the oil that was poured out upon it in libation, or the priest who was consecrated to its service. The worship of these Sacred Stones was common to all the branches of the Semitic family. The famous Black Stone of the Kaaba at Mecca is a standing witness of the Fact. The Muslim pilgrims make Seven circuits around the Kabba. Islamic Tradition holds that it Fell from Heaven to show Adam and Eve where to build an altar.

In the Mountain of the Sunset, it is said, those Seven were born ; in the Mountain of the Sunrise those Seven grew up ; in the Hollows of the Earth they have their dwelling ; on the high-places of the Earth their names are proclaimed. As for them, in Heaven and Earth they have no dwelling,

256

hidden is their name. Among the sentient Gods they are not known. Their name in Heaven and Earth exists not. Those Seven from the Mountain of the Sunset gallop forth, those Seven in the Mountain of the Sunrise are bound to rest. In the Hollows of the Earth they set the foot ; on the high-places of the Earth they lift the neck. They by naught are known ; in Heaven and Earth there is no Knowledge of them.

The Primitive Hieroglyphs out of which the Cuneiform Characters were evolved have no resemblances to the Hieroglyphs of Egypt. With the exception of such obvious symbols as a circle to denote the Sun, which occur in every pictorial system of writing, the Ideographs of Chaldea and Egypt have nothing in common. Even the idea of divinity is represented differently in them. The Chaldea it is expressed by an eight-rayed Star ; in Egypt, by a Stone-Headed Axe. [They are Connected, the other Bright as the Sun Star and the Thundering Stone Bolide.]

"Incantation. – The storm-like-ghost, the tormentor of all things, and the demon who Disturbs the Disturber of Anu [Above], the Plague-demon the beloved son of Mul-lil, the begetter of Nin-ki-gal (the Goddess of Hades), above Destroy like Consumption [Tuberculosis 1918] and below cut down. They are the creation of Hades, even they ! Above They Roar, below they peep ; the bitter breath of the Gods are they. The Great Worms who have been let Loose from Heaven are they ! The mighty ones whose Roar is in the city ; who Cast Down the Waters of Heaven, sons who have come forth from the Earth ! The Lofty Beam, the Broad Beam they Encircle like a crown. From house to house they make their way. As for them, the door restrains them not, the bolt turns them not back. Into the door like a Snake they glide, into the socket like a wind they blow.

The Strong Serpent of the Sea drives the foe before it. . . . . . . The Weapon, the Terror of whose Splendor Overwhelms the Earth. . . . . . . Thou who Rained Fire and Stones upon the enemy, may thy heart be exalted! . . . . His Lord Mounted and Rode Upon the Mountain. [Connecting the Mountain to the Bull] . . . . . . .The Dragon (Mamlu) which Shines Brightly. . . . . . . His face is that of the God of Destruction. . . . . . . His eye is filled with the shadow of the forest. . . . . . . Who Hurls Down Terror, whose Clothing is Splendor ; the Forceful Fire-God, the exalter of the Mountain peaks, the uplifter of the Torch, the Enlightener of the Darkness. . . . . . . The Great Serpents, the evil spirits, were their huntsmen.

The Religion of Ancient Egypt and Babylonia, by A. H. Sayce, The Gifford Lectures, 1902

The mother of Amon-hotep III was of Asiatic origin ; we read, therefore, on the Walls of the Temple of Luxor, that he was Born of a Virgin and the God of Thebes.

Primitive Man does not distinguish as we do between the Animate and the Inanimate. He Projects His Own Personality into the things he sees about him, and ascribes to them the same motive forces as those which move himself. He knows of only one source of movement and activity, and that source is Life. The Stars which travel through the Firmament, the Arrow that Flies through the Air, are either Alive or else are directed and animated by some Living power. Movement, in fact, implies Life, and the moving object, whatever it may be, is a Living thing.

The title "follower of Horus" would take us back to the earliest Traditions of Egyptian history. The "followers of Horus," according to the later texts, were the predecessors of Menes and the First Dynasty of united Egypt, the Pharaohs and princes of the southern kingdom whose very names were forgotten in after days. Nevertheless, it was remembered that they had founded the great sanctuaries of the country ; thus an inscription at Dendera declares that in the reign of king Pepi of the Sixth Dynasty there was found in the wall of the palace a Parchment on which was a plan of the temple drawn upon it in the time of "the followers of Horus." The Legends of Edfu told how these followers of Horus had been Smiths, Armed with Weapons of Iron, and how they had driven the enemies of their leader before them until they had possessed themselves of the whole of Egypt. Mesnitiu – Blacksmiths. The Mesnit of "Forge" was the name given to the passage opening into the shrine of the temple of Edfu.

Horus the son of Isis and his twin brother Set. But the confusion between the two Horuses must have arisen at an early time. In the Rock Drawing, south of El-kab, the two Horus hawks stand on the symbol of "Gold," the one wearing the crown of Southern Egypt, the other that of the North. " the Horus who Issues From the Two Horizons" The conception of the Twin-Mountains between which the Sun-God comes forth every morning, and between which he passes again at nightfall, is of Babylonian origin. On early Babylonian Seal-Cylinders we see him stepping through the door, the two leaves of which have been flung back by its warders on either side of the Mountains, while rays of glory shoot upward from his shoulders, the Mountains were called Mas, "The Twins," in Sumerian. Horus has much in common with the Babylonian Sun-God Nin-ip, they are both Warrior-Gods ; and just as the followers of Horus were Workers in Iron, so Nin-ip also was the God of Iron. Between the Babylonian and the Egyptian schemes of creation, the differences are slight. Both denote that Watery Chaos out of which, it was believed, all things have come and the Sun-God is the most praised. Between the Cosmological doctrines of Babylonia and Egypt, a connection of some sort must have existed. One of the old formulae embedded in the Pyramid Texts (Teta 86) reads like a passage from a Sumerian hymn : "Hail to thee, Great Deep (Ageb), Moulder of the Gods, creator of Men." It belongs to Babylonia rather than to Egypt, where the "Great Deep" could have been a matter only of Tradition.

Astro-Theology once played a considerable part in the religion of the Egyptians. In the Historical Age it has Lost its Importance ; the Stars have been identified with the official deities, who have accordingly absorbed their individual attributes ; but echoes of the worship formerly paid to them are Still Heard in the Pyramid Texts. Sahu or Orion is still remembered as a mighty hunter, whose hunting-ground was the Plain of Heaven, and whose Prey were the Gods Themselves. When he rises, it is said in the Pyramid of Unas, "the Stars fight together, and the "Searchers Patrol" the Sky which drops with rain ; the smaller Stars which form his Constellation pursue and Lasso [Snake eating its Tail.] the Gods as the human hunter Lassoes the Wild Bull ; they Slay and Disembowel their booty, and boil the flesh in glowing Caldrons. The "Greater Gods" are hunted "in the morning," those of less account at mid-day, the "lesser Gods" "at evening, and Sahu refreshes himself with the divine banquet," feeding on their bodies and absorbing "their magic virtues." "The Great Ones of the Sky" launch "the Flames against the Caldrons wherein are the haunches of the followers" of the Gods ; the Pole Star, "who causes the Dwellers in the Sky to March in Procession Round" Orion, "throws into the Caldron the legs of their wives." We are transported to the cannibal's kitchen of some African chieftain, such as that represented on a curious stela found in Darfur, and

now in the museum of Constantinople. The whole description takes us back
to a period in the history of Egypt long anterior to that of the Pyramids,
when the Pharaonic invaders were first beginning to mingle with the older
population of the land and become acquainted with its practices. One of the
Constellations frequently mentioned in the Pyramid Texts is "the Bull of
Heaven," which was also an important Constellation in early Babylonian
Astronomy, where the name formed part of an Astronomical system ; in
Unas 421 the "Bull of Heaven" is called the Acor "Column" of Heliopolis.
We hear also of "the Fresh Water of the Stars" (Unas 210). So far as we
know, the only people who have ever systematically mapped out the
Heavens, dividing the Stars into groups, and giving to each group a name of
its own, were the Babylonians ; and it was from the Babylonians that the
Constellations as known to Greeks and Romans, to Hindus, or to Chinese,
were ultimately derived. The inference, therefore, is near at hand, that the
Primitive Egyptians also were indebted for their map of the Sky to the same
source. And the inference is supported by more than one Fact. Several
names of Constellations were the same among both Babylonians and
Egyptians. Still more striking are the thirty-six Egyptian decans, the Stars
who Watched for ten days each over the 360 days of the ancient Egyptian
year, and were divided into two classes or hemispheres, those of the day
and those of the night. Not only did the early Chaldean year similarly
consist of 360 days ; it to was presided over by thirty-six "councilor" Stars,
half of which were Above the Earth, while the other half were Below it.
Such a Coincidence cannot have been Accidental ; the Babylonian and
Egyptian decans must have had the same origin. It is the same with a
curious echo of ancient Babylonian Cosmology, that begins with the
words –

"At that time the Heaven above was not known by name, the Earth beneath
was not named, in the beginning the Deep was their generator, the Chaos of
the Sea was the Mother of Them All."

On the walls of the Pyramid of Pepi I. we read again almost the same words.
Pepi, it is said, "was born of his father Tum. At that time the Heaven was
not, the Earth was not, Men did not exist, the Gods were not born, there
was no Death." But here the words have been introduced without
connection with the context ; they cohere neither with what precedes nor
with what follows them, and are evidently nothing but an old formula torn
from the Cosmogony to which they once belonged, and repeated Without a
Clear Understanding of What they Really Meant.

260

The Persian Gulf, it was believed, was the cradle of Babylonian culture ; it was also the source of that cosmogony which saw in the Deep the "mother" of all things ; it was from the "Deep" that the Gods had come, and the Deep was still the home of the Culture-God Ea. [Valley of the Persian Gulf.]

. . . . all the Earth was Sea, while in the Midst of the Sea was a Water-Course . . . . Holy Mound in the Midst of the Deep . . . .

Tiamat's name signifies, the Chaos of Waters.

It is impossible not to be struck by the many points of similarity between the Babylonian ritual and arrangement of the temples and that which existed among the Israelites. The temple of Solomon, in fact, was little more than a Reproduction of a Babylonian Sanctuary. And just as the place of the Hebrew king adjoined the temple in which he claimed the right of offering sacrifice, so too at Babylon the place of Nebuchadnezzar – who, it must be remembered, was a pontiff as well as a king – stood close to the temple of Merodach. Even the Bronze Serpent which Hezekiah destroyed finds its parallel in the Bronze Serpents erected in the Gates of the Babylonian temples. The internal decoration of the sanctuary, moreover, was similar in both countries. The walls were made gorgeous with enameled bricks, or with plaques of Gold and bronze and inlaid stones. Sometimes they were painted with vermilion, the Monsters of the Epic of Creation being pictured on the walls. [Like the ones in Mexico that the priests thought so demonic !] But more often the painted or sculptured figures were, as at Jerusalem, those of Cherubim and the Sacred Tree or other vegetable devices. At Erech, Bull-headed colossi guarded the Doors.

The Sabbath-rest was essentially of Babylonian origin. The word Sabbath itself was Borrowed from Babylonia, where it had the form Sabattu, and was derived by the native lexicographers from the Sumerian sa, "heart," and "bat, to cease," and so explained as "a day of rest for the heart." The derivation is, of course, absurd, but it indicates the antiquity of the term.

Winged Lion Probably Signifying the -13K Years BP event
Precession Dated When the Sun was in the Sign of Leo
Actually Between the Virgin and Leo Plus Time to Recover
Thus the Virgin/Lion Composite Egyptian Sphinx

Winged Bull Probably Signifying the 2,300 BC Event
Precession Dated When the Sun was in the Sign Taurus
The Cherub or pl. Cherubim

263

Light on the Old Testament from Babel, by Albert T. Clay, 1906

All of which impresses us with the Fact that while we have reached far back into the misty past, the Oblivion which Hides the beginnings of the human race seems to grow Deeper and Deeper. This Early Literature goes back to an Exceedingly Remote Antiquity.

Jahweh is represented as having contended with a Great Primeval Monster, who is called in some passages Rahab, and in others Leviathan, Tihom, and the Dragon.

When the Waves thereof arise, thou (Jahweh) stillest them. Thou hast broken Rahab in pieces, as one that is slain ; Thou hast scattered thine enemies with the Arm of thy strength. The Heavens are thine, the Earth also is thine : The World and the fullness thereof, thou has founded them. The north and south, thou hast created them.

Psalm 89 : 9

Arise, arise put on strength, O Arm of Jahweh ; Arise as in the days of old, the generations of ancient times. Art thou not he who cut Rahab in pieces, Pierced the Dragon ? Art thou not he who dried up the sea, the waters of the great Tihom, Who made the Depths of Sea a way for the redeemed to Pass Over ?

Isaiah 51 : 9

He Stirreth up the Sea with his power, And by his understanding he Smiteth Through Rahab. By his spirit the Heavens are garnished ; His Hand hath Pierced the Swift Serpent.

Job 26 : 12

Thou didst Divide the Sea by thy strength : Thou Brakest the Heads of the Dragons in the Waters. Thou Brakest the Heads of the Leviathan in Pieces. The day is thine, the night also is thine : Thou hast prepared the Light and the Sun. Thou hast set all the borders of the Earth : Thou hast made Summer and Winter.

Psalm 74 : 13

The creation story of Genesis, while it makes no reference to the conflict between Jahweh and the primeval power referred to in other parts of the Old Testament, does mention a Chaotic state, an Abyss of Waters, prior to the creation of the Heavens and the Earth. The word translated "Deep" (Tihom, Genesis 1: 2), by which is meant the Primeval Ocean, is generally recognized to be the same as the Babylonian Tiamat, which is the equivalent to the Feminine of the Hebrew Tihom.

Babylon in the inscriptions as Babilu means "Gate of God." The Hebrews called it Babel because "Jahweh did there confound the language of all the Earth" (Gen. 11 : 9).

Some scholars hold that the Ziggurat is symbolical of the Heavenly seat of the Gods. The Deities being Astral, the whole Constellation represents the God. The Ziggurat they claim is the God's Heavenly Shrine. The figures cut in relief on the upper part of boundary Stones which represent the Deities seem to express this theory. In some instances the shrine, God, and the weapon are given. In other, the shrine and the weapon, or even one symbol. A Shrine on one of the Stones appears to be a good representation of a Ziggurat. This has led some scholars to conclude that the Ziggurat is an Earthly symbol of the God's Heavenly Seat.

The Beginnings of History according to the Bible and the Traditions of Oriental Peoples. From the Creation of Man to the Deluge, by Francois Lenormant, 1882

The idea of the Edenic happiness of the first human beings constitutes one of the Universal Traditions. Among the Egyptians, the terrestrial reign of the God Ra, who inaugurated the existence of the World and of human Life, was a Golden Age to which they continually looked back with regret and envy ; to assert the superiority of anything above all that imagination could set forth, it was sufficient to affirm that this belief in an age of happiness and of innocence in the infancy of Mankind may likewise be found among all peoples of the Aryan race. It was among the beliefs held by them anterior to their dispersion, and it has been long since remarked by all scholars, that this is one of the points where their Traditions find themselves most evidently on common ground with the Semitic stories which we find in Genesis.

 The Aryan nations have a belief in Four Successive Ages of the World, the gradual degeneracy of Legend which marks them is expressed by the Metals, the names of which are applied to them are – Gold, Silver, Brass, and Iron.

"Then the Earth did Shake and Quake, The foundations of Heaven did Tremble ; they were Shaken, because He was Wroth. Smoke arose up in His Nostrils, and Fire out of His Mouth did Devour ; coals Flamed forth from Him. He Bowed the Heavens also, and Came Down ; and Thick Darkness was Under His Feet. and He Rode upon a Cherub [Bull], and did Fly ; yea, He was Seen upon the Wings of the Wind. And He made Darkness Pavilions round about Him, gathering of Waters, Thick Clouds of

266

the Skies. At the Brightness before Him Coals of Fire Flamed forth. The Lord Thundered from Heaven, and the Most High gave forth His Voice. And He sent out Arrows, and Scattered them ; Lightning, and discomfited them. And the channels of the Sea appeared, the foundations of the World were laid bare, by the Rebuke of the Lord, at the Blast of the Breath of His Nostrils."   2 Samuel 22 : 8-16   1917

"Then the Earth did Shake and Quake, the foundations also of the Mountains did Tremble ; they were Shaken, because He was Wroth. Smoke arose up in His Nostrils, and Fire out of His Mouth did Devour ; Coals Flamed forth from Him. He Bowed the Heavens also, and Came Down ; and Thick Darkness was Under His Feet. And He Rode upon a Cherub, and did Fly ; yea, He did Swoop Down upon the Wings of the Wind. He made Darkness His Hiding-Place, His Pavilion Round about Him ; Darkness of Waters, Thick Clouds of the Skies. At the Brightness before Him, there passed through His Thick Clouds Hailstones and Coals of Fire. The Lord also Thundered in the Heavens, and the Most High gave forth His Voice ; Hailstones and Coal of Fire. And He sent out His Arrows, and Scattered them ; and He Shot forth Lightnings, and Discomfited them. And the Channels of Waters appeared, and the Foundations of the World were laid bare, at Thy Rebuke, O Lord, at the Blast of the Breath of Thy Nostrils."   Psalm XVIII 8 : 16   1917

"Then Solomon began to build the house of the Lord at Jerusalem in Mount Moriah, where the Lord appeared unto David his father; for which provision had been made in the Place unto David, in the threshing-floor of Ornan the Jebusite. And he began to build in the second day of the second month, in the fourth year of his reign. Now these are the foundations which Solomon laid for the building of the house of God. The length by cubits after the ancient measure was threescore cubits, and the breadth twenty cubits. And the porch that was before the house, the length of it was according to the breadth of the house, was twenty cubits, and the height was an hundred and twenty ; and he overlaid it within with pure Gold. And the greater house he covered with cypress-wood, which he overlaid with fine Gold, and wrought thereon palm-trees and chains. And he garnished the house with precious stones for beauty : and the Gold was Gold of Parvaim. He overlaid also the house, the beams, the thresholds, and the walls thereof, and the doors thereof, with Gold ; and graved Cherubims [Winged Bulls] on the walls. And he made the most Holy place; the length whereof, according to the breadth of the house, was twenty cubits, and the breadth thereof twenty cubits: and he overlaid it with fine Gold, amounting

267

to six hundred talents. And the weight of the nails was fifty shekels of Gold. And he overlaid the upper chambers with Gold. And in the most holy place he made two Cherubim of image work ; and they overlaid them with Gold. And the Wings of the Cherubim were twenty cubits long : the Wing of the one Cherub was five cubits, reaching to the wall of the house ; and the other Wing was likewise five cubits, reaching to the Wing of the other Cherub. And the Wing of the other Cherub was five cubits, reaching to the wall of the house ; and the other Wing was five cubits also, joining to the Wing of the other Cherubim. The Wings of these Cherubim spread themselves forth twenty cubits ; and they stood on their feet, and their faces were inward. And he made the veil of blue, and purple, and crimson, and fine linen, and wrought Cherubim thereon. Also he made before the house two pillars of thirty and five cubits high, and the capital that was on top of each of them was five cubits. And he made chains in the Sanctuary, and put them on the tops of the pillars ; and he made a hundred pomegranates, and put them on the chains. And he set up the pillars before the temple, one on the right hand, and the other on the left ; and called the name of that on the right hand Jachin, and the name of that on the left Boaz."   2 Chronicles 3   1917

"Therefore the Lord God sent him forth from the garden of Eden, to till the ground from whence he was taken. So He drove out the Man ; and He placed at the East of the Garden of Eden the Cherubim, and the Flaming Sword which turned every way, to keep the way to the Tree of Life."
Genesis 3 : 23-24   1917

"And thou shalt make an Ark-Cover of pure Gold : two cubits and a half shall be the length thereof, and a cubit and a half the breadth thereof. And thou shalt make two Cherubim of Gold ; of beaten work shalt thou make them, at the two ends of the Ark-Cover. And make one Cherub at the one end, and one Cherub at the other end ; of one piece with the Ark-Cover shall ye make the Cherubim of the two ends thereof. And the Cherubim shall spread out their Wings on high, screening the Ark-Cover with their Wings, with their faces one to another ; toward the Ark-Cover shall the faces of the Cherubim be. And thou shalt put the Ark-Cover above upon the Ark ; and in the Ark thou shalt put the testimony that I shall give thee. And there I will meet with thee, and I will speak with thee from above the Ark-Cover, from between the Two Cherubim which are upon the Ark of the Testimony, of all things which I will give thee in commandment unto the children of Israel."
Exodus 25 : 17-22   1917

"Moreover thou shalt make the tabernacle with ten curtains : of fine twined linen, and blue, and purple, and scarlet, with Cherubim the work of the skilful workman shalt thou make them." Exodus 26 : 1 1917

"And when Moses went into the tent of meeting that He might speak with him, then he heard the Voice speaking unto him from above the Ark-Cover that was upon the Ark of the Testimony, from between the Two Cherubim ; and He spoke unto him." Numbers 7 : 89 1917

"So the people sent to Shiloh, and they brought from thence the Ark of the Covenant of the Lord of Hosts, who Sitteth upon the Cherubim ; and the two sons of Eli, Hophni, and Phinehas, were there with the Ark of the Covenant of God." 1 Samuel 4 : 4 1917

"And David arose, and went with all the people that were with him, from Baalejudah, to bring up from thence the Ark of God, whereupon is called the Name, even the Name of the Lord of Hosts that Sitteth upon the Cherubim." 2 Samuel 6 : 2 1917

"And in the Sanctuary he made Two Cherubim of olive-wood , each ten cubits high. And five cubits was the one Wing of the Cherub, and five cubits the other Wing of the Cherub ; from the uttermost part of the Wing unto the uttermost part of the other were ten cubits. And the other Cherub was ten cubits ; both the Cherubim were of one measure and one form. The height of the one Cherub was ten cubits, and so was it of the other Cherub. And he set the Cherubim within the inner house ; and the Wings of the Cherubim were stretched forth, so that the Wing of one touched the one of the other wall ; and their Wings touched one another in the midst of the house. And he overlaid the Cherubim with Gold. And he carved all the walls of the house roundabout with carved figures of Cherubim and palm-trees and open flowers, within and without." 1 Kings 6 : 23-29 1917

In an Accadian text is a song of triumph, a sort of dithyrambic, of a Warrior God to his victorious arms ; perhaps it may be Marduk, when about to engage in his Cosmogonic struggle against the Monster Tiamat. He is armed with a complete panoply, Grappling-Hook, Lance, Lasso, Bow, Club, and Shield ; furthermore, he holds a Disk in each hand. This is his most Formidable Weapon, the one which assures to him the victory, one upon which he dwells with most satisfaction, describing it with a perfect wealth of metaphors. These varied metaphors, which seem at first sight contradictory, are reconcilable only when allowed to apply to a Weapon for

269

Slinging, shaped like a "Disk" or Like the "Sun," moving horizontally with a Gyratory Motion, like that of a "Waterspout," having a hollow centre, that the tips of the fingers can pass through, whence Seven divergent rays issue toward a circumference, about which are studded "fifty heads," – fifty sharp points.

"In my right hand I hold my Disk of Fire ; in my left hand I hold my Disk of Carnage. The Sun with fifty faces, the High Weapon of my Divinity, I hold it. The Weapon which Devours Entirely, like the Ogre, I hold it. That which Breaks the Mountains, the powerful Weapon of the God Anu, I hold it. That which Bends the Mountains, the Fish with the Seven Fins, I hold it. The littu of the battle, which Devastates and Desolates the rebellious land, I hold it. . . . . . . The Whirlpool of the battle, the Weapon of fifty heads, I hold it. Like unto the Enormous Serpent, with Seven heads, unto a Wave which divides itself into Seven branches. Like unto the Serpent which Lashes the Waves of the Sea, attacking the enemy in front. Devastating in the Violence of Battles, Dominatrix of Heaven and of Earth, the Weapon of Seven Heads, I hold it. . . . . . . The Weapon which fills the land with Terror of its Vast Strength. In my right hand powerfully, the Projectile of Gold and of Onyx, I hold it."

This "Disk of Fire" and this "Disk of Carnage" are so highly esteemed, as having in themselves "a spirit" like the wheels of Yehezqel's vision, a Life of their own like the lahat hahareb of Genesis, that they are finally invoked, as personal Gods, side by side with Shamash [Sun] and his spouse Gula. There are two verbal roots for this Weapon, one signifying "to Flame," the

270

other "to Envelope," the latter intimately associated with that of "Surrounding" and of "going Around," which might agree perfectly with the Gyratory Motion of the object to which the name applies.

Thus we have in one of the most ancient Texts of Chaldaic poetry the Distinct Allusion to a Mythological Weapon, Entirely Analogous to the Tchakra of the Indian heroes, and corresponding, in a very remarkable manner, to the idea which is most naturally evoked by the Very Expressions of the Bible texts as to the Kerubim at the Gate of the Garden of Eden.

India's account of the Deluge found in the Shatapatha Brahmana translated by Max Muller :

"One morning Water was brought to Manu to wash with ; and when he had washed, a Fish remained in his hands ; and it addressed these words to him : 'Protect me, and I will save thee.' 'From what wilt thou save me ?' – 'A Deluge will carry off all creatures ; it is that from which I will save thee.' 'How shall I protect thee' The Fish answered : 'So long as we are small, we live in great danger ; for Fish swallow Fish ; keep me at first in a vessel. when I am too large for that, hollow out a basin to put me in. When I have become still larger, carry me to the Ocean. Then I shall be preserved from Destruction.' Very soon it grew to be a Large Fish. It said to Manu : 'In the very year when I shall have attained my full growth the Deluge will overtake us. Build then a vessel and worship me. When the Waters rise, enter into this vessel, and I will save thee.' "After having thus kept him, Manu carried the Fish to the Ocean. In the year which it had indicated, Manu built a vessel, and worshiped the Fish ; and when the Deluge came he entered into the vessel. Then the fish came swimming toward him, and Manu fastened the cable of the vessel to the Fish's Horn, and by this means the Fish caused him to pass over the Mountain of the North. The Fish said : 'I have saved thee ; fasten the vessel to a Tree, that the Water may not carry it away while thou art upon the Mountain ; as the Waters fall, thou shalt descend.' Manu descended with the Water, and that is called the descent of Manu on the Mountain of the North. The Deluge had carried away every creature, and only Manu remained."

In the Cosmogony of Hieronymus, the Egyptian, is mentioned the form of a Dragon with the heads of a Bull and a Lion joined, and between them the face of a God (anthropomorphic), with Wings on his shoulders, and they call him time.

The First of Empires "Babylon of the Bible" In the Light of Latest Research, by W. ST. Chad Boscawen, 1906

Within the Adapa story : On his arrival in Heaven he is met by two Gods, who guard the Gate of Heaven – Tammuz and Giz-zida. The mention of these two Gods as the guardians of Heaven is important. Tammuz, the son of life, was the God of flesh, Verdant Nature, and a Tree-God. Giz-zida, the Firm Tree, or Tree of Life, and was especially the God who presided over the growth of Trees. So these Two Tree-Gods are the guardians of the Gate of Heaven. The reason why the guards start crying is because they are the two Gods missing from Earth that Adapa informs them when explaining why he is dressed in morning rags while passing through the Gates. These two Gods are especially connected with Eridu, and were no doubt represented by the two pillars at the entrance of ancient temples.

The whole Tradition of the Garden of Eden, with its Trees of Life and Knowledge, is based on the Babylonian Tree worship, especially associated with Eridu. The Yaveh of Hebrew Tradition is an agricultural God, who plants his garden in Eden. The name Eden is the Sumerian Edina, the equivalent of the Semitic Zeru, "open land," plain, desert, and especially applied to the lowlands of South Chaldea. The garden is planted by Him (Genesis 2 : 8), and Man is appointed to till it exactly as a Babylonian landlord might appoint his gardener (Code, sec. 60-65), giving him his share for sustenance. "Of every Tree of the garden thou mayest eat freely" (Genesis 2 : 16). It must be remembered that the profession or gardener was a vary noble one in Babylonia. Sargon of Agade (3800 BC), according to a Legend, was brought up as a gardener. Babylonian kings claimed the title of "Gardener of the Sacred Tree," and Nebuchadnezzar the Great calls himself the "Gardener of Babylon."

272

From an inscription in the British Museum relating to the sacred grove of Eridu and the Sacred Tree which grew there :

"In Eridu growth the Dark Kiskanu (Tree), that growth up in a Holy place. Its summit was bright Lapis Lazuli ; it stretched into the Ocean (Abyss) from Ea, its path was in Eridu bountiful in luxuriance. Its site is the place of the Earth it is the place of the couch of the Goddess JD. In a holy abode like a forest grove. Its shade spreadeth, and none may enter it, within it are Samash and Tammuz. At the mouth of two rivers the Gods Ka-khegal, Si-dugal . . . . of Eridu have gathered this Kiskanu (Tree). They have recited the Incantation of the Deep. At the head of the Wanderer (Delirious one) they have set it, that a propitious Guardian and a favorable Spirit may stand at the side of the Man the son of his God."

Although not directly mentioned in the above inscription there appears to have been a River associated with this sacred garden or grove. This was the Mythic River of creation, shown in an interesting fragment which reads :

"O thou River, thou didst Create all things. When the Great Gods Dug thee out, on thy banks they placed prosperity. Within thee Ea, King of the Ocean, Created his dwelling. The Deluge they sent not before thou wert. Fire and Wrath, Splendour and Terror, have Ea and Asar (Marduk), the good being, presented to thee. Thou Judgest the cause of Mankind, River, thou art mighty ; O river, thou art supreme ; O river, thou art righteous."

It is upon material such as these, and we must remember that Ur, the birthplace of Abram, was only a few miles away from the sacred city of Eridu, that the Hebrew writer founded his story of Eden and the River of Life and the Sacred Trees.

In a Tablet of Ea cycles a certain Atarpi who had offended the God Ea in some way, and for whose sake a curse is put upon the Earth : "He turned to Mankind. From their stomachs he Minished Vegetables. On high Adar (Rain-God) Drank up his Rains. The field was Barren, and there was no Water in the fountains. Destroyed was the Wealth of the Harvest-God, Devastated the Fields. The open land (Edina) was rebellious and produced Blackness ; Vegetables sprung not up, no corn grew, upon all Men was Fever and Pestilence."

This text, short as it is, contains all the essential features of the Curse when Man was Driven from the Garden of Eden. (Genesis 3 : 17, 18.)

"Cursed is the ground for thy sake ; in toil shalt thou eat of it all the days of thy Life. Thorns also and thistles shall it bring forth to thee ; and thou shalt eat the herb of the field. In the sweat of thy face shalt thou eat bread"

Thus Man goes forth to battle against nature, to Struggle for Existence, and to Adapt Himself to his [Changed] Environment.

Istar, the Voluptuous Goddess, queen of love, the sensual Goddess, with her attendants Samkhat ("pleasure"), Kharimat the devotee, and her bands of harlots (kadistu) and the ensnarers (kizrite).

The Vengeance of the Goddess is brought about in another way, unfortunately not clearly revealed to us in the broken state of the tablets. The hero is afflicted with leprosy, and from this time onwards the progress of the hero is one of disease, Misery, and Disaster. His giant Strength Wanes, his Luxuriant Locks, the sign of his strength, fall off, and he is filled with the Dread of Death and with a terrible yearning for the knowledge of the Secret of Immortality.   (Gilgamesh)

The Daevas of the Avesta "are born in the Gloom of Sunset or in the Dark Clouds of the North, in burial-places or in the places where the Dead are placed, in all corners where Light does not penetrate, in the Darkest places of Earth, or in the Abyss. To them belong Cold and Gloom, Drought, Barren Land and Wilderness, Poisonous Plants and Herbs, Hunger and Thirst, Sickness and Death."

Surely this entourage of Ahriman, like that of Tiamat, is the old demon horde of the magical litanies, who are described as bringing "cold and rain" and Floods, Destructive Blasts and Evil Winds, Raging Storms, Fever, Poison, pain sorcery, evil malaria.

The "Higher Criticism" and the Verdict of the Monuments, by Rev. A. H. Sayce, 1894

About ancient writers and modern interpreters:

An exactitude was required of them which would not and could not be demanded of many modern writers of history. A single error in detail, a

274

single inconsistency, a single exaggeration, a single anachronism, was considered sufficient to overthrow the credit of the whole narrative.

Old Accado-Sumerian hymn Fragment :

In Eridu a palm-stalk grew overshadowing ; in a holy place did it become green ; its root was of bright lapis which stretched towards the Deep ; before the God Ea was its growth in Eridu, teeming with Fertility ; its seat was the central place of the Earth ; its Foliage was the couch of Zikum the Primeval Mother. Into the heart of its holy house which spread its shade like a forest hath no Man entered. There is the home of the mighty Mother who Passes Across the Sky. In the midst of it was the God Tammuz.

Mr. Boscawen found a Babylonian fragment forming part of the third tablet in the Creation-Seris, in which the fall of Man seems to be described in plain terms. He gives the following translation of it -

In sin one with another in compact joins. The command was established in the garden of the God. The Asnan-tree they ate, they broke in two, its stalk they destroyed, the sweet juice which injures the body. Great is their sin. Themselves they exalted. To Merodach their Redeemer he the God Sar appointed their fate.

The Chaldean Account of Genesis, by George Smith & revised by A. H. Sayce, 1880

It is now five years since the present volume was first laid before the public by Mr. George Smith, just before setting out on his last ill-fated expedition to the East. It naturally awakened extreme interest and curiosity. The earlier chapters of Genesis no longer stood alone. Parallel accounts had been discovered by the author among the clay records of ancient Babylonia, which Far Exceeded in Antiquity the venerable histories of the Bible. All those who had a theory to support, or a Tradition to overthrow, turned eagerly to the newly-discovered documents, which possessed an equal interest for the students of history, of religion, and of language.

The Babylonian text, which relates to the Destruction of a Country by Rain of Fire, though long contained in the British Museum Collection, was first noticed by myself [Sayce] as being apparently the Babylonian version of the Biblical account of the Destruction of Sodom and Gomorrah.

275

The name of the pilot of Xisuthrus is Nes-Hea, "the Lion of Hea" in which
the second part of the name is invariably written with the Numeral 40, the
symbol of the God Hea. [The Sun in Leo is ~13,000 years BP]

Mr. Smith translated the text he had so laboriously pieced together, and
published his discovery to the world at a meeting of the Society of Biblical
Archaeology, December 3rd, 1872. The interest excited by Mr. Smith's
discovery was naturally very great.

. . . . the Star . . . . may he Seize that which has the Head in the Tail
[The Zodiacal Trail] since that in the Midst of the Sea he Passed Over . . . . .
His name accordingly is Nibiru the Passer Over, the possessor . . . . . may he
confirm the precepts (or laws) of the Stars of Heaven. Like sheep may he
feed the Gods all of them ; may he Exorcise the Sea, its treasures may he
hedge in and summon among Men hereafter through length of days.

A hymn put into the mouth of Merodach :

The Sun of Fifty Faces, the Lofty Weapon of my Divinity, I bear. The hero
that Striketh the Mountains, the propitious Sun of the morning, that is mine,
I bear. My Mighty Weapon, which like an Orb Smites in a Circle the
Corpses of the fighters, I bear. The Striker of Mountains, my Murderous
Weapon of Anu [The Sky], I bear. The Striker of Mountains, the Fish with
Seven Tails, that is mine, I bear. The Terror of battle, the Destroyer of
rebel lands, that is mine, I bear. The defender of conquests, the Great
Sword, the Falchion of my Divinity, I bear. That from whose hand the
Mountain escapes not, the land of the hero of battle, which is mine, I bear.
The delight of heroes, my Spear of Battle, I bear. My crown which Strikes
against Men, the Bow of the Lightning, I bear. The Crusher of the Temples
of rebel lands, my Club and Buckler of Battle, I bear. The Lightning of
Battle, my Weapon of Fifty Heads, I bear. The Feathered Monster of Seven
Heads, like the Huge Serpent of Seven heads, I bear. [The Feathered
Serpent from Americas also in Mesopotamia.] Like the Serpent that Beats
the Sea, which attacks the foe in the face, the Devastator of Forceful Battle,
Lord over Heaven and Earth, the Weapon of Seven Heads, I bear. That
which Maketh the Light come forth Like Day, God of the East, my Burning
Power, I bear. The established of Heaven and Earth, the Fire-God, who
has not his rival, I bear.

Merodach is then ordered to fetch "the laurel, the baleful Tree that breaks in pieces the Incubi, the name whereof Hea remembers in his heart, in the mighty enclosure, the Girdle of Eridu," in order that the Seven Evil Spirits may be driven away. It must be remembered that Hea was "the Lord of Wisdom," and under the form of a Fish as Oannes or Hea Khan was supposed to have ascended from the Persian Gulf, and taught the primitive Babylonians the elements of culture and civilization. [Ascended from the Valley of the Persian Gulf as the sea level rose 400 Feet.]

An Overthrow came from the Midst of the Deep. The Fated Punishment from the Midst of Heaven Descended. A Storm like a Plummet the Earth (overwhelmed). Towards the four winds the Destroying Flood like Fire Burnt. The inhabitants of the city it had caused to be Tormented ; their bodies it Consumed. In city and country it spread Death, and the Flames as they rose Overthrew. Freeman and Slave were equal, and the high places it filled. In Heaven and Earth like a Thunderstorm it had rained ; a prey it made. To a place of refuge the Gods hastened, and in a throng collected. Its mighty onset they fled from, and like a garment it concealed the guilty. They Feared, and Death overtook them. Their feet and hands it embraced. . . . . Their body it Consumed . . . . as for the city, its foundations it defiled . . . . with glory and breadth his mouth he filled. This Man the Voice of the Thunder called ; the Thunderbolt Descended ; during the day it Flashed ; Grievously it Fell . . . .

Sargon I was a Babylonian monarch who reigned in the city of Agane about 1800 B C This curious story is found on fragments of tablets from Kouyunjik, and reads as follows : [Woodworker Version]

Sargina the powerful king, the king of Agane am I. My mother was a princess, my father I did not know, a brother of my father chose the Mountains. In the city of Azupiranu which by the side of the River Euphrates is situated my mother the princess conceived me ; in an inaccessible place she brought me forth. She placed me in a basket of rushes, with bitumen my exit she sealed up. She launched me on the River which did not drown me. The River carried me, to Akki the Irrigator it brought me. Akki the Irrigator in tenderness of bowels lifted me up ; Akki the Irrigator as his child brought me up, Akki the Irrigator as his woodman set me, and in my woodmanship Istar loved me. Forty five years the kingdom I ruled, the people of the black heads I governed, I . . . .

277

over rugged countries in many chariots of bronze I rode, I governed the upper countries, I ruled over the chiefs of the lower countries. To the sea coast three times I advanced, Dilvun (in the Persian Gulf) submitted, Durankigal bowed, ...

Only fragment of Berosus's Oannes, Accadian Hea-Khan, "Hea the fish," Sumerian Ea. [Lion-Fish]

To the Waters their God has returned : to the house of bright things he descended as an Icicle : on a seat of snow he grew not old in Wisdom.

Other stories apparently relate to the Great Period Before the Flood, when Celestial Visitors Came to and From the Earth [Fly Bys], and the inhabitants of the World were very distinctly divided into the good and bad, but the stories are only fables with a moral attached. Two of these stories are very curious, and may hereafter turn out to be of great importance ; one is the story of the sin committed by the God Zu, and the other the story of Atarpi.

According to Berosus several of the Babylonian cities were built before the Flood, and various arts were known, including writing.

The Monuments and the Old Testament ; Light from the Near East on the Scriptures, by Ira Maurice Price, 1899

The Rosetta Stone was found in 1799, in 1818 Jean Francois Champollion began the task of deciphering it and he eventually succeeded in finding the long-lost combination that opened the Creaking Old Door to the civilization of the Nile Valley, in 1822 he published his discovery to the World. A new era of ancient history was immediately made available.

In 1887 a peasant woman in Egypt discovered a collection of about three hundred cuneiform tablets at Tell el-Amarna on the Nile. These proved to be a collection of letters written in Babylonian language by governors, officers, and individuals from many cities in Asia to the then reigning kings of Egypt, Amenhotep III and IV (1411-1358 BC). They describe their political distress in the face of Invaders who are crowding into the domain of the Egyptian ruler, and make pathetic appeals for help against the treachery of some of Egypt's ambitious officers.

278

Henry C. Rawlinson, made a discovery in 1835 in the Zagros Mountains. Rawlinson resolved at once to copy the mysterious inscriptions from which would become known as the Behistun Rock, 350 feet up a near vertical cliff face. Henry soon discovered, however, that he had not one language but three in the 1,200 lines of inscriptions which he copied. In 1847, the text, translation, and commentary appeared in the Journal of the Royal Asiatic Society.

As in all cases of great advance in any one department, there were doubters and skeptics as to the validity of the alleged results of ten years of additional work translating Persian, Susian, and Babylonian Cuneiform. To make a final test of scholars' ability to read and interpret these inscriptions, four men, H. C. Rawlinson, Edward Hincks, Julius Oppert, and H. Fox Talbot met in London in 1857. The trustees of the British Museum gave each a fine lithographic copy of a long historical Inscription (Tiglath-pileser I, 1120-1100 BC) and asked that he work independently and present at a specified time the results of his work. No translation of that text had been published. At the given date all appeared, submitted their translations, and a commission compared the results. To the surprise and profound satisfaction of every one, their translations agreed substantially from beginning to end. The triumph was almost incredible ; the victory was complete ; and the whole was published by the Royal Asiatic Society in 1857. This new philological achievement was the greatest ever made in the field of language or archeology. It was as great a discovery in the field of ancient philology and history as that of the telegraph or telephone in the commercial world. This is no exaggeration. Before this achievement the Babylonian-Assyrian valley was merely a cemetery of vanished nations, covered with tombs of ancient cities and towers, whose identities even were mere matters of conjecture.

The four rivers of Eden - Euphrates, Tigris, Pishon, and Gihon. [Possibly the Riyadh and Mond rivers when the area was green and flowing into the Persian Gulf Valley ?]

Chaldea means "Sea-Lands"

605 BC beginning of captivity of Jews in Babylon, go home 538-537 BC.

279

Stone Tablet from the Temple of the Sun at Sippara.

Hebrew and Babylonian Traditions   The Haskell Lectures
by   Morris   Jastrow   Jr.   1914

Archaeological research, in combination with the ascertained and generally
accepted results of Biblical studies, has demonstrated the Close Bond
existing between Hebrew and Babylonian Traditions to be Beyond Question.
The evidence is Overwhelming and is Idle at this stage to Deny either the
composite character of the stories in the early chapters of Genesis, or the
late date at which they must have received their present form ; it is equally

280

Futile to Deny the factor of Evolution in the Development of religious ideas among the Hebrew. One can readily understand how even learned and conscientious scholars through a determination to cling to certain views can acquire an attitude of mind which prevents them from weighing evidence Judiciously and Fairly. This observation applies particularly to those who Deceive Themselves by imagining that they are pursuing studies in an open-minded spirit, whereas in reality they are merely seeking a confirmation of views which they hold quite independently of their studies, and generally held antecedent to any investigation.

We must keep a frame of mind Free from Bias and without any predilections for any special theological postulates and strive with a spirit of pure historical inquiry to understand the Struggle of Man Everywhere and at all times to reach out to an Understanding of the Mysteries by which he is Surrounded – Mysteries that even in early stages of culture are Dimly Perceived, and that become more clearly defined and correspondingly more Profound as with Enlarged Experience and with Increasing Knowledge Man Realizes how much must always remain for him within the Shadow of the Unknown and the Unknowable.

A writer intent upon giving an answer to two fundamental questions, how Mankind came to be dispersed over the face of the globe, and why there are so many different languages, tells the curious tale in the tenth chapter of Genesis – itself a combination of two stories, one about the building of a city, the other of a high tower – which represents the dispersion as radiating from the city of Babylon in the land of Shinar (a general term for the Euphrates Valley) as a center, and the confusion of languages as a device of Yahweh to prevent the people from carrying out their design to build the tower. The city of Babylon symbolized for the writer the entire civilization of the Euphrates Valley. The tower that the writer had in mind was a characteristic feature of the Sacred Architecture with broad terraces, heaped one above the other in Imitation of a Mountain, with a winding road leading to the top where the deity to whom the tower was dedicated had his seat. The story thus not only takes us back to Babylonia, but represents a characteristic Protest of the Old Testament writers against Babylonish Customs. It voices the feelings of these writers towards Babylonia as a Wicked place, as a source of Mankind's misfortunes and ills.

The language of the oldest historical inscriptions is Sumerian, the commercial documents down to about 2000 BC are likewise largely in Sumerian. To this oldest period belong Sumerian votive inscriptions,

Sumerian hymns and lamentation, ritual Appealing to the Gods to Desist from their Wrath which had manifested itself in some political Catastrophe or in Havoc Wrought by Destructive Storms ; and it is fair inference that the script developing from a Pictorial or Hieroglyphic form of writing was the invention of the Sumerians, though developed with Semitic co-operation. For, even in this earliest period, Semitic influences may be detected. We find Semitic names and Semitic words in very early inscriptions.

Curiosity is, indeed, the beginning of Wisdom, and the most modern and most advanced scientific spirit is merely curiosity, plus the application of a proper method to satisfy it.

At the very beginning of this account we have perhaps the most striking evidence of the ultimate identity of the Hebrew and Babylonian Creation Traditions, for in the statement that the Earth was Tohu and Bohu ("Void and Waste") and that Darkness was over the face of the Deep (Tehom), we have the Hebrew counterpart to the Babylonian description of Primeval Chaos. At the same time the description furnishes the evidence for the thesis that in the Biblical account the Mythical element has been reduced to the utmost possible minimum. This is indicated by the use of the terms Tohu and Bohu in place of personifications like Apsu and Mummu, and more particularly in the entirely impersonal use of the term "Tehom" in the sense of "Watery Deep," as against the personification of the Primeval Waters as Tiamat, and this despite the Fact that the Hebrew version still uses the very same term, "Tehom," as the Babylonian.

There are traces elsewhere in the Old Testament that Tehom was once personified, though the personification became, in the advanced Hebrew thought, merely a Poetical Metaphor. In the beautiful twenty-eighth chapter of Job, where Man's search for Wisdom is so impressively described, we read: "But Wisdom, - where may She be found, and where is the place of Understanding ? Man does not know Her way and She is not found in the land of the living ; Tehom says, "She is not in me," and the Sea says, 'Not with me.'" Further on we read: "Abaddon ("Destruction," a name for the nether world, where the Dead are huddled together.) and Death say, 'We have heard a rumor about Her : God understands Her way and He knows Her place,'" Elsewhere, as in the 104th Psalm as well as in the various references to Rahab and the Leviathan and the Dragon, particularly in Isaiah and Job, we have the further Proof that the Hebrews were Well Acquainted with the Nature-Myth in its more primitive form, for such figures as Rahab and Leviathan pictured as Huge Serpents are merely the reflections, in the form of Poetical Metaphors, of Primeval Chaos as a period in which Monstrous Beings were in Control.

When Job, in one of his descriptions of the divine Power which lay so heavily on him in his unbearable sufferings, exclaims :

"The shades Tremble Beneath the Waters and the Inhabitants thereof. The nether-world is naked before Him, and Destruction hath no covering. He stretcheth out the North over empty space, and hangeth the Earth over nothing. He bindeth up the Waters in His Thick Clouds ; and the Cloud is not rent under them. He Closet in the Face of His throne, and Spreadeth His Cloud upon it. He hath described a Boundary upon the face of the Waters, unto the confines of Light and Darkness. The pillars of Heaven Tremble and are Astonished at His Rebuke. He Stirreth up the Sea with His power, and by His understanding He Smiteth Through Rahab. By His breath the Heavens are serene ; His hand hath Pierced the Slant Serpent. Lo, these are but the outskirts of His Ways ; and how small a whisper is heard of Him ! But the Thunder of His Mighty Deeds Who Can Understand ?"

Job 26 : 5-14 1917

The lines Imply a conflict with Rahab in which God is Triumphant. By His power He subdues the Monster, just as Marduk vanquishes Tiamat ; and we have a further reminder of the Babylonian Myth in the reference to the Bolts of Heaven which, it will be recalled, Marduk attaches to the Gates established at either side of the Heavenly Expanse, and at which he places watchmen as guards.

In another speech of Job, portraying the irresistible force of God's Anger, the "Helper of Rahab" are described as to "stoop" under the Divine Wrath, a definite indication that among the Hebrews, as among the Babylonians, Rahab-Tiamat was represented as having an Army of Monsters to assist Her, and which Marduk captures after he has overcome Tiamat.

"Who Shaketh the Earth Out of her Place, and pillars thereof Tremble. Who commandeth the Sun, and it Riseth Not ; and Sealeth Up the Stars. Who alone stretcheth out the Heavens, and Treadeth Upon the Waters of the Sea. Who maketh the Bear, Orion, and the Pleiades, and the chambers of the South. Who doeth great things past finding out ; yea, marvelous things without number. Lo, He goeth by me, and I see Him not ; He passeth on also, but I perceive Him not. Behold, He snatcheth away, who can hinder

283

Him ? Who will say unto Him : 'What doest Thou ?' God Will Not Withdraw His Anger ; the Helpers of Rahab did Stoop under Him."

Job 9 : 6-13   1917

Even more explicit is a passage in a late chapter of the postexilic portion of Isaiah in reference to Rahab as a being that belongs to Primeval Days, to the Very Beginning of Time.

"Awake, awake, put on strength, O Arm of the Lord ; awake, as in the days of old, the generations of ancient times. Art thou not it that Hewed Rahab in Pieces, that Pierced the Dragon ? Art thou not it that Dried up the Sea [No Rain], the Waters of the Deep ; that made the Depths of the Sea a way for the redeemed to Pass Over ?"   Isaiah 51 : 9-10   1917

The picture here forms a complete analogy to the Babylonian Myth – even to the conception of Rahab as a Dragon.

"For Who in the Skies can be Compared unto the Lord, who among the Sons of Might can be Likened unto the Lord, a God Dreaded in the great council of the Holy Ones, and Feared of All Them that are Round about Him ? O Lord God of Hosts, who is a Mighty one, like unto Thee, O Lord ? And thy faithfulness is round about Thee. Thou rulest the proud swelling of the Sea ; when the Waves thereof arise, Thou stillest them. Thou didst Crush Rahab, as one that is Slain ; Thou didst scatter Thine enemies with the Arm of Thy strength.   Psalms 89 : 7-11   1917

In the course of time the term loses its original force of a proper name, as Tehom Lost it, and Rahab Becomes a Poetical Synonym for Wickedness, Violence, and Hostility to Yahweh's kingdom of justice and order. It is so used in Psalm 40 : 5, which is rendered as follows :

"Happy the Man who makes Yahweh his trust, and turns not to the Rahabs and to Lying Rebels." "Happy is the Man that hath made the Lord his trust, and hath not turned unto the Arrogant, nor unto such as Fall Away Treacherously."   [1917]

"Thou, O Yahweh, art my king from of old, working salvation in the Midst of the Earth. Thou hast divided the Sea with thy Arm, Thou has Broken the Heads of the Dragons in the Waters. Thou hast Crushed the Heads of Leviathan, gavest him as food for the people of the wilderness, Thou hast split fountain and brook, Thou hast Dried Up the Streams of primeval time.

284

Thine is the day, aye thine is the night. Thou hast fixed the Moon and Sun, Thou hast set all the bounds of the Earth. Summer and winter thou hast formed."   Psalm   74 : 12-17

"On that day Yahweh will visit with his Sword the Cruel, the Mighty and the Powerful, - Leviathan, the Winding Serpent, and Leviathan, the Twisted Serpent, and he shall Kill the Dragon in the Sea."
                                                                    [Greek rendering...?]

To illustrate the Weakness of Man in contrast with the Deity, whom alone could subdue the Primeval Monster, and therefore the Folly of Man to question God's ways, the poet says :

"And the Lord answering Job out of the Whirlwind, said : Gird up thy lions like a Man: I will ask thee, and do thou tell me. Wilt thou Void my judgment : and condemn me, that thou mayst be justified ? And hast thou an Arm like God, and canst thou Thunder with a Voice like him ? Clothe thyself with beauty, and set thyself up on high and be glorious, and put on goodly garments. Scatter the Proud in thy Indignation, and Behold every Arrogant Man, and Humble him. Look on all that are Proud, and Confound Them, and Crush the Wicked in their place. Hide them in the dust together, and plunge their faces into the Pit [Crater]. Then I will confess that Thy Right Hand Is Able To Save Thee. Behold Behemoth whom I Made with thee, he eateth grass like an Ox. His strength is in his lions, and his force in the navel of his belly. He Setteth up his Tail like a Cedar, the sinews of his testicles are wrapped together. His bones are like pipes of Brass, his gristle like plates of Iron. [S]He is the Beginning of the <u>Ways of God</u>, Who Made Him, he will apply his Sword. To him the Mountains bring forth grass : there all the Beasts of the field shall play. He sleepeth under the shadow, in covert of the reed, and in moist places. The shades cover his shadow, the willows of the brook shall compass him about. Behold, he will Drink up a River, and not wonder : and he trusteth that the Jordan may run into his mouth. In his eyes as with a hook he shall take him, and bore through his nostrils with stakes. Canst thou draw out the Leviathan with a hook, or canst thou tie his tongue with a cord ? Canst thou put a ring in his nose, or bore through his jaw with a buckle ? Will he make many supplication to thee, or speak soft words to thee ? Will he make a covenant with thee, and wilt thou take him to be a servant forever ? Shalt thou play with him as with a bird, or tie him up for thy handmaids ? Shall friends Cut him in Pieces, shall Merchants Divide him ? [Asteroid mining] Wilt thou fill his skin, and the cabins of fishes with his head ? Lay thy Hand upon Him [Three times so

285

far] : Remember the Battle [Yes], and speak no more. Behold his hope shall fail him, and in the sight of all be cast down. I will not stir him up, like one that is cruel : for who can resist my countenance ? Who hath given me before that I should repay him ? All things that are under Heaven are mine. I will not spare him, nor his Mighty Words, and framed to make supplication. Who can discover the face of his garment ? Or who can go into the midst of his mouth ? Who can open the doors of his face ? His teeth are round about. His body is like Molten Shields, shut close up with scales pressing upon one another. One is joined to another, and not so much as any air can come between them : They stick one to another and they hold one another fast, and shall not be separated. His sneezing is like the Shining of Fire, and his eyes like the eyelids of the morning. Out of his mouth Go Forth Lamps, like Torches of Lighted Fire. Out of his nostrils Goeth Smoke, like that of a pot heated and boiling. His breath kindled Coals, and a Flame cometh forth out of his Mouth. In his neck strength shall dwell, and want goeth before his face. The members of his flesh cleave one to another : he shall send Lightnings against him, and they shall not be carried to another place. His heart shall be as Hard as a Stone, and as Firm as a Smith's Anvil. When he shall raise him up, the Angels shall Fear, and being affrighted shall purify themselves. When a sword shall lay at him, it shall not be able to hold, nor a spear, nor a breastplate. For he shall esteem Iron as straw, and Brass as rotten wood. The archers shall not put him to flight, the stones of the sling are to him like stubble. As stubble will he esteem the hammer, and he will laugh him to scorn who shaketh the spear. The beams of the Sun shall be under him, and he shall Strew Gold under him like mire. He shall make the Deep Sea [Sky] to Boil like a pot, and shall make it as when ointments boil. A Path shall Shine after him, he shall esteem the Deep as growing old. There is no power upon Earth that can compared with him who was made to fear no one. He Beholdeth Every High Thing, he is King over all the Children of Pride."

Job 40 and 41 Douay – Rheims 1899

Be this as it may, enough evidence has been brought forward to show that up to a late period the Hebrews were perfectly familiar with the Old-Myth of the conflict with the Monster Tiamat, or whatever name we choose to apply to it ; and it is also a justifiable conclusion that what has become a Metaphor in Hebrew poetry was once popularly regarded as an Actual Occurrence, to account for the existence of law and order in the World in place of Primeval Chaos and Lawlessness. No conflict is required, the suggestion of a conflict would mark a limitation to the supreme majesty of the divine command.

Hence the addition to the description of Primeval Chaos, in the second verse of the first chapter, of the words "and Darkness was upon the Face of the Deep ; and the spirit of God hovered over the face of the Waters," Since Water and the Atmosphere Above the Waters are supposed to be in existence earlier than the land, the animals of the water and of the air are mentioned first. It is, however, of importance to note that among the Life that swarms in the waters, "the Great Dragons" are singled out for special mention. The word used for Dragons (Tanninim, plural of Tannin.) is Identical with the term occurring in the Poetical Allusions to the Nature-Myth of the Conflict between Yahweh and the Great Primeval Monster, pictured as a Dragon and accompanied by an Army of Dragons. The introduction of the term is hardly accidental, and I have no hesitation in recognizing in the specific mention of the "Great Dragons" as the creation of Yahweh, a further protest against the Nature-Myth which assumed the Great Dragons, including their leader Tiamat or Rahab or Leviathan, as Pre-Existent. This again, therefore, a Deliberate Effort to Expunge the Mythical Element which we have seen to be one of the characteristic aims of the creation version in the priestly code.

"And God said: 'Let the waters swarm with swarms of living creatures, and let fowl fly above the Earth in the open firmament of Heaven,' And God created the great Sea-monsters, and every living creature that creepeth, wherewith the waters swarmed, after its kind, and every winged fowl after its kind ; and God saw that it was good. And God blessed them, saying : 'Be fruitful, and multiply, and fill the waters in the seas, and let fowl multiply in the Earth.'"   Genesis 1 : 20-22   [1917]

The wide departure from Babylonian Traditions is, however, particularly apparent in the spirit of the transformed Hebrew Tradition which changes the Creator from a Vanquisher of Hostile Forces, and from an Artificer after the fashion of a human workman, into a spiritual Power, acting by His 'Word' alone. The Word brings about Light, the Word causes the dry land to appear and clothes the fields with Verdure, the Word brings forth Trees and plants, and fills water, air and land with living beings. This 'Word of Yahweh' is frequently introduced in the Prophets and Psalms to describe not merely the power but the very essence of the Deity, conceived as a Universal Being and pictured as a spiritual force. To be sure, in Babylonian and Assyrian hymns the 'Word' of Enlil, of Marduk, of Ea, of Shamash, and so through the list of the chief Gods of the pantheon, also plays a Prominent part. Compositions bewailing some Great Catastrophe that has Overtaken the land describe the power residing in the Word of a God, which causes Heaven and Earth to Tremble and spreads Terror on All sides :

"The Word that causes the Heavens on High to Tremble, The Word that makes the Earth below to Quake, The Word that brings Destruction to the Anunnaki (a lower order of divine beings), His Word is beyond diviner and seer, His Word is a Tempest without a rival."

The conception, however, remains on a materialistic basis, and when applied to other than Storm-Gods whose 'Word' is the Thunder, it is the actual strength and power of the God that is meant. We have a trace of this conception of the Word in Poetical Metaphors occurring in Psalms such as the twenty-ninth :

"The Voice of the Lord is upon the Waters ; The God of glory Thundereth, even the Lord upon many Waters. The Voice of the Lord is Powerful ; the Voice of the Lord is full of majesty. The Voice of the Lord Breaketh the Cedars ; yea, the Lord Breaketh in Pieces the Cedars of Lebanon. He maketh them also to skip like a calf ; Lebanon and Sirion like a young Wild-Ox. The Voice of the Lord Heweth out Flames of Fire. The Voice of the Lord Shaketh the Wilderness ; The Lord Shaketh the Wilderness of Kadesh. The Voice of the Lord maketh the Hinds to calve, and Strippeth the Forests Bare ; and in His temples all say : 'Glory.' The Lord sat enthroned at the Flood ;"

Psalm 29 : 3-10 1917

In the eighth chapter of the book of Proverbs, celebrating the power of Wisdom, Wisdom is personified (verse 23) :

"The Lord made me (i.e., Wisdom) as the beginning of His way, the first of His works of old. I was set up from everlasting, from the beginning, or ever the Earth was. When there were no Depths (Tehomot, the plural of Tehom), I was brought forth ; when there were no fountains abounding with Water. I was in honor (Conjectural emendation of the Hebrew text, suggested by the parallelism.) before the Mountains were settled, before the hills was I brought forth ; while as yet He had not made the Earth, nor the fields, nor the beginning of the dust of the World. When He established the Heavens, I was There ; when He Set a Circle upon the Face of the Deep, when He made firm the Skies above, when the Fountains of the Deep showed their Might, when He gave to the Sea His decree, that the Waters should not transgress His commandment, when He appointed the foundations of the Earth ; then I was by Him, as a Nursling ; and I was Daily All Delight, Playing always before Him, Playing in His habitable Earth, and my Delights are with the Sons of Men."

It is clear that Wisdom is here used almost as a synonym for the Divine 'Word,' which naturally is the 'Word' of Wisdom. The description given of creation may be regarded as a poetical paraphrase of the account of creation in Genesis. It is based on this account, and Wisdom thus associated with every phase of the work of creation, existed even before Primeval Chaos, is the spirit of God Himself "Brooding Over The Waters," as well as the Divine 'Word' through which everything is Created. The three terms, God, Word, and Wisdom, are Almost Identical. Word and Wisdom become theological concepts, endeavours to picture the workings of a Power conceived entirely as a spiritual force. This Personification of Wisdom as the Companion [Tiamat] of God in the work of creation, the medium through which the Divine transforms His desires into Actions, is reflected in the twenty-eighth chapter of Job to which a reference has already been made. After describing the hopeless search of Man for Wisdom – not to be found in the Sea nor in the Depths nor in the hidden recesses of the Mountains to which Man penetrates in search of Gold and precious Stones – poet in a sublime height of rapture exclaims :

"When he fixed a bound to the rain, and a Path for the Flash of the Thunder, then He saw and celebrated Her. He established and searched Her out, and said to Man : 'Behold the Fear of the Lord is Wisdom (Evidently a paraphrase of Proverbs 9 : 10 : "The Fear of the Lord is the Beginning of Wisdom, and the Knowledge of the Holy – Understanding.") removing from Evil – Understanding.'"

Concomitant, therefore, with the minimizing of Myth in the development of Hebrew views of creation, we have the process which leads to the personification of the 'Word' of God – more specifically pictured as 'Wisdom' – as the associate of the Deity in the work of creation. The further growth of this personification of the Word or of Divine Wisdom leads to the Famous Doctrine of the Logos or 'Word' as set forth in the writings of Philo of Alexandria and which finds its reflection in the opening words of the Gospel of John that so succinctly and admirably sum up the entire process of thought involved :

"In the beginning was the Word and the Word was with God and the Word was God."

A comparison with the chapter from Proverbs, from which we have quoted, shows the identity of the 'Word' and 'Wisdom,' for Wisdom (like the 'Word') was in the beginning ; She was "with God" and, as we have seen, was Not To Be Distinguished from God. God, Word, and Wisdom are three in one. We thus have, under the influence of the higher conception of divine government of the Universe as voiced in the utterances of the Hebrew Prophets, the transformation of the 'Word' of power and strength – such as the 'Word' of the Babylonian and Assyrian Gods is, and as the 'Word' of Yahweh at an earlier stage of the 'Word' that is 'Wisdom' ; and along with this transformation the personification of the Word, suggested in the Genesis account of creation and receiving its theological formula in John's definition of the Logos.

"Doth not Wisdom call, and Understanding put forth Her voice ? In the Top of High places by the way, where the paths meet, She standeth ; besides the Gates, at the entry of the city, at the coming in at the Doors, She Crieth Aloud : Unto you, O Men, I call, and my Voice is to the Sons of Men. O ye Thoughtless, Understand Prudence, and, ye Fools, be ye of an Understanding Heart. Hear, for I will Speak Excellent things, and the opening of my lips shall be Right Things. For my mouth shall Utter Truth, and Wickedness is an Abomination to my Lips. All the Words of my mouth are in Righteousness, there is nothing Perverse or Crooked in them."

Proverbs 8 : 1-8 1917

"Wisdom hath Builded Her House, She hath hewn out Her Seven pillars;"

Proverbs 9 : 1 1917

Many of the Cuneiform characters have this (shapattum) double value, either with a hard or a middle sound of the palatals, labials, or dentals, as e.g., uk or ug or bal, ta or da, ect.

Aspects of Religious Belief and Practice in Babylonia and Assyria, by Morris Jastrow Jr. 1911

The Cuneiform Texts from approximately 1500 BC recorded the number of Thunder-claps, the place in the Heavens whence the sound proceeded, the month or day or special circumstances when heard, were all carefully noted, as was also the quarter whence the Lightning came, and the direction it took, the course of the winds and rain and so on, without end. And especially when Extraordinary Phenomena Appeared in the Skies, such as Thunderclap Out of a Clear Sky.

The reference to the dwelling of Utnapishtim "in the distance at the Confluence of the Streams" [Zodiacal Stream] is exceedingly interesting. We may properly assume that the Streams meant are the Euphrates and Tigris, and perhaps other rivers known to Babylonians. The Confluence is the Great Ocean [Space], which, for the Babylonians, began with the Persian Gulf. Is the destined, a counterpart of the Greek idea of the Island of the Blest, the first faint beginnings of a Paradise reserved for those who had secured divine favor ? It is not impossible that such is the case, though it may be added that beyond this Vague Indication No Other Evidence Exists [19th Century]. The mere Vagueness, however, of the Description is Suggestive. The story is intended to voice a hope that through special favor some may escape the ordinary fate, but nothing more. The narrator feels that he is In the Presence of a Mystery. Utnapishtim [Noah's Antecedent] Explicitly states that the story which he is about to tell to Gilgamesh is Mysterious, and Ea Emphasizes that through a dream "a Wise One Among Men Learned the Secret of the Gods." The distant place at the Confluence of the Streams is also a Mystery [The Space Between the Mouth and the Tail midway of the Pleiades and the Goat-Fish, the Fishes or THE DEEP.] – perhaps the greatest of all in the mind of the compiler – and for this reason he desists from any further description.

This is an extract from one of the episodes of the Gilgamesh epic, in which the advice is given to the hero to desist from the attempt to seek immortality and to content himself with the joys and pleasures of this world.

"Thou, Oh, Gilgamesh, let thy belly be full. Day and night be merry, daily celebrate a feast, day and night dance and make merry. Clean be thy clothes, anointed be thy head ; be washed daily in pure water. Look joyfully on the child that grasps thy hand ; be happy with the wife in thy arms."

The passage reminds us of the spirit of the book of Ecclesiastes 9 : 7-9 which, in fact, gives the same advice in almost the same words :

"Go thy way, eat thy bread with joy, and drink thy wine with a merry heart. Let thy garments be always white, and let thy head not lack ointment. Live joyfully with thy wife whom thou lovest, all the days of thy life of vanity which He hath given thee under the Sun, for that is thy portion."

At the close of my task I am even more painfully aware than at the beginning of the Futility of the Attempt to give an Exhaustive Treatment of this Important and Fascinating Theme. The Exhaustive Treatment of the Subject

291

would be Exhausting to the Reader as well as to the Author. The last word of True Science should always be the emphasis on the Open Mind and the Expectant Disposition. The test of a Genuine Desire for Truth is the Willingness to Reinvestigate Our Conclusions, the Maintenance of a Sympathetic Attitude Towards New Light, in the firm assurance that the Truth which is the Goal of Mankind, and which it should be the Aim of Each One of Us to realize so far as possible in our Life, will also be the Means of Our <u>Salvation</u>.

The Old Testament In the Light of the Historical Records and Legends of Assyria and Babylonia, by Theophilus G. Pinches, 1902

In Eridu a dark vine grew, it was made in a glorious place, Its appearance as Lapis-Lazuli, planted beside the Abyss, Which is Ea's Path, filling Eridu with Fertility. Its seat is the central point of the Earth, Its dwelling is the couch of Nammu (River – God). To the glorious house, which is like a forest, its shadow extends, No Man enters its midst. In its interior is the Sun-God, and the peerless mother of Tammuz. Between the mouths of the Rivers which are on both sides.

When within the Sea there was a Stream, in that day Eridu was made, Esagila was built – Esagila which the God Lugal-du-azaga had founded within the Abyss.

1st line of series of Gilgamesh : He who Saw the World, the Legend of
Gilgamesh. the hero who knew the Wisdom of the Whole . . . . & saw
Secret and Hidden things . . . .

In Larsa and Sippar the temples of the Sun-God Samas were named E-
Barbara.

The Legend of Chedorlaomer
Cuneiform Text

". . . . . . and they pressed on to the Supreme Gate. He Threw Down,
Removed, and Cast Down the Door of Istar in the holy places, He
Descended also, like Ura the Unsparing, to Du-maha ; He stayed also in
Du-maha, looking at the temple ; He opened his Mouth, and Spake with the
children of the place. To all his warriors then he hastened the message : -
'Carry off the spoil of the temple, take also its goods, Destroy its Barrier,
cause its Enclosure to be Cut Through.' To the Channel . . . . they
Pressed On . . . . He drove away the director's overseer, he took away
the Vail. The enemy pressed on Evilly to Ennun-dagalla. The Gods were
Clothed with Light before Him, He Flashed like Lightning, and Shook the
Holy places. The enemy feared, he hid himself. There Descended also its
chief Man, and he spake to him a command . . . . the Gods were Clothed
with Light, He Flashed like Lightning, and Shook the Holy places. Draw
near unto his temple, seize his hand ! . . . . , he did not fear, and he
regarded not his Life. He shall not approach Ennun-dagalla, he shall not
remove his crowns. . . . . . . (the Elamite, the wicked Man, proclaimed . . . . .
to the lands and stayed in Du-nmaha . . . . When the guardian spoke
peace . . . . There Came Down his Winged Bulls, which . . . . the
temple. The enemy, the Elamite, multiplied evils, and Bel allowed evil to
be planned against Babylon. When Righteousness was Absent, then was
decided also the Destruction of the temple, the house of the multitude of the
Gods. Then Came Down his Winged Bulls. The enemy, the Elamite, took
its goods – Bel, dwelling upon it, had displeasure. When the magicians
repeated their Evil Words, Gullum and the Evil Wind performed their evil.
There Came Down also their Gods, they Came Down like a Torrent. Storm
and Evil Wind went Round in the Heavens. Anu, their Creator, had
Displeasure. He made Pale their Face, he made Desolate his place, He
Destroyed the barrier in the shrine of E-anna, He . . . . the temple, and
the platform Shook . . . . he decreed Destruction, ... he had
disfavor. The . . . . of Bel of E-zida barred the road to Sumer. Who is
Kudurlahgumal, the doer of the evils ? He has gathered also the Umman-

293

manda against the . . . . of Bell – He has Laid in Ruin . . . . by their
side. When the enclosure of E-zida was Broken Down, and Nebo was Ruler
of the Host, there Came Down his Winged Bulls. Down to Tiamtu he set
his face. Ine-Tutu, whom the Sun-God (?) hastened within Tiamtu, entered
Tiamtu, and founded a pseudo-capital. The enclosure of E-zida, the
everlasting temple, was caused to be Broken Through. The enemy, the
Elamite, caused his Yoke of Horses to be Directed, and set his Face to go
Down to Borsippa. He traveled also the road of Darkness, the road to
Mesech. The tyrant Elamite Destroyed the palace, he subdued the princes
of . . . . with the Sword, he carried off the spoil of all the temples. He
took their goods, and carried them away to Elam . . . . ruler, he
Destroyed the ruler, ... filled also the land." . . . .

After the sacrifice at Bethel God reveals Himself to Jacob as El-shaddai, His
name in the text of "the priestly narrator" (Genesis 17 : 1), and in many
other passages. The word Shaddai here is generally connected with the root
Shadad, "to act powerfully," and the translation "God Almighty" is based
on this. As the word is a very difficult one, however, there have been many
attempts to find a more satisfactory etymology. It is to be noted, therefore,
that there is in Semitic Babylonian a word sadu, often applied to deities,
and expressed, in the old language of Akkad, by means of the same
ideograph (KURU) as is used for "Mountain," as that which towers up
commandingly, a Mighty Mass (sadu or saddu in Semitic Babylonian).

**The Bible and the Monuments. The Primitive Hebrew
Records in Light of Modern Research. by W. St. Chad
Boscawen 1895**

The word for Family being the small circle of individuals united by the tie of Relationship. This word is Preserved in the word Kimmah of Job, the Family of the Pleiades.

The Being Tiamat Corresponds Exactly to the Tehom of Genesis, the Watery waste which covered the surface, and is also to be identified with Tavthe, the wife of Apason, in the cosmogony of Damascios. In the tablet She is called Muallidat, "the Bearing Mother" of all the Heaven and Earth ; and in the older Legend from Kutha She is called Musenik, "the Nutrice of them all." She is represented on the monuments as having the body of a Woman, Terminating in the Coiled Tails of Two Serpents [Vortices], similar to the figures on the sculptures from Pergamos. In this form She represents the Great Nature-Serpent of Darkness, who Coils Round the Earth like an Egg, and Hold the Earth in its Toils, until Slain by Merodach, the Lord of Light. As the personification of Chaos and Darkness, Tiamat becomes the Spirit of Evil, against whom Merodach, the God of Goodness, the "protector of good Men," wages eternal war.

To the Mountains whose form is double. To the double Mountains in his course he came, which each day guard the Sun. Above them is the threshold of Heaven ; below them the house of Death embraces them. Scorpion Men, they guard the Great Gate, whose Terror is Terrible and their beholding Death.

The great temple in the city of Sippara known as E Barbara, "the House of Light," which, according to Tradition, had Existed Before the Deluge, but which, at any rate, was an ancient edifice in as remote a period as 3800 BC. The explorations of M. de Sarzec at Tello on the Shatel Hie, in Southern Babylonia, brought to light the ruins of a very ancient city. This city Sirpurra, "the Bright Light or Flame," as its name indicates, was dedicated to the God Ningirsu. Most of the Inscriptions are those of a monarch named Gudea (Prophet), whose reign was about 2800 BC ; but there are many monuments of a far greater antiquity, reaching back to about 4000 BC. The most Archaic of these have inscriptions in a curious Linear Character, almost Pictorial, which preceded the elaboration of the Cuneiform Writing. All the monuments contain dedications to "Ningirsu, the warrior of Ellila" ("the Lord of the Ghost land"). This God was the Fire God of Babylonia, and his worship was closely associated with the Working of the Metals. The name Ningirsu means simply "the Piercer of the Flesh," or Mass. The city is sacred to the Fire-God, and from the Inscriptions we learn that its temple was called "the House of the Fire-Brand."

Merodach, in his character as the son of Ea, occupies a position but slightly inferior to that of his father, repeatedly assuming the divine epithets of his father ; and in a hymn to Merodach, "Mankind (even), the human race, the Living creatures, all that by name are called, and in the land exist, is thine." It would appear, therefore, that to Ea and Merodach, or the pair conjointly, the Babylonians attributed the creation of the human race. It would seem also from a passage in a magical text of Considerable Antiquity, being certainly of Akkadian origin, that the story of the creation of Woman from the rib of the Man was known to the Babylonians, for we read, Assat ina udli nis uttam, "the Woman from the flank of the Man was called" – certainly this is a curious parallel to Genesis 2 : 21, 22.

The Legend of Eridu
Cuneiform Text

The holy house, the house of the Gods, in a holy site had not been made. A reed had not sprung up, a tree was not made. A brick was not laid, a beam was not made. A house was not constructed, a city was not built. A city was not made, an abode was not made strong. Nipur had not been built, E Kurra was not constructed, Uruki had not been built, E Anna was not constructed. The Absu was not made. Eridu was not built. The holy house, the house of the Gods, its site was not made. The Whole World, the Sea also in the Midst of the Sea was a Flowing (tide). At that time Eridu was built, E Sagila was constructed. E Sagila which the God Lugal-du-azagga within the Absu raised up. Babylon was built. E Sagila was made perfect. The Gods and the Anunaki together he made. The holy city, the abode of the joy of their hearts, supremely he proclaimed. Merodach a wide space on the Face of the Deep Bound (it) Round. He made dust, and poured it on the space. The Gods in the abode of the joy of heart he seated. He made Mankind. The Goddess Aruru created the seed of humanity by him. The Cattle of the field, the Living creatures of the field he made. The Tigris and Euphrates he made, and in (their) places he placed. Their names as good he declared. Grass, marsh plants, reeds, and forest he made. The Verdure of the field he made. The land, the pool, and the jungle (?). Oxen, the young Steer, the humped Cow and her Calf, the Sheep of the fold. The plantation, and the forest also. The Wild Goat and the Gazelle were protected by him. The Lord Merodach around the Sea made an Embankment.

This remarkable text bears on its face an indication of being an ancient document incorporated into a magical library relating to the purification of

296

the Temple of Nebo at Borsippa ; but a very little examination is necessary to see that it is not an original product of this school. The great prominence given to Merodach, who is represented as the Creator of the World and the human race, as well as the frequent mention of the Absu, or Mystic Ocean, and of Eridu, show that we have to deal with an adapted version of one of the Oldest Legends of the great priest-city of Eridu.

There is a very interesting relic of older times preserved in the last lines of the Fragment, where we read, "The Wild Goat and the Gazelle were protected by him." This carries us back to the days of Totemism, and again serves to identify this Legend with the Oldest School of Chaldea. In Chaldea, as in Egypt, most of the Gods had their Sacred Animals or Totems in one form or another. In the Mythological Inscriptions Merodach is called "the Mighty One of the Gazelle God," and as such the "Gazelle" was his Totem. So also as a Solar deity "the Goat" was one of his Totems, and the Goat-Skin was the Sacred Robe of the Babylonian Priests, as the Panther Skin was of the Priests of Egypt. [And the Leopard in America.]

The Fact of this Legend being, in its Older Form, a product of the school of Eridu is of Great Importance when we come to make comparisons with the Biblical Writings as are possible. Eridu, the Eridugga of the Akkadians, was the "Holy City," the abode of the God Ea and his son Merodach. Ea bore the titles of "the God who Knows All Things," "the Lord of the Deep Knowledge" – the Wise, and his abode was the Absu, or "House of Deep Knowledge" (Bit nemiki) ; it was, therefore, pre-eminetly the city of Wisdom, and it is, therefore, Most Interesting to find a Curious Parallel, or series of similar thoughts and expressions, between this Tablet and the "Beginnings of Wisdom," as described in the eighth chapter of Proverbs.

The Legend of Kutha
Cuneiform Text

"(He is the Lord) of all that is above, and which is below, the Lord of the spirits of Earth ; who Drinks Turbid Waters, and Drinks Not Clear Waters. He whose field is that where the Warrior's Weapon (rests not), he Captures, he Destroys. On a Tablet he wrote not, his mouth and bodies and produce he caused not to the land, and I drew not near him. Warriors with the bodies of a Bird of the valley, Men with the faces of Ravens [The Norse equate Crows with Death] did the Great Gods Create. In the Earth the Gods Created his city. Tiamat was their Nurse ; their Progeny the Mistress of the Gods Created. In the Midst of the Mountains they grew up and became

297

heroes, and increased in number ; Seven kings begotten appeared as fathers ; six thousand in number were their Hosts ; the God Banini was their father ; their mother, the queen Niehili."

Here follow the names of the Seven brothers. They are all in Akkadian and difficult of explanation, and may therefore be omitted. The various generations created seem to have been Destroyed one after the other in much the same manner as Berosos describes the Destruction of the Composite Creatures who preceded the organized creation. The God then laments that all his efforts have only produced War and Destruction, as each of these successive generations are Destroyed. "Verily now, and I, what have I left to reign over ? I am king who brings Not Peace to his land, a prince who brings Not Peace to his Hosts. Why have I established (only) Corpses and left a Desert ? Terror of Men : with Night, Death, and Plague I Have Cursed It."

The Serpent, or, more properly speaking, different kinds of Serpents, held a considerable place in the religions of Antiquity. The role of the Serpent varies considerably in different systems ; in some it appears as Divine, Protective, and Benign. To this class belongs the Serpent of Ea – "The Wise One," which is an emblem of Life and Wisdom. In other systems, on the contrary, it is the emblem of all that is Evil and Dark. In All Religions we meet with the Hostile night Serpent and Dragon – the Wicked Principle, which is the Emblem of Death and Darkness. In the Mythology of Babylon this Wicked Serpent is represented by the Great Dragon, Tiamat, which for Myriads of Years had Coiled Round the Earth like a Serpent around its Egg, and whom, as I have already stated, is represented on the monuments as a Serpent-Limbed Woman. The connection between the Serpent and Night, and, consequently, with the Long First Night which preceded the work of Creation, is proved by the monuments, for Two Great Mystic Serpents are mentioned in the inscriptions. The first is called Zir Zalamtum, "the Serpent of Darkness," or "the Shadow of Death" – the Hebrew Zalmoth ; the second is called the Zir Musi, or "Serpent of Night." There is little trace of the war against the Evil Serpent in the Hebrew writings ; only a reference to it in the passage, "A Sign was Seen in the Heaven : and behold, a Great Red Dragon, having Seven heads and ten horns, and on his heads Seven diadems ; and his Tail draws the third part of the Stars of the Heaven ; and he Cast them To the Earth . . . . and there was War in the Heaven ; Michael and his Angels went to War with the Dragon. And the Dragon fought, and his Angels ; and he Prevailed Not, nor was their place found any more in the Heaven. And the Great Dragon was Cast Out, the ancient

Serpent, he who is called Devil and Satan, he who Deceives the Whole Habitable World, he was Cast Out Into the Earth, and his Angels were Cast Out with him." Revelation 12 : 3-9 Darby translation 1890

Tiamat's husband Kingi, whose name means the "Maker of Darkness."

Then Arose the Water of dawn at daylight ; it Arose Up like a Black Cloud from the Horizon of Heaven ; the Thunder-God (Rimmon) in the Midst of it Thundered ; Nebo and the Wind-God (Sar) march in front ; the Throne Bearers (Guzalli) (Cherubim) Traverse Mountain and Plain ; the Pestilence-God (Dibbara) brings with him Affliction ; the War-God (Ninip) in front Cast Down. The Angels of Earth (Annunaki) bear Flaming Brands ; in their Wild Course they Burn Up the Earth ; the Deluge of the Rain-God Reaches to Heaven ; all that is Visible to Darkness ("a Thick, Impenetrable Darkness") is turned.

Other Cuneiform Fragments and not necessarily directly associated with above Fragment :-

"The Tempest from the Midst of Space (absu) [Abyss], the Fatal Decree (Mamit) from the Midst of Heaven proceeds. It Sweeps the Earth as the Verdure is Swept ; to the Four Winds its Terror Spreads like Fire. To the Men of the Habited Earth it Causes Affliction to their Body. In the city and the country is causes Destruction to small and great ; strong one and menial bewail it. In the Heavens and Earth like a water-spout it pours down rain. To the Holy place of their God they hasten and Cry Aloud".

"Like a cup of wine poured out [Broken] upon them. Country unto country looks Afraid ; the female servant to her chamber flees upward ; the head of the house by the entrance of the house it ushers forth ; the son of the house from the house of his father it drives forth ; the Doves in their Cotes it takes ; the bird on its wing it caused to mount upward ; the swallow in its nest it caused to fly ; the Ox it struck down, the young ass it smote ; Great Dragons, evil spirits, were their huntsmen".

The sacred city of the Ghost-God [Probably the commemoration of the Dead from the Deluge.] was the city of Nipur, in Central South Babylonia, the site being marked by the mounds of Nuffar. This city was dedicated to the Ghost-God, whose name occurs on all the bricks and inscriptions found there. There is an inscription of Sargon I., the king of Akkad, which belongs to the remote period of 3800 BC, as follows ; "To Mullil, the

299

Great Lord, Sargani (Sargon), the king of the city, the mighty king, king of Akkad, the builder of the temple, the house of Mullil, in Nipur. Whosoever this tablet shall remove, Mullil and the Sun-God and the Goddess (Istar) his foundation shall tear up, and his seed obliterate." These inscriptions show plainly that the worship of the "Ghost-God" was fully established as early as 3800 BC. Another inscription from this city supplies further information with regard to this peculiar worship. It is inscribed upon a block of Lapis Lazuli, by order of the Kassite king, Kadasman- Tergu, who reigned about 1380 BC : "To Mullil of Nipur, father of the Gods, king of the great Anunas, king of the World ; his king, Kadasman-Turu, king of Babylon (gave)." With the mention of the Anunas the first knowledge of any Chaldean idea of the future state is acquired. The word Anuna signifies the "master," or "great one," and corresponds to "the chief ones of the Earth" (alim) of Isaiah 14 : 9 - "The nether-world from beneath is moved for thee to meet thee at thy coming ; the shades are stirred up for thee, even all the chief ones of the Earth;". The Anunas, who dwelt in the realm of Mullil, were called the Anunage, or "Masters of the Under-World." They sat on golden thrones beside the stream of the "Waters of Life," in a land of Darkness and decay. The creed of Eridu, with its "Ocean-God," and that of Nipur, with the worship of the "Ghost-God," were blended together, with a third element was added, viz., that of the "Mountain of the World," where the Gods met in the subterranean recesses of which was the land of Arallu, "the House of Death." This combination must have taken place very early, for in the inscriptions of Urbahu and Gudea, 2800 BC, the " Lady of the Mountain of the World" is frequently mentioned. In the statue of the king Urbahu the inscription reads, "For the Goddess Nin-garsag (Lady of the Mountains), Mother of the Gods." It is probably to this form of the Myth which the Prophet Isaiah refers in the words : "How art thou Fallen from Heaven, O Day-Star, son of the morning ! How art thou Cut Down to the Ground, that didst cast lots over the nations ! And thou sadist in thy heart : 'I will ascend into heaven, above the Stars of God will I exalt my throne ; and will sit upon the Mount of meeting, in the uttermost parts of the North;"

Isaiah 14 : 12, 13 1917

On the summit was the place of the Assembly of the Gods, with the "Temples of the Place of Light," and "the House of the Host of Heaven." In the interior was the abode of the Anunas, "the Host of Earth," and their meeting place, "the Temple of Darkness." The Mountain of the Stream, the place of the Destines, the World Mountain, the meeting place of the Gods, and in whose interior was the ghost-kingdom of Mullil.

300

"O mighty Mountain of Mullil Im Kharsag (the Sky Mountain),
whose head rivals the Heavens, the Pure Deep is Laid at its Foundations.
Among the Mountains it Couches as a Strong Bull, Its peaks Glisten like the
Sun-God ; like the Stars of Heaven that proclaims the day, it is Full of
Glittering Rays. The Mighty Mother Ninlil (the Lady of the Ghost World),
the reverence of E Sara (the House of the Host of Heaven), the glory of
E Kura (the Temple of the Host of Earth), the adornment of E Giguma (the
Temple of Darkness), the heart of the Temple Ki-gusura (the temple of the
land of Light). "The North was regarded as an Evil Death-Dealing Quarter,
for Thence Came the Wind Iltanu or Istanu, from Satanu, "Hostile Evil."
The Mountain of the North and North-East, the Mountain of the World, in
whose interior was the land of Aralli, the House of Death, situated in the
Evil North. The Akkadian word lil within the names of the above king and
queen, meant, "a Ghost," "a Dust Cloud," and the Root of Lilith, the first
wife of Adam, "the Night Demon," and "the Vampire," who lived on the
blood of children whom she Slew at night. The concept conveys only the
idea of a vast, Dark place of the Gods of the Ghost-World, in which the
Great Dead sit on thrones in silent conclave and to each new-comer hail with
the cry, "Art thou become weak as we ?"

The King and Queen of The Dry Fog.

A Fragment of Mythological Text found at Tel el-Amarna from 1400 BC, or
about a century before the age of Moses, may be read as follows : "When
the Gods had appointed a banquet to their sister Eris-kigal they sent a
messenger." But she being the wife of the God Nergal, the Lord of the
Under-World, is forbidden to come to the banquet in the "Highest
Heavens." The Gods are Angry that one of their number should refuse to be
present at the feast, and send to fetch Her. The ambassador chosen is the
God Namtar, "the Pestilence God," who is the messenger between the
Under-World and Heaven. Namtar corresponded to the "Angel of Death."
The reverse side of the Tablet names fourteen Gods then : "In the Gateway
was standing the God Khuduma, who in the couch cuts off. Namtar to his
Host a command made, the Gates. In the midst of the palace he seized Eris-
kigal by her hair and dragged her from the throne to the ground, her head to
cut off. 'Do not slay me, O my brother ! a word may I speak to thee' Heard
Nergal, and lifted his hand he wept . . . . 'Thou art my husband, I truly
thy wife. Then take to thyself sovereignty in the wide Earth, and establish,
good for power is at thy hand. Then thou shalt be Lord and Lady.' Nergal
gave ear to her words. He took her and kissed her, her tears, he covered :
'Whatsoever thou askest of me in future for all time it is done." This was the

301

city of the Dead, called Unugal, or "the great city," and also called Tigabba, or the "city of the bowing down of the head," which was Encircled by Seven walls, with Seven sets of double Gates, each guarded by a pair of Gods thus the chief necropolis of Chaldea. Nergal is also known as the War-God and his wife is the sister of Istar.

The position of Tammuz and Giz-zida reminds us, as Professor Sayce has pointed out, of the pillars Jachin and Boaz at the Gates of the Temple : "And he set up the pillars at the porch of the temple ; and he set up the right pillar, and called the name thereof Jachin ; and he set up the left pillar, and called the name thereof Boaz. And upon the top of the pillars was lily-work ; so was the work of the pillars finished." 1st Kings 7 : 21, 22. [1917]. It is also curious to find the Gods of the Tree of Life forming the guardians of the Gate of Heaven, for after the Fall, Man was shut out from eating of the Tree, 'Behold, the Man is become as one of us, to know good and evil ; and now, lest he put forth his hand, and take also of the Tree of Life, and eat, and live forever.' Genesis 3 : 22 [1917]. There are other Inscriptions which show that the Assyrians had a clear idea of a place of happiness to which those who had "eaten of the food of Life or drank the waters of Life" would go to dwell. In a hymn of the late age of Assurbabipal 668 BC there is a passage which indicates this belief : "As a Man may he Live and be at peace. Over kings and princes may he exercise wide-spread dominion. May he come to grey hairs. For the Men who utter these prayers may the land of the silver sky, oil unceasing, and wine of blessedness be their food, and a perpetual noon-day their light. Health to thy body and prosperity is my prayer to the Gods who dwell in the land of Assyria."

We cannot compare these passages with any in the Old Testament, for it is remarkable to note how lacking these books are in any description of the future abode of the blessed ; indeed, only one text can be quoted with any certainty. "Thou makest me to know the path of life ; in Thy presence is fullness of joy, in Thy right hand bliss for evermore." Psalm 16 : 11. [1917]. It was not until the advent of Christianity, with its wider hopes, with its grand doctrine of the resurrection and the kingdom of Heaven, that the true conception of the life of Heaven was realized.

The Early History of the Hebrews   by A. H. Sayce   1899

The practice, horrible as it seems to us, was nevertheless founded on a
Truth. The victim, if he were to be accepted, must be the most precious
that the offerer could present. The Gods did not require that which cost him
nothing. It needed to be the most costly that could be given ; it needed to be
also, in the words of the prophet, the fruit of the sinner's own body.
Nothing else would suffice : the Gods demanded the firstborn son, still
more the only son. In no other way could Ball be satisfied that the sinner
had repented of his guilt or had made him an offering which was of equal
value to his own Life.

The belief that the scene of Abraham's sacrifice was the spot whereon the
Jewish temple afterwards stood went back to an early date. When the book
of Genesis assumed its present form it had already become fixed in the
Jewish mind. This is clear from the proverb quoted to explain the name
Yahveh-yireh. 'To this day,' we are told, it was said : 'In the mount of the
Lord it shall be seen.' For the Jew there was but one 'Mount of the Lord,'
that Mountain whereon Yahveh revealed Himself above the Cherubim of the
Ark. It was 'the Hill of God,' wherein He desired to dwell "A Mountain of
God is the Mountain of Bashan ; a Mountain of peaks is the Mountain of
Bashan. Why look ye askance, ye Mountains of peaks, at the Mountain
which God hath desired for His abode ?" Psalm 68 : 16, 17. [1917], the
seat of the sanctuary of Yahveh the God of Israel. When the Samaritains set
up on Gerizim their rival temple to that of Jerusalem, it was necessary that
the scene of the sacrifice of the Hebrew patriarch should be transferred to the
new site. It was a proof how firm was the conviction that the Temple-Mount
had been consecrated to the sacrifice of the firstborn by the great ancestor of
the Israelitish family. The spot whereon the victims of the Jewish ritual were
offered up was the very spot to which Abraham had been led by God that he
might offer there the terrible sacrifice of his only son. Its name had been
given to it by Abraham, and this name found its explanation in a saying that
was current at Jerusalem about the Temple-Mount. The actual meaning of
the name is not certain, nor indeed is the original signification of the
proverb itself. Already in the time of the Septuagint translation the meaning
of the latter was doubtful, and the Greek translators have made the divine
name the subject of the verb, reading, 'In the Mountain the Lord was seen.'
But the fact that the Chronicler calls the Temple-Mount Moriah shows that
such a rendering was not accepted in Jerusalem. It may be that the name
'Mount of the Lord' goes back, at all events in substance, to patriarchal

times. Among the places in Southern Palestine conquered by the Egyptian Pharaoh, Thothmes III., of the eighteenth dynasty, and recorded on the temple walls of Karnak, is Har-el, 'the Mountain of God.'

Abraham at 2153 BC   Exodus at 1280 BC

"Oh, that wouldest Break the Heavens, and Come Down, and that the Mountain might Melt at Thy Presence ! As the Melting Fire Burned, as the Fire caused Waters to Boil, that thou mightiest declare the name to thine adversaries the people did Tremble at Thy Presence. When Thou didst Treble Things, which we looked Not for, Thou Camest Down, and the Mountains Melted at thy Presence. For Since The Beginning of the World, they have not Heard nor Understood with the ear, Neither hath the eye Seen Another God beside thee, which doeth so to him that waiteth for him. Thou didst him, that rejoiced in thee, and did justly : They Remembered thee in Thy Ways : behold, thou art Angry, for we have sinned : yet in them is continuance, and we shall be saved. But we have all been as an unclean thing, and all our righteousness is as filthy cloths, and we all do fade like a leaf, and our iniquities like the wind have taken us away. And there is none that calleth upon thy name, neither that stirreth up himself to take hold of thee : for thou hast hid thy face from us, and Hast Consumed Us because of our iniquities. But now, O Lord, thou art our father : we are the clay, and thou art our potter, and we all are the work of thine hands. Be not Angry, O Lord, Above Measure, neither remember iniquity forever : Lo, we Beseech Thee, behold we are all thy people. Thine holy cities lie Waste : Zion is a Wilderness, and Jerusalem a Desert. The house of our sanctuary, and of our glory, where our fathers praised thee, is Burnt Up with Fire, and All our Pleasant Things are Wasted. Wilt thou hold thyself still at these things, O Lord ? Wilt thou hold thy Peace and [Not] afflict us above measure ? "
                                                          Isaiah 64   Geneva 1599

"God is our hope and strength, and help in troubles, ready to be found. Therefore will not we fear, though the Earth Moved, and though the Mountains Fall Into The Midst Of The Sea, though the Waters there of Rage and be Troubled, and the Mountains Shake at Surges of the same. Selah . . . . When the nations raged and the kingdoms were moved, God Thundered, and the Earth Melted . . . . Come and behold the works of the Lord, what Desolations He Hath Made in the Earth".
                                                     Psalm 46 : 1-3, 6, 8. Geneva 1599

304

"The Lord reigneth : let the Earth rejoice : let the multitude of the isles be glad. Clouds and Darkness are round about Him : righteousness and judgment are the foundation of his throne. There shall go a Fire before Him, and Burn Up his enemies round about. His Lightning gave Light unto the World : The Earth Saw It and was Afraid. The Mountains Melted like was at the Presence of the Lord of the Whole Earth. The Heavens declared his righteousness, and All the people See his glory. . . . . For thou, Lord, art most High Above all the Earth :"   Psalm 97 : 1-6, 9. Geneva 1599

"The Earth Trembled, the Heavens also Dropped Water. The Mountains Melted from the Face of Yahveh, even Sinai itself from before Yahveh the God of Israel. . . . . . . From the Heavens Fought the Stars, in their courses they Fought against Sisera." The idea is the same as that of the Sun and the Moon standing still while Joshua defeated the kings at Makkedah : "Then spake Joshua to the Lord, in the day when the Lord gave the Amorites before the children of Israel, and he said in the sight of Israel, Sun, stay thou in Gibeon, and the Moon, in the valley of Aijalon. And the Sun abode, and the Moon stood still, until the people avenged themselves upon their enemies : And there was no day like that before it, nor after it, that the Lord heard the voice of a Man : for the Lord fought for Israel."
                                    Joshua 10 : 12-14 Geneva 1599

Babylonian astrology taught that events in this World were dependent on the motion of the Heavenly bodies.

The entrance of Solomon's temple was approached by steps, and consisted of a porch, on either side of which were two lofty columns of bronze, called Jachin and Boaz, dedicated to the Sun and associated with the worship of Asherah and Baal and mentioned in a Palmyrene inscription. Similar columns were planted before the entrance of a Phoenician temple where they symbolized the fertilizing power of the Sun-God, and Herodotos (2:44) states that the two which stood in front of the temple at Tyre were made of Gold and emerald glass. Two similar columns of stone, though of small size, have been found in the Temple of the Giants in the Island of Gozo, one of which still remains in its original place. In the outer court was a bronze 'Sea' or Basin, thirty cubits in circumference, and supported on Twelve Oxen. The 'Sea' had been imported into the West from Babylonia, where it similarly stood in the court of a temple, and represented the Apsu or 'Watery Abyss,' out of which Chaldean philosophy taught that all things had been evolved. A Babylonian hymn which describes the casting of a Copper 'Sea' for the Temple of Chaos tells us that, like the 'Sea' at

Jerusalem, it rested on the heads of Twelve Bulls. Along with the 'Sea' bronze Lavers and Basins were provided for the ablutions of the priests and the vessels of the sanctuary. Image Pg. 59.

Cuneiform Texts :-

"Seven are the gods the sons of Bel who is the Voice of the Firmament ; they heap up the seat. Twelve are the sons of Copper ; on the heart of the rim they lay the Copper. The rim of the Copper is dark (tekil). The Great Bull, the supreme Bull, who Treads Down the Pure Pasture [Verdure], has opened the heart (of it), spreading wide (its) fertility, planting the corn, and beautifying the field ; my pure hands he purified before thee ! The mouth of the Deep ('the Sea') which is between the ears of the Bull is made ; on the right is it made ; a rim of Copper I found. On a reed whose head is cut thou shalt press a good reed. The Bull, the offspring of the God Zu, art thou ! At thy command am I carrying the pails for thee. For ever is the Lady of the Eternal Tree thy comrade ; The great (Gods?), who determine the boundaries, who establish (musim) the Laws of Heaven and Earth . . . . May the rim be watched over, and . . . . to Bel may He present (liqdhais) . . . . of the Bull is made, on the left hand it is made ; the rim of Copper I found. How long, O Lord of Shade, shall the shade be a cover ? How long, O Mighty Mountain, father of Mul-lil, who art a shade? O shepherd that determinest destiny, who art a shade, how long ? . . . . At the time when thou Bringest the Bull to the Temple of Mummu (Chaos). The work of the Gallos-Priest."

. . . . "The chief Mubarra ("the Fire-God"), the exalted male, who Hurls Down Terror, whose Clothing is Splendor ; the forceful Fire-God (Mubarra), the exalter of the Mountain-peaks, the uplifter of the Torch, the Enlightener of the Darkness."

"Who can escape from thy message ? Thy word is the Supreme Snare which is stretched towards Heaven and Earth. It turns to the Sea, and the Sea dreads it. It turns to the marsh, and the marsh mourns. It turns to the Channel (literally, "Band.") of the Euphrates, and the word of Merodach disturbs its bed. O Lord thou art supreme ! Who is there that rivals thee ? O Merodach, among the Gods as many as have a name thou art he that Coverest them !"

Mythology Among the Hebrews and Its Historical Development, by Ignaz Goldziher, 1877 Translated from the German, with Additions by Russell Martineau

Al-Meydani informs us that 'the old Arabs say that the Star al-Dabaran wooed the Pleiades, but the latter Constellation would have nothing to do with the suitor, turned obstinately away from him, and said to the Moon, 'What must I do with that poor devil, who has no estate at all ?' Then al-Dabaran gathered together his Kilas (a Constellation in the neighborhood of al-Dabaran), and thus gained possession of an estate. And now he is constantly following after the Pleiades, driving the Kilas before him as a wedding present.' 'The Constellation Capricorn killed the Bear, and therefore the daughters of the latter encircle him, seeking vengeance for their slain father.' 'Surely gave the female Star al-Jauza a blow ; the latter returned it and threw him down where he now lies ; but he took his Sword and cut his adversary in pieces.' 'The Southern Sirius was walking with her sister the Northern Sirius ; the latter parted company and crossed the Milky Way. Her sister, seeing this, began to weep for the separation, and her eyes dropped tears ; therefore she is called the Wet-eyed.

"How art thou fallen from Heaven, O Lucifer, son of the morning and cut Down to the Ground, which ? Didst last lots upon the nations ? . . . . . But thou shalt be brought Down to the Grave, to the Side of the Pit". [Crater]

Isaiah 14 : 12..15. Geneva 1599

"And I will rise up against them, saith the Lord of Hosts, and cut off from Babylon name and remnant, and offshoot and offspring, saith the Lord. I will also make it a possession for the bittern, and Pools of Water ; and I will Sweep it with the Besom [Broom/Comet] of Destruction, saith the Lord of Hosts". [Pleiades]   Isaiah 14 : 22, 23 1917

"In that day the Lord with his Sore and Great and Mighty Sword shall visit Leviathan, that Piercing Serpent, even Leviathan, that Crooked Serpent, and he shall Slay the Dragon that is in the Sea [Sky]. In that day sing of the vineyard of red wine. I the Lord do keep it every moment : lest any assail it, I will keep it night and day. Anger is not in me : who would set the biers and the thorns against me in battle ? I would go Through them, I would Burn them together".   Isaiah 27 : 1 Geneva 1599

"For I will rise up against them and will cut off from Babel (the Gate of God) the name and the remnant, and the son, and the nephew, saith the Lord : and I will make it a possession to the Hedgehog, and Pools of Water, and I will Sweep it with the <u>Besom</u> of Destruction, saith the Lord of Hosts".
                                        Isaiah 14 : 22, 23. Geneva 1599

When e.g. Isaiah says, 'I will Sweep it with the <u>Besom</u> of Destruction,' this is what we call a poetic figure – Destruction being pictured as a <u>Broom</u> that Sweeps away from the Surface of the Earth those who are to be Destroyed. But from another side it is seen to be something more and different from mere poetical figure, since its Origin is due, not to an artistic idea of the speaker, but to an Old-World Mythical conception here employed figuratively, a conception which occurs in many cycles of Mythology. For instance, the Maidens of the Plague are represented with <u>Brooms</u> in their hands, with which they Sweep before House-Doors and bring Death into the village. On the German Legends in which this idea occurs see Henne-Am-Rhyn, Die deutsche Volkssge, Leipzig 1874, p.268. [Halloween Witch ?]

"O Lord our God, Other Lords beside thee, Have ruled us, but we will remember thee only, and thy name".   Isaiah 26 : 13 Geneva 1599

"Rejoice not, because the Rod of him that did beat thee is broken : for out of the Serpent's root shall come forth a Cockatrice, and the fruit thereof shall be a Fiery Flying Serpent. For the first born of the poor shall be fed, and the needy shall lie down in safety : and I will Kill thy root with Famine, and it shall Slay thy remnant. Howl, O Gate, cry, O city : thou whole land of Philistia art Dissolved, for there shall come from the North a Smoke, and none shall be alone, at his time appointed". Isaiah 14 : 29-31 Geneva 1599

Chaos is named – a word signifying according to its original sense 'Darkness' – and Tartarus – the subterranean place to which the souls of the Dead go. It may denote Darkness, but not Dead, cause all were Dead in the beginning and then Life again...

On Semitis ground the Assyrian Divine name Rammanu or Raman must be mentioned here. If this name has any etymological connexion with the root ram 'to be high,' as hesychius and some modern scholars say, though others derive it from ra'am 'Thunder,' Ra'aman 'the Thunderer,' then we find here again the Primitive Mythological idea that the Intrinsically High is the Dark Stormy Sky, or, personified, the God of Storms [Rams Crack their horns together an analogy to Thunder.]. So also in the Old Hebrew Myth the 'High' is the nightly or rainy Sky. The best known Myth that the Hebrews told of their Abh-ram is the story of the intended sacrifice of his only son Yischak, commonly called Isaac. But what is Yischak ?
[Ta Ta Ta ?] Literally translated, the word denotes 'he Laughs,' or 'the Laughing.' In the Semitic languages, especially in proper names and epithets, the use of the aorist is frequent where we should employ a participle. So here. Now whi is the 'He Laughs,' the 'Smiling One' ? No other but 'He who sits in Heaven and Laughs' "He that sitteth in Heaven Laugheth, The Lord hath them in Derision. Then He will speak unto them in His Wrath, and Affright them in His Sore Displeasure : truly it is I that have established My King upon Zion, My Holy Mountain.' Psalms 2 : 4-6.
[1917], whom the Mythology of almost all nations and their later poetry too likes to call the Laughing or Smiling one. When, as Plutarch tells in his Life of Lycurgus, that legislators consecrated a Statue to Laughter which enjoyed divine honours at Sparta, we are certainly not to understand it of the laughter that plays round the lips of mortals, but of the Celestial Smile with which Mythology endows the Sun, as when the Indian singer calls Ushas (the Sun, strictly the Dawn) the Smiling (Rigveda, 6.64.10). With regard to the Sun's Laughing in the Aryan Mythology, we can refer to the learned work of Angelo de Gubernatis, 'Zoological Mythology' (vol. 1.1.1).

"I will tell of the decree : The Lord said unto me : 'Thou art My Son, this day have I begotten thee. Ask of Me, and I will give the nations for thine inheritance, and the ends of the Earth for thy possession. Thou shalt break them with a Rod of Iron ; Thou shalt dash them in pieces like a Potter's Vessel. Now therefore, O ye kings, be Wise ; Be Admonished, ye Judges of the Earth. Serve the Lord with Fear, and rejoice with Trembling. Do homage in purity, lest He be Angry, and ye Perish in the Way, when Suddenly His Wrath is Kindled'." Psalms 2 : 7-12 1917

The Semitic designations of Darkness are mostly formed from roots denoting 'to Cover,' and also in the Aryan languages, the Sanskrit, and Greek denote the Overclouded Sky, are from the root var 'to Cover,' in Opposition to the Bright Day-Sky, Mitra. In the old classical Arabic, nights which either have No Moonshine at All, or have none at the beginning and only a little quite at the end, are called layalin dur'um ; and when a verb is required, adra'aal-shahr ia said. This adra'a is unquestionably a denominative verb from dir', which signifies a 'breast-plate,' or a breast-covering of any sort.

1520 Painting portraying Sodom and Gomorrah

"The Sun did rise upon the Earth, when Lot entered into Zoar. Then the Lord Rained Upon Sodom and Gomorrah, Brimstone and Fire from the Lord Out of Heaven and overthrew those cities, and All the Plain, and All the Inhabitants, of the cities, and that Grew upon the Earth. Now his wife behind him looked back, and she became a pillar of salt. And Abraham rising up early in the morning went to the place, where he had stood before the Lord, and looking toward Sodom and Gomorrah, and toward all the land of the plain, behold, he saw the Smoke of the land Mounting Up as the Smoke of a Furnace".   Genesis 19 : 23-28. Geneva 1599

If the conception of Kerubhim (Cherubim) [Winged Bull] is native to the Hebrews, and not borrowed at a later period from foreign parts – a question which must be regarded as still an open one – then we may find here also the Coverer (compare kerubh has-sokhekh 'the Cherub that Covereth,') "Thou hast been in Eden the Garden of God : every precious Stone was in thy garment, the Ruby, the Topaz, and the Diamond, the Chrysolite, the Onyx, and the Jasper, the Saphire, Emerald, and Carbuncle, and Gold : The workmanship of thy timbrels, and of thy pipes was prepared in thee : in the day that wast created. Thou art the anointed Cherub, that Covereth, and I have set thee in honor : Thou wast upon the Holy Mountain of God : thou hast walked in the Midst of the Stones of Fire. Thou wast perfect in thy ways from the day that thou wast Created, till iniquity was found in thee. By the multitude of thy merchandise, they have filled the midst of thee with cruelty, and thou hast sinned : therefore I will Cast Thee as Profane Out of The Mountain of God : and I will Destroy Thee, O Covering Cherub, from the Midst of the Stones of Fire. Thine heart was lifted up because of the Beauty, and thou hast <u>Corrupted</u> thy <u>Wisdom</u> by <u>Reason</u> of thy Brightness : I will Cast thee to the Ground. I will lay thee before kings that they may Behold Thee. Thou hast defiled thy sanctification by the multitude of thine iniquities and by the iniquity of thy merchandise : therefore will I bring forth a Fire from the Midst of Thee, which shall Devour thee : and I will bring thee to Ashes upon the Earth, In the Sight of All them that Behold Thee all they that know thee among the people, shall be Astonished at Thee : thou shalt be a Terror, and Never Shalt Thou Be Anymore".
                                                   Ezekiel 28 : 13-19. Geneva 1599

The Covering Cloud ; and hence may be Derived the Function of Concealing and Covering which was given to the Cherubim in the later ceremonial, as also their Connexion with the Curtains. 'Jahveh Rides On The Cherub,' says one of the later religious poets, 'and appears on the Wings of the Wind ; he makes Darkness Round About Him, tents, Collections of Water, Gloomy Clouds.' Here the Dark Overclouded Rainy Sky is described ; and when Jahveh sends Rain Over the Earth, he Rides on the Cherub, and 'mists are beneath his feet,' and the Dust which he Turns Up while riding, forms the Shechakim (properly the Dust), the Overcast

311

Sky. Jahveh is described in other passages also as riding on clouds "Behold, the Lord Rideth upon a Swift cloud," Isaiah 19 : 1 [1917]. Accordingly Kerubh would originally Denote the Covering Cloud, and whatever is connected with the Cherubim in later theological conceptions would be a transformation of ancient Mythological ideas. Now the root krb is used in Himyarite inscriptions in titles of kings, as Mukrib Saba, or Tobba' Kerib, i.e. as Von Kremer explains them, 'Protector of Saba,' 'Protecting Tobba'.' This is easily explained by the fact that in the Semitic languages words signifying 'to protect' are often derived from the fundamental idea of 'Covering.' 'The Cherubim spread forth their Wings' "For the Cherubim spread forth their Wings over the place of the Ark, and the Cherubim covered the Ark and the staves thereof above." 1 Kings 8 : 7. [1917], i.e. they Cover. To spread out the Wings (kenaphayim) over someone is in Biblical language the usual expression for the protection which is allotted to him. In Arabic the same word (kanaf) signifies not only a Bird's Wing, but also Concealment, Shade, "O thou that Dwellest in the Covert of the Most High, and Abidest in the Shadow of the Almighty;" Psalm 91 : 1. [1917], and protection.

The opinion that the Cherubim were borrowed from foreign parts is accordingly much less probable than that which maintains that they originated with the Hebrews ; and the latter view receives further support from the fact that the Cheribum can be easily fitted without any violence into the system of Hebrew Mythology. It is again supported by the Connexion between Cheribum and Seraphim, the latter of which are originally Hebrew. This connexion agrees moreover with the results of our Mythological researches. As Kerubh as 'Coverer' belongs to the Cloudy Sky, so the Seraphim must be a Mythological conception pertaining to the same series, if we adopt the correct interpretation of them as Dragons, and remember the Mythological significance of Cheribum and Seraphim belongs to the remains of the very earliest form of Hebrew religion. This scholar wishes to explain the Assyrian divine name Anu as etymologically identical with the Hebrew 'Anan 'cloud' which certainly well suits the two epithets of the deity, 'Lord of Darkness.'

One of the Solar heroes of the Persian Myth of civilization is Jemshid, whose character can scarcely be doubtful to the Mythologist, after the consentaneous characteristics of giving to Iran, till then savage, the benefits of civilization as being the first builder of cities, the inventor of the fine arts, especially of music, navigation (which belongs especially to the solar Myth), and cultivation of the vine ; thus putting an end to the nomadic tribal

312

life. The Prometheus – side of the Jemshid story is surprising. The Persian hero, like the Greek, is chastised and Hurled Down by God for his presumption ; his Fall is occasioned by Zohak, who conquers him, from whose shoulders Dragons grow up. After a hundred years he appears on the coast of the Chinese Sea. The Sun is devoured by the Monster waiting for him at the Bottom of the Sea, but afterwards rises again out of the sea, like Jonah in the Hebrew Myth.

Again God said, "Let there be a Firmament in the midst of the Waters, and let it Separate the Water from the Waters. Then God made the Firmament, and Separated the Waters, which were Under the Firmament, from the Waters which were Above the Firmament and it was so".

Genesis 1 : 6,7. Geneva 1599

"Or who hath begotten the Drops of Dew ? Out of whose womb came the Ice ? And the Hoar-Frost of Heaven, who hath, gendered it ? The Waters are Congealed like Stone, and the Face of the Deep is Frozen. Canst thou Bind the Chains of the Pleiades [Can You Stop the NEO's?], or loose the bands of Orion ? Canst thou lead forth the Mazzaroth (Constellations) in their season ? Or canst thou guide the Bear with her sons ? Knowest thou the Ordinances of the Heavens" ? Job 38 : 28 – 33. [1917]

The Dew, also, has a connexion with the anwa' 'Stars' (plural of nau'). It is not without interest to find this view in a Jewish-Arabic writer of the middle ages ; Sa'adia, who translates Job 38, egle tal 'stor-house of dew,' by the Arabic anwa' 'Stars,' Gesenius, Thesaurus, p. 21. The worship of the kokhabh 'Star' by the Hebrew nomads must therefore have a special connexion with the rain.

The story of little Red Riding Hood, mutilated in the English nursery version, but known more perfectly by old wives in Germany, who can tell that the lovely little maid in her shining red satin cloak was swallowed with her grandmother [Two Ages] by the Wolf, but they both came out safe and sound when the hunter cut open the sleeping beast. Anyone who can fancy with prince Hal, 'the blessed Sun himself a fair hot wench in flame-coloured taffeta,' and can then imagine her swallowed up by Skoll, the Sun-Devouring Wolf of Scandinavian Mythology, may be inclined to class the tale of Little Red Riding hood as a Myth of sunset and sunrise. There is indeed another story in Grimm's Marchen, partly the same as this one, which we can hardly doubt to have a quaint touch of Sun-Myth in it. It is called the Wolf and Seven kids, and tells of a Wolf swallowing the kids all but the youngest of the Seven, who was Hidden in the clock-case. As in Little Red Riding hood, they cut open the Wolf and fill with Stones. This tale, which took its present shape since the invention of clocks, looks as though the tale-teller was thinking, not of real kids and wolf, but of days of the week swallowed by night, or how should he have hit upon such a fancy as that the Wolf could not get at the youngest of the Seven kids, because it was hidden in the clock case ? Tylor, Primitive Culture [Hidden in Darkness for a Time.]

314

It is greatly to be desired that an Unprejudiced Conception of the matter of Hebrew Mythic Stories may be promoted by the discovery of the Cuneiform Texts. But to attain to the result of true freedom from old errors, it is essential to Put Away All Fears, and to be guided solely and simply by the interests of the Holiest of Holies, namely, Scientific Truth, in forming a Judgment on the Priority or Simultaneous Origin of such Stories in different nations.

The Philistines avenge the destruction of their cornfields, vineyards, and olives by Samson, by burning his bride and her father. This causes Samson to inflict a great defeat on his enemies ; but after the victory he flies and hides in a cavern (Judges 15: 8). What means this behavior, for which no motive is assigned ? What had Samson to fear in any case, but especially after such a victory ? But let it be remembered that Apollon flies after killing the Dragon ; so also Indra after killing Vrtra, according to the Indian Legend in the Vedas ; and that even El, the Semitic supreme God, has to fly. Thus Samson's retreat, mentioned, but not very clearly expressed because not understood, by the Biblical narrator, appears to indicate this often-recurring flight of the Sun-God after victory. In the tempestuous phenomena, in which two powers of nature seemed to be contending together, Men felt the presence of the Good God ; but after his victory, when all was quiet again, he seemed to have withdrawn and gone to a distance. [Waiting for the Atmospheric Loading to Dissipate.]

If the hair is the symbol of the growth of nature in Summer, then the cutting off of the hair must be the disappearance of the power of Nature in Winter. Samson is blinded at the same time, like Orion : this again has the same meaning, the cessation of the power of the Sun. Again, Samson and the other Sun-Gods are forced to endure being bound : and this too indicates the tied-up power of the Sun in Winter. [Not Annual]

To the foe he is the scathing Sun-God. This is the sense of the story of the Foxes, which Samson caught and sent into the Philistine' fields with firebrands fasted to their Tails, to burn the crops. [Or possibly hot Meteorites.] Like the Lion, the Fox is an animal that indicated the Solar heat ; being well suited for this both by its colour and by its Long-Haired [Comet] Tail. At the festival of Ceres at Rome, a Fox-hunt through the Circus was held, in which Burning Torches were bound to the Foxes' Tails : 'a symbolical reminder of the damage done to the fields by mildew, called the "Red Fox" (robigo), which was exorcised in various ways at this momentous season (the last third of April). It is the time of the Dog-Star, at

315

which the mildew was most to be feared ; if at that time great Solar heat follows too close upon the hoar-frost or dew of the cold nights, this mischief rages like a Burning Fox through the corn-fields. On the twenty-fifth of April were celebrated the Robigalia, at which prayers were addressed to Mars and Robigo together, and to Robigus and Flora together, for protection against devastation. [From dew?] In the grove of Robigus young dogs of red colour were offered in expiation on the same day.' Ovid's story of the Fox which was rolled in straw and hay for punishment, and ran into the corn with the straw Burning and set it on Fire, is a mere invention to account for the above-mentioned ceremonial Fox-hunt ; still it has for its basis, though in the disguise of a story, the original Mythical conception of the divine Fire-Fox that burns up the corn. The Fox was in many nations sacred to the Evil Sun-God, Moloch or Typhon, on account of his red colour, from which his name in Hebrew is taken. Rahabh, etymologically denoting the Noisy, Defiant, was originally the name and description of the Storm-Dragon ! [The Myth's meaning was lost, the Sun isn't noisy and doesn't set fields on Fire, Plus Moloch is a Bull and Typhon is a Snake.]

A prayer of Habakkuk the prophet. "Upon Shigionoth. O Lord, I have Heard the Report of Thee, and am Afraid ; O Lord, revive Thy work in the midst of the years, in the midst of the years make it known ; in Wrath remember compassion. God cometh from Teman, and the Holy One from Mount Paran. Selah His glory Covereth the Heavens, and the Earth is full of His praise. And a Brightness Appeareth as the Light ; Rays hath He at His side ; and there is the hiding of His power. Before Him goeth the Pestilence, and Fiery Bolts go forth at His feet. He standeth, and Shaketh the Earth, He beholdeth, and maketh the nations to Tremble ; and the everlasting Mountains are Dashed in Pieces, the ancient hills do bow ; His goings are as of old. I see the tents of Cushhan in affliction ; the curtains of the land of Midian do Tremble. Is it, O Lord, that against the Rivers, is it that Thine Anger is Kindled Against the Rivers, or Thy Wrath Against the Sea ? That thou dost ride upon Thy Horses, upon Thy chariots of victory ? Thy bow is made quite bare ; sworn are the Rods of the word. Selah Thou dost Cleave the Earth with Rivers. The Mountains have seen Thee, and they Tremble ; the Tempest of Waters Floweth Over ; the Deep Uttereth it Voice, and lifted up its Hands on high. The Sun and Moon stand still in their habitation ; at the Light of Thine Arrows as they Go, at the Shining of Thy Glittering Spear. Thou Marchest through the Earth in Indignation, Thou Thresheth the nations in Anger. Thou art come forth for the deliverance of Thy people, for the deliverance of Thine anointed ; Thou woundest the head out of the house of the wicked, uncovering the foundation even unto the neck. Selah Thou hast stricken through with his own Rods the head of his rulers, that come as a Whirlwind to Scatter me ; Whose Rejoicing is as the Devour the poor Secretly. Thou hast Trodden the Sea with Thy Horses, the Foaming of Mighty Waters. When I Heard, Mine Inward Parts Trembled [Shock Wave / Concussion], my lips quivered at the Voice ; rottenness entereth into my bones, and I Tremble where I stand ; that I should wait for the day of Trouble, when he cometh up against the people that he Invadeth. For though the fig-tree shall Not Blossom, Neither shall Fruit be in the Vines ; the labour of the Olive shall Fail, and the fields shall yield No Food ; the Flock shall be cut off from the Fold, and there shall be No herd in the Stalls ; Yet I will Rejoice in the Lord, I will exult in the God of my salvation. God, the Lord, is my strength, and he maketh my feet like hinds' feet, and he maketh me to walk upon my high places. For the Leader. With my string-music." Habakkuk 3 [1917]

Moses causes manna, sweet as honey, to be rained down with the Dew ; this again reminds us of the nectar and the mead of the Gods.

Analogy with Old Heathen elements in the popular ideas of the later age. It results from the preceding historical investigation that the Oldest Hebrews were Heathens, and that elements belonging to Heathen Mythology are even present in the Bible. To gain a clearer idea of the nature of this Fact, I will refer to a precisely similar case – the relation of our age to the Old German Heathen times.

The Germans had originally Gods, worship, Myths and Legends – in short, a Heathen Faith, of their own. But for more than a thousand years all the German tribes have been Christian. Nevertheless, Heathen Practices still Survive among them everywhere and in most various forms ; and are so closely interwoven with Christian practices as to be almost Ineradicable. I will only select a few instances. The Old German Gods still live in the names of the days of the week. In English Tues-day, Wednes-day, Thurs-day, Fri-day, Satur-day, from Anglo-Saxon names of Gods, Tiu or Teow, Woden, Thunor, Frige, and Saetern. Churches and convents were founded at places which had been Heathen Sanctuaries ; Christian feasts were fixed on days sacred to Heathen Deities, and thus the Heathen name 'Easter' has maintained its existence as a designation for the Highest Christian Feast. Heathenism is preserved chiefly in the popular Legends both of the hills and of the lowlands, in popular customs, usages, games and superstitions ; all which has been lately collected in special books and periodicals. Kuhn's collections made in North Germany and Westphalia are of especial scientific value. The Gods, however, have been Converted into Devils and Monsters, the Goddesses into Night-Hags and Witches. But religious stories, Christian Legends, are also often Utterly Heathen ; there are deeds and occurrences belonging to Gods and Heroes, which are attributed to the Saints and to Christ himself. Thus the Killing of the Dragon, which is known as a Myth to all the Aryan nations, is ascribed to Saint George. The office of the God Thor, who pursued and bound Giants, is filled in Christian Norway by Saint Olave. Christ and Saint Peter wander about unrecognized in human form, to reward virtue and punish vice, as the Heathen Gods did before them. Mary, especially, had a multitude of lovely and charming features ascribed to her, which under Heathenism were attributes of Freyja and Venus, are called Mary's attributes. In short, 'now Christian substance appears disguised in a Heathen Form, now Heathen substance in Christian form.

The thought 'God' forms the apex of the Pyramid of ideas ; it possesses the highest and widest dominion – for this very reason unfortunately often the weakest – and therefore shapes every province of consciousness in accordance with what it contains. Now, let an altered character come over the contents of one of these domains, say of the ideas concerning our relation to our fellow-Men, or concerning Causality in Nature ; then that domain can no longer tolerate to be ruled and moulded by the thought previously connoted in the word 'God,' standing as it now does in contradiction to that thought. It set up the sway of a new form of thought, which fits its new contents, because growing out of them ; there arises a new conception of God, a new Theology. But the old Theology has still its seat in all the other provinces of consciousness ; so that, before any further advance, the New Idea has still to bring all these other provinces under its sway, to dissolve the shape given them by the Old Principle, and replace it by one which is congenial with itself. This may, nay must, produce a long conflict, which demands much labour. Of many a concept the intension will have to be Entirely Cancelled, - of all to be at least remodeled. Yet with many ideas the association has through long habit become quite fixed. Severed they must be, the new God requires it ; but it can only be done very gradually. A thousand forbidden combinations find lurking-places and remain ; they maintain themselves in contradiction to the new order of thing, and perhaps half accommodate themselves to it in order to Avoid a Shock.

In Germany it was told of the God Wuotan, that he was called Long-Beard, and as such fell asleep inside a Mountain.

If the stream of time carries off the subjects and meanings into the Ocean of Oblivion, then by the psychological law the unattached predicates and sounds must fasten themselves on to any other subjects and meanings by which they can be supported. This takes place Without any one Intending it, and Without any one Observing it.

Earliest Intellectual Man's Idea of the Cosmos, by Samuel A. B. Mercer, 1957

Of Sumero-Babylonia it is recorded in documents of the reign of Sargon of Agade that "At the wharf of Agade he caused to moor ships from Meluhha, ships of Magan and ships of Dilmun" ; and that Gudea of Lagash, in building a Temple of Ningirsu, brought Cedar logs 60 cubits long (104') from Amanus (south-central Turkey), the Cedar Mountain.

Evidence of physical Man in Sumero-Babylonia back to eighth millennia BC. Clay tablets have been excavated with pictographic signs, which are taken to be fore-runners of cuneiform writing. In this pre and protoliterate period, Sumero-Babylonian objects have been found in Egypt.

Code of Hammurabi – a charter of human rights. [Worth looking up, much longer than the Ten Commandments, the Eyptian Codes are also good.]

The earliest relief sculpture is found on sculptured stone maceheads and slate-palettes. They belong to the Very Early Dawn of History. One of the earliest represents a Bull Trampling on a Human Enemy. The conventionalized form of the same scene on the Palette of Narmer is excellent.

In the case of Re-Atum, we have Two Creator-Gods or Two Sun-Gods, a combination which becomes a pantheon, such as also in the case of Ptah-Nun of Memphis, Re being a personification of the Sun, with the obelisk as his symbol, and Atum also a Sun-God, creator of the Gods, who made the deceased pharaoh "to Endure and to Live," and the begetter of all, both things and people, and he who Arose Out of the Primeval Watery Abyss. The name Ptah means "to Open." The name Atum is difficult to define, although Kees has hit upon a reasonable equivalent, "he who is not yet existent", or "the not-yet existing one", in reference to the way in which he Arose Out of Nun on the Primeval Hill or Pyramidion. Shu, a personification of air or dryness, was pictured as Holding Up the Sky ; and his consort Tefnut, is moisture personified. Nut is a personification of the Sky, as Geb, prince of the Gods, is the Earth.

The ancient Egyptians recognized, thought of, and treated All Cosmic Objects as Gods or Goddesses, which were Worshipped as such, and Ninety Percent of the Myth and Legend was Cosmic. Perhaps the oldest of all the Cosmic Gods, Hr, the "Face of Heaven," was at first represented under the form of a Falcon.

A Sumerian seal of about 2300 BC shows the Sun-God Babbar emerging from the Wooded Mountains of the East, holding in his hand the key with which he unlocks the gate of Sunrise. The Sumerian Enlil, whose "Word" issues from his Mouth was also the Agent of Calamities, such as Flood, Hurricane, Fire, Pillage, Hunger, and Exile. [Locked away for a Time.]

Not a single reference to an eclipse has been found in the documents of ancient Egypt. [Maybe proof of how the good stuff was top secret.]

In the Sumerian account of creation there was first a Primeval Sea, and this Sea is said to have Begot a Cosmic Mountain which seemed to embrace Heaven and Earth.

In the Sumero-Babylonia the World was thought of as a Vast Mountain, named Ekur, "House of the Mountain", in the midst of which stood the Hursag Mountain, the place where the Winds Dwell. [Bet the Evil Wind.]

The Mythology of all Races – Semitic, by Stephen Herbert Langdon, 1931

The entire Mythology of Astarte goes back to the Sumerian Ininni = Ashdar = Ishtar, Goddess of Venus and mother, wife, and lover of the Sumerian dying God Tammuz. And also a Virgin and mother of Tammuz.

Ishtar, "Queen of Heaven," "Goddess of Fate," as the Morning Star she is Goddess of War, and as Evening Star patroness of Love and Harlotry. In Babylonia the Morning Star is called the "Male Venus," and the Evening Star the "Female Venus." Ishtar stands on a Lion holding in one hand Serpents, symbolic of the life of Earth, and in the other Lotus blooms,

320

symbolic of love. [That's not right it should be death for the Serpents and resurrection of verdure for the Lotus !]

"To the pure Flame that Fills the Heavens, to the Light of Heaven, Ishtar, who Shines Like The Sun . . . . The Long Bow, Mighty of Battle she holds in her hand. With her left arm she lays low the foe. The queen of Battle, the Loud Crying, Utters a Cry of Wailing. She Descended, she Mounted on High, while Raged the Roar of her Voice. At the reins she stood Not, but went Forth in her Might."

Suidas, the Greek lexicographer says that the object of Dusares' worship was a Black Stone, four feet high and two feet wide, standing on a base of Gold. Moreover Epiphanius states that Dusares was the offspring of the virgin Chaabou and only son of the "Lord." The panegyrarchs of Nabataean cities came to Petra to assist in the festival of his birth, which was celebrated on the twenty-fifth of December.

The Semitic word for "God" meant originally, "he who is High." In Sumerian, the word for "God," Dingir, also means, "Shining," "Bright," and the sign used for writing Dingir also stands for An, the Sky-God ; the word also means "High," "Heaven." The Ideogram for Writing "God," and for the God An, was the picture of a Star. On seals of the Pictographic Tablets and on painted pots of that Prehistoric Period, the picture of a Star Constantly Occurs. This Star is Almost the Only Religious Symbol in this Primitive Age.

The Astronomers divided the fixed Stars into three parallel bands called the "Way of Anu," "Way of Enlil," and "Way of Ea." The band of Anu included those Stars in what seemed to them the highest parts of Heaven along the Ecliptic. The Northern band was the 'Way of Enlil," and the Southern the "Way of Ea."

"O Great Enlil, im-hur-sag , "Wind of the Underworld Mountain," whose head rivals the Heavens, whose Foundation is Laid in the Pure Abyss, who Reposes in the Lands like a Furious Wild Bull, whose Horns Gleam like the Rays of the Sun-God."

The stage tower of his temple Ekur at Nippur bore the name E-im-hur-sag, and one of his titles was "Wind of the Earth." Ningirsu, "Lord of Floods," was his son, and his father named him "King of the Storm of Enlil." In the liturgies he has almost exclusively the character of a Terrible, Wrathful God

321

who brings Disaster Upon His Own people for their Sins and upon the Enemies of Sumer. The agent of his Anger is always the "Word" which issues from his mouth, and goes though the World causing Calamity, Flood, Hurricane, Fire, pillage of cities, Hunger, and exile. The Word of Wrath may be uttered by any one of his great sons, but it is primarily the prerogative of the "Earth Mountain" of Ekur.

Prevalent in Babylonian Mythology is that of the Monster called Darabzu, "Antelope of the Nether-Sea." Fore-parts of a Goat and body of a Fish, bearing the names Kusarikku and Suhurmashu were also used for Capricorn and one of the Monsters of Chaos in the Train of the Dragon Tiamat.

Mushussu, "Raging Serpent," or Serpent Dragon, which is one of the eleven Dragons of Tiamat in the Epic of Creation. Another is Basmu (Viper) & good image of the type similar to Set in Egypt.

The Mace of Seven Heads. Like the Mighty Serpent with Seven Heads Murder does, my Divine Kurrashurur [ta ta ta sound?] ('God who Causes the Mountain Distress'), whose Brightness like Day-Light is Sent Forth, I bear. Many of the Weapons are called "Gods." The Poisonous Tooth of the Sky Thou hast Broken. Casting Shadow of glory Over the Land. The Lord went Forth like a Cyclone. Like a Storm he Raged on the Foundation of Heaven. Heaven and Earth Tremble as Thou Comest. When Thou Liftest thy Arm a Shadow Stretches Far. [Contrail Shadow?] The self-exalted Stone thou didst Destroy and the Plants Altogether Thou has Crushed. The Gods of Earth at thy call Lapsed into Silence. The Wild Cow of Battle, my wicked net of the hostile land, I bear.

[The Poisonous Tooth also is in the Myth of Etana and Zu, the Eagle, which prey upon the carcass of a Bull and was Ensnared by a Serpent.]

A poem from the age of Hammurabi at Babylon :

Irra the Slayer desired Battle and Spoke to his Weapons, "the Seven Gods," to smear themselves with the Poison of Death. They urged him forth to Destroy the Land. But Irra wished to repose and enjoy himself with Mami his wife. Here the Dreadfulness of the "Seven Gods," that is the Seven Weapons of Irra, is described. Anu, the father of the Gods, begat them, gave them their names, and Decreed their Fates. The Seven Fates are : (1) "On High Appear and go Without Rival" ; (2) "Be like the God Mes the Furious Bull" ; (3) "The appearance of a Lion has been provided for thee . .

322

. . . . . carry out the order" ; (4) "When thou Liftest thy Raging Weapons let the Mountain Perish" ; (5) "Rush like the Wind and Spy out the Regions" ; (6) "Enter above and beneath and Spare No Thing" ; (7) "The Seventh he filled with Poison of a Dragon Serpent saying 'cause to Perish the Soul of Life.'" Anu gave the Seven Gods to Irra for his helpers because Irra was Enraged against the people and had decided to Slay Man and Beast. And Seven Weapons Arose and urged Irra to Destroy Men ; they will not sit in the city like pale-faced old Men or like children at home, or eat bread of Women . . . . Mountains and lands, Gods, demons, kings, Men, and cattle shall be Terrified . . . . After the Flood the Pestilence of Heaven and Earth are let loose to Kill the Survivors, but Marduk saved Seven Wise Ones (Ummani) by causing them to Descend to the Apsu, and the precious Mes-Tree which had its roots in the Wide Sea, in the Depths of Arallu, and its top attained High Heaven, by "changing their places" and then asks Irra where are the Lapis Lazuli [Blue Skies], the Gods of the Arts, and the Seven Wise Ones of the Apsu. . . . . . .

The name Tammuz is derived from dumu, "son," and zi, which has three principal meanings ; it may stand for zid, "faithful," "true" ; or for zig, "to go forth," "to rise up" ; and also "breath of life." Tammuz may mean, therefore, "Faithful son," or "Risen son," or "Son of life." The last interpretation is most improbable, for no Accadian phrase mar napishti, "son of life," is known. [Tammuz is Greenery and life.]

A hymn to Tammuz :

"She of the Dawn, she of the Dawn, Daily with Weeping is Surfeited. Sobbing goes the daughter of Kullab ; "O Heavenly psalmist, Lord of the Earth (Ninsubur), O my holy psalmist, thou of the Lapis Lazuli sandals (?), my messenger, who turns my words to good account. My herald who established my words. Herald of counsel, Man of woe. O my exalted one, in thy Resurrection, in thy Resurrection, O my exalted one, in thy Rising to the Bosom of the Mother that Bore Thee, To the Bosom of thy Mother, to the Bosom of thy Beloved Rise. O my exalted one, Who is like Shamash ? Thou art like Shamash. O my exalted one, Who is like Nannar ? Thou art like Nannar.'" [Weeping for Life at the time of the Sun in Virgo and return.]

Sumero-Babylonian Mythology :

"Cold, Fever Diminishing All Things, Evil Devil whom Anu begat. Namtaru, beloved son of Enlil, borne by Ereshkigal. On High they have

323

Decimated, on Earth they have laid Misery. They are the creation of Hell. On high they Roar, on Earth they Shriek. Bitter Poison sent by the Gods are they. Great Storms which have been let loose from Heaven are they. Owl (?) which cries in the city are they. Begotten by Anu, children, offspring of the Nether World are they. Giants Seven times two are they. All one begetting, Created by the begetting of Anu, are they. They are Surging Blasts of Wind. A wife they married not, children they begat not. Child they know not. Horses which grew up in the Mountain are they. They are Wicked ones of Enki. Throne-Bearers of the Gods are they. To trouble the streets they stand in the ways. They stalk before Nergal, strong hero of Enlil."

Winged Bull also called Sedu :

"Decimating Heaven and Earth, Sedu Decimating the Land, Sedu Decimating the Land, whose Power is of Heaven, Whose Power is of Heaven, whose Roving is in Heaven. The Gallu, the Goring Ox, the mighty ghost, ghost which violates all houses. Shameless Gallu, Seven are they. They Grind the Land like meal, they know not mercy. Raging against the people. Eaters of the flesh, causing Blood to flow like rain, drinking the Arteries. Once on a time, in the place of the forms of the Gods, in the house of the God of the holy chamber, of the Goddess of flocks and grain, they grew fat. The Gallu, who are full of Wickedness, are they. Ceaselessly they Eat Blood. Cause them to Swear the Curse, and may they not return outside or inside (the house). May they be Cursed by the Life of Heaven and Earth."

Here the Sedu are Identical with the Seven Devils, and are Explicitly Described as Ghosts who Ravage the Land in the Shape of Bulls. They are described as Evil and Merciless, and Associated with Ghosts from the Grave. The Ideogram employed in writing Sedu probably means "Strong One of the Pit," [Meteorite / Crater] a Spirit whose Abode is in Hell. The Ideogram for "Bull" has also the value Alad (=Sedu) and may be used besides as a title of Nergal, Lord of the Dead. The Good and Evil Sedu was, therefore, a Genius of the Underworld, usually conceived of as a Bull and, like all other Demons, Connected with Wandering Souls of the Dead. These then were the Mythical beings of Canaanitish Mythology. The writer of the song attributed to Moses, but of a later age, Deuteronomy 32 : 17, accused the Hebrews of sacrificing to the Sedim (Devils) "which are no God." The writer of Psalm 106 : 37 states that, in the Old Paganism of Canaan, sons and daughters were Sacrificed to the Sedim, from which the inference may be drawn that here also the Sedim were associated with Nergal, or with Malik (Moloch) the Terrible God of Plague, Fiery Heat, and Inferno.

Many believe that Yahweh means "He Who Causes To Fall Fire From Heaven."

Mythology of the Babylonian People,
by Donald A. Mackenzie, 1915

Scientific expeditions in Russia and Chinese Turkestan have accumulated important archaeological data which clearly establish that vast areas of desert country were at a remote period most Verdurous and Fruitful, and Thickly Populated by organized and apparently Progressive Communities. From these ancient centres of civilization wholesale migrations must have been impelled from time to time in consequence of the gradual encroachment of wind-distributed sand and the increasing shortage of water. At Anau in Russian Turkestan, where excavations were conducted by the Pumpelly expedition, abundant traces were found of an Archaic and Forgotten Civilization reaching back to the Late Stone Age.

Enlil, whose name is translated "Lord of Mist," "Lord of Might," and "Lord of Demons" by various authorities. The name of Enlil's temple at Nippur has been translated as "Mountain House," or "like a Mountain."

Shamash [The Sun] was exalted as the Great Judge, the Lawgiver, who Upheld Justice ; he was the Enemy of Wrong, he Loved Righteousness and hated Sin, he inspired his worshippers with rectitude and punished evildoers. The Sun God also Illuminated the World, and his rays penetrated every quarter : he Saw All Things, and Read the Thoughts of Men ; Nothing Could be Concealed from Shamash.

The "Dragon of Babylon" which was portrayed on walls of temples, had a Serpent's head, a body covered with Scales, the fore legs of a Lion, hind legs of an Eagle, and a Long Wriggling Serpentine Tail. Ea had Several Monster Forms [Shape Shifter]. The following description of one of these is Repulsive enough : The head is the head of a Serpent, from his nostrils Mucus trickles, his mouth is Beslavered with Water ; the ears are like those of a Basilisk, his Horns are Twisted into Three Curls [Vortices], he wears a Veil in his head band, the body is a Suh-Fish full of Stars, the base of his

325

feet are Claws, the sole of his foot has No Heel, his name is Sassu-Wunnu, a Sea [Space] Monster, a Form of Ea.   R. C. Thompson's Translation

After Eating of the Dragon's Heart [Meteorite] One is Inspired with its Cunning and Wisdom.

Beowulf with a Gigantic magic Sword Slays the mother Dragon, whose Poisonous Blood afterwards Melts the "Damasked Blade." [Meteoric Iron]

In Brazil, Monan, the chief God, Sent a Great Fire to Burn Up the World and its wicked inhabitants. To Extinguish the Flames a magician caused so much rain to fall that the Earth was Flooded.

In an Eddic poem, the Voluspa, the Vala tells of a Sword Age, an Axe Age, and a Wolf Age which is to come after the Battle of the Gods and Demons, the Sun is Darkened and the Earth Sinks in the Sea.

In India the Ghosts of the "Seven Rishis," who were semi-divine Patriarchs, formed the Constellation of the Great Bear, which in Vedic times was called the "Seven Bears." The Wifes of the Seven Rishis were the Stars of the Pleiades. [Came from the Pleiades and Struck in the North aka Ursa Major.]

In Phoenician Astronomy the Vulture was "Zither" known as Lyra.

Myths & Legends of Babylonia & Assyria, by Lewis Spence, 1916

It is possible also that the Great Sea-Dragon, or Serpent, which was Slain by the Creator, may have Flooded the Earth with his Blood as he expired : there is an Algonquin Indian Myth to this effect. In an Old Cuneiform Text, in Fact, the Year of the Deluge is Alluded to as "the Year of the Raging Serpent."

The Legend of the Confusion of Tongues is to be traced in other Folk-Lores than that of Babylon. It is found in Central America, where the story runs that Xelhue, one of the Seven Giants rescued from the Deluge, built the Great Pyramid of Cholula in order to Besiege Heaven. The structure was, however, Destroyed by the Gods, who Cast Down Fire upon it and Confounded the Language of its Builders. [Sounds Corrupted, but is it?]

326

The Gods, it is said, urge Adar on, he Descends like the Deluge, the champion of the Gods Swoops Down upon the hostile land. A fine hymn to Adar describes the Rumbling of the Storm in the Abyss, the 'Voice' of the God :

The Terror of the Splendor of Anu in the Midst of Heaven. Thy chariot is as a Voice of Thunder. To the Lifting of thy Hands is the Shadow turned. The spirits of the Earth, the Great Gods, return to the Winds.

The Noise of the Storm was spoken of as his 'Word.' Probably, too, because he was a Very Old God he was regarded in some localities as a Creator of the World. The Great Winged Bull of Assyrian art may well often represent En-lil : no symbol could better typify the Tempest which the Babylonians regarded as Rushing and Rioting Unrestrained over country and city, Overturning even Tower and Temple with its Violence, and Tumbling the wretched reed huts of the lower caste into the Dust. [Atomic Bomb Blast type of Destruction, that is why they Built with such Huge Stones.]

Nin-lil, the wife of En-lil, shared his authority over Nippur, where she had a temple which went back in Antiquity to the First Dymasty of Ur. In certain Inscriptions She is described as 'the Mother of the Gods,' and was also called the 'Lady of the Mountain.' [The Sky Mountain.]

It is quite possible for a Solar Deity to have an Underworld Connexion, seeing that the Sun is supposed to travel through that gloomy region during the Night. Nergal, God of the Dead, Spreading Pestilence and War, where he goes Violent Death Follows in his Wake, 'God of Fire,' the 'Raging King,' he who Burns,' the 'Violent One,' and Fierceness of Flame.

327

Below : The Twelve Tablets of Gilgamesh corresponding to the Zodiac.

The Zodiacal significance is in all probability a superficial one merely, added to the poem by the scribes of Assur-bani-pal, and not forming an integral part of it. At the same time it is not hard to divide the epic naturally into Twelve episodes, thus : (1) Gilgamesh's oppression of Erech ; (2) the seduction of Eabani ; (3) the slaying of the monster Khumbaba ; (4) the wooing of Ishtar ; (5) the fight with the Sacred Bull ; (6) Eabani's death ; (7) Gilgamesh's journey to the Mountain of the Sunset ; (8) his wanderings in the region of Thick Darkness ; (9) the crossing of the Waters of Death ; (10) the Deluge-story ; (11) the Plant of Life ; (12) the return of Eabani's spirit.

[American Thunderbird , Arabian Knights Roc or Rukh, and Zu-bird]

The Legend of the God Zu that on one occasion ambition awaking in his breast caused him to cast envious eyes on the power and sovereignty of Bel, so that he determined to Purloin the Tablets of Destiny, which were the tangible symbols of Bel's greatness. In the Creation Legend how Apsu, the Primeval, and Tiawath [Tiamat], Chaos, the First Parents of the Gods, afterward conceived a hatred for their offspring, and how Tiamat, with her Monster-Brood of Snakes and Vipers, Dragons and Scorpion-Men and Raging Hounds, made War on the Hosts of Heaven. Her son Kingu she made captain of her hideous army –

"To march before the forces, to lead the Host, to give the battle-signal, to advance to the attack, to direct the battle, to control the fight. Now when Bel was pouring out the clear water, and his diadem was taken off and lay upon the throne, (Zu) seized the Tablets of Destiny, he took Bel's dominion, the power of giving commands. Then Zu fled away and hid himself in his Mountain." Bel was Greatly Enraged at the Theft, and the Gods with him. Anu, Lord of Heaven, summoned about him his divine sons, and asked for a champion to recover the Tablets. But though the God Ramman [The God of Thunder] was chosen, and after him several other deities, they all refused to advance against Zu.

This Legend is of the Prometheus type, but whereas Prometheus (once a Bird-God) Steals Fire from Heaven for the Behoove of Mankind, Zu steals the Tablets of Destiny for his own. [Stable power is overcome by Chaos.]

328

"At Nippur there developed an elaborate lamentation ritual for the occasion when national Catastrophes, defeat, failure of crops, destructive storms, and pestilence revealed the Displeasure and Anger of the Gods. At such times earnest endeavourers were made, through petitions accompanied by Fasting and other symbols of Contrition, to bring about a Reconciliation with the Angered Power".

- Morris Jastrow

Ninib as an Assyrian War-God :
Such a deity as Ninib (another name for Ningirsu, the God of Lagash) was certain to find favour among the Assyrians by virtue of those characteristics which would render him a valuable ally in war. We find several kings extolling his prowess as a warrior, notably Tiglath – pileser I , and Assurrishishi, who allude to him as "the courageous one," and "the mighty one of the Gods." His old status as a Sun and Wind God, in which he was regarded as Overthrowing and Leveling with the Ground everything Which Stood in his Path, would supply him with the reputation necessary to a God of Battles.

The Stars / Constellations possess volition, and even although omens were looked for out of their movements, it may have been believed that these were the outcome of volition on the part of the Stars themselves as deities or deific individuals.

Jupiter, the largest of the planets, was identified with Merodach, head of the Babylonian pantheon. We find him exercising control over the other Stars in the creation story under the name Nibir. Ishtar was identified with Venus, Saturn with Ninib, Mars with Nergal, Mercury with Nabu.

We find in this Early Star-Worship of the ancient Babylonians the Common Origin of Religion and Science. [!] Just as magic partakes in some measure of the nature of real science (for some authorities hold that it is Pseudo-Scientific in Origin) so does Religion, or perhaps more correctly speaking, Early Science is Very Closely Identified with Religion. Thus we may believe that the religious interest in their Early Astronomy spurred the ancient Star-Gazers of Babylonia to Acquire More Knowledge Concerning the Motions of Those Stars and Planets which they Believed To Be Deities. We find the Gods so Closely Connected with Ancient Chaldean Astronomy as To Be Absolutely Identified with It in Every Way. A number was assigned to each of the chief Gods, which would seem to show that they were Connected In Some Way With Mathematical Science. Thus, Ishtar's number is fifteen ; that of Sin, her father, is exactly double that. Anu takes sixty, and Bel and Ea represent fifty and forty. Ramman is identified with ten.

As civilization proceeded and theological option took shape, religious ceremonial began to take the place of what was little better than sorcery. It has been said that magic is an attempt to force the hands of the Gods, to overawe them, whereas religion is an appeal to their protective instincts.

Professor Robert Smith has put it on record in his Religion of the Semites, that sacrifice among that race was regarded as a Meal Shared Between the Worshipper and the Deity.

An Early Ideal was to Reproduce in Miniature the 'Mountain of all Lands' – Khursag-kurkura, the Birthplace of the Gods – and to this end the temple was Erected on a Mountain-Like Heap [Pyramid] of Earth.

The Babylonian Tablet with the history of the Seven Evil Gods or spirits, though much mutilated and impossible to decipher the context, gives us a hint of the attack made by them Upon the Moon. They dwelt in the lower part of Heaven, and were rebellious in heart. Shaped like Leopards, Serpents, and Angry Beasts of Prey, they went from city to city on the Wings of an Evil Wind, Destroying and Smiting. And into the Heaven of Anu they Burst, but Bel and Ea took council, and Sin the Moon, Shamash the Sun, and Ishtar the Planet Venus in the Lower part of Heaven to govern and control it along with Anu. No sooner had this been accomplished than the Seven Evil Spirits Fiercely Attacked the Moon-God. But Bel saw the Peril of Sin, and said to his attendant, the God Nusku, "Carry Word of this thing to the Ocean, to the God Ea." Ea Heard the message, and called his son, the God Merodach. "Go, my son Merodach," quoth he, "each into the Shining Sin, who in Heaven is Greatly Beset, and expel his enemies from Heaven."

In the Babylonian magical records we have by far the most complete picture of the magic of the ancient World. It is a wondrous story that is told by those bricks and cylinders of stamped clay – the story of civilized Man's First Gropings for Light. [After the Event] For in these Venerable Writings We Must Recognize the First Attempts at Scientific Elucidation of the Forces by which Man is Surrounded. Science, like Religion, has its roots Deep in Magic. The primitive Man believes Implicitly in the Efficacy of Magical Ritual. What it brings about once it can bring about again if the proper conditions be present and recognized. Thus it possesses for the

330

Barbarian as much of the element of certainty as the Scientific Process does for the Chemist or the Electrician. Given certain <u>Causes Effects</u> must follow. Surely, then in the Barbarous Mind, Magic IS Pseudo-Scientific – of the Nature of Science. The Seven Storm-Demons were the Children of Ea [Ubaid Period Tiamat]. In a magical incantation describing the Primitive Monster form of Ea it is said that his head is like a Serpent's, the ears are those of a Basilisk, his Horns are Twisted into Curls, his body is a Sun-Fish Full of Stars, his feet are armed with Claws, and the sole of his foot has No Heel. [Like Image at Pg. 164 - aka Vortices of the Bolide.]

The Origin of the Worship of Yahwe, by William Hayes Ward, The American Journal of Semitic Languages and Literatures, Vol. XXV April 1909

For a study of the Earliest character of the Yahwe worship we are driven to but one source, that of the indications of it that remain in the Hebrew Literature. We must consider in what figurative way the people had continued to represent to themselves their national God. Some ideas and expressions under which they pictured Yahwe to themselves are likely to have come down from a Primitive Source, while other expressions will have come in later. I regard that Pictorial form which we now and then find by which Yahwe is represented with Wings, as of a comparatively later period, that is, as having arisen considerably after the Exodus ; because such expressions as "under the Shadow of thy Wings," "healing in his Wings," have in view the figure of the Winged Solar Disk. This design was modified from the Egyptian Solar Disk by the Omission of the Asps, and did not come into use in Syria until, I think, considerably later than the conquest of Syria by Egypt and the Nineteenth Dynasty. This Biblical Representation of Yahwe is peculiar and quite apart from others, and is to be dismissed from our discussion.

The following are the more general and Special Descriptions or Attributes of Yahwe which seem to have come down from a Primitive Source. In the first place, he is a God of the Mountains. So he is represented at Sinai and Horeb, and also often elsewhere. Abraham went to Moriah to sacrifice Isaac in the story which relates itself to the killing of the first-born. Elijah goes to Mount Carmel to contend with the priests of Baal, and later flees to Horeb, the Mount of God. The theophanies are related naturally to Mountains. "God came from Teman, the Holy One from Mount Paran." We seem to have the definite statement that such was the view of Yahwe in the story of the defeat of the soldiers of Benhadad by those of Ahab. His advisers explained his defeat to the Syrian king by saying, "Their God is a God of the hills, but he is not a God of the valleys." Historically and Figuratively he was a deity of the Mountains.

The next point to observe is that he was particularly a God of Storms, Thunder, and Lightning. This relates itself to the Mountains which are the scenes of Storm. So he appeared to Moses in Sinai, and to Elijah at Horeb. In the earliest bit of Hebrew Literature that has come down to us we read.

Yahwe, when thou wentest forth out of Seir, when thou marchedest out of the field of Edom, the Earth Trembled, the Heavens also Dropt, yea the clouds dropt Water, the Mountains flowed down at the presence of Yahwe, even you Sinai, at the presence of Yahwe, the God of Israel.

In the book of Job, in which the name of Yahwe is avoided, and El Shaddai so often takes its place, the name which we are told was the earliest name of Yahwe, God twice (38:1 ; 40:6) addresses Job from the Whirlwind, even as Elijah was taken up into Heaven in a Whirlwind ; and in 36 : 26-37 Elihu gives a long description of God as the ruler of Lightning, Storm, and Rain. Indeed, it was the Lightning and the Tempest, and also the Hosts of the Sabeans and Chaldeans, by which the wealth of Job was Destroyed. Amos begins his prophecy (1 : 2) : "Yahwe shall Roar from Zion, and Utter his Voice from Jerusalem ; and the pastures of the shepherds shall moan, and the top of Carmel shall wither." In 4 : 13 he it is that "formeth the Mountains and Created the Wind," "that maketh the morning Darkness and Treadeth upon the High Places of the Earth [Like the 1960's Footage of a Bolide seemingly touching the mountain peaks.]," a God of both Mountain and Storm. Again we have the Mountain and the Storm in the Theophany of Micah 1 : 3, 4:

"Behold the Lord cometh forth out of his place, and will Come Down and Tread Upon the High Places of the Earth. And the Mountains shall be Molten under him, and the valleys shall be Cleft, as Wax before the Fire, as Waters that are Poured Down a steep place."

Nahum's prophecy begins with a similar Theophany :

"The Lord hath his way in the Whirlwind and the Storm, and the Clouds are the Dust of his feet. He Rebuketh the Sea and Maketh it Dry, and Drieth up

332

All the Rivers ; Bashan languisheth and Carmel, and the Flower of Lebanon Languisheth. The Mountains Quake at him and the hills Melt ; and the Earth is Upheaved at his presence. Yea, the World and All that Dwell Therein . . . . His Fury is Poured out like Fire, and the Rocks are Broken Asunder by him." (1 : 3-6).

Habakkuk's Theophany (3:3-13) develops the picture of Storm, Lightning, Thunder, and Earthquake, when Yahwe went forth to victory, "with the "Light of his Arrows" and "the Shining of his Glittering Spears," when "Fiery Bolts went forth at his feet."

And yet it is in the Psalms that we have the Most Numerous Descriptions of Yahwe as God of Storm, Lightning, and Rain. It is sufficient to call attention to Pss. 7:12, 13; 11:6; 18:6-15; 29:3-10; 48:7; 50:3; 65:5-13; 68:7-17; 33; 81:7; 83:15; 93:1-4; 97:3-5; 104:1-13, 32; 107:33-37; 147:15-18. Of these we may specify Ps. 29 which is entirely devoted to a description of Thunder as "the Voice of Yahwe."

"The Voice of the Lord is upon the Waters ; the God of glory Thundereth, even the Lord upon many Waters. The Voice of the Lord is full of majesty. The Voice of the Lord Breaketh the Cedars ; Yea, the Lord Breaketh in Pieces the Cedars of Lebanon".   Psalms 29 : 3-5 1917

Closely allied to the representation of Yahwe as the God of Thunder and Storm is that which makes him a Fighting God, a God of battles. The Lightnings are Weapons ; they are "Arrows" and "Glittering Spears" with which he confronts his enemies and those of his people. Accordingly one of the most common Attributes given to him is that of "God of Hosts," [Pleiades] that is "God of the Armies of Israel," I Sam. 17 : 45. In the song of Moses, Exod. 15:3 we are told : Yahwe is a Man of War ; Yahwe is his name.

Another of the more important indications as to the origin of the worship of Yahwe is to be found in the way he was represented in art. We are told that when Moses delayed to come down from the mount Aaron made a Golden "Calf," that is, a young Bull, which Represented Their God to the people. Then, in some way the Bull was the symbol of the God they worshiped. Also when Jereboam separated from the Southern Kingdom, in order to prevent the people from resorting to Jerusalem to worship Yahwe, he set up shrines in Bethel and Dan, and represented Yahwe by Golden "Calves." Whether the earliest worship at Dan with an image, Ephod, and Teraphim

333

was with a Calf we do not know. But the Fact of the worship of the Bull at Bethel and Dan is again and again substantiated in the denunciations of the prophets, especially in Hosen and Amos. In Hos. 13:2 we learn that the kissing of the Calf was an act of worship. In Hos. 8 : 5, 6 the "Calf of Samaria" is mentioned. It is generally recognized that the Bull must have been from the earliest times related to the popular worship ; and that the Bull-God was supposed to have brought the children of Israel out of Egypt, and the representation by a Bull could not have been derived from an Egyptian God, but belonged to an Asiatic type of worship. We are not told what was the form of the "graven image and molten image" which, with the Ephod and Teraphim, were stolen by the Danites from the house of Micah and taken to Dan (Judges, chaps. 18 and 19) ; but from the fact that Dan was later the seat of worship of the Calf it is likely that this was a Bull. The 1,700 shekels of Gold with which Gideon made an Ephod in Ophrah in the land of Manasseh, which became a Snare to Gideon and his house," must have gone for an image also, but we are not told what was its nature.

These Facts are Patent in the story as to the Figuration or symbolic worship of Yahwe : He was a God of Mountains ; he was a God of lightning, Thunder, Storm, and Rain, and so necessarily a God of War, a God of Armies who led the Israelites to battle ; and he was Figured as a Bull. These are Our Data ; and it is now our duty to see how these attributes agree with those of any of the Gods of the Region.

one   two

three   four

We have no satisfactory figures of an early time of the Gods of Phoenicia or Palestine which would sufficiently identify them. In Egyptian Monuments Resheph is figured as a Syrian deity. But we know from a multitude of seals of which are known to have come from the Hauran or other neighboring regions, what were the Gods worshiped. They are, whatever their names, principally three (and are all seen in the seal cylinder, Fig. 1), a dignified standing deity usually with no weapon, the God to the left in Fig. 1 ; a more active and militant deity as the one to the right in the same figure ; and a Goddess, who stands between them. These were worshiped under various names from Tigris to the Mediterranean, and apparently for many centuries beginning back even of the Twelfth Dynasty of Egypt, that is, Long Before the Exodus from Egypt. It is the second militant God whom I would compare with the Primitive Yahwe or Yahu, or Yah.

This deity was known under various names, but is the same under whatever name. He is Adad or Addu, or Ramman or Rimmon, under the Babylonians, Assyrians, and in Damascus. He is Teshub among the Hittites and kindred peoples, and he was the Resheph of Humath. Whether he was one or more of the local Balls, or whether he was Moloch is by No Means Certain. He was also identified for his Militant Character, with Egyptian Set or Sutekh.

It has been said that Yahwe is described as God of Mountains, as the God of Thunder, Lightning, Rain, and Storm, and so a Fighting Deity ; and that as an Idol he was Represented by the Bull. These characteristics unite in Ramman-Adad-Teshub and in no other deity.

In the first place he is the God of the Mountains. So he is characteristically represented in Figs. 1, 2, 3, 4. He Stands or Walks on Mountains as his regular Home. In the language of Micah, he "Treads on the High Places of the Earth." This does not resemble the cases in which in early Babylonian art we see the rising Sun Shamash coming out of the Gates of the East and stepping on a Mountain, of lifting himself up between two Mountains by his hands, to indicate the rising of the Sun, for they are Adad's Regular Abode, as Olympus was the Abode of the Hellenic Deities, and Particularly of Zeus, the God who Wields the Thunderbolt, and who is most closely related to Adad-Ramman.

Adad-Ramman also was the God of Thunder, Lightning, Wind, and Rain. This appears frequently in the Babylonian Inscriptions, for he is a western God imported into Babylonia at an early period. As a single example we may refer to the case on the boundary stones asked for from him, praying that the harvests of any violator may be washed away. The derivation of Ramman is supposed to be from Ramamu, to Bellow, to Thunder, and we find such expressions as that of "Ramman Thundered in the Heavens." In a Tablet giving the titles of the Gods we have the following titles of Adad: "God of Clouds ; God of the Storm Cloud ; God of Earthquake (?) ; God of Thunder ; God of Lightning ; God of Inundation ; God of Rain ; God of Storm ; God of the Deluge." The later, Abubu is the Great Deluge, which we learn from Genesis was brought upon the Earth by Yahwe. We also learn that under the names Sumukan, Martu, and Amurru, Adad was recognized as "God of Lightning" and "God of Mountains." In Babylonian art he is represented as carrying a Thunderbolt (see Figs. 5, 6), and not infrequently the Bident or Trident Thunderbolt appears alone as his emblem (Fig. 9), and, occasionally, is placed above his Ashera. In the Syro-Hittite art the Thunderbolt is not known, but various other Weapons appear, as in the Biblical descriptions of Yahwe. So in Figs 1, 2, 4, 7, 8.

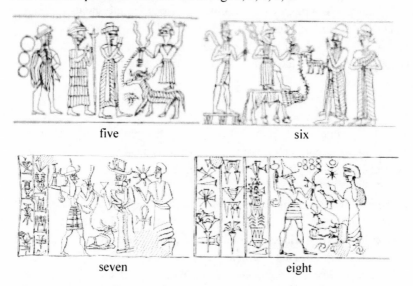

five   six

seven   eight

Equally, and naturally, he is a God of War. The Thunderbolt is itself a Weapon, and Adad carries the Weapons, the Bow and the Club and the Ax. He is in the act of War in Fig. 3, swinging a foe by the hair of his head.

There remains to be considered the Bull which was the animal emblem of Yahwe. But the Bull is the special animal belonging to Adad. When Adad is represented in his most complete form, as in Fig. 4, he stands on Mountains, in one hand he lifts a Weapon over his head and carries in the other hand a Club, Ax, Serpent, or other Weapon, and in the same hand

336

holds a cord attached to a ring in the nose of the Bull. In a multitude of
cases of Babylonian Seals we have the Thunderbolt and the Bull (Figs. 5, 6),
but in the case of the Syro-Hittite seals other Weapons, with the Bull, as in
Figs. 4, 7, 8. Nor is the Bull omitted in the inscriptions as the animal Sacred
to Adad. On the kudurru of Nazimaruttash, col. iv. 16, "the Mighty Bull of
Adad" is appealed to. The reason why the Bull belongs to him is plain ; as
he needs the zigzag [Wavy] Weapon for Lightning, so he needs the Bull to
provide him with the bellowing of the Thunder [No, It's the Origin & Time].
When the exigency of art requires the omission of the figure of the God, we
may have the figure of the Bull with the Thunderbolt above it, thus
suggesting both Lightning and Thunder, or the Thunderbolt alone, as in Fig.
9. It was as the God of Thunder that the Hebrews used the familiar
representation of the Bull, which was well known to every inhabitant of
Palestine and all the region as far as Peria and Elam At the Time of the
Emergence of the Israelite people. We have the Bull alone as the emblem
probably of the same God in Figs. 10, 11. As a herm ashera we see him in
Fig. 12.

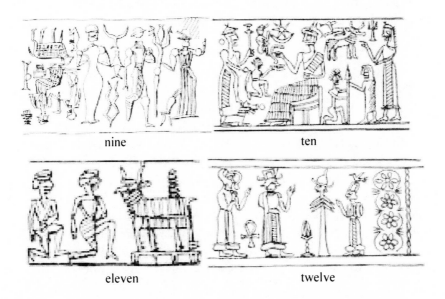

nine   ten

eleven   twelve

We thus have Every One of the Distinguishing Marks of the early character
of Yahwe in the Characteristics of Adad-Ramman I cannot help Believing
that he Was the Pagan Yahwe, before Yahwe emerged as the Universal God
of Monotheism.

If, then we may presume that Yahwe was, in origin of worship, the God
Ramman, or Adad, we get an easier explanation of one or two points in

337

Hebrew history. Not only do we find an explanation of the representation of Yahwe in the Desert and later at Bethel, and Dan by the Bull, but we may see how it was that Ahaz Copied the Altar at Damascus. We are told, II Kings 16 : 10-16, that when after Tiglath-pileser had conquered Damascus, and Ahaz had gone to Damascus to pay homage to the Assyrian king, he saw a magnificent altar there, of which he had Urijah, the priest, make a copy in the temple at Jerusalem for the worship of Yahwe. This altar at Damascus was with Little Doubt an altar for the worship of Adad, and the Relation of Yahwe and Adad would have made it easier for Ahaz to make such an altar for Yahwe.

Another more Definite case we have in the story of Naaman. After he had been healed by Elisha of his leprosy, we are told, II Kings 5 : 17-19, that Naaman declared that henceforth he would worship only Yahwe, nevertheless "when my master goeth into the house of Rimmon to worship there, and he leaneth on my hand and I bow myself in the house of Rimmon, Yahwe pardon thy servant in this thing. And he (Elisha) said unto him, Go in peace." This is a Surprising Concession, and may be explained if there was supposed to be any relation between the Gods of Damascus and the God of Israel.

As an evidence of the presence of the worship of Adad in Palestine before the entrance of the Israelites, it is to be observed that he is the principal deity of that land of whom we have Evidence From the Amarna Letters. One of them, No. 149, 13, extols the king of Egypt, who "lifts up his Voice like Addu, so that all the land Trembles at his Voice," Addu being the usual and Correct name for Adad, with the case-ending. There are, I think, as many proper names in those letters composed of Addu as of all other Gods combined. Thus we have A-Addu, Abd-Addi, Addu-.-ia, Addu-asharidu, Addu-daian, Addu-dan, Addu-mihir, Amar-Addi, Yadi-Addi(?), Yaha-Addi, Yapahi-Addu, Yapti-Addu, Natan-Addu, Pu-Addi, Shanu-Addu, and Shipti-Addi. The evidence seems clear that he was the prevailing deity of the country. As such the Yahwe worship would be likely to come from the worship of this God.

It has become Very Evident that All of Mankind Globally were Witness to the Actual Events and Embedded the Information into their Traditions in to which Amazingly Survived Millennia. From what I've read it seems that most consider the 2300 BC event to be the time of The Deluge, without a doubt that was a Space Fall climate changing event, but it is clear that civilization didn't change that much given the Cuneiform and Hieroglyph texts continued on after a relatively short silence. Furthermore the meaning behind the Traditions had already been half forgotten when the historical written language evolved. The Huge Conflagration and Flood had to Coincide with the Extinction of the Mega Fauna and the Formation of the Carolina Bays. It may be hard to comprehend such Legends surviving for such a span of time ; yet it is the way it is adding up.

The story goes, that the World had a stable climate and with entirely different trade winds and Ocean currents in which the mid latitudes globally where green and vibrant from the deserts of China through Egypt and also the Americas at the time that the World was slowly pulling out of an Ice Age. Then a Comet came out of the Pleiades over Taurus the Bull and got by Orion and flew over the North at least one time as stated in at least one of the Legends that it came for a visit and went back into the Stars. It must have been a wildly spectacular scene that everyone saw and up close because Mankind built Pyramids to emulate the Sky Mountain they saw sailing by spewing Fountains of 'water' and spinning releasing a huge trail of debris that lasted at least long enough so that the Worldwide Snake with its Tail in its Mouth Circuit Ideograph was implanted and is the very faint Zodiacal Light before Man made light pollution.

There are maps made by the radar imaging that show two streams wherein at probably the time of the first impact of one part of it was perturbed from the orbit of the other to form the Northern and Southern Taurid Streams caused by passing over the North Pole. It most likely broke up into three major pieces with the first striking at the Great Lakes around 13,000 years ago, the second part responsible for the 2350 BC Event, and the surviving 2P/Encke Comet. It is said via the Belfast Ireland Dendrochronologist that there are other smaller Events at 540 AD, 210 BC, 1160 BC, and 1630 BC, in which two would correspond with the English Myth of King Arthur and the Hebrew Exodus. [New Light on the Black Death is one of his books.]

Mankind played Sympathetic Magic to the spectacle and it should be realized that there are at least two different types, one being the physics of the magnificent phenomena in outer space and the terrifying spectacle of Atmospheric plethora of possibilities even modern Man has yet to witness or venture to guess. The latest Airburst over Russia is a prime example, what if it comes straight down in the Atlantic, just as a thought. The Scientist assure us that the frequency, as in a sharp instant impact not in time of occurrence of centuries or millennia, of the blast is far too short to cause a Tsunami to make the sea come prodigiously across the land as all the testimony you have just read. The emulation and or presuppositions are rampant, such as Copernicus relentlessly trying to make the elliptical or parabolic orbits of the planets to fit into the assumed perfect God's principle that had to be Circular. It is the same with the Sky Mountain and Mankind made almost perfect triangular monuments around the World and also made huge glyphs such as the Nazca Lines and Serpent mounds so that the God Flying above could see our work. There is a modern example in the Pacific at the end of WW2 of islanders making airstrips and aircraft to entice the cargo airplane back to their islands, so the behavior must be ingrained into us in a primitive form.

Mankind didn't understand what was happening and related to whatever was around him to analogize the events to his fellow man that missed it or saw it from a different area and gave it different names. I think this may have really kicked off the advent of language of mankind onto a new level because We all saw it and talking about the same phenomena would have bridged the gap of different communication skills with a common story wherein the receiver after awhile of trying to Understand would realize that they are describing the same event. It is not so farfetched, as I just said. We use it all the time even today, is it so hard to understand a concept that is thrown way out in left field (baseball) and is so farfetched (dog play) that you are incredulous ?

Personally I find that countless aspects of the Hypothesis fit so nicely together that it is mind boggling that this isn't already common knowledge. I was profoundly set back while researching this and have yet to figure out how Mankind as a whole cannot fathom this paradigm if that is indeed what it is. It is almost as if there is a conscious conceited effort to suppress the truth, first the church and now academic bureaucracy and fear of change. Such as pathetic reaches to explain say the Carolina Bays as an organized fish fin wave action or Man wiping out the Saber Toothed Cat and other predators so that the herbivores over populated and died of disease which is just silly because the Cat alone is twice as big or bigger than Man with two huge Canine Teeth and 20 huge razor sharp claws and Man with a flint spear plus the cat is nocturnal.

While researching this it was evident that there is a multitude of spin offs to the subject and at the time it became difficult not to deviate off the path. It reminds me of when I lived with the Step Dad who told me about the Taurid Stream and when the 4th grade teacher asked the class to invent new game board games, I thought it was a grand idea, finally school will be fun. I made up a high risk Egyptian Pyramid game and got a Fail, the other kids with rubber stamped Parcheesi clones they all got A's, perplexed when the teacher told me it was too complicated.

I thought I would work on it some more in my free time at home and asked her for it back when she snapped it up and folded it then told me with a scolding voice that she was going to put it into my permanent secret file along with my other defiant acts they have been collecting on me. Also, probably the very next year I got my very own small Television Set and when after waiting a week to watch a PBS show on how engineers cut up the colossal statues that were going to be flooded by the Aswan Dam in Egypt and move them to higher ground, I wasn't allowed to watch it and had to sit in the living room like some kind of trophy and no one even talked to me of any consequence. I see now that it is online, but still peeved and to find out they didn't really get into the good stuff about how they actually cut it and held onto the pieces isn't worth it. Strange, but since I'm on the subject, I recall the Step Father praising the oriental architect at his achievement of the completion of the Twin Towers and saw it on TV. I just wanted to touch on this one spin off, maybe it is just an intrinsic quality of Mankind to hold onto mediocrity and not a conscious effort to nip the bud of innovative curiosity.

Before I regress I found a beauty while fruitlessly trying to find just one image of the symbol of the Snake with its Tail in its Mouth that isn't under copyright law, hopefully the reader knows what I'm talking about. From *What Every Man and Woman Should Know About the Bible,* by Sidney C. Tapp 1917 : "The ancient Pagans symbolized the thought of eternity through a Serpent. They placed the Tail of the Serpent in the Mouth of the Serpent and thereby made a circle out of the Serpent. The circle symbolizes eternity, in that it has neither beginning nor end. The ancients were so Carnal that their conception of eternity was eternal Lust in the consciousness of the Soul ; hence the Serpent with his Tail in his Mouth was their symbol of eternity. There is a Serpent in Nature that places his Tail in his Mouth and thus forms a circle when he wishes to strike at a human being. He comes at

342

you rolling like a hoop with all his force that the Poison of his Mind can produce. When he strikes and throws his fangs into you he Breaks the Circle and his Poison is Death. In the Countries where the Serpent of this species are found human beings frequently dodge behind Trees when they see a Serpent of this species coming at them. The Serpent is So Blind with the Poison of his Mind that he throws his fangs into the Tree, thinking the Tree the human being, and cannot extract his fangs from the Tree ; both Tree and Serpent die".

This is what Mythology has been reduced to in modern language, as an outright lie. The word is synonymous with False, Untrue, 'Oh, that's just a Myth'. Well, I think I have proven that perception wrong by dredging through seemingly endless Texts to find the shortest, oldest, and least corrupted testimony of Mankind. Over all these Legends are so diverse, involving different animal characters, and concepts to their same ends it couldn't possibly have be orchestrated behind the scenes by so many different anthropology minded people that recorded them into print over the millennia, especially the Cuneiform Text which were buried and completely forgotten and can't possibly be altered. Matter of fact their text are remarkably true to Life and ring of reality and detail unlike the Hebrew prayers and psalms, not to mention the Egyptian text chiseled into their monuments are much more elaborate. I feel like I should have incorporated some to show how really heartfelt they can be, but as I've mentioned there are many spin offs that distract from the cause of showing that there is a record of the Cataclysmic Tragedy that Happened to Mankind on Earth.

These ancient cylinder seals have perplexed the scholars, at least the ones back in the late 19th and early 20th centuries. I believe the Winged Gates represent the unpredictability of when the Space Falls will occur and these are the Gods deciding when and where they will release the Raging Bull. Like the Minotaur of the Minoans in which it is unknown when the Bull would emerge from the Labyrinth or the mosaic scenes of them leaping over the Bull as if Life hinged on the actions of the Beast. Along with the Traditions today with Bull Fighting and Running with the Bulls !

The Egyptians had grand ceremonies for sacrificing the Bull and even parading it around Seven times symbolizing Its origin of the Pleiades. They even had a Manmade Lake right next to the Temple of Karnack, which is

343

still there to the South, in which they no doubt reenacted the scenes that played out in the Heavens of the past in elaborate boats remotely similar of the Chinese and Japanese floating lanterns on the water during their modern festivals for the Dead. This is probably the reason for the Pools of Water in the court yards of the great temples on a miniature level and as one author's testimony of the people of India only watching an eclipse via the reflection in the water, this makes since because the Over Powering Light from Bolides and watching phenomena with the Sun will damage the eyes.

Many of the people in the Old World sacrificed the bull to propitiate the Gods so that they would not send the causation of the chaotic weather and especially the bombardment and Killing of Life. In the New World this custom seems to be missing and I believe it to be one piece of evidence that there was no frequent intercourse between the two 'Worlds'. It could be a lack of Bovine around the Equator of the Americas that they used human sacrifices or possibly mimicking the Gods who outright killed the people. The North American Indigenous people as far as I know didn't actually sacrifice their favorite prey, the Buffalo. There are some interesting connections though, such as Ursa Major both named after strangely a long tailed Bear and I've noticed the striking similarity between the large Stone work of Peru and the Hittites masonry. That is all extraordinary, but beyond the scope of this book as I've mentioned there are many many paths that stray "away," for a lack of a better term, from the subject.

The footage of the Chelyabinsk Bolide was extraordinary and its timing was perfect for me reading about all this at the time. It must be my aviation background and as a kid use to flag for crop dusters from Dawn 'till Dusk

and witnessed aircraft Vortices hundreds of times a day that I instantly recognized the phenomena and connected it to these ancient guilloche (Above Left) which are represented World Wide. Obviously larger Bolides produce Two Spinning Vortexes as I would assume the Space Shuttle did, I searched in vain for any images at all of high altitude reentry of any space craft to see if this is inherent in the field. Many times within the Mythological Stories it is stated that there were seen Two Serpents Fighting with themselves in the Water and with the Chinese Dragons a Bright Pearl

344

Leads the Two, which to the primitive mind perfectly describes a Bolide. As already mentioned with the Columbia Disintegration would produce the illusion of the sparkling treasure of Gold, Silver, and Pearls associated with Dragons.

This twisting of lines could have a Dualistic form as in the hypothesis of the spinning Triskelion and Swastika being the spinning Comet and the atmospheric Vortices which could easily be mistaken by primitive / ignorant Man's interpretation of the spectacle. Lest we forget the Roar and Shout of the God as demonstrated with the Chelyabinsk Super Bolide. If Man believed that he could hear messages from rustling leaves, ocean waves, and Thunder/Airburst he had to recognize as demonstrated in the American's, as 'The One Who Must Be Obeyed.' The Norse churches are covered with intricate carvings in wood of Serpents and Dragons at the gables. There are many instances of intertwined Serpents and stories of Weaving in the Sky like lattice work : that could be small, numerous contrails, from different angles over time, and mixing and twisting in the multi-layered atmospheric air currents. These in the past have been interpreted as maidens spinning the clouds which is probably the changing of the meaning of the Myth for a current phenomena, as how the Gods became the Planets after the true phenomena had faded from the Heavens and from the memory of the collective mind of Man through many new generations.

345

One thing that I have yet to place is the mention of Reeds, almost in every culture, they mention Reeds, Swamps, and the Dragon. Even in many of the St. George stories the Dragon lives in the swamp, could it be associated with the beginnings of creation (after the Deluge) wherein everything is cold, wet, and slimy mud and the Reeds where the first Re-building materials or maybe some skyward image? They also are used in many floatation devices that saved the last Man and Woman and even antediluvian as Ea speaks through the primitive Reed shelter to warn Man of the decision of the Gods to bring on the Flood, 'Reed Wall, Reed Wall, Hear'... Which brings up another subject of the Green Verdure of the Middle East and Egypt before and after the Deluge and then continually turning to drought and desert. Even in more recent times as in the Americas as researchers are now understanding that Equatorial parts turned dryer and the South Western North American to deserts wherein the indigenous peoples had mostly abandoned their abodes for the lack of rain such as the meaning of Las Vegas being the Marsh or Meadows which today never crosses one's mind.

There are numerous Legends, images on the Monuments, and Petroglyphs of shallow lakes with animals and verdure abounding in the 'Fertile Crescent' which is mostly desert today. Stories of Colossal Cedar Trees in Lebanon, Turkey, and even in Iraq mountains to the east which is even more hard to realize because the Cedar tree is usually a tree which thrives in swamps and needs plenty of water. The ancient text all cry out to God for more rain and how the climate has changed for the worst and nothing but worthless desert plants survive anymore. Along with animals being outright killed in the fields, probably from the Meteorite Scorpion Men, and the Shock Waves making the animals give birth before gestation. The prayers are replete with propitiations to please stop punishing us, and Men being at wits end to what they have done to deserve such treatment and call out by name of all fifty of their Gods hoping at least one will hear. By the way, I agree with the curly haired scientist who says the Sphinx was eroded by water, not just only by looking at the evidence which surely looks correct, but that it was made at the time when the sky began to clear when the Sun emerged again between the Virgin and the Lion at the Spring Equinox which it stares toward and when Egypt was Green. The acid rain from myths could explain some of it... Now it's just sand.

Another perplexing issue is that academia seems to be at a consensus that the Worlds Salt Water Rose Four Hundred Feet in the last 13,000 years and yet they ignore that that means the Persian Gulf, the Red Sea, and Mediterranean would be Above that height ! The Sumerians speak of the Fish-Man Ea coming from the Persian Gulf to teach them how to farm and the arts, the Egyptians say the Iron Workers came from the East, and the

Hellenistic people have Legends of their kind coming from the lower lands to the South. The Persian Gulf and the Red Sea are a certainly being that they are only at most 200 feet deep and the Mediterranean a complex issue even though the strait of Gibraltar had to be dry, there being most likely huge fresh water lakes in the bottom of the valley.

Every time I see the Egyptian monuments under water it is said, 'earthquake', and that is the end of the explanation, I say bull ! There are other monuments underwater South of India and I wouldn't doubt and more, most of the past I bet is underwater. Fishermen dragging the English Channel pull up artifacts, the Baltic Sea was most assuredly empty also and the Vikings were forced into being sailors ! I bet with all the war ships and high technology hanging out in the Persian Gulf, that somewhere it is known where if there are any structures under that gulf it is known and yet secret like the veil that has been over the Mysteries for all this time. I often wonder if while making those Manmade islands there if they bothered to scan somehow if they were sucking up artifacts. Also a probability is that when the Mediterranean Sea started to fill up that the water and the volcano of Santorini mixed and that was the reason for such a colossal explosion and now dormant and also with the gases that are not coming up any more for the Delphic Prognostications. In addition, just maybe Pompeii, also...

 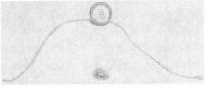

I'm at a loss why it isn't obvious, to the left is a symbol from Persia and the one to the right a Stone Megalith at Avebury England just a degree or two off from straight twenty seven miles north of Stonehenge. Sure looks like a Serpent Going Around The Sun. And there are others as the Serpent Eating the Sun, the Earth, or possibly the Bolide it is chasing of the Serpent Mount in Ohio, and the World Wide representations of the Serpent and Dragon eating Mankind. This isn't some immoral, psychological or spiritual demon, that Man should be afraid for his soul. It is a Real Physical Threat of Inner Solar System Space Debris Influencing the Climate of Our World. With eight billion people, the next time it occurs the old legends of family turning on family will be child's play in comparison. Which serves all the more to reinforce the importance of the message within this book. We need to stop the cycle of Disinformation and Misunderstanding to insure that if there are new initiates that they can get back on their feet faster or hopefully we can solve the problem.

347

The Dolmans and massive Stone structures also seem to be misinterpreted as initially tombs and not for the living hiding from the real threat from Above, if not for the Wise Shaman to survive the periodic down fall of material while they Watched the Heavens for the next attack. The temple and or city walls are made to withstand just about anything from colossal earthquakes to flying boulders. There had to be a reason to go to such extents ! Not just the Imaginary or Solar God watching down on them to do their best, but a real need and probable fear factor of all the people not just stories they heard. Which goes back to the interaction between the Continents, if a ship load or two of people from the 'Old World' show up and tell of fantastic stories, that wouldn't be enough for the locals to believe if their Traditions say nothing but Blue Sky dominated the past, then to perpetuate for eons, it would have to be indoctrinated from a substantial group to get going without eyewitnesses. I believe without doubt that it was a Global Spectacle Observed by All Tribes of the World and of course observed from their specific orientation to the Sun and the Space Debris contact or fly by temporal situations to their geographic locations and cloud cover. Some stories are clearly from the witnesses trying to understand what is happening with overcast skies.

I decided to cut back as the book was going to be much larger and I was afraid the size would scare many away. I wanted to put in a full length version of Gilgamesh, some other longer stories, and a number of prayers, psalms, and the humanitarian codes of Babylonia and Egypt to show the complexity of the ancient people which were far beyond only Ten Commandments. They had litigation in courts that would remind one of current problems, Women had rights, even slaves had rights, they had mail service and many were literate, they wrote about common family problems like lazy teenagers and cheating spouses, and I gathered mostly the declining climate from a farming and herding perspective.

Camera Obscura

This subject could easily take a life time to explore towards being comprehensive and if finding copyright free images wasn't a problem it could go on into Volumes. This is a great illustration of the Camera Obscura which from the Pyramid text that I read though, took copious notes from, and then lost in a computer crash illustrates what I think some of the mysterious text are talking about. They had huge long temples as one author explains as alike a telescope and another author, Lockyer, says that the temples where set up for similar observations with a long (football field long) corridor to obscure outside light so that the Star Light, either ours or Night Stars could be observed in a darkened room. From reading the Pyramid Texts it seems like they talk about Sun spots and mass coronal ejections in an obscure way. Lockyer tells how they even moved these colossal structures to realign them for the Precessional Retrograde yet doesn't tell how he came to these conclusions. Even though, the Egyptians and Babylonians had the technology to grind lenses without doubt. To prove it they frequently state in their texts that they have circular Crystal rings that had to be made on some sort of Lathe and they had the technology to make Glass also. There is even an extant example from the Americas of a Highly Polished Toroid in a Green Stone. Mankind was much more advanced than is let on, matter of fact I bet the Meteoric Iron Age should be before the Bronze Age. I find it very hard to believe the Egyptians made the Great Pyramid without extensive Iron and diamond usage. For example no one seems to ever talk about the Huge Hollow Pyramid just North of there on top of a Mountain. From the few pictures that I've seen it looks like a massive foundry wherein it is designed to draft air from the bottom and surely appears like blackened interior walls all probably designed for Iron production even if just one charge at a time.

The 1871 Fires of Chicago, Peshtigo, and Huron are not commonly considered related, the academia will say meteorites come down Cold from their Fiery Entry, how short our recall is. Does anyone suppose that three people planned on that night hundreds of miles away from each other to set fires simultaneously? Or could it have been some part of the Comet Biella?

I wonder if the reader caught the significance of the Battle between Tiamat and Marduk, the first time I read it I sat in Awe. It is one of the oldest stories known to Mankind and to me describes a Massive Super Bolide Air Burst. It has all the elements of the Chelyabinsk Bolide and more that we have yet to witness, the Blinding Light, the Serpent Trail coming down, the Loud Shrieks and Shouts, the Host of Fragments along with Her, the Thunder Claps, the Seven Winds filling Her (Expansion of the Blast), the Evil Wind (the Shock Wave that rips the cloths right off Man, the innocuous demon statue in that scary movie in the early 70's, Pg. 255), the Net (Like a circular casting net of fragments smoking and flying away from the blast.), and Marduk standing on her head as the Heat rising alike an Atomic Explosion!

I forgot to mention the Shape Shifters back while discussing the phenomena of the Beautiful Space Spectacles and the Atmospheric Terror Ridden Results of the Entry into Our World. Many cultures speak of the Shape Shifters and the above is my theory of why it is so prevalent within Mythology along with another strange story I read from the Norse Sagas. I believe it was similar to the Tiamat story when Marduk was given unlimited powers and the other Gods tested him by making the cloak disappear and reappear with his Word, but this one was as if watching the Sky Mountain flying by and they analogize it as alike a Man sewn up in a leather bag and moving around and being visible and then vanishing and then reappearing as I would envision a tumbling Asteroid flying through the shade of the Earth as if lit, dark, and lit again. The story seems to be lost in my piles of notes and going off memory. The shape shifting could also explain why Ishtar takes on opposing attributes as the giver and taker of Life and a virgin and a whore. In Space the Phenomena would bring on a Angelic quality and when it entered into our Atmosphere it would change into a Demonic attribute.

There was also a book I read, *The Cave and the Cathedral*, that I thought would prove that the Mediterranean Sea was practically an empty valley and yet there was no corroborating evidence that I could find. It talked about an underwater cave South of France that has ancient Petroglyphs in it, but there were no details of what the images are of or how deep and if that could be the only access. Guess it will have to be categorized with the underwater Egyptian monuments and Atlantis which is probably on the bottom of that sea. Myths are strange, from what little I've read, Atlantis is supposed to be beyond the Pillars of Hercules in which Hercules broke apart the Mountain of Atlas thus connecting the Mediterranean Sea to the Atlantic, but yet it could have meant the isthmus is where the water flowed in from. I'll admit that I sidestepped a lot of the Greek and Roman Mythology as I'm sure most know how intertwined and complicated it can be and reads like three modern soap operas combined.

Then there is the Lapis Lazuli, Turquoise, Egyptian Faience Blue, Han Blue, and Maya Blue usage around the World, they weren't just implying they liked Sunny Blue Sky days, they had a set Tradition to be ecstatic that the Blue Sky came back. Not from a week of overcast weather, but from long periods wherein crops were failing and people were starving and certainly not just the Sun coming up everyday type of thing, sure, the majority didn't have a clue and to them it was mostly diurnal or seasonal. Alike today in the USA on the night of October 31 people celebrate Halloween without a clue to what it really means, Its New Years Eve and if we don't get clobbered by a Space Fall till Sunrise (Or the Five Unliucky days.) then we are safe for one more year. Not the first of January when Jesus was circumcised. Isn't it strange that the Most Important Festival of the year is considered Taboo Heathenism, the Festival of the Dead, the Dead as the Slaughter of Mankind Thirteen Thousand Years ago by the progenitor of 2P/Encke. The other Festivals of the Dead around the World such as the Bon Festival are celebrated at different dates and the only logical reason must be the huge time interval and the Precession of the Equinoxes with the slippage of the seasons at one degree per 72 years and the great distance between the cultures.

It is also strange how in history books about calendars it seems Man had a tough time at figuring it out, the Sumerians, the Egyptian, and the Mayans had it slam dunked, they watched the Skies incessantly, looking for trouble,

351

and all most likely used 360 days (The Chaldeans used a base 60 math which is far more accurate than our 10.) plus the 5 unlucky days and every 4 years had the Festival a day earlier by checking the Stars (Sidereal), done! If they could calculate the Sun moving from the background 1/72 of a degree per year I seriously doubt we had to wait for the Gregorian Calendar to clear things up, if it wasn't for setbacks from Above !

It is said that the Tunguska and Chelyabinsk Super Bolides smelled like Gun Powder or Sulphur alike testimony from the Apollo missions to the Moon and Dragon stories. At Chelyabinsk eyewitnesses testified that it was Brighter than the Sun, one could feel the Intense Heat, and had to look way from the Fire Ball. The academia will tell you that such occurrences are extremely rare and will give statistical numbers to prove something they know nothing about such as the equation that will tell you the odds of the possibility of other intelligent life in the universe, please... People watched as the Kaali meteorite slammed nine times into the Island of Saaremaa, Estonia back around 500 BC, and the South West USA is littered with craters, plus the Tens of Thousands of Carolina Bays, the countless stories I have dug up of eyewitnesses, Tunguska with a blast radius of eighteen miles of fallen trees, and many other instances in the very resent past and yet they will assure you this kind of thing doesn't happen, why is that, Plausible Denial ? The Comet that caused all this had to just show up and get perturbed by Jupiter to swing it into the Inner Solar System to establish its short 3.3 year orbit. It doesn't matter really how they show up, the fact is, is that they do on occasion and we better be ready. I've never heard of it being discussed, but it seems that NEO's are attracted to our Goldilocks orbit and or our Magnetic Field draws them more than our sister planet Venus which doesn't have a Magnetic Field, nor does Mars and Mercury, or I'm just unaware of the missing data. The last one had a Iron chunk in the middle of it, makes since that they would be attracted to a huge Iron Magnet in Space, the Earth.

What harm is it to Open One's Eyes ? Bet Academia's eyes will be as wide as those Babylonian statues with the Huge Eyes when they finally see it for themselves ! Blind denial will get us Nowhere. Burying one's head in the sand and giving it all up to Fatalistic Fate is just plain stupid and not Science. It seems like the majority of the people of the World are just Waiting and Prodding for the End... Sigh. They will probably attack the messenger even though most of this information was written down at least One Hundred Years Ago and seemingly forgotten already ! It just needed someone who wasn't afraid to lift up the Veil and take a Good Look. I can hear it in Movies, Rock N Roll songs, and in modern magazines that show of ancient people preserving their kings and bring them out once a year and

yet never mention why...? Like as I've said about the Cock of the
Weathervane on top of the barn, it is a long lost reminiscent of the Pleiades
influencing our weather ! I have no idea if the reader will be able to grasp
this from this book, but for me it shows up almost every day without
looking, it is literally echoing still around the World as the last blast did on
the scientists nuclear detection devices and it is because it was much more
pronounced. Man certainly heard it the same way without hearing aids, they
state that the Sky even shook along with the waves of the water, the H20
water, and figuratively shattered the Earth like a ceramic pot. Alike the
huge Egyptian carving with the king (God) with a mace beating the enemy
(Mankind) and they (Man) is expressed visually like violent vibration.

   Chichen Itza is a fantastic site with a Pyramid that Illuminates the Serpent
on the staircase on the Spring Equinox, sorry I can't find a non-copyrighted
image. I do have one of the Ball Court Goal with Serpents around it, below.
The one on the Right seems to be a Dragon or Eagle. This is the same site
wherein they switched the Tsunami Wave noses for big upper lips to throw
off the public, I can't show that either, you'll just have to look the waves up
in the Codex if interested.

Gobekli Tepe, is an extraordinary site said to be 10,500 – 11,500 years old, as when the Sun was between the Virgin and Leo on the Spring Equinox, the Dawn after the Deluge. One is dressed as Gilgamesh with a Lion tied around his waist and on the base in which he stands are Seven Birds representing the Pleiades. The other has to be his friend Enkidu with a Bull on his chest. It seems obvious to me that the two pillars are of them who fought against the Raging Bull of Anu that Ishtar asked for to Kill the Sun (Gilgamesh). It appears to me that these Two Pillars are the oldest example of Jachin and Boaz or of Tammuz and Giz-zida the Two Tree Gods at the Gates of Heaven when Adapa went by for breaking the Southern Wind's wings, the Tree of Life and the Tree of Knowledge. Without the latter the former may go extinct and thus taking both down !

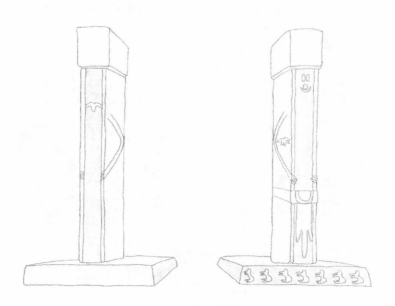

Viking Sword

Tanun Rock Carving Sweden

From Ancient Seal Cylinders at the Top Left is the Most Horary Ideograph
for God and representations of Vortices from Bolides and Taurus.

356

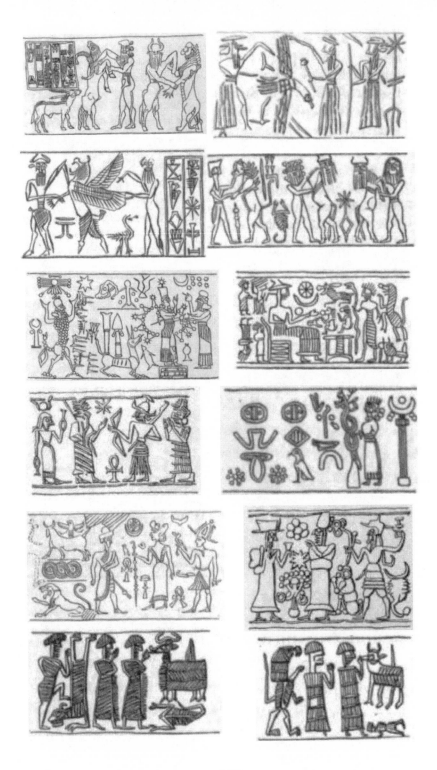

357

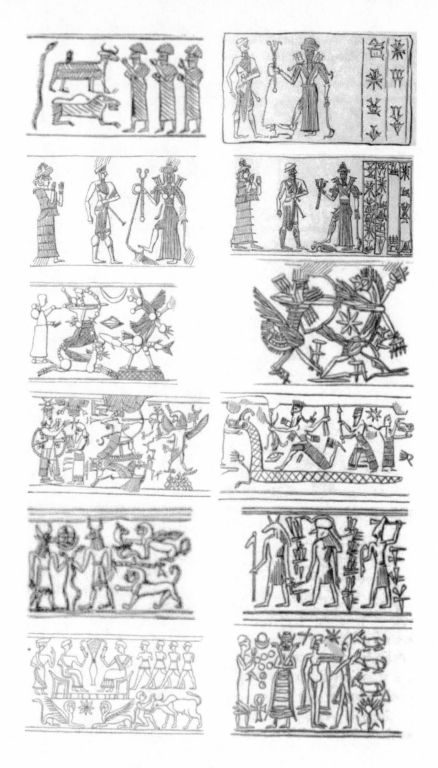

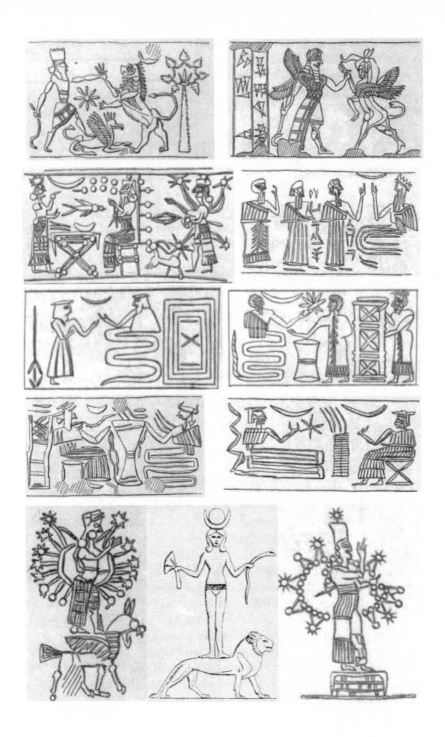

359

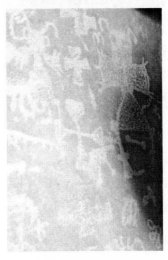

Barringer Crater Winslow Arizona

Bibliography / Books Read for this Project / Index

The Early Dawn by Elizabeth Rundle Charles 1864   Pg. 4

The Sibylline Oracle Books 3-5 by Herbert Bates 1918   Pg. 16

New materials for the History of Man Derived from a Comparison of the Calendars and Festivals of Nations by R. G. Haliburton 1863   Pg. 19

The Holy Scriptures According to the Masoretic Text A New Translation with the Aid of Previous Versions and with Constant Consultation of Jewish Authorities 1917   Pg.25 plus

Astronomical Myths, based on Flammarion's "History of the Heavens." by John Fredrick Blake 1877   Pg. 29

The Elder Edda of Saemund Sigfusson translated by Benjamin Thorpe, and *The Younger Edda of Snorre Sturleson* translated by I. A. Blackwell 1907   Pg. 39

Astronomy and Religion Among the Greeks and Romans by Franz Cumont 1912   Pg. 44

362

Legends, Traditions, and Laws of the Iroquois, or Six Nations, and History of the Tuscarora Indians by Elias Johnson a Native Chief 1881 Pg. 45

Myths and Marvels of Astronomy by Richard A. Proctor 1903 Pg. 47

Myths of the North American Indians by Lewis Spence 1914 Pg. 49

The Sacred Tree or The Tree in Religion and Myth by Mrs. J. H. Philpot 1897 Pg. 50

The Myths of Mexico and Peru by Lewis Spence 1914 Pg. 54

Symbolism of the East and West by Mrs. Murray-Aynsley 1900 Pg. 59

Myths of the New World : A Treatise on the Symbolism and Mythology of the Red Race of America by D. G. Brinton 1876 Pg. 64

The Mythology of All Races North America by Hartly Burr Alexander 1916 Pg. 69

The Migration of Symbols by The Count Goblet D'Alviella 1894 Pg. 79

The Seal Cylinders of Western Asia by Ward William Hayes 1910 Pg. 84

Ragnarok : The Age of Fire and Gravel by Ignatius Donnelly 1882 Pg. 86

The Dawn of Astronomy : A Study of the Temple-Worship and Mythology of the Ancient Egyptians by Sir Norman Lockyer 1894 Pg. 101

Star Lore of All Ages A Collection of Myths, Legends, and Facts Concerning the Constellations of the Northern Hemisphere by William Tyler Ocott 1911 Pg. 102

Sun Lore of All Ages A Collection of Myths and Legends Concerning the Sun and Its Worship by William Tyler Olcott 1914 Pg. 108

Myths of China and Japan by Donald A. Mackenzie 1923 Pg. 111

The Mythology and Rites of the British Druids Ascertained by National Documents and Compared with the General Traditions and Customs of Heathenism, as Illustrated by the Most Eminent Antiquaries of Our Age by Edward Davies 1809 Pg. 113

New Light from the Great Pyramid by Albert Ross Parsons 1893 Pg. 113
The Golden Bough a Study in Comparative Religion by J. G. Frazer vols. 1 & 2 1894 Pg. 116

The Holy Bible Translated from the Latin Vulgate Diligently Compared with the Hebrew, Greek, and other editions in Diver Languages. 1906 Pg. 140 plus

The Zonal-Belt Hypothesis A New Explanation of the Cause of the Ice Ages by Joseph Y. Wheeler 1908 Pg. 142

The Hymns of the Rigveda Translated with a popular commentary by Ralph T. H. Griffith 1889 Pg. 155

The Thunderweapon in Religion and Folklore A Study in Comparative Archaeology by Christopher Blinkenburg 1911 Pg. 160

The Serpent Symbol and the Worship of the Reciprocal Principles in America by E.G. Squier 1851 Pg. 165

The Evolution of the Dragon by G. Elliot Smith 1919 Pg. 171

The Mysteries of Mithra by Franz Cumont Translated from the Second Revised French Edition by Thomas J. McCormack 1903 Pg. 183

The Angel-Messiah of Buddhists, Essenes, and Christians by Ernest De Bunsen 1880 Pg. 186

Ancient Calendars and Constellations by The Hon. Emmeline Plunket 1903 Pg. 192

The Origin of all Religious Worship Translated from the French of Dupuis 1790 Containing also A Description of the Zodiac of Denerah 1872 Pg. 192

Development of Religious and Thought in Ancient Egypt by James Henry Breasted 1912 Pg. 197

The Gods of the Egyptians or Studies in Egyptian Mythology by E. A. Wallis Budge Vols. 1 & 2 1904 Pg. 198

Egyptian Literature comprising Egyptian tales, Hymns, Litanies, Invocations, The Book of the Dead and Cuneiform Writings 1901 Pg. 213

Religion of the Ancient Egyptians by Alfred Wiedemann 1897 Pg. 214

Isis Serpent Ra Pg. 216

The Threshold Covenant or The Beginning of Religious Rites by H. Clay Trumbull 1896 Pg. 218

Saint George Pg. 223

Tiamat – The Seven Tablets of the History of Creation Pg. 224

Tammuz Ishtar Pg. 229

Ishtar Pleads Love Pg. 232

The Deluge Pg. 233

The Adapa Legend Pg. 236

Enuma Elish : The Seven Tablets of Creation, or the Babylonian and Assyrian Legends Concerning the Creation of the World and of Mankind. vol. 1 & 2 L.W. King 1902 Pg. 238

The Religion of Babylonia and Assyria by Morris Jastrow, Jr. 1898 Pg. 239

The Origin and Growth of Religion as Illustrated by the Religion of the Ancient Babylonians, by A. H. Sayce   The Hibbert Lectures, 1887 Pg. 246

The Religions of Ancient Egypt and Babylonia The Gifford Lectures on the Ancient Egyptian and Babylonian Conception of the Divine by A. H. Sayce 1902 Pg. 254

Light on the Old Testament from Babel by Albert T. Clay 1906 Pg. 264

The First of Empires "Babylon of the Bible" In the Light of Latest Research an Account of the Origin, Growth, and History of the Ancient Babylonian Empire, from the Earliest Times to the Consolidation of the Empire in B.C. 2000 by W. St. Chad Boscawen 1906 Pg. 272

The "Higher Criticism" and the Verdict of the Monuments by A. H. Sayce 1894 Pg. 274

The Chaldean Account of Genesis Containing The Description of The Creation, The Deluge, The Tower of Babel, The Destruction of Sodom, The Times of the Patriarchs, and Nimrod ; Babylonian Fables, and Legends of the Gods ; from the Cuneiform Inscriptions. by George Smith A New Edition, Thoroughly Revised and Corrected (With Additions), by A. H. Sayce 1880 Pg. 275

The Monuments and the Old Testament Light from the Near East on the Scriptures by Ira Maurice Price 1899 Pg. 278

365

Hebrew and Babylonian Traditions The Haskell Lectures by Morris Jastrow, Jr. 1914 Pg. 280

Aspects of Religious Belief and Practices in Babylonia and Assyria by Morris Jastrow, Jr. 1911 Pg. 290

The Old Testament In the Light of the Historical Records and Legends of Assyria and Babylonia by Theophilus G. Pinches 1902 Pg. 292

The Bible and the Monuments The Primitive Hebrew Records in the Light of Modern Research by W. St. Chad Boscawen 1895 Pg. 294

The Early History of the Hebrews by A. H. Sayce 1899 Pg. 303

Geneva Bible 1599 Via – Tolle Lege Press Pg. 304 plus

Mythology Among the Hebrews and Its Historical Development by Ignaz Goldziher Translated from the German, with Additions by the Author by Russell Martineau 1877 Pg. 307

Earliest Intellectual Man's Idea of the Cosmos by Samuel A. B. Mercer 1957 Pg. 319

The Mythology of All Races Semitic by Stephen Herbert Langdon 1931 Pg. 320

Mythology of the Babylonian People by Donald A. Mackenzie 1915 Pg. 325

Myths and Legends of Babylonia and Assyria by Lewis Spence 1916 Pg. 326

The Origin of the Worship of Yahwe by William Hayes Ward The American Journal of Semitic Languages and Literatures Vol. XXV April 1909 Pg. 331

Other books read for this research project -

The Beginnings of History According to the Bible and the Traditions of Oriental Peoples. From the Creation of Man to the Deluge. by Francois Lenormant Translated from the Second French Edition by Francis Brown 1882

Sumerian Mythology A Study of Spiritual and Literary Achievement in the Third Millennium B. C. by Samuel Noah Kramer 1961

The Voice of the Seven Thunders : or, Lectures on the Apocalypse by Elder J. L. Martin 1874

Thunder and Lightning by W. De Fonvielle 1867

The Wild Huntsman A Legend of the Hartz by Julius Wolff Translated from the German by Ralph Davidson 1905
Myths and Legends of the Celtic Race by T. W. Rolleston 1917

A Miracle in Stone or The Great Pyramid of Egypt by Joseph A. Seis 1877

The Viking by Tre Tryckare 1972

Myths of the Norsemen From the Eddas and Sagas by H. A. Guerber 1914

Assyrian and Babylonian Literature Selected Translations 1900

The Legends of Genesis by Hermann Gunkel Translated from the German by W. H. Carruth 1901

Religion in the Heavens ; or, Mythology Unveiled in a Series of Lectures, by Logan Mitchell 1881

The Ascent of Man by J. Bronowski 1973

The Buried Book The Loss and Rediscovery of the Great Epic of Gilgamesh by David Damrosch 2006

Gilgamesh A New Rendering in English Verse by David Ferry 1992

Cosmos by Carl Sagan 1980

Comet by Carl Sagan and Ann Druyan 1985

The Dragons of Eden Speculations on the Evolution of Human Intelligence by Carl Sagan 1977

The Age of Reason by Thomas Paine 1880

Mythologies of the Ancient World edited by Samuel Noah Kramer 1961

The Witness of the Stars by Ethelbert William Bullinger 1893

Between the Planets by Fletcher G. Watson 1941

The Mystery of Comets by Fred L. Whipple 1985

Irish Druids and Old Irish Religions by James Bonwick 1894

Sacred Mysteries Among the Mayas and the Quiches, 11,500 Years Ago Their Relation to the Sacred Mysteries of Egypt, Greece, Chaldea and India. Free Masonry In Times Anterior to the Temple of Solomon. by Augustus Le Plongeon 1886

Egyptian Magic by E. A. Wallis Budge 1901

The Fate of the Mammoth Fossils, Myths, and History by Claudine Cohen 1994

The Cave and the Cathedral how a Real-Life Indiana Jones and a Renegade Scholar Decoded the Ancient Art of Man by Amird D. Aczel 2009

Egyptian Religion Egyptian Ideas of the Future Life by E. A. Wallis Budge 1899

The Deciding Voice of the Monuments in Biblical Criticism an Introduction to the Study of Biblical Archaeology by Melvin Grove Kyle 1924

The Study of Religion by Morris Jastrow, Jun. 1902

The Lay of the Nibelungs Metrically Translated from the Old German Text by Alice Horton 1898

The Harvard Classics Epic and Saga Beowulf, The Song of Roland, The Destruction of Da Derga's Hostel, The Story of the Volsungs, and Niblungs 1909

Star-Names and Their Meanings by Richard Hinckley Allen 1899

The Exact Sciences in Antiquity by O. Neugebauer 1952

The Comets of God New Scientific Evidence for God Recent Archeological, Geological and Astronomical Discoveries that Shine New Light on the Bible and Its Prophecies by Jeffrey Goodman 2011

Origin and Growth of Religion as Illustrated by the Religion of the Ancient Babylonians by A. H. Sayce The Hibbert Lectures 1887

Babylonian Religion and Mythology By L. W. King 1899

Atlantis the Antediluvian World by Ignatius Donnelly 1882

Dolmens for the Dead Megalith-Building throughout the World by Roger Joussaume 1985

Babel and Bible by Friedrich Delitzsch 1903

Teutonic Myth and Legend by Donald A. Mackenzie 1912

Myths and Legends of China by Edward T. C. Werner 1922

The Codex Nuttall A Picture Manuscript from Ancient Mexico edited by Zelia Nuttall 1902   1975

The Codex Borgia A Full-Color Restoration of the Ancient Mexican Manuscript by Gisele Diaz and Alen Rodgers 1993

Light from the East or The Witness of the Monuments An Introduction to the Study of Biblical Archaeology by C. J. Ball 1899

The Pyramid Texts by Samuel A. B. Mercer 1952

Rain of Fire and Ice by John Lewis 1996

The 2300 B.C. Event Vols. 1, 2, & 3 by M. M. Mandeckehr 2006

Worlds in Collision by Immanuel Velikousky 1950

The Book of Enoch by R.H. Charles 1917

The Apocrypha Translated out of the Greek and Latin Tongues Being the Version Set Forth A.D. 1611 Compared with the Most Ancient Authorities and Revised 1894

Hamlets Mill by De Santillaca 1969

The Cosmic Serpent by Victor Clube and Bill Napier 1982

The Cosmic Winter by Victor Clube and Bill Napier 1990

Comets and the Origin of Life by Janaki and Chandra Wickramasinghe and William Napier 2010

The Celtic Gods : Comets in Irish Mythology by Mike Baillie and Patrick McCafferty 2005

Myth and Geology by L. Piccardi and W. B. Masse 2007

Comet / Asteroid Impacts and Human Society : An Interdisciplinary
Approach by Peter T. Bobrowski and Hans Rickman 2007

Exodus to Arthur by Mike Baillie 2003

New Light on the Black Death by Mike Baillie 2006

The Cycle of Cosmic Catastrophes : Flood, Fire, Famine in the History of
Civilization by Richard Firestone, Allen West, and Simon Warwick-Smith
2006

Man and Impact in the Americas by E. P. Grondine 2005

The Epic of Gilgamesh by N. K. Sanders 1960

The Serpent Myths of Ancient Egypt being a Comparative History of These
Myths by W. R. Cooper 1873

Warriors of Old Japan and Other Stories by Yei Theodora Ozaki 1909

*Researches into the Origin of the Primitive Constellations of the Greeks,
Phoenicians and Babylonians* by Robert Brown Vols. 1 & 2 1844

Comets, Their Origin, Nature, and History by H. W. Elson 1910

A New Theory of the Earth, from Its Original, to the Consummation of All
Things. Wherein the Creation of the World in Six Days, the Universal
Deluge, and the General Conflagration as Laid Down in the Holy Scriptures,
are Shown to be Perfectly Agreeable to Reason and Philosophy. by William
Whiston 1696-1737 Quote much too hard to read the whole book...

The Tale of the Argonauts by Apollonius of Rhodes   first printed 1496
Translated from the Greek by Arthur Sway 1901

Istar

The Statue of Liberty Has Seven Spikes on Her Diadem.

CPSIA information can be obtained
at www.ICGtesting.com
Printed in the USA
LVOW12s0046210917
549487LV00003B/496/P